ENGINES
OF
DEMOCRACY

Politics & Policymaking
in State Legislatures

Alan Rosenthal

Eagleton Institute of Politics
Rutgers University

D1216858

CQ PRESS

A Division of SAGE
Washington, D.C.

CQ Press
2300 N Street, NW, Suite 800
Washington, DC 20037

Phone: 202-729-1900; toll-free, 1-866-4CQ-PRESS (1-866-427-7737)

Web: www.cqpress.com

Cover design: designfarm
Composition: Auburn Associates, Inc.

∞ The paper used in this publication exceeds the requirements of the American National Standard for Information Sciences—Permanence of Paper for Printed Library Materials, ANSI Z39.48-1992.

Printed and bound in the United States of America

12   11   10   09   08   1   2   3   4   5

Library of Congress Cataloging-in-Publication Data
Rosenthal, Alan
     Engines of democracy : politics and policymaking in state legislatures / Alan Rosenthal.
        p.   cm.
     Includes bibliographical references and index.
     ISBN 978-0-87289-459-4 (pbk. : alk. paper) 1. Legislative bodies—United States—States. 2. State governments—United States. I. Title.

     JK2488.R665 2009
     327.73—dc22

                                                          2008036598

To those who work at

representative democracy and

make representative democracy work

About the Author

Alan Rosenthal is professor of public policy and political science at the Eagleton Institute of Politics, Rutgers University. He has consulted with legislatures and participated in legislative ethics training and new-member orientations for many years. He has written extensively about state legislatures, including *The Decline of Representative Democracy* (1998) and *Heavy Lifting* (2004). In 1995 he received the American Political Science Association's Charles E. Merriam Award, which honors a person whose published work and career represent a significant contribution to the art of government through the application of social science research. In 2006 he was given an award for lifetime achievement from the National Conference of State Legislatures and the State Legislative Leaders Foundation. In 1993 he received the New Jersey Governor's Award for Public Service, and in 1992 and 2001 he was selected to be the independent member and chair of the New Jersey Congressional Redistricting Commission.

Contents

Tables and Figures

Tables

Figures

Preface

This book is the product of my observing, trying to make sense of, and teaching and writing about legislatures and the legislative process in the states. It covers most of what I think needs to be communicated to people about legislatures, the people who make these institutions work, and how public policy is made. It includes what legislators are like as individuals; how they relate to and represent their districts; the roles of political parties and partisan competition; the influence of interest groups and lobbyists; the effects of organization and structure; the challenges of ethics; the job of leadership; the power of the governor; and the processes of study, deliberation, negotiation, compromise, and bargaining that are critical to building majorities in the lawmaking process.

Engines of Democracy is informed by a rich scholarly literature, and it is also informed by my observations of and work with legislatures throughout the nation. I have tried to make this book comprehensive but also readable, so that legislatures are as alive for the reader as they have been for me. It should serve as an introductory exploration for undergraduates, a survey of the field for graduate students, and a guide for members of the "legislative community" including new and veteran legislators, professional staff, lobbyists, and statehouse reporters. If this book gets the picture of state legislatures right, it is because of the great help I have received and continue to receive.

For *Engines* and my books that preceded it, my greatest debt is to members of the legislative community. Legislators and their staffs invited me to observe them in their natural habitats, and lobbyists shared perspectives on their jobs and the legislative process. Just about all of the men and women I encountered on legislative terrain appreciate and respect the legislature as an institution, just as I do. They were most generous to me with their time, patience, and trust.

I owe them all, and would like to thank each and every one of these people who did so much to educate me. To acknowledge them, I would have to mention hundreds of names. Still, I want to name those legislators whose influence on my explorations has been most profound. They are listed here, not by state or seniority, but alphabetically, as follows: Hunter Andrews, Stan Arinoff, Rich Bagger, Dick Bagley, Sam Bell, Peter Berle, John Brandl, Wayne Bryant, Bill Bulger, Al Burstein, Mike Busch, Jack Cade, Ben Cardin, Betty Castor, Lawton Chiles, Joe Clarke, Dick Codey, Jack Collins, Kevin Coughlin, JoAnn Davidson, Larry DeNardis, Alan Diamonstein, Don DiFrancesco, Sal DiMasi, Joe Doria, Tom Dowd, Bill Doyle, John Paul Doyle, Cary Edwards, George Edwards, Mike Egan, Jeanne Faatz, Dick Finan, Herb Fineman, George Firestone, Dave Frohnmeyer, Bob Garton, Bob Graham, Ted Gray, Art Hamilton, Bill Hamilton, Chuck Hardwick, Joe Harper, Kevin Harrington, Marshall Harris, Chuck Haytaian, Bubba Henry, Barbara Hoffman, P. J. Hogan, Gerry Horton, Cal Hultman, Harry Johnston, Phyllis Kahn, Vera Katz, Gerry Kaufman, Bill Kelley, Bill Kenton, Harriet Keysterling, Kurt Kiser, Howard Klebanoff, Bob Knowles, Nancy Kopp, Madeline Kunin, Chuck Kurfess, Jack Lapides, Cal Ledbetter, Jerris Leonard, Larry Levitan, Tom Loftus, Thomas Hunter Lowe, Harris MacDowell, Gordon MacInnes, Jodie Mahoney, Mike Maloney, Marvin Mandel, John Martin, Buddy McKay, Mike Miller, Don Moe, Roger Moe, Dick Moore, Bob Moretti, Ted Morrison, John Mutz, James Nowlan, Frank O'Bannon, Dave Obey, Norma Paulus, Dick Pettigrew, John Pittenger, Bill Ratchford, Pete Rawlings, Jody Richards, Dick Riley, Fred Risser, George Roberts, Joe Roberts, Lew Rome, Sandy Rosenberg, Kenneth Royall, Buzz Ryan, Martin Sabo, Pat Saiki, Steve Saland, Raymond Sanchez, Paul Sarbanes, Bill Schluter, Dick Schneller, Peter Shumlin, Alan Simpson, Bob Smalley, Kevin Sullivan, Steve Sviggum, Gaye Symington, Cas Taylor, Alan Thompson, James Harold Thompson, Jim Townsend, Jesse Unruh, Ruben Valdez, Jack Veneman, Jerry Warner, and Ralph Wright.

In practically every state I have benefitted from help and information provided by the men and women who staff the legislature, just about all of whom show dedication in serving members and the institution. The staffs of three national organizations that represent and promote the interests of legislatures also deserve my thanks. It has been a real pleasure to work with people at the National Conference of State Legislatures, the Council of State Governments, and the State Legislative Leaders Foundation.

I am also in debt to my political science colleagues, on whose research I have drawn extensively in this and earlier books. Many of these colleagues are cited in these pages, and I am grateful to them for all their help. Without the literature that political scientists have produced, a work like this could not have been written. Special gratitude is extended to Bruce Anderson, Diana Evans, Thad Kousser, Gary Moncrief, James Nowlan, John Redifer, and Paul Soper.

Faculty and staff at the Eagleton Institute of Politics at Rutgers University have my gratitude as well. If Eagleton had not been in the picture, I never would have had the opportunity to carve out the career I have had as a student of legislatures.

Finally, I want to mention members of my family, who cannot be blamed for my folly. They neither encouraged it nor discouraged it. They were just around, and it has always been wonderful having them around. They deserve much more than mention, but mention is all they will come away with here. My children: John, Kai, Tony, and Lisa, and their spouses, Lisa, Kathleen, and Garrison. Then, of course, their children—my grandchildren, a motley crew—in order of age: Patrick, Kelly, Chas, Dylan, Tori, Mason, Ian, and Emily. My first wife, Vinnie, fits in here. My greatest debt is to Lynda, my present wife, who so expertly typed and proofed *Engines* in manuscript. Thanks to her, I have been blessed with additional family: Jim and Dorothy, Lynda's parents, and her sons, Nick and Jeremy; Nick's partner, John, and Jeremy's wife, Deb; Lynda's brother, Jim, his wife, Susan, and their daughter, Marisa; and especially Lynda's sister, Carol, who is doing such great work with youngsters in Laos. And last but not least, two more grandchildren: Mac and Emmett.

I only hope that the quality of this book comes close to the quality of all the people I thank here.

Introduction

GENERATIONS OF AMERICAN TODDLERS have enjoyed the story about the little engine that rescued a train that had broken down while climbing a steep hill. The *Little Engine That Could* chugged and puffed, "I think I can, I think I can, I think I can," as it pulled the train over the crest of the hill. Boys and girls in the valley town, who eagerly awaited the toys, food, and other goodies that the train was bearing, cheered when it finally arrived.

Much like the little engine, the legislature chugs and puffs along. The legislature (and not the executive or the judiciary) is truly the engine of democracy. It tugs and pulls a heavy load, uphill much of the way. Like the little engine that could, the legislature usually delivers the goods—a mixed bag, depending largely on one's tastes. The legislature, however, upon its arrival is far more likely to be greeted by jeers than by cheers.

Legislatures are the key agencies of representative democracy in America. They have been in the business of governing for 250 years, which stands as testimony to their resilience as political institutions. They are not the only institutions of governance in the nation and states. State constitutions, like the federal constitution, provide for systems of separated powers with three branches of government, each with its own role but sharing power and balancing one another. Along with legislatures, the executive and judicial branches also govern.

Yet in the order in which provisions are specified in constitutions, the legislative branch comes first, ahead of the executive and judiciary. The legislature is not only the first branch of government, it is the branch closest to the people. It is the most representative, with members firmly rooted in their constituencies. It is the most democratic, with each member having an equal vote and power substantially dispersed. And it is the most accessible, subject to continuing pressures and demands from a multiplicity of groups and individuals.

1

Along with the executive, and to a lesser extent the judiciary, the legislature makes law. No major policy can be adopted, no major program undertaken without legislative involvement and approval. No taxes can be levied or monies spent without the legislature's go-ahead. Not much can happen in state government unless the legislature is on board.

A Perspective on Legislatures

My career as a political scientist has mainly been spent observing, studying, consulting with, and teaching and writing about state legislatures. Congressional scholar Richard Fenno characterizes his approach to studying Congress as "poking and soaking." I too have poked and soaked—and even wallowed in the process—as I explored legislatures in the states.

It was fortunate for me to have become involved with state legislatures during the late 1960s, the beginning of a period of legislative modernization. The Eagleton Institute of Politics at Rutgers University, under the directorship of Donald Hertzberg, forged a relationship with Jesse Unruh, California's speaker of the assembly, and the National Conference of State Legislative Leaders. Eagleton became the research and development arm of the conference and played a key role in the reform movement that was then getting underway.

I was hired to direct Eagleton's legislative efforts, and I started learning close-up about legislative organization, procedures, and operations. I conducted a comprehensive study commissioned by the Maryland General Assembly and then supervised studies for legislatures in Arkansas, Connecticut, Florida, Mississippi, and Wisconsin. I benefited from my association with legislators who were specially selected to participate in annual institutes from 1966 to 1975. Funded by the Carnegie Corporation, these ten institutes were attended by almost 450 legislators from all fifty states. Thanks to grants from the Ford Foundation, I was able to work with legislatures in a dozen states— especially in Connecticut and Virginia—on the development of a method to oversee the administration and assess the effectiveness of programs that had been enacted into law. These endeavors got me started on the study of legislatures, which I have continued until today.

Working in a consultative capacity has obviously shaped my perspective; I've been close to the phenomena that I have been studying and about which I have been writing. Perhaps I have been too close to maintain the detachment and objectivity required of a legislative scholar; after all, familiarity is said to breed contempt. Not in this case, however, nor in most cases. Familiarity encourages empathy, which I for one have developed with regard to legislative people and legislative institutions. I have tried to put myself in their shoes, but I have also been able to step back to make judgments. I have come to respect these political institutions, which truly are the engines of American democracy, and those who man (and woman) them. The people and the institutions, of course, are hardly perfect. They could use tweakings here and changes there, but all in all, state legislatures do a remarkable job for our political system. I can only hope that my outsider-insider perspective is a helpful one.

Understanding Legislatures

It is not easy to understand one legislature, let alone fifty of them. Legislatures differ one from another. New Hampshire's legislature is not like California's, nor is Montana's like Kentucky's. Indeed, within each legislature (except Nebraska's, which is unicameral), the senate and house are very different bodies. Legislatures also differ over time. They are not the same today as they were in the 1940s or the 1970s. Each legislature differs from session to session, depending upon its composition, partisan control, leadership, and circumstances.

Although legislatures are moving targets, it is possible to acquire an understanding of how they work, how they govern, and the problems they confront. That is my objective in this book.

There is no better place to start than by considering Americans' views of their legislators and legislatures; this is the goal of chapter 1. In exploring what people think and why they think it, it becomes clear that legislatures have an uphill battle as far as the public is concerned. Not only is it difficult for citizens to understand their legislatures, it is even difficult for them to appreciate their legislatures.

In chapter 2 I address what legislators themselves are like, no matter how they are perceived by the public or portrayed by the media. Why do people run for the state legislature? Once elected, how—and how well—do they adapt to life in the legislature? Why do they stay, why do they leave? On balance, what do they derive from their legislative careers?

Probably the most important characteristic of legislators is their relationship to their districts. As I argue in chapter 3, virtually all of them are rooted in their districts. Indeed, what legislators and legislatures both do best is the job of representation. They perform superbly in responding to the needs of their constituents and constituencies. They do almost as well in expressing the views of their constituents, at least those of most of their constituents, and at least on the relatively few issues on which constituents have views.

It used to be that the processes of getting elected on the one hand and governing on the other were differentiated. In today's political world, the two processes are intertwined. The nature of political parties and the effects of partisan competition help determine how legislatures govern and how policies are made in the states. It is a high-stakes, contentious enterprise, as shown in chapter 4.

No other aspects of American politics suffer as much from media derision and public disapproval as lobbyists and lobbying. Yet these elements are key in a political system that permits people to organize into interest groups and try to influence governmental policies and programs. Chapter 5 explores lobbying, focusing on the approaches and techniques that are used and on the influence interest groups and lobbyists exercise.

To understand state legislatures, it is necessary to have a sense of the most significant features of the terrain on which representational and policy-making processes take place. Chapter 6 considers matters of professionalism, including staffing and term limits and the contrast between professional and citizen bodies. It also examines organizational features, including differences between the two chambers, the question of size, and the role of committees. Finally, matters of legislative ethics and the ways in which legislators make ethical choices are discussed.

Legislative leaders have much to do with how legislatures run. Nothing can substitute for effective leadership. Chapter 7 reviews the multiple responsibilities that legislative leaders have—from getting members reelected to appointing committee members to strategizing and negotiating. I examine how leaders fulfill their responsibilities and ask whether they have too much or too little power.

Just about everywhere the governor is legislator in chief. The executive usually shapes the budget that the legislature reviews and enacts. The executive has an agenda that is presented to the legislature for its consideration. The executive can also veto measures that the legislature enacts. The governor's role in the legislative process gives him or her a strategic advantage. I explore just why governors normally have the upper hand in relating to the legislature, the various approaches governors take, and the difficulties legislatures face in trying to maintain their independence as coequal branches of government.

The legislative job most familiar to many of us is making law. It is the legislature's most important job, and is the subject of the next three chapters.

In chapter 9, on just what goes into law, we start with the sheer volume of bills that are introduced and the many sources of legislation. Important here is the notion that legislators are not only subject to pressures from without but also from within. They themselves are advocates, and have arrived at advocacy in a number of ways. What affects their efforts, as much as anything else, is the degree of controversy surrounding measures they introduce.

Once legislation is introduced, the game begins, as is discussed in chapter 10. No metaphor accurately describes it, but the most frequent comparison is to sausage making. But, unlike the manufacture of sausage, lawmaking is premised on differences and disagreements, which are expected in a political system where people have different values, interests, and ideas. Such differences are manifest in the pros and cons of legislation. Even if everyone agreed at a general level, what would still make the process difficult would be the complexity of problems addressed and the range of differences over detail.

All it takes to pass a bill is a majority of members voting for it. As chapter 11 details, successive majorities must agree to pass a bill, while a single majority ordinarily can derail it. What determines whether legislators vote to make a majority for or a majority against a proposal? What determines how the legislature decides? Study, deliberation, negotiation, and compromise all are critical to the process that takes place in the legislature, and all are key to building majorities.

Chapter 12 concludes with an assessment of how well legislatures work. How should we judge their performance—by what the media reports, by what is reflected in public opinion polls, or by trying to determine just how well they do their principal jobs of representing, lawmaking, and balancing the power of the executive? In addition to examining standards that can be used for assessment, we discuss the problems legislatures confront and the ways in which legislatures might be reformed. My judgment in these matters is that legislatures do a much better job than they are given credit for and significant institutional improvement is far more difficult than most people imagine.

This book ranges broadly, although undoubtedly important aspects of legislative life have been overlooked. More attention, for instance, could have been devoted to legislative oversight or the legislature's role in confirming gubernatorial appointments. Still, my primary objective here is to give the reader a basic understanding of institutions, processes, and people that are not easy to understand. Perhaps with a better understanding will come a realization of how effectively the system works in a representative democracy, such as our own.

My interpretation of state legislatures draws on the research of many legislative scholars, who are cited throughout this book. Today, legislative studies is a thriving field. I owe a particular debt to the political scientists and others who worked on the term limits study, which had the sponsorship of three national legislative organizations—the National Conference of State Legislatures (NCSL), the Council of State Governments (CSG), and the State Legislative Leaders Foundation (SLLF). As part of that study, a survey was conducted of legislators in the fifty states. I make use of some of this survey's results.

My interpretation also draws on the observations of legislators themselves. Memoirs by former legislators, such as Harriet Keyserling of South Carolina, Tom Loftus of Wisconsin, Ralph Wright of Vermont, and William Bulger and John E. McDonough of Massachusetts, are invaluable source materials for me. So are James Richardson's biography of Willie Brown of California, Taylor Pensoneau's of Russ Arrington of Illinois, and Richard

Hyatt's of Tom Murphy of Georgia. Over the years, I have had interviews or conversations with hundreds of legislators, staffers, and lobbyists, all of whom informed my views. I have observed legislators, and in particular legislative leaders, in a number of states and in connection with a variety of projects.

For the past decade or so, I have been involved with NCSL on several projects designed to bring a better understanding of representative democracy to government, history, and civics teaching in middle schools and high schools throughout the nation. One of the products of this enterprise was a book, *Republic on Trial*, that I coauthored with three political-scientist colleagues. I draw on material in this book, as well as on simulations and scenarios that I prepared for classroom teachers.

Engines of Democracy plows some new ground. I spent a session in 2005–2006 observing the Massachusetts legislature—formally called the General Court of the Commonwealth of Massachusetts—which helped flesh out this examination of policymaking. This book also covers old ground, building as it does on my previous work. Most important, in this respect, is *Heavy Lifting*, which focused in particular on legislatures in Maryland, Minnesota, Ohio, Vermont, and Washington. What I learned there is very relevant here, especially the findings of a survey of legislators in these five states on matters related to their representational roles.

I have had the opportunity to spend my career as an academic trying to make sense out of state legislatures. I have also tried to convey what sense I've made of the subject to others—members of the "legislative community" (that is, legislators, legislative staff, lobbyists, and journalists), undergraduate and graduate students, and colleagues who share my fascination with legislative institutions and processes that continue to chug and puff along.

1

Why Legislatures Are Not Appreciated

LEGISLATURES ARE IMPRESSIVE POLITICAL INSTITUTIONS, but they are not at all popular ones. As the comedian Rodney Dangerfield might put it, legislatures get no respect. They get little support. They are probably the most unappreciated institutions in the country.

Most people view state legislatures, including their own, from a distance. The impression they have of legislatures and legislators is not a favorable one. Just what people think and why they think it are the subjects of this chapter, so let's take a look at state legislatures from the public's perspective before approaching closer for an inside view.

The Practices of Representative Democracy

There is a huge difference between how people feel about the abstract principles of American democracy on the one hand and the nitty-gritty practice of American democracy on the other. When democracy and related principles, such as liberty, majority rule, minority rights, freedom of speech and religion, and even equality, are expressed in general terms, support is widespread. But as these values are related to concrete applications and more specific situations, support diminishes and cleavage replaces consensus.[1] For Americans, democracy is surely the best form of government. We take pride in our democratic system and in our government's structure and believe that our democratic framework is worthy of export. Why doesn't everyone enjoy a democratic political system, as we do?

Our enjoyment, however, is only skin deep. If we probe beneath the political surface to the actual practices and agencies of democracy, agreement declines and unquestioning pride turns to unquestioning cynicism. It is necessary to look at the central elements, rather than the general notions, that characterize democracy in the United States, and how they are popularly regarded.

Diversity and Disagreement

There is probably no more basic feature of American democracy than the diversity of people in the nation and the differences among them in terms of values, interests, and preferences. Disagreement among people is natural and to be expected in our system. Moreover, disagreement is healthy in a democracy—in California and New York or in Wyoming and Vermont. We would expect, therefore, that Americans acknowledge differences in the views people hold and the political conflicts that come about as a result.

While many Americans do recognize the existence of differences and conflicts, many do not. Research conducted by John R. Hibbing and Elizabeth Theiss-Morse[2] indicates that people overestimate the degree of agreement in society, in large part because their social and political views tend to coincide with those of people with whom they associate. They assume that others believe as they do. Nowadays, not only do the media and blogs tend to cater to people's individual political values, but increasingly Americans are clustering in homogenous communities.[3]

An Internet survey conducted for the National Conference of State Legislatures (NCSL) by Knowledge Networks[4] shows how Americans feel about political disagreement as well as about other issues. Selected questions and responses to the Knowledge Networks survey appear in Figure 1-1, which reports on public attitudes toward representative democracy. These attitudes are illustrative.

Respondents were asked to agree with either one or the other of two statements, whichever came nearer to their own view on representative democracy. As shown in the table, 60 percent agreed with the statement, "People disagree, so it's difficult to resolve issues." But about 40 percent did not, or had no opinion on such a basic assertion. Similarly, 60 percent agreed with "Many competing groups make conflict unavoidable," but 40 percent did not agree, or had no opinion on a related statement.

A number of people who do acknowledge the existence of disagreement and conflict, nevertheless, do not regard views other than their own as

Figure 1-1 Public Attitudes toward Representative Democracy

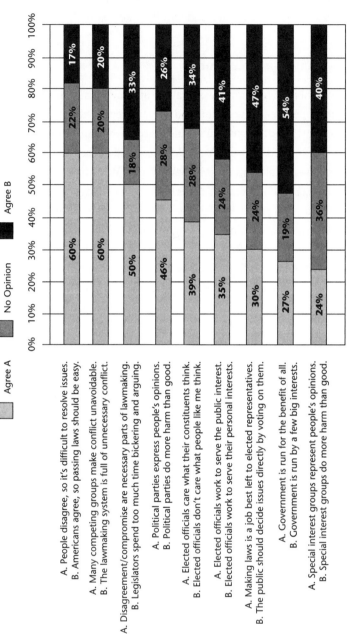

Source: Karl T. Kurtz, Alan Rosenthal, and Cliff Zukin, *Citizenship: A Challenge for All Generations* (Denver: National Conference of State Legislatures, September 2003), 9.

legitimate. They see their own values, interests, and priorities as the only genuine ones. Especially in the heat of an election campaign or an issue campaign, those who feel strongly sometimes demonize their opponents. They not only question their opponents' judgment but their motives as well. At the very least, they are uncomfortable with opposing views.

While a majority of Americans rationally accept the existence of disagreement and conflict, fewer are accepting at the gut level. Somehow, they believe, "everyone ought to agree with me." Even legislators, particularly those who are new to public office and the process, tend to think that their views are the only correct ones. Indeed, every legislator believes his or her ideas are right. As expressed by Bruce King, a former legislator and governor of New Mexico, "We all felt that if the others would just listen to our presentations and follow our recommendations to the letter, things would turn out just fine." Yet "it rarely worked out like that," or so King discovered early on.[5]

Political Parties

One of the most important operating features of representative democracy is the two-party system. Political parties play a critical role in representing people, conducting campaigns, organizing government, and formulating and enacting public policy (see chapter 4). The framers of the U.S. Constitution never anticipated that political parties would develop as they have. Nor would they have welcomed the division that has accompanied parties. Yet parties arose, gained strength, and persevered. This was not always the case. Twenty-five years ago political scientists were so convinced that parties were in decline that David Broder, one of the nation's foremost journalists, wrote a book titled *The Party's Over*. Today, the American party system is strong, perhaps as strong as ever.

Despite the fact that most Americans affiliate with or lean in the direction of the Democratic or Republican Party and vote along party lines, many of them are unhappy with the party system. In the Knowledge Networks survey, as shown in Figure 1-1, 26 percent believe "political parties do more harm than good," as compared to 46 percent (less than a majority, it should be emphasized) who believe that parties "express people's opinions." While people are willing to live with political parties, the same survey shows,

59 percent think that parties have too much power, only 3 percent think that they have too little power, and only 19 percent think they have the right amount. From time to time, public opinion polls have revealed that a number of people would go as far as to ban political parties altogether.

Interest Groups

James Madison anticipated the importance of "factions" in the American political system, and he wanted to minimize their negative effects. Interest groups are the contemporary manifestation of Madison's factions. As Samuel P. Huntington wrote, "interest-group politics account for most of American politics most of the time . . . although not all of American politicians all of the time." [6] The fact is that interest groups provide a channel of representation for most of us (see chapter 5). Seven out of ten Americans belong to one interest group or another and four out of ten belong to multiple groups. Whether a person is a member or not, his or her interests may be represented by one or a number of groups operating in the political system.

For example, as a college professor, I belong to the American Association of University Professors, and as a political scientist I am a member of the American Political Science Association. These groups represent my economic and professional interests. My political views, however, are represented by a diversity of groups, none of which I am a card-carrying member. Indeed, I doubt that I have any political view that is not spoken for, and spoken for by multiple groups.

Nevertheless, "special interests," as interest groups are pejoratively labeled, upset citizens mightily. They rank as Public Enemy Number One. In the Knowledge Networks survey, 48 percent thought that interest groups had too much power, compared with 12 percent who thought they had too little and 14 percent who thought they had about the right amount. (Even a higher percentage, 62 percent, felt that business and corporations had too much power.) Figure 1-1 shows that 40 percent agree with the statement, "Special interest groups do more harm than good," while only 24 percent agree with "Special interest groups represent people's opinions." The picture is bleaker, because Americans believe that their government is a captive of special interests—the big ones, that is. While only 27 percent agree with the statement that government is run "for the benefit of all," twice as many agree that it is run "by a few big interests."

Kevin Coughlin, a member of the Ohio Senate, tells of an encounter with an elderly constituent shortly after he was first elected to represent Akron in the legislature.

"Kevin," the senior citizen implored, "when you get to Columbus, you have just got to get rid of all those special interests—they're killing us."

The senator paused and then asked his constituent, "You're a member of AARP—isn't that a special interest?"

"Not on your life," the senior replied, "AARP isn't a special interest, it's for the public interest."

Apparently, groups to which we ourselves belong, or those that express our views, act in the public interest. Those to which other people belong are special interest groups and therefore act selfishly. Many of us make a distinction based upon our own affiliations and preferences. But, as the comic strip possum Pogo would put it, "We have met the enemy [special interests], and they are us."

Deliberation, Conflict Resolution, Negotiation, and Compromise

As long as disagreements exist—whether in the family, in the workplace, or in small groupings—they have to be worked out. In one way or another, people deliberate, negotiate, compromise, and manage to resolve conflict or simply live with it. It is not terribly different in political institutions, such as legislatures.

In each state, start off with individual legislators. These legislators have different and conflicting values, interests, and priorities. Add to this mix the fact that these legislators represent constituents who have different and conflicting values, interests, and priorities (usually organized and channeled by interest groups). Spice it all up with partisan conflict, which both reflects and contributes to public differences. Lay on top of all this the element of accountability, which is enforced by the requirement that legislators have to run for reelection if they want to keep their jobs. In this environment legislators try to reach settlements that promote public policy objectives and will not harm them politically. In this endeavor they advocate, deliberate, negotiate, compromise, trade, and decide. Usually, but not always, settlements are reached.

Americans, however, have serious doubts about the process. As shown in Figure 1-1, only 50 percent agree with the statement that "disagreement/ compromise are necessary parts of lawmaking," while 33 percent agree that "legislators spend too much time bickering and arguing." Lee Hamilton, a former member of the U.S. Congress and currently director of the Center on Congress at Indiana University, explains the problem:

> Pretty much every time I address an audience, someone complains, "I'm sick and tired of all the bickering. Those guys are always fighting." And everyone around will nod. Most people are uncomfortable with disagreement and debate. As individuals, this is fine; but as citizens, I would argue that we should not only get used to it, we should be pleased by it. It has been a constant in American politics, and let us hope it always will be.[7]

People are also suspicious of "compromise," which they regard as "selling out." Yet they do not like the idea of stalemate, which involves not getting much done. Their attitude toward legislators and the legislature is: "Just do what's right; we know what's right, so why don't you?" The problem, of course, is that among the public, as well as among their representatives, disagreement exists as to what is right.

Representation

People in the nation and states do not directly decide policy but rather choose those who decide on their behalf. That is the essence of *representative* democracy, which is how governance is mainly structured in the United States. Varieties of direct democracy also exist from place to place. New England town meetings allow all citizens to participate in deciding local questions. Citizen initiatives and referenda, which are provided in one form or another in twenty-four states, permit the voters to decide on selected issues as well.

Madison envisaged a system in which people would elect the most virtuous among them to represent the rest. Americans today are hardly convinced that legislators are the most virtuous among them, or that they are virtuous at all. They are distrustful of politicians generally, although they tend to like their own representatives.[8] They do not believe that those who are elected care about or represent them or their interests. In the Knowledge Networks survey, as shown in Figure 1-1, only 39 percent agreed that "elected officials care what their constituents think," while 34 percent felt that they did not care. Only 35 percent agreed that "elected officials work to serve the public interest," while 41 percent thought that they "work to serve their personal interests."

A large percentage of Americans believe that public officials are not only self-interested but also corrupt. Political humor, which is popular among legislators themselves, reinforces public beliefs. Quite to the point is a Tennessee story in which "Uncle Joe" is boasting about his sons: "I've got two fine boys and I'm mighty proud of them. Neither of them has ever been in the penitentiary or the legislature." [9] Uncle Joe might just as well have said that neither had ever been in the legislature *and then* in the penitentiary. Depending on the wording of the question and the state population surveyed, from one to three or four out of ten people express a lack of confidence in the integrity of their legislators. In New Jersey, for example, citizens were asked what percentage of legislators in Trenton they thought took bribes. One-third of the respondents said that they believed that anywhere from 50 to 100 percent of New Jersey legislators took bribes.[10] The question was asked, and answered, at a time when no scandals were being reported in the media, so the people had no immediate reason to be so distrustful. Years later, during a period in which several legislators were under indictment and more were under fire, New Jerseyans were asked what percentage of state legislators were willing to sell out to lobbyists in return for free meals, free trips, or campaign contributions. The responses averaged about 60 percent (an increase from 52 percent four years earlier).[11] Not a very flattering impression of the integrity of the people voters elect to the legislature.

People feel they are getting the short end. As many as 77 percent think that "ordinary people" have too little power, according to the Knowledge Networks survey. They feel that they are taken advantage of by those who are supposed to serve them and thus are ambivalent about the "representative" part of democracy.[12] When asked, as Figure 1-1 indicates, whether "making laws is a job best left to elected representatives" or "the public should decide issues directly by voting on them," only 30 percent chose the former, while 47 percent chose the latter. People want to have more control, even though few of them exercise that which they already have.

Where Americans Stand

Many people realize that disagreement among individuals is natural, but they still do not see why there is so much conflict in legislative bodies. People find conflict entertaining on television, in the movies, and on playing fields; but they are impatient with it in the governmental processes. "Deliberation," for the public, is bickering and a waste of time. "Bargaining" refers to back-room deals, in which the public is likely to be sold out to special interests, and "compromise" is one way of selling out. Americans are cynical about organizations and groups that are not their own and toward elected public officials, with the exception of those for whom they themselves vote. They do not seek to be involved in politics; they want the power to make laws on their own, however, rather than through representative assemblies. They do not trust those who have the power to decide or the processes by which decisions are made.

It is understandable then that people do not express much confidence in, let alone support for, their political institutions generally or their legislatures in particular. It is the rare state poll that reveals a legislature that is positively rated.[13] Some, like New York, have been in the doghouse for decades. According to Richard Brodsky, a member of the New York Assembly:

> We've been very effectively Swift-boated [the technique used in the 2004 presidential elections to discredit Democratic candidate John Kerry's war record] as dysfunctional, ineffective and corrupt. And it's our fault. We have never gotten the message out in a coherent way of what we do well and right.[14]

Not all state legislatures are in the public's doghouse. In some of the smaller states, such as North Dakota and Vermont, people think well of the legislature. But for the most part, disapproval is normal, especially in the larger states with more professionalized legislatures. Table 1-1 reports public

Table 1-1 Job Performance Ratings of Legislatures in Selected States

State and year	Disapprove	Approve	No opinion	Ratio D:A
California				
2007[a]	43	38	19	1.1
2006[a]	52	28	20	1.9
2005[a]	55	28	17	2.0
Connecticut				
2007[a]	36	46	18	0.8
2004	33	48	19	0.7
2003[a]	51	34	15	1.5
Florida				
2008	48	32	20	1.5
2007[a]	39	39	22	1.0
Kentucky				
2008	66	22	12	3.0
New Jersey				
2008	54	26	20	2.1
2007[a]	52	30	18	1.7
2006	71	20	10	3.5
New York				
2008	51	32	17	1.6
2007[a]	48	32	20	1.5
Ohio				
2007[a]	36	37	27	1.0
2006	55	25	20	2.2
Pennsylvania				
2008	42	37	21	1.1
2007[a]	48	34	18	1.4

Sources: California: The Field Poll, December 28, 2007; Connecticut: Quinnipiac University Poll, May 9, 2007; Florida: Quinnipiac, April 10, 2008; Kentucky: *Herald-Leader*/WKYT Kentucky Poll, May 14, 2008; New Jersey: Quinnipiac, February 20, 2008; New York: Quinnipiac, April 17, 2008; Ohio: Quinnipiac, May 15, 2007; and Pennsylvania: Quinnipiac, February 28, 2008. The questions ask whether respondents "approve" or "disapprove" of the way the state legislature is doing its job. Other state polls frame the question differently, asking whether respondents would rate the performance of the state legislature as "excellent," "good," "fair," or "poor."

[a] Average of several polls.

approval ratings for eight selected states where citizens are polled on a regular basis as to their approval or disapproval of the way the legislature is handling its job. Only in Connecticut do more people approve than disapprove, at least in two of the three years for which data are reported. Legislatures in Florida and Ohio, in one of two years, have equal percentages approving and disapproving. In contrast, the percentages disapproving in California, New Jersey, New York, Pennsylvania, and even Kentucky (a smaller state) are substantially higher than the percentages approving. The last column of Table 1-1 presents a ratio that shows rates of disapproval higher than approval in all but three of the data points (and more than twice as high in five instances and more than one and a half times as high in six other instances).

John E. McDonough, a former member of the Massachusetts House, recounts how when Speaker George Keverian traveled around the state he displayed official license plates with the words "The Speaker" on them. At the outset he would get beeping horns and thumbs up from passing drivers. That soon became beeping horns and raised middle fingers. Like many members with "House" plates, he too had his car plates changed so that he was unidentifiable.[15] Years later, even when the Massachusetts legislature was on the way to enacting major health insurance reform, the public was not satisfied. Two-thirds of those polled thought that the legislature was doing no better than an "only fair" or "poor" job, while only one-quarter believed it was doing an "excellent" or "good" job.[16]

Why Americans Are Cynical

It would be surprising if Americans viewed politics, the political system, political people, and legislatures much differently than they do. Given the nature of human beings, the nature of the environment in which they live, and the nature of the legislature itself, cynicism can be considered normal, not abnormal.

People who view politics positively are the deviants today. They constitute a distinct minority of the population. *Political heritage* may account for how some of them turn out. Such people tend to come from political families where their father, mother, and/or a close relative have enjoyed an involvement in politics. If one grows up hearing positive accounts about campaigning or governing within the family, one's orientation is likely to be positive. The glass, for them, is half full rather than half empty. Political institutions and processes are so complex that one can discern all kinds of things. The positively oriented will fasten on the pluses, the negatively oriented, the minuses. *Political experience* itself may also work to shape an orientation in a positive way. High school students who work as pages in Congress or at a state legislature or college students who intern on campaigns or in the legislature get a different impression from those who do not participate at all. I recall a page in the Washington House who described how "cool" his experience was carrying messages on the floor of the chamber and running errands for members. As an adult, he may regard the legislature with more empathy than others. I also remember college interns I met with in Minnesota and Ohio who observed how hard legislators worked and how well motivated they appeared to be. These interns may turn out to be more supportive of legislatures than the average citizen. Finally, *political instruction* may affect later attitudes. It is possible that a solid grounding in a high school civics course or a college American government course or an advanced seminar would make an impression. Probably, the teaching would have to be inspirational to make a sizable difference, but it does happen from time to time.

Yet one's normal experience in most parts of the country today runs in the negative direction. There are a number of compelling reasons why people today are cynical about legislatures and legislators.

An Ideal Whipping Boy (or Girl)

First, the legislature is an ideal whipping boy (or girl). Everyone can displace frustration or anger on a political institution such as a legislature. It is remote, an abstraction, not the flesh and blood of an individual. Its feelings can't be hurt. That is why public opinion polls and election returns show that people like their own legislators, rather than the rest of the legislators or the legislature. They do not have to know their legislators personally or even their names; it is enough that the legislators are theirs. In an analogous vein, surveys of public education find that estimates by respondents vary by their proximity to the subject. When asked for their assessment of education in the state, they generally award a C rating; when asked about public schools in their community, they give a B; and when asked about public schools that their children attend, they award an A.

Along similar lines, because governors are perceived as individuals rather than as faceless institutions, they generally have higher job approval ratings with the public than the legislatures. For example, if one were to match the disapproval scores of governors (which are not presented in Figure 1-1) with those of legislatures in the eight states, in every comparison lower percentages would disapprove of the way individual governors handled their jobs. Occasionally, as in Connecticut, where Gov. Jodi Rell was extremely popular, it appears that legislatures may have benefited from gubernatorial coattails. While gubernatorial approval can rub off on legislatures, it is unlikely that legislative approval would ever benefit governors' ratings.

Everyone Can Run against It

Second, with the possible exception of majority party leaders, who are responsible for what takes place, everyone can run against the legislature. Years ago Richard Fenno pointed out the phenomenon of members running against Congress. It is not difficult to see why challengers to incumbent legislators attack the institution in their campaigns. But some incumbents do so as well, in the belief that the legislature is defective and reform needed, because institution-bashing appeals to the electorate, or both. Again, the legislature is a sitting duck for someone who wants to take aim. If the process is too slow, major bills appear stalled, legislators travel to out-of-state events, funds are solicited for a campaign, legislative salaries or *per diem* expenses are raised, or for any number of other reasons, criticism and attacks are predictable. "The system needs reform, and I am the one to do it!" is heard from candidates in just about every state legislative election. The legislature does not fight back, or even defend itself. Nor do individual members.[17] What, then, are citizens to think if not where there's smoke there's fire?

The Minority Party Hammers Away

Third, in order to win seats and take control, the minority party in the senate or house will run against the majority party. The line between castigating the governing party and castigating the legislature itself is a thin one. Charges of a do-nothing legislature, a culture of corruption, or a legislature beholden to special interests resonate with the public. They reinforce notions that people already hold, not just about one party, as intended, but about the legislature as a whole.

In a campaign, unlike in basketball, defense is not a winning strategy. So the majority party takes a preemptive posture and attacks the minority. The legislature as an institution probably suffers more from the minority's assault on the majority, but it suffers from the attacks of partisans on both sides. If the political discourse becomes uncivil enough, we can expect negative effects on political trust and lower levels of support for political institutions.[18] The public response to that tends to be "a plague on both your houses."

Mobilizing the Troops

Fourth, many interest groups also act to undermine the standing of the legislature as an institution and the lawmaking process. The intensity of the struggle among groups for policy and funding is such that the legislature cannot make everybody happy. Occasionally all the groups are satisfied with an outcome. For example, when the Massachusetts legislature enacted comprehensive medical insurance legislation in 2006, each of the major stakeholders expressed approval. The Republican governor; the Democratic senate and house; the coalition of advocacy groups; and hospitals, physicians, insurance companies, and business all seemed satisfied and prepared to join in efforts to implement the state's ambitious program.

Normally, however, most interest groups feel that they are not getting as much as they need or deserve. Even though they probably get something, they want more. The process, they may believe, doesn't work for them and therefore is defective. Regardless of whether a group's leadership is sincerely critical of the legislature or the legislative process, a critical position can be organizationally advantageous. How else can a group with a grassroots membership mobilize its troops? Many interest groups today rely on members, employees, families, and friends for the outside part of their lobbying effort. A group has to motivate its grassroots if it wants them to act—to contact their legislator, visit the capitol, join in a rally, or sign a petition. Not getting a fair shake will motivate people far more than a sense of satisfaction with the process. And the very idea that the legislature has to be pressured, rather than acknowledging the merits of an interest group appeal, suggests that there must be something wrong with the legislative system.

Rank-and-File Legislators Complain

Fifth, legislators themselves complain about the process. A number feel marginalized or excluded. This is especially true for members of the minority party in a two-party, competitive state. The majority party organizes the chamber, sets the calendar, and has predominant influence over what bills get enacted. Republicans in chambers controlled by Democrats feel left out, as do Democrats in chambers controlled by Republicans. And they let it be known that they are not content with the way the legislature is working.

Even members of the majority party, if they are not in positions of leadership or on the leadership team, can feel out of the loop. They may be consulted in caucus, but still they are not in the office of the speaker of the house or president of the senate when strategy is discussed, negotiations take place, and the final deal is made. They tend to be critical of the process until they have achieved leadership.

Finally, some legislators are purists by conviction and mavericks by disposition. For them the process is not sufficiently transparent or democratic. Their criticism is ongoing.

Accentuating the Negative

Sixth, legislatures are undermined by the news media. We are fortunate in the United States to have a free and unfettered press. People get enormous amounts of information from a diversity of sources expressing a variety of views. An independent press serves to keep politicians and political institutions accountable. I cannot conceive of a political system such as ours without such media. But there are downsides, which are problematic for American politics.

Too often it appears that the media operate to highlight the bad and, perhaps, make it appear worse than it is.[19] How Americans orient themselves toward their political institutions depends in large part on the impression they get from the media.[20] The media are the principal storytellers about government, politics, and political institutions. No single story in print, on television, or on a blog shapes people's orientation, but the cumulation of coverage—especially if it runs in a negative direction—has an effect over time. There is some evidence that young people are less cynical than older people; that may be because they have consumed less of the media's coverage of politics.

For the media the very definition of news is a negative one. The cliché that "no news is good news" has a corollary: "good news, by and large, is no news." [21] When legislatures are working satisfactorily, they are not at all newsworthy. When there is controversy, conflict, or deadlock, then they are newsworthy. According to Thomas E. Patterson, an expert in this area, the media's focus on bad news has heightened Americans' disillusionment with their political institutions.[22]

It used to be that cynicism was the province of political cartoonists, whose avowed role was to lampoon politicians and politics. Now the media in general play the role of cynic, not just a small coterie of cartoonists. Whereas state house reporters once wrote "straight" news accounts, chronicling events in the legislative process, now they write with an emphasis on drama, disagreement, and criticism. Joseph Cooper describes contemporary coverage of Congress as follows: "Politics and politicians are covered in ways that highlight conflict and controversy, on the one hand, and personal ambition and ethical lapses, on the other. . . . The defining impression created is of Congress as a bunch of politicians squabbling over the distribution of benefits to special interests and jockeying for personal power while the needs of the country are ignored." [23] For the media the more negative the better, and the most scandalous the best.

The media behave the way they do partly for commercial reasons. The business environment—with newspapers, television, cable, and now blogs all competing for an audience—is frenzied. The print press still covers the state house, while electronic media have largely withdrawn. Newspapers try hard to give the public what it wants—investigative reporting and revelations of scandal and corruption. This is what editors insist on, and what journalists search for, if they hope to get ahead in their careers. What gets acknowledged in the profession of journalism? In 2006 the Pulitzer Prizes, for instance, were awarded for stories about scandalous and secretive behavior. The *Washington Post* won awards for revelations about lobbyist Jack Abramoff and the existence of secret military prisons; the *New York Times* won for exposing wiretapping by the National Security Agency; and the *San Diego Tribune* and *Copley News Service* won for the probe of California representative Randy "Duke" Cunningham. It is plain to see what the incentives are.

In addition to having their motives shaped by the professional marketplace, journalists also share a cynical orientation endemic to the profession. It goes with the territory. Illustrative is the question, "Why didn't the legislature pass the budget on time?" that was posed to fifty reporters and twenty-five legislative staffers. Respondents could choose either: (a) "Because democracy is a messy process. We all hold our values dearly and want what's best for our constituents"; or (b) "Because they spent too much time bickering and being stubborn instead of coming to consensus." All but a few reporters chose option (b), with "bickering" the explanation. All but a few legislative staffers chose (a), explaining why the budget was late in terms of the messiness of it all.[24]

Journalists are a distrustful lot. They are especially distrustful of what they cannot see. The legislative process goes on everywhere, concurrently, so it is not possible to see it all. And although the legislature is far more open than it used to be, the most important negotiations still are conducted in private (although the rooms are no longer smoke-filled). Since they are not witnesses to what is happening, journalists suspect the worst—or almost the worst. For them the legislative story is rather simple: follow the money. Most anything, they believe, can be explained by gifts and campaign contributions. No need to look for nuances; money tells the story. Huntington adds to this mix his contention that the media have an anti-authority attitude, which inclines toward an adversarial relationship with government. The level of government that receives the most media attention (i.e., the legislature) will over time experience the greatest public disdain.[25]

Students of the media, like Patterson, Joseph N. Cappella, and Kathleen Hall Jamieson, point to the negative news coverage by the media as responsible for the unfavorable attitudes people have toward politics. Public cynicism is the inevitable result of a journalism that emphasizes self-interest, strategy, inside-dope, and worse.[26]

The effects of the media are felt not only by the public, but also by legislators themselves. The coverage can be demoralizing to lawmakers who feel that they are trying to do a good job and accomplish something. Political scientist Grant Reeher interviewed such a lawmaker, who is worth quoting at some length:

> Knowing what I went through and what we went through to try to give birth to those bills, and to get those bills through the process and to the senate, and then to take the rap that we were ineffective. . . . The sad thing I learned about politics, and it didn't take me long to learn it: When you're in the legislature and you're concerned about the issues, you eat, sleep, and breath [sic] the issues, the people—you think that everybody out there on the street has the same level of understanding and cares as much as you do. The fact of the matter is they don't know and they could care less. And that becomes frustrating. Until it gets to the point where the press feeds what they fed on this year, all the negatives that went on, then that's when the average Joe gets all the sound bites, and then, bam, it comes back to you and you're continually explaining yourself. That part for me is frustrating.[27]

Generalizing from the Worst

Seventh, people generalize from the worst cases, not the best cases. In other words, they do not generalize from their own legislator, whom they regard positively, to the rest. They generalize from the relative few who are convicted or indicted in a court of law, reprimanded by a state ethics commission, or are accused explicitly or inferentially in the media.

Among the 7,382 members of the fifty state legislatures, there would have to be some "worst" cases and also some that are simply bad. A few legislators, no doubt, are personally corrupt. A number more probably cross the line in raising funds for campaigns. Some are oblivious to ethical considerations, and some are just stupid. From time to time, these legislators are outed by a sting operation, such as California's "Shrimp-gate," Kentucky's

"Operation Boptrot," South Carolina's "Operation Lost Trust," or Arizona's "AzScam," all of which occurred over twenty-five years ago. More recently, "Operation Tennessee Waltz" captured the nation's attention. These erring legislators may be subjects of a federal or state prosecution. Many more are targeted by opponents in an election for alleged misconduct or taken to task by the press for crossing an ethical line, or even getting too close to it.

These convicted, indicted, and even accused legislators constitute a very small percentage of the total, but they are the ones the public reads and hears about. People generalize from these few to the many others, assuming that those who are exposed are only the tip of the iceberg. Things look even worse below the water line, people suspect. This is a principal reason why public opinion polls reveal such large percentages believing that public officials are self-serving, dishonest, or corrupt.

It Is Messy and Has to Be

Eighth, neither the legislature nor the legislative process is appealing to people. In a society where standards of beauty dominate, the legislature is anything but beautiful. Indeed, to anyone who has been exposed to the dominant cultural standards, the legislature looks pretty ugly.

The legislative process is seldom what people think it ought to be. I recall, for example, the time I spent observing the Florida Legislature in the 1980s. Visitors in the gallery, looking down toward the floor of the house, would see legislators scurrying around, talking to one another, paying little attention to the proceedings, and rushing back to their desks to cast a vote by pressing a green, red, or yellow button. From the perspective of the visitors, it was not a reassuring sight. But the legislature was doing its job. Members already knew how they were going to vote on the bills that were brought up; they did not have to listen to the proceedings. Instead, they used the time to lobby and strategize with their colleagues on other issues that were at other points in the process. They were doing important legislative work but not the work the public expected them to be doing.

What the public sees on the floor or in committee is truly only the tip of the iceberg. The process is everywhere. It goes on in individual offices, in the lobbies outside the legislative chambers, in the cafeteria and corridors, on the run. It goes on in leadership suites and in caucus rooms. Unlike the old Ringling Bros. and Barnum and Bailey Circus, the process is not confined to three rings (and certainly not to the one ring of the Big Apple Circus). It is wherever legislators, lobbyists, and others talk to one another about bills, amendments, and all sorts of issues connected to public policy. The process is concurrent, complicated, unpredictable, human, and—last but not least—messy. It is hardly a sight for sore eyes; rather, it is a sight that makes eyes sore.

Years ago, I examined public opinion data to discern patterns in how New Jerseyans viewed the performances of their legislature in Trenton. The Eagleton Institute of Politics at Rutgers University asked a statewide sample of citizens on a quarterly basis how they would rate the job of the New Jersey Legislature: "excellent," "good," "only fair," or "poor." In examining data collected over the course of a decade, I could detect only one pattern. Legislative performance was rated "only fair" every month of the year, except for the summer months. Then, the ratings improved significantly. What was the explanation for this pattern? During July and August the legislature was not in session. When it was not doing its job, the New Jersey Legislature looked better and was rated higher. When it was doing its job, it looked worse and was rated lower. Hibbing points out that the more Congress is in the news, wrestling with tough problems and trying to check the president, the more support for Congress declines. His explanation: "People do not like to see the debate and conflict that are inevitably part and parcel of representative democracy. . . ." [28]

The View from Within

It is entirely understandable why Americans think the way they do. Political institutions, and especially legislatures, are easy to misperceive and to criticize. Those who see legislatures differently are likely to have been close to the process or to people who have participated in the process. There is no substitute for firsthand experience. But in lieu of that, the following chapters are intended to give readers a close-up view of the legislature, one that should challenge the view that prevails today.

Notes

1. Samuel P. Huntington, *American Politics: The Promise of Disharmony* (Cambridge: Harvard University Press, 1981), 18.

2. John R. Hibbing and Elizabeth Theiss-Morse, *Congress as Public Enemy* (Cambridge: Cambridge University Press, 1995) and *Stealth Democracy: American Beliefs about How Government Should Work* (Cambridge: Cambridge University Press, 2002).

3. See Bill Bishop, *The Big Sort: Why the Clustering of Like-Minded America Is Tearing Us Apart* (New York: Houghton Mifflin, 2008).

4. Karl T. Kurtz, Alan Rosenthal, and Cliff Zukin, *Citizenship: A Challenge for All Generations* (Denver: National Conference of State Legislatures, September 2003).

5. Bruce King, *Cowboy in the Roundhouse* (Santa Fe, N.M.: Sunstone Press, 1998), 41.

6. Huntington, *American Politics,* 105.

7. Lee Hamilton, newsletter, November 9, 2007.

8. See John R. Hibbing, "Images of Congress," in *The Legislative Branch,* ed. Paul J. Quirk and Sarah A. Binder (New York: Oxford University Press, 2005), 477.

9. Roy Herron and L. H. "Cotton" Ivy, *Tennessee Political Humor* (Knoxville: University of Tennessee Press, 2000), 132.

10. Alan Rosenthal, *Drawing the Line: Legislative Ethics in the States* (Lincoln: University of Nebraska Press, 1996), 43.

11. Monmouth University/Gannett New Jersey Poll, "New Jersey Sees Corruption Flourishing," October 7, 2007.

12. Hibbing and Theiss-Morse, *Stealth Democracy.*

13. For public attitudes toward Congress, see Hibbing, "Images of Congress," 472.

14. *New York Times,* February 9, 2007.

15. John E. McDonough, *Experiencing Politics: A Legislator's Stories of Government and Health Care* (Berkeley: University of California Press, 2000), 139.

16. State House News Survey, reported in *The Boston Globe,* July 31, 2006.

17. There is no political gain but substantial risk for legislators who defend their institution.

18. See Diana C. Mutz and Byron Reeves, "The New Videomalaise: Effects of Televised Incivility on Political Trust," *American Political Science Review* 99 (February 2005): 1–15.

19. Thomas E. Patterson, *Out of Order* (New York: Vintage Books, 1994).

20. The following paragraphs draw on Alan Rosenthal, Burdett A. Loomis, John R. Hibbing, and Karl T. Kurtz, *Republic on Trial: The Case for Representative Democracy* (Washington, D.C.: CQ Press, 2003), 20–21.

21. Reported in State House News Service, Massachusetts, "Weekly Roundup," July 17, 2006.

22. See Patterson, *Out of Order.*

23. Joseph Cooper, "Performance and Expectations in American Politics," in *Congress and the Decline of Public Trust,* ed. Joseph Cooper (Boulder: Westview Press, 1999), 150.

24. An online survey of reporters and legislative staff, in Nicole Casal Moore, "Adversaries Always," *State Legislatures* (May 2005): 21–23.

25. Huntington, *American Politics,* 217–218.

26. See Joseph N. Cappella and Kathleen Hall Jamieson, *Spiral of Cynicism: The Press and the Public Good* (New York: Oxford University Press, 1997).

27. Grant Reeher, *First Person Political* (New York: New York University Press, 2006), 103.

28. Hibbing, "Images of Congress," 462. Also see Robert H. Durr, John B. Gilmour, and Christina Wolbrecht, "Explaining Congressional Approval," *American Journal of Political Science* 41 (January 1997): 175–207.

2

Lives of Legislators

IT IS NOT POSSIBLE to have a sense of legislatures without an appreciation of the people who serve in legislative office. One way to begin is by exploring the careers of members, as related in biographies and memoirs. Not many are out there to choose from, because the lives of state legislators have as little appeal to the publishing industry as they do to the reading public.

In examining what makes legislators tick, we shall draw here on the careers of three legislators in particular—Willie Brown, Harriet Keyserling, and Tom Loftus.[1] Their careers illustrate why legislators run, the ways they adapt to legislative life, what they like and dislike about their jobs, and why they leave legislative service.[2]

Willie Brown served in the California Assembly from 1965 to 1995, including fifteen years as speaker. He followed his legislative tenure with two four-year terms as mayor of San Francisco. His biographer, James Richardson, who covered Brown and the California Legislature for the *Sacramento Bee*, writes in the prologue: "No politician dominated California politics longer or more completely. . . . No politician in California was more flamboyant or controversial or relished wielding power with more joy and zeal."[3] Harriet Keyserling was a member of the South Carolina House in Columbia, almost three thousand miles away from Sacramento, where Brown exercised command. She was sworn into office in December 1976 and left at the end of her term in 1992. Keyserling, in many respects the antithesis of Brown, was "more given to quiet research, serious conversation, and careful organization" in pursuing objectives in which she believed.[4] Tom Loftus spent his fourteen-year career in the Wisconsin Assembly rising quickly through the ranks, being elected by his Democratic colleagues majority leader after just four years and speaker two years later. A man of principle, Loftus was also a pragmatic leader and one who through his service developed great affection and respect for the legislature as an institution.

What Motivates People to Run

I recall being interviewed about state legislatures for a television program some years ago. Referring to my expertise on the subject, the interviewer asked me why I, myself, didn't run for a seat in the state where I lived. I responded, "If I ran, I don't think I could win a primary in order to get the nomination." I continued, "Let's assume that I won the primary and the nomination, I don't think I could win a general election." After a pause, I went on, "But let's just say I won both the primary and the general election, I don't think I could govern. It's harder than it looks."

A number of my fellow citizens might agree with me. It is harder than it looks. Others might believe that, if they wanted to, they could win an election and do the job. But they would not choose to get their hands dirty. The largest number of citizens, however, is elsewhere entirely. They are not at all interested in the prospects of a campaign and/or governance. They pay politics little or no attention, perhaps because politics repels them, because their energy is consumed by other pursuits, or for both reasons. Only a small proportion of the population in the country or in any single state would consider running for the legislature or other public office. These are the people who need explaining. What motivates them to do so?

Power as an Explanation

Political scientists recognize the centrality of power in the lives of politicians. But not many of them have been able to explore the motivations of politicians seeking power. Probably the major work along these lines was done more than a half-century ago by Harold D. Lasswell who, among other things, posited that people with weak egos attempt to compensate by seeking and exercising power in the public sphere.[5] Years later, James David Barber, in his study of Connecticut legislators, used a psychological approach to reveal the motivations of political candidates. One set of influences related to personal needs, such as that for power, which might be satisfied in politics. For Barber an individual's sense of self is central. Political candidacy, in his view, draws toward it exceptional people—exceptional in their high abilities and/or their strong needs and exceptional in their high or low level of self-esteem.[6] Barber's "lawmaker," one of four legislative types he portrays, has a strong ego and thus is unlike Lasswell's politicians who seek power to compensate for weak egos.

For some politicians the prospect of exercising power has great appeal. Willie Brown is one such politician. Having grown up poor and black in East Texas, he had much for which to compensate psychologically. During his childhood, he suffered the stings of racial discrimination. Much that followed, including his involvement with civil rights demonstrations, his election campaigns, and his self-image as an outsider, can be traced to his experiences as a young boy. When later in his career Brown was accused of having a racial "chip on his shoulder" about whites, he replied, "I don't have a chip, I got a redwood forest on my shoulders . . . it's permanent." [7] At the age of seventeen, Brown made his way to San Francisco, where he went to live with an uncle. There, he began developing political relationships and political experiences that helped launch him in his pursuit of power. For Brown power was not only a goal in and of itself, it was also a means of serving the needs of his district, members of his race, and the public. In addition, it provided a way in which Brown could prove himself by showing everyone just what he was made of and what he could do. Power, for Brown, was a means of receiving attention, approval, and support. He enjoyed its exercise immensely, which he exhibited in the most public of places as well as in the back rooms and watering holes in Sacramento. Even when he had lost his Democratic majority in the assembly and was leaving legislative office, Brown succeeded for a year in preventing Republican leaders from taking the control that should have been theirs. He wanted to show that he could wield power even after his legislative party had lost it.

Harriet Keyserling is probably unusual among those who run for legislative office in that not only was she not power hungry, she was power averse. Perhaps because she did not receive the same level of attention as her brother, or perhaps because she was a poor student in school, Keyserling grew up with a low sense of self-esteem. But a weak ego did not drive her, as it drove Lasswell's political man, to project her psychological needs onto public objects. She stumbled rather than strode into the political arena, but she did eventually run for local and then legislative office and succeeded in getting elected. But neither ambition, nor purposefulness, nor a drive for power had much to do with her candidacies. She was pulled and pushed by others. She had to be persuaded to run. Keyserling fortunately found a vocation that she liked and a means by which she managed to build self-confidence. By the time she left the legislature, she was much more comfortable with power and appreciated that it had to be used in order to accomplish public good.

Political candidates will not admit publicly, even if they do privately, that they want power. That is because most Americans are suspicious of power, believe that it corrupts, and would prefer that politicians manage the public's business without resorting to it. Madeleine M. Kunin, a former legislator and governor of Vermont, illustrates how politicians refuse to admit to seeking power: "I could not bring myself to acknowledge that I wanted power; it was not a desire I could articulate even to myself." So she translated her ambition into "more comfortable language"—that she wanted to get something done, to have an impact.[8]

In view of its public reputation, it is impossible to discover just how much power motivates candidates. What proportion of legislative candidates are like Brown? What proportion are like Keyserling? My guess is that for a good number of aspiring politicians, the prospect of exercising power has appeal independent of what power can help accomplish. Jesse Unruh, the legendary speaker of the assembly in California (and one of Brown's mentors), was surely one of them. Power seemed to gravitate to him and he luxuriated in its exercise. But it is not the only motive and probably not the dominant one for most of those who run and are elected. However they start out, as they serve in office, politicians become more comfortable with power.

Bill Bulger, who served as president of the Massachusetts Senate for over twenty years, certainly was comfortable with power. In his view, there are three types of power in politics. First is the power of acquired political knowledge that derives mostly from experience, although it is partly intuitive. Second and third are the powers inherent in office and those that are perceived to exist there. The perception, according to Bulger, usually exceeds the reality, but it is important nonetheless.[9] If and when legislators achieve positions of leadership, they are likely to derive pleasure from exercising power. It is part of the job. Ralph Wright certainly enjoyed wheeling, dealing, and cajoling as speaker of the house in Vermont.[10] But "power" in legislative politics does not confer the ability to command or control. It does offer increased responsibility, along with a greater say as to what gets done and especially what does not get done.

Sociology as an Explanation

People who run for the legislature are not a sociological cross-section of the population. Candidates generally come from the ranks of upper- and upper-middle-class Americans. Those from impoverished backgrounds, like Brown, are few and far between. A survey of nonincumbent candidates for state legislatures some years ago reported that the most common types of candidates were white (less than 7 percent were not), male (22 percent were women), in their forties or fifties (only 5 percent were under thirty), had attended college (only 22 percent had no college at all, and only 6 percent had less than a high school degree), and had incomes of more than $50,000 (12 percent earned less than $30,000 and 15 percent more than $120,000). Three-quarters had lived in their community for more than ten years.[11]

A former Wisconsin legislator recalls that although the public perceived of legislators as dunderheads and hacks, his experience was the opposite: "As a class of people," he writes, "they seemed to me on the whole to be nuanced, subtle and sophisticated; able to think three to four moves ahead in any given direction." [12] In fact, by and large those who run for public office are well-educated, intelligent, and resourceful. When they first run for the legislature, they hold a variety of jobs. Their most frequent occupation is business employer or owner (30 percent) followed by attorney (10 percent). Another 45 percent are spread across other professions and occupations: real estate, insurance, health care, farming, ranching, education, and government. The remaining 15 percent are retired.[13]

In terms of their backgrounds, those who are elected are fairly representative of those who run for the legislature. As part of a study of the effects of term limits, a survey mailed to all 7,382 legislators in the spring of 2002 was completed by 2,982, for a response rate of 40 percent.[14] According to the survey, 77.4 percent are male, 89.6 percent are white (with 5.5 percent African American and about 3 percent Hispanic), and 47.5 percent Protestant, 28.5 percent Roman Catholic, 6.7 percent Fundamentalist Christian,

3.7 percent Jewish, 4.5 percent "none," and 9.1 percent "other." Of the 89.7 percent reporting their family income, only 11.8 percent receive less than $50,000, while 42.3 percent receive between $50,000 and $100,000, and 35.7 percent receive over $100,000. Occupationally, the percentage of attorneys in the legislature today is about 16 percent, down significantly from the 25–30 percent in the 1960s.

The major change in the composition of legislative bodies has been the increased number of women in office and the slightly higher proportion of African Americans and Hispanics. Brown and Keyserling were exceptional in winning office when they did. In the past thirty years, the situation for women has undergone substantial change. In 1970 only 4 percent of legislators were female and in 1980 only 10 percent. Since then the percentage has doubled, and then plateaued at just about a quarter. The proportion of African Americans has inched up, so that now it is likely that districts with sizeable African American populations are represented by one of their racial own in the state house. Hispanics never had much of a foothold in state legislatures, but today they have sizeable delegations in New Mexico, Arizona, Colorado, and Florida, and they may be the dominant political force ethnically in California.

Proponents of term limits, which are now in effect in fifteen states, had hoped that the composition of legislative bodies would be transformed as a result of limiting the number of terms legislators could serve. But the demographic shape of legislatures is not very different in these states after term limits than it was before.

The trend has been toward younger legislators. Practically everywhere the average age of legislators has been declining and the number of members under forty, and under thirty, increasing. More and more young people have been running and getting themselves elected. Part of the reason for current legislators who are not so long in the tooth is that at least some young people want to make careers out of politics. Young people who gravitate to politics still are precious few, but they are numerous enough to give the younger generation a toehold in legislative bodies.

Tom Loftus exemplifies the kind of young person who heads for politics. His generation came of political age in the 1970s and 1980s. Loftus and a number of his Democratic colleagues in the Wisconsin Legislature all spent time working in politics before running for office. David Clarenbach was an intern and Stan Gruszynski and David Travis both served as staff directors of the Senate Democratic Caucus. Loftus did graduate work in public affairs at the LaFollette School at the University of Wisconsin before being hired by the speaker of the assembly. He was committed to politics, poised to run, and waiting for his chance. As described by Alan Ehrenhalt: "For a liberal Democrat in Wisconsin in the 1970s, government was fun. It turned dozens of academics and staff aides into active political candidates willing to invest their efforts in moving from the sidelines to the more exhilarating experience of holding office." [15] Grant Reeher, in his engaging study of legislators in Connecticut, New York, and Vermont, confirms the importance of youthful experience in stimulating political candidacy. A number of his interviewees tell of an "early, poignant, epiphanic experience" that spurred them on. Particularly salient, along these lines, is the opportunity of a politically related internship.[16]

Perhaps even more important than youthful experience outside the family is what transpires within the family. Many candidates emerge from the ranks of political dynasties. We can all think of the nation's leading political families, the Kennedy and Bush clans, and others as well. State by state, families transmit political predispositions from generation to generation. For example, Fred Risser, Wisconsin Senate president, in 2007 serving his fiftieth year in the legislature, was the fourth generation of his family to represent Madison in the legislature. (Risser is a Democrat, his father was a Progressive, his grandfather a Republican, and his great grandfather a Unionist.) In the study mentioned above, Reeher asked where legislators originally got their political commitment and interest. He found that about two-thirds of those he interviewed in the three states inherited their political tendencies from their parents and grandparents as well as their parents' close friends.[17] In the case of John E. McDonough of Massachusetts, "inheritance" worked very indirectly. McDonough's mother was a maid and cook in the Jamaica Plain home of James Michael Curley, the former mayor of Boston, governor of Massachusetts, and legendary political boss. Curley took McDonough's mother under his wing and hosted her wedding, and undoubtedly made an impression on her son. Since his early youth, McDonough had wanted to live in Curley's neighborhood; he finally was able to move to Jamaica Plain, where he was elected in 1984 to represent the Twelfth Suffolk District.[18]

I can think of students I taught, each of whom was pursuing a master's degree in political science or public policy at Rutgers University in New Jersey. Steve Adubato's father was a political leader in the North Ward of Newark and his uncle a member of the New Jersey Legislature. His grandmother wanted Steve to become the first Italian American governor in the state. Steve chose a legislative district where he had a possibility, worked hard, ran against an incumbent, and won a seat in the assembly, but two years later he lost his bid for reelection. William Hughes, son of a New Jersey congressman who later became ambassador to Mexico, ran for a seat in the state senate from a district that his father had previously represented. He lost. Ellen Karcher, the daughter of a former speaker of the New Jersey Assembly, moved from her father's district, settled elsewhere, and won local office. When an opportunity presented itself, she ran against an incumbent senator and beat him, but was defeated in her next election.

A number of New Jersey legislators are descendants of former legislators. Sen. Thomas Kean Jr. is the son of former assembly speaker and governor Tom Kean. Assemblyman Christopher "Kip" Bateman is the son of Ray Bateman, a former president of the senate and candidate for governor. Sen. Leonard Lance is the son of a former senator. Sen. Robert Littell's father served earlier, and his daughter was recently elected to the assembly. Bonnie Watson Coleman fills the assembly seat her father once held. Leonard Connors Jr. is a member of the senate, while his son is a member of the assembly.[19]

Who a person is and where he or she comes from has a lot to do with running and getting elected to the legislature. Coming from a political family, getting involved in a political campaign, serving as an intern in the legislature, and having friends who care about politics all serve to spur one's candidacy.

Ambition as an Explanation

"Ambition" is defined as an "ardent desire for rank, fame, or power" and as a "desire to achieve a particular end." Joseph Schlesinger has written about ambition for political office in terms of three directions ambition may take. First, ambition may be *discrete,* with individuals wanting to serve in a particular office for a limited term and then return to private life. Second, ambition may be *static,* with individuals seeking to make long-term careers in a particular office. Third, ambition may be *progressive,* with individuals striving to attain office higher than the one they are holding.[20]

Legislators tend to be self-starters. Among candidates for the legislature, only one-fifth or so say they had not thought about running until someone had suggested it to them.[21] These individuals may have been recruited by local party activists, legislative leaders, or interest group representatives, or simply had been talked into candidacy by friends. They were asked to run and likely promised support. Many of them, no doubt, lived in districts that were safely in the hands of the other party, districts they had little chance of winning. Their party still wanted to field a candidate. In helping their party as sacrificial lambs, they might anticipate "losers' benefits" of one kind or another—a chance to run elsewhere, an appointment to a board or commission, or simply getting known by people who mattered.

According to Reeher, recruitment by local and state party leaders is very important for a few legislators in Connecticut, New York, and Vermont. But it is not a prominent feature in most candidates' paths to the legislature.[22] Ralph Wright, as Democratic leader in Vermont, worked to recruit candidates. But Wright himself recognized that people normally want to run; they do not have to be begged to run. "Don't believe any of those guys," Wright suggests, "that try to tell you they ran for office because a lot of folks begged them." [23]

Most candidates either got their idea to run for the legislature entirely on their own or got some help from the encouragement of others. The fact is that, in most cases, people recruit themselves. "Who sent us the political leaders we have?" Ehrenhalt asks. The answer for him is simple: "They sent themselves. And they got where they are through a combination of ambition, talent, and the willingness to devote whatever time was necessary to seek and hold office." [24] These individuals are rare in that they are willing, and can also afford, to forgo other opportunities and put all their eggs in a candidacy basket. Although percentages vary by state, a considerable number have embarked upon political and electoral careers prior to running for the legislature. A few have worked as staffers in the legislature or for Congress. A few have held local or state party office. Many more have been elected to positions in local or county government. The motivation to involve oneself in politics is general, not specific to the legislature as the only political office.

Brown and Loftus certainly did not have to be talked into running. Each wanted to make a mark in politics. Each worked tirelessly toward that goal. Each took a different avenue. For Brown it was through law practice, involvement in church affairs, and adoption by political mentors like Phil Burton, one of California's principal Democratic leaders. For Loftus it was working on a campaign, writing speeches for the speaker of the assembly, and being prepared to move when the opportunity arose. The ambitions Brown and Loftus brought with them continued throughout their careers in the legislature. For Brown capturing the speakership took a change in behavior after an unsuccessful try. For Loftus achieving first one and then another leadership position looked relatively easy.

By contrast, Keyserling could not possibly have planned the way her career developed. She migrated from New York City, where she grew up and went to college, to the town of Beaufort, South Carolina, where she married a local physician. No fire burned within her, as it obviously had in Brown and less obviously, but no less strongly, in Loftus. Keyserling was happy to become involved in the study and activity of the local League of Women Voters, still without much thought of running. She was truly a recruit to politics.

Despite the anomaly of Keyserling, ambition usually helps in candidacy for legislative office. Without ambition, it is unlikely that someone will devote the time, energy, and perhaps money to an election campaign, as well as make the sacrifices of professional, family, and personal life required for running. Term limits were intended to dampen political ambitions and diminish political careers. Limiting terms, however, does neither; it only makes people who want to be in public office worry more about where they will go next and how they will get there. The fire continues to burn. Even Keyserling developed a taste for office; otherwise she would have left years before she did.

Public Service as an Explanation

People run for the legislature because they have a commitment to public service. A former speaker of the Michigan House of Representatives put it this way: "Most people run with some level of idealism—to leave the state and the community better for their children than they found it. Why do people teach or go into the ministry? I think it's very much the same thing. . . ." Legislators with whom Reeher talked were pursuing a path of public service that reflected a commitment to civic engagement and attachment to their communities.[25]

As part of their commitment, many who run want to improve some facet of public policy. Keyserling exemplifies those who run with the objective of reforming policy. When the state representative from Beaufort, who was going to retire, asked Keyserling to run for his seat, she was uncertain. But she realized, from her stint on the county council, that there had to be policy changes at the state level before the problems at home could be remedied. Education led her list of problems, followed by the environment. Others, who have been members of local school boards or have taught at elementary or secondary levels, harbor their own ideas about what should be done to make education right. Businesspeople who become candidates are likely to want to focus on the promotion of a healthy business climate and economic development, and farmers are inclined to seek improvements in agriculture policy. Candidates impelled by personal situations and experiences to go into politics may want to improve health care or family services.[26] Whatever their objectives, participating in the making of public policy can be a very gratifying experience. Recalling his many years in the Massachusetts legislature, Bulger writes: "To make law, to make what you believe is *good* law, to see laws you have sponsored or effectively supported improve the happiness of people, is the ultimate satisfaction." [27]

Beyond policy *per se,* many of those drawn to legislative candidacy are critical of the incumbent. They think they can do a better job than the one being done. Keyserling, for example, had as one objective ridding the South Carolina General Assembly of the good ol' boys system, "which protected the status quo and vested interest at the expense of the public interest and open government." Furthermore, she wanted to do something about the underrepresentation of women in elected and appointed positions, an issue about which she cared passionately. "There was so much to do," she writes, "and I wanted to do it all."

Others who run are people-oriented rather than policy-oriented. Mainly, they want to hold office in order to be able to help their constituents. They enjoy being available, helping out, trying to solve problems. They like seeing tangible results. As former New Jersey legislator Gordon MacInnes observed, most of his colleagues were ombudsmen, not lawmakers, and they knew that was what they wanted to be when they ran in the first place.[28]

Some individuals develop a public-service ethos within their families or in their communities. Loftus is very much of this breed. Although his father sold farm machinery, family values and Democratic roots in Dane County were responsible for the direction Loftus set for himself. As he matured, it never occurred to him that there was any other place to go than into public life.

Doing Good and Doing Well

Ralph Wright explains the motivations that impelled him to seek office:

> I made the decision to run for the Vermont legislature in 1978 because I wanted to be a player in the great American game of politics. To me it was an opportunity to get involved in an arena that offered the chance to make people's lives more rewarding—including my own.[29]

Practically every legislator wants to do "good" and also do "well." "Doing good" involves public-regarding motivations, such as improving policy, reforming government, solving problems, and helping people. On a number of issues this brings to bear ideology, core values, and beliefs. There are liberal "goods" and conservative "goods," public school "goods," charter school "goods," and so forth. Interpretations of what constitutes "good" vary, according to the legislator's concept of the public interest—whether left or right, expansive or modest, district focused or state focused.

Doing "well" involves self-regarding motivations, rather than public-regarding ones. Reelection is one such motivation. Legislators who run for reelection have as their objective winning, not losing. Although the desire to be reelected can be justified as a prerequisite for doing "good," it is fundamentally in one's personal interest. There is nothing wrong with that. After all, winning reelection indicates plurality (or majority) support in one's constituency. In aspiring to do "well," legislators are also in pursuit of careers in politics, power within their institutions, or the attainment of higher public office. The sheer enjoyment of the game of politics—the competition, the risk, the excitement, and the exercise of power—is part of doing "well." Satisfaction and ego gratification are important benefits that derive from public life. Finally, legislators want to do "well," or as "well" as possible, by their families. Some seek to enhance their incomes, but the large majority settles for trying to cut the economic losses that go with service in the legislature.

Both public- and private-regarding motives exist in just about everyone who seeks elective office. The question is, how do these two types of motives balance out in each individual? On a public- versus private-regarding continuum, Keyserling can probably be placed as near to the public end as possible, as can Loftus.

Both, of course, were concerned about reelection. Loftus, at least, sought power and had no compunctions about wielding it. And both enjoyed their service in the legislature. Brown, by contrast, falls nearer to the private-regarding end of the continuum, because power and ego played such a large part in his motivational set. Brown was more self-concerned than public-regarding. Some legislators, who are primarily interested in using public office to advance their outside careers or who fixate on the game of politics as an end itself, are even more private-regarding in their motivations.

However, estimating political motivations is not like baking a cake, where there is a recipe that measures out all the ingredients. When it comes to political motivations, there is no way to measure the ingredients. All that can be said with confidence is that they are mixed.

Opportunities and Resources

Motivations are one thing, opportunities another, and resources still another. Opportunities and resources are intertwined. If there is a real opportunity to achieve office, then fewer resources will be needed to get there. However, if there is little opportunity, far greater resources will have to be brought to bear. Schlesinger has examined the opportunity structure state by state for political office, taking into account the number of offices and turnover rates.[30] Here, the question is narrower, whether or not individuals—in view of their motivations, their chances of winning, and the likely costs—will choose to run for a seat in the legislature.

An individual's personal opportunity structure is determined at the outset by the match of his or her own political identification with that of the district. If one lives in a place dominated by the opposite party, opportunities are limited indeed. It is possible for an aspirant to change parties, as a number of Democrats in southern states have done in the past decade or so, but this occurs infrequently.[31] The best hope for those individuals, who have public office as an objective but who live in enemy territory, is to move to a more politically compatible district. A few individuals do just that, shopping around until they find a place to set down political roots.

If a person is in political sync with his or her district, chances are that the legislative seat is filled already. The choice is either to challenge the incumbent of one's own party or wait until the incumbent moves on or out and the seat becomes vacant. Then the challenge is to win a party nomination for which a number of people may be vying. In the meantime, the potential candidate works in partisan politics, serves on appointed boards, and perhaps runs for and is elected to local office. After a while a chance to run for the legislature may open up. If it does not, the aspirant may shift his or her energies away from public life.

Joseph Lieberman, at the outset of his political career in New Haven, Connecticut, took advantage of the opportunity when it arose. He explains that opportunities cannot be created but have to be seized:

> So much is luck, particularly in timing. Hard work is important; so are personal skill, issue development, and organization. But without luck in timing, the rest cannot produce victory. By luck in timing, I mean the coming together of a politician's goals with the historical environment that makes these goals obtainable.[32]

As a rule, an individual's best chance comes when the office sought is vacant. If the district is politically safe for one's own party and if the nomination can be secured, victory is probable. No better opportunity for an aspirant could be imagined. If the district is politically competitive, one usually has a better chance running if the seat is vacant than if it is held by an incumbent. But even a race against an incumbent, assuming that the district is reasonably competitive, offers an opportunity to someone who is motivated and resourceful. Even if one loses, one can always try again.

A candidate, of course, has to be legally qualified. Written into every state constitution or statute are age requirements for the state senate and state house. In state houses, minimum age requirements range from eighteen years old (in thirteen states) to twenty-five years old (in three states). In state senates, the range is from eighteen (in thirteen states) to thirty (in five states). Half the states require American citizenship, four-fifths set a residency period in the state, and nearly all require that the legislators have residence in the district or county to be represented for some period of time prior to the election.[33]

Beyond these legal requirements, the rest is optional. In order to be credible to the electorate, it helps if a candidate can tap into a variety of resources. At the legislative level, probably the most important resource is one's reputation within the local community. Most legislators are not new arrivals; they have lived in their communities for quite some time. In a 2001 survey of 364 legislators (of the 848 who were mailed questionnaires) in five states—Maryland, Minnesota, Ohio, Vermont, and Washington—I asked members just how long they had lived in the district they represented. This Five-State Survey revealed that as many as 27 percent had lived their entire lives in their district; another 40 percent had lived there twenty-five years or more. All told, 83 percent had lived in their districts twenty years or longer. Even at the time they were first elected, most legislators from these five states tended to have solid groundings in their communities.[34] Loftus is typical of those with local reputation and roots. He writes:

> After all I did not arrive in Sun Prairie, Wisconsin from Persia, a follower of Zoroaster, intending to sell band instruments to the high school and then end up somehow getting elected to the legislature. No, I represented the district where I was born. Like many of those I represent, I was raised a Lutheran and married a Catholic, can eat lutefish with a smile, speak some Norwegian and some German, know how to play euchre, and, with the help of beer, can dance the polka. Like most of those I represent, I understand everything Garrison Keillor has to say.[35]

One's political base in the community is enhanced by having held public office prior to running for the legislature. Many legislators have experienced public office before being elected to the state legislature. The 2002 State Legislative Survey found that 46.7 percent had held elective public office (including the 8.5 percent who had held elective office in their political party) immediately prior to their election to the legislature. (Incidentally, 11.6 percent had been on the state legislative staff before running for the legislature.) In the Five-State Survey, about half the respondents reported that the legislature was not their first elective office. They had either been mayors, members of municipal councils, county commissioners, or school board members. The variations among the states in terms of prior local-office experience are substantial. In Vermont 67 percent had been elected previously to another office, in Ohio 52 percent, in Washington 36 percent, in Minnesota 31 percent, and in Maryland 29 percent. In other words, from one- to two-thirds of these legislators had some political reputation in their communities. Reeher's data from Connecticut, New York, and Vermont run along similar lines, indicating that 51 percent had held elective office before coming to the legislature. In addition, nearly all of these legislators had previously been involved in social and political organizations. Only three of the seventy-seven legislators interviewed by Reeher said that running for the state legislature was the first serious political activity in which they had engaged.[36]

While having family, friends, and a following in the district is important, status and celebrity can count even more as a resource. Celebrity certainly has left its mark on statewide elections, as the candidacies of John Glenn in Ohio; Bill Bradley in New Jersey; and Ronald Reagan, George Murphy, and Arnold Schwarzenegger in California attest. Only a few celebrities run for the state legislature; they are more likely to cut their political teeth on congressional races or running statewide. Money also matters, although in most states and for most races campaign expenditures, as we shall explain in chapter 4, are rather moderate. Only in the large states with professionalized legislatures and only in districts with competitive races does campaign funding become an arms race between the two parties and the two candidates. Still, a candidate who can afford to contribute to or entirely finance his or her campaign has a resource advantage over the rest of the field wanting to run. State, local, and legislative party leaders will be more likely to solicit as candidates those who can bring such resources to the table.

Personal, as well as monetary, resources count. The ability to devote one-self wholeheartedly to the pursuit of elective office is usually requisite. It helps considerably if a fire is burning in the belly of the person seeking a seat in the legislature. He or she has to want it badly to be willing to commit the time and energy demanded by campaigns and thereafter by legislative duties. If the candidate's health is questionable or energy depleted, chances are that his or her ambitions for office will weaken and drive diminish.

Loftus, for example, had a base that had largely been established by his family in Sun Prairie, Wisconsin. He had experience on a campaign, a plan for running, and boundless energy. And he fit, as far as the voters in his district were concerned. "The winner is not necessarily the one with the best pitch," Loftus writes, "but the one the voters feel most comfortable with." Perhaps because of his youth, his enthusiasm, and his roots, people felt very much at home with him. Brown hungered for the nomination, and he had in his favor the support of Phil Burton and his Democratic organization. Brown campaigned tirelessly and everything he "did was intentional, serious, and totally committed to winning." [37] Keyserling, likewise, had a commitment. Her commitment was to the many issues in which she believed, and not primarily to winning. However, when she finally was persuaded to run, Keyserling worked hard and narrowly won first a primary and then the general election.

Adapting to Legislative Life

The motivational mix of legislative candidates ranges widely. It depends on whether the legislature is a full-time, professional one or a part-time, citizen one. It also depends on the political culture of the state. In states with political cultures categorized by Daniel Elazar as "moralistic," motivational mixes probably lean somewhat more toward public-regarding. In states categorized by Elazar as "individualistic," motivational mixes probably lean somewhat more toward private-regarding.[38]

Once candidates have won their elections in November and get sworn in, their legislative sessions begin in January (except in Florida, Louisiana, Nevada, and Oklahoma, where they begin later). The job of adapting to legislative life is then underway. For nearly everyone who begins service in a state legislature, major adjustments have to be made. Even for those who have experienced local office, the differences are substantial.

The Time Required

There is a tremendous variation among the fifty states in the time an individual has to spend serving in the legislature. In some states being a legislator is essentially a full-time job, although members everywhere are permitted to earn income from employment outside. In California, Illinois, Massachusetts, Michigan, Ohio, and Pennsylvania, being a legislator entails full-time work. In these states the constitution does not limit the amount of time legislatures can meet in session. Consequently, these legislatures tend to be in session for much of the year. The normal schedule is for rank-and-file members to spend Tuesdays, Wednesdays, and Thursdays meeting at the capitol and be at home in their districts Fridays, Saturdays, Sundays, and Mondays. Legislative leaders, committee chairs, and members of standing committees responsible for the budget spend additional time at the capitol. Legislative recesses occur periodically, and almost always the legislature is in recess over the summer months and in the fall of alternate years when members campaign for reelection. In Ohio, for example, nine out of ten members put in forty hours or more each week when the legislature is in session, and the legislature is in session about forty weeks during the year.

At the other end of the continuum are legislatures where session length is restricted by constitution or statute. The legislatures of Arkansas, Montana, Nevada, North Dakota, Oregon, South Carolina, and Texas are limited to meeting biennially or every other year. These biennial sessions are limited to a specified number of days (60, 90, 120, or 140) in all but Oregon, where the legislature may stay in session as long as it wants.

Most legislatures have limits on the number of days they can be in session. For example, Georgia is limited to forty legislative days, New Hampshire to forty-five legislative days, and Hawaii to sixty legislative days a year. South Dakota is limited to forty legislative days the odd year of the biennium and thirty-five legislative days the even year, Wyoming to forty and

Table 2-1 Hours per Week on the Job during the Session and the Interim (in percentages)

Hours per week	Total	State				
		Maryland	Minnesota	Ohio	Vermont	Washington
Session						
Thirty-nine or less	5	3	0	11	11	1
Forty to forty-nine	20	14	18	20	38	0
Fifty to fifty-nine	29	20	31	44	35	19
Sixty or more	46	63	51	25	16	80
Total	100	100	100	100	100	100
Interim						
Fourteen or less	30	16	30	6	66	9
Fifteen to twenty-four	28	31	35	23	24	28
Twenty-five to thirty-four	22	31	21	28	10	26
Thirty-five or more	20	22	14	43	0	37
Total	100	100	100	100	100	100

Source: Alan Rosenthal, *Heavy Lifting: The Job of the American Legislature* (Washington, D.C.: CQ Press, 2004), 22.

twenty legislative days during the two years of the biennium. (A legislative day is any day in which either house is actually in session.) Utah's limits are forty-five calendar days and West Virginia's and Florida's sixty. New Mexico is limited to sixty calendar days one year and thirty the next, Indiana to sixty-one and thirty. (A calendar day is any day, including Saturdays and Sundays.)[39]

As far as the length of legislative sessions is concerned, other states fall somewhere between the essentially full-time legislature on the one hand and the more part-time legislature on the other. For example, Colorado is able to meet 120 calendar days a year, Delaware about 180, Iowa 110 one year and 100 the next, Maryland 90, and Mississippi 125 and 90.

During the course of a legislative session, being a legislator is essentially a full-time job, and even more than that for many members. Table 2-1 reports data collected in the Five-State Survey. It shows that during the session, very few members spend fewer than thirty-nine hours per week on the job. At least half in each state put in over fifty hours a week. In Maryland 83 percent are putting in this much time for three months, in Minnesota 82 percent for three or four months, in Ohio 69 percent for nine months, in Vermont 51 percent for four or five months, and in Washington 99 percent for about two or three months.

Just how full-time the job actually is depends largely on what legislators do when they are not in formal session. In most places today, legislators meet periodically in the capitol during the interim period. They are on legislative committees or commissions exploring problems, conducting studies, or preparing for an upcoming session. In addition to their days at the state capitol, they are at work in their districts, meeting with constituents and handling their requests, attending functions, and generally doing politics. In most states nowadays people expect their legislators to be available year-round, night and day. In only a few states, such as Montana, New Hampshire, North Dakota, South Dakota, Vermont, and Wyoming, do constituents regard their representatives as "citizen legislators" who have other lives to lead. Only in these places do constituents appreciate that when the legislature is not in session their representatives are not on call, but are instead attending to their regular professions and occupations and trying to earn a living. But even in these states members may choose to work a good part of their time even when the legislature is not in session. Two-thirds of Vermont's legislators, as Table 2-1 shows, spend fewer than fourteen hours a week on legislative business during the interim, but another quarter spends as much as fifteen to twenty-four hours on it. One out of ten chooses to put in between twenty-five and thirty-four hours a week, even when their citizen legislature is not in session. The latter group consists of virtually full-time legislators.

In legislatures that meet year-round, no interim period really exists. But even when the legislatures are not specifically in session, members tend to work on legislative and/or constituency matters. When Ohio's legislature is not meeting, for example, only 43 percent spend anything approaching the amount of time that they spend in session. The rest attend to private matters for the most part. But a majority of the nation's legislatures are at neither the almost full-time end nor the very part-time end of the continuum. They are located somewhere in the middle. Maryland, Minnesota, and Washington are illustrative. In each legislature, there is significant variation in how much members work during interim periods.

Some (almost a third in Minnesota) put in relatively little time, fourteen hours or less each week. Others continue to put in the equivalent of full time, thirty-five hours or more (25 percent in Maryland, 14 percent in Minnesota, and 37 percent in Washington). In each of the three states most legislators devote between fifteen and thirty-four hours per week to the varieties of legislative and political work that can be done in the time between sessions.

Depending mainly on the length of the session, a basic amount of time has to be allocated to legislative work. Beyond that, individuals have discretion in just how much time they choose to commit. Those who are in leadership put more time in. Those who are not employed outside of the legislature are able to devote more time, and many of them are full time. Brown worked full time in the full-time California Legislature. But Keyserling and Loftus were full time in South Carolina and Wisconsin, which in their day were still part-time legislatures. Legislators have to adapt to time demands, but how they do so depends on the choices they make. In the 2002 State Legislative Survey, legislators were asked, "What proportion of a full-time job is your legislative work, averaged over an entire year?" It was less than 30 percent of a full-time job for only 5 percent of the respondents and under half a full-time job for a total of only 26 percent. It was over half a full-time job for 74 percent, among whom it was just about full time for 22 percent. An index of legislators' perceptions of their time on the job, state by state, is shown in Table 2-2.[40] On the basis of responses, state by state, the percentages of legislators spending 90 percent or more of their time on the job—70–90 percent, 50–70 percent, 30–50 percent, and less than 30 percent—are shown in the columns. The last column presents a summary indicator for each state.

Financial Adjustment

Not many legislators come out ahead financially as a result of their legislative service. Only a few earn more money being in the legislature than they would have earned depending solely on income outside. Some legislators also benefit because their membership helps their professional or business reputation. But the large majority sacrifices financially in order to serve. This is because, except in a few states, legislative salaries are low, and particularly so

Table 2-2 State Legislators' Perceptions of Their Time on the Job

State (n of cases)	Percentage of a full-time job					Composite index
	>90	70–90	50–70	30–50	<30	
Alaska (34)	20.6%	26.5%	50.0%	2.9%	0.0	71.73
Alabama (45)	15.6	33.3	31.1	20.0	0.0	68.19
Arkansas (78)	17.9	24.4	33.3	23.1	1.3	65.87
Arizona (44)	45.5	29.5	18.2	4.5	2.3	79.71
California (31)	64.5	19.4	6.5	9.7	0.0	83.99
Colorado (48)	25.0	50.0	22.9	2.1	0.0	78.23
Connecticut (72)	22.2	30.6	33.3	13.9	0.0	70.68
Delaware (28)	21.4	17.9	50.0	10.7	0.0	68.82
Florida (43)	34.9	27.9	27.9	9.3	0.0	75.65
Georgia (56)	3.6	26.8	44.6	25.0	0.0	61.53
Hawaii (37)	24.3	32.4	32.4	8.1	2.7	72.31
Iowa (70)	5.7	38.6	32.9	21.4	1.4	64.73
Idaho (46)	6.5	19.6	41.3	32.6	0.0	59.44
Illinois (46)	47.8	34.8	15.2	2.2	0.0	83.12
Indiana (61)	9.8	21.3	41.0	27.9	0.0	61.94
Kansas (92)	7.6	19.6	43.5	26.1	3.3	60.00
Kentucky (55)	14.5	21.8	47.3	14.5	1.8	65.73
Louisiana (45)	22.2	35.6	26.7	15.6	0.0	71.73
Massachusetts (60)	60.0	18.3	10.0	10.0	1.7	81.79
Maryland (63)	14.3	36.5	31.7	14.3	3.2	67.97
Maine (91)	17.6	27.5	30.8	24.2	0.0	66.65
Michigan (51)	58.8	19.6	17.6	3.9	0.0	83.66
Minnesota (80)	17.5	41.3	27.5	13.8	0.0	71.41
Missouri (77)	31.2	37.7	22.1	9.1	0.0	76.57
Mississippi (37)	8.1	18.9	32.4	35.1	5.4	57.30
Montana (83)	3.6	12.0	22.9	38.6	22.9	47.71
North Carolina (69)	30.4	34.8	24.6	10.1	0.0	75.16
North Dakota (83)	0.0	4.8	15.7	49.4	30.1	40.53
Nebraska (30)	20.0	26.7	36.7	16.7	0.0	68.59
New Hampshire (192)	8.9	16.7	22.4	37.5	14.6	53.58
New Jersey (126)	30.8	3.8	46.2	19.2	0.0	67.23
New Mexico (55)	1.8	25.5	23.6	43.6	5.5	54.88
Nevada (30)	6.7	16.7	43.3	26.7	6.7	57.76
New York (77)	67.5	16.9	9.1	5.2	1.3	85.41
Ohio (63)	49.2	33.3	14.3	3.2	0.0	83.14
Oklahoma (67)	35.8	32.8	22.4	7.5	1.5	76.95
Oregon (43)	32.6	25.6	23.3	16.3	2.3	72.23
Pennsylvania (86)	62.8	22.1	8.1	5.8	1.2	84.83

(Table continues)

Table 2-2 (continued)

State (*n* of cases)	Percentage of a full-time job					Composite index
	>90	70–90	50–70	30–50	<30	
Rhode Island (37)	0.0	13.5	48.6	32.4	5.4	54.32
South Carolina (46)	19.6	23.9	37.0	17.4	2.2	67.13
South Dakota (57)	1.8	3.5	8.8	52.6	33.3	37.10
Tennessee (45)	11.1	22.2	51.1	15.6	0.0	65.04
Texas (60)	25.0	28.3	28.3	15.0	3.3	70.54
Utah (51)	2.0	9.8	27.5	47.1	13.7	48.08
Virginia (65)	13.8	21.5	33.8	29.2	1.5	62.51
Vermont (74)	2.7	10.8	52.7	33.8	0.0	56.21
Washington (44)	20.5	38.6	31.8	9.1	0.0	72.78
Wisconsin (51)	49.0	31.4	11.8	5.9	2.0	81.35
West Virginia (43)	14.0	14.0	32.6	32.6	7.0	58.44
Wyoming (58)	0.0	3.4	17.2	46.6	32.8	39.89
Total (2,925)	21.7	23.9	28.0	21.3	5.1	

Source: The 2002 survey of state legislators by the Joint Project on Term Limits. Reported in Karl T. Kurtz et al., "Full-Time, Part-Time, and Real Time: Explaining State Legislators' Perceptions of Time on the Job," *State Politics and Public Policy Quarterly* 6 (Fall 2006): 326–327.

Note: The composite index score for each state is the mean value of all individual responses from that state, using the midpoint for the first four categories (95 percent, 80 percent, 60 percent, and 40 percent) and 30 percent in the final category. The total composite score is weighted by the number of responses in each state.

in relation to the responsibilities that members of state legislatures bear and the time they devote to their legislative jobs.

The compensation that legislators earn is made up mainly of their base salaries. At the top of the scale is California, which pays $110,880 a year, followed by Michigan at $79,650, New York at $79,500, Pennsylvania at $69,647, Illinois at $57,619, Ohio at $56,260, and Massachusetts at $55,569. At the bottom of the scale are New Mexico, which pays legislators nothing at all, and New Hampshire, which pays them $100 a year. Wyoming, Nevada, Montana, Utah, and North Dakota pay their legislators by the day ($76 to $150) and Vermont pays $589 per week during the session. In Texas legislators receive $7,200 a year, in Mississippi $10,000, in South Carolina $10,400, and in Nebraska $12,000.

In most states legislative leaders receive additional compensation. For example, the New York Senate president and assembly speaker receive an ad-

Table 2-3 Estimated Legislator Compensation, 2007

$50,000–100,000	$30,000–50,000	$20,000–30,000	$10,000–20,000	$10,000 and below
California	New Jersey	Alabama	Virginia	Maine
New York	Wisconsin	Connecticut	Louisiana	Kansas
Michigan	Oklahoma	Florida	Tennessee	Texas
Pennsylvania	Delaware	Alaska	Georgia	New Mexico
Illinois	Washington	Arizona	Kentucky	South Dakota
Ohio	Hawaii	Iowa	Idaho	North Dakota
Massachusetts	Missouri	(6)	Oregon	Utah
(7)	Maryland		West Virginia	Nevada
	Minnesota		North Carolina	Montana
	Colorado		Arkansas	Wyoming
	(10)		Vermont	New Hampshire
			Nebraska	(11)
			Indiana	
			Rhode Island	
			South Carolina	
			Mississippi	
			(16)	

Source: Adapted from Peverill Squire and Keith E. Hamm, *101 Chambers; Congress, State Legislatures and the Future of Legislative Studies* (Columbus: Ohio State University Press, 2005), 73.
Note: Estimates compensation as of 2003.

ditional $41,500, and twenty-three other senate and thirty-three other assembly leaders also receive additional compensation. The presiding officers in Hawaii receive $37,000 in addition to their base salaries, those in Massachusetts and Pennsylvania $35,000, and in Louisiana $33,000.

Finally, compensation is supplemented in forty-five states by living-expense allowances during both the session and interim periods. These payments compensate legislators for the costs of rented apartments or hotel rooms, meals, and some travel. If legislators manage their finances carefully—by rooming together and taking advantage of the food available at the almost daily receptions during the course of the session—they can pocket a portion of the *per diem* expense money as a supplement to their salaries.

In only a few states is legislative compensation at all substantial (although it should be pointed out that forty-three states do provide legislators retirement benefits). Table 2-3 supplies estimates of total compensation, including both salary and expenses, for the fifty states. Except in a very few states, such as California and New York, not many legislators would choose to live entirely on the compensation they receive. In no more than one-third could they afford to live without supplementary income. Most, therefore, have to supplement their legislative compensation with other income—investment income, savings, retirement benefits, a spouse's earnings, or outside employment.

Somehow, most do adjust financially. According to the 2002 State Legislative Survey, only 14 percent report family incomes below $50,000. Another 48 percent report between $50,000 and $100,000 and 38 percent report family incomes over $100,000. The majority of legislators would not be classified as financially needy, even though legislative service may entail financial sacrifice on their part.

Occupational Adjustment

In the 1960s and 1970s most state legislators had spent considerable time on the jobs they held outside of the legislature. They found time, after their election to the legislature, to continue practicing law, running a business, ranching and farming, and so forth. Today, however, the demands of legislative office are greater than they used to be. The amount of time that legislative matters, and in particular constituency service, can consume is almost unlimited. The number of states where legislatures meet practically year-round has increased, sessions in other states have lengthened, and interim work requires additional time in the capital. Consequently, fewer legislators pursue outside employment while in office. Responses to the 2002 State Legislative Survey indicate that 61.2 percent still work for pay on the outside but 38.8 percent do not. For example, Brown, even when serving as speaker of the assembly, managed to derive income from a law firm with which he was associated. But neither Keyserling nor Loftus were employed outside the legislature. Reeher's survey suggests that where legislative salaries are higher and legislatures are practically full-time enterprises, fewer members pursue outside employment. In New York only 30 percent had another occupation, while in Connecticut and Vermont 67 percent and 73 percent, respectively, worked outside.[41]

Those who are employed are spread among a number of professions and occupations. According to a 1999 estimate, 27 percent of those employed are in business and services; 15 percent in law; 17 percent in government; 9 percent in education; and the rest in farming, fishing, and health services.[42] It is interesting that as many as 1,250 legislators in the nation have governmental jobs that, together with their legislative salaries, allow them to piece together a living without wandering far afield from politics. In a few states legislators are not only allowed to have jobs with government but also to hold other elective positions. In New Jersey, for example, one-sixth of the 120 members of the legislature receive income from a government agency besides the legislature, including a number who are employed as attorneys for local jurisdictions.[43] The norm, however, is for states to ban dual office holding. Recently, New Jersey banned holding another elective office.

Those who continue to work have to juggle their regular jobs in order to serve in the legislature. Attorneys, for instance, cut back on their practice. If they are partners in large firms, they may be compelled to leave and go into private practice or team up with another attorney in a smaller practice. If they are insurance brokers, their availability to clients is reduced and their sales tend to suffer. If they own a business, although they may remain in it, they have to get someone else to run it. And if they are college professors, despite their flexibility in scheduling, the time they can spend on research and publication shrinks considerably and they lose out professionally.

One of Reeher's interviewees mentions the tension between having to pursue two careers and acknowledges that he couldn't go on that way, that at some point he would have to choose between business and politics.[44] The case of Rich Bagger, a former assemblyman in New Jersey, illustrates the balancing that has to be done between public and private occupations. Bagger had the advantage of serving in a legislature that met only about thirty-five or forty days a year. He chaired the assembly's Republican majority caucus for a time and then chaired its Appropriations Committee. His full-time job was at Pfizer pharmaceuticals, whose offices were in New York City. Bagger estimated that he spent about thirty-five hours a week on his legislative job and another thirty-five hours a week on his job at Pfizer. Not much time was left for family or leisure pursuits. When he was offered a promotion at Pfizer, he had to choose between public and private careers. He chose the latter.

Individuals who serve in the legislature have to find time for their regular jobs. Those in very part-time bodies have long interim periods, when the legislative workload is light. They manage pretty well. Those in more full-time bodies have less uninterrupted time. They have to cut back on their outside employment. And those in essentially full-time bodies may have Mondays, Fridays, and weekends to pursue outside jobs. They hang on, but only by stealing large chunks of time from their families.

Family Life Adjustment

As noted above, legislators have to readjust their family lives as well as their professional and occupational lives. Frank Smallwood, a former Vermont legislator, recalls a conversation he had his twelve-year-old son while Small-wood was deciding whether to run for the legislature. The son told his father that he hoped that he wouldn't go into politics. Why? Smallwood asked. "Because I will miss you," his son replied matter-of-factly.[45] Legislators simply have less time and energy for spouses or children. A majority of them have to spend many nights at the state capital in a hotel, motel, or condominium, while the family remains in the district. For example, when the legislature is meeting, legislators from New York City and its suburbs will take the train to Albany on a Monday and return on Friday. California legislators, unless they represent the local area, spend many nights each year in Sacramento. Most of Florida's legislators fly into Tallahassee on Monday and fly back home on Thursday evening until the sixty-day session heats up and members have to stay in Tallahassee over the weekend. Members of the Texas Legislature also have to travel back and forth during their long odd-year session and during special sessions.

Many legislators may not have to stay away from their home overnight. During the session they can drive to the capitol on a daily basis, and during the interim they do so on occasion. If the state capitol is located in a population center, a number of members will represent urban and suburban districts within commuting distance. Legislators from the Twin Cities, that is the Metro region, in Minnesota; those in the Lincoln-Omaha area in Nebraska; Atlanta and its suburbs in Georgia; Honolulu, Hawaii; Anchorage, Alaska; or the greater Boston area all drive back and forth the same day. If the state is geographically small, members commute from their home to the capitol. This is the case in New Jersey, where any legislator can get home from Trenton within two-and-one-half hours, and in Delaware and Connecticut. It is certainly the case in Rhode Island, where every legislator's district is practically within shouting distance of Providence.

Commuters manage to sleep in their own beds at night, but they have little disposable time at home during the period of the legislature session. By the time they arrive home from the capitol, their children are asleep and both they and their spouses are exhausted and ready to turn in. On those days when the legislature is in recess, they are either working at their outside employment, meeting with constituents, or attending functions in the district. Not much time is available for little league baseball, football, soccer, or hockey games, or for school plays and concerts. As one legislator commented: "There are people up here that don't see their kids grow up, including myself." All of this puts strain on a legislator's family: first, the amount of time spent away from home; second, the emotional drain of legislative work; and third, the personal attacks that legislators receive and family members feel.[46]

Other Adjustments

Time, work, and family require the biggest adjustments. But other adjustments also have to be made.

Legislators live in a fish bowl. Almost everything they do is or can be made public. In every state but Vermont they are required to file a financial disclosure statement, which usually lists their financial holdings and sources of income, including that of members of their immediate family. This information is available to the public. The media, in particular the print press, may take interest in a legislator's private life. Frequently, a challenger in an election that can go either way will try to dig up anything that can make a difference in a campaign. As public people, legislators must give up the ordinary citizen's right to privacy.

Legislative work itself requires psychological adaptation. The workload is heavy. Members cannot be on top of all the issues on which they have to vote. They must trust the information and advice they get from legislative leaders, colleagues, constituents, lobbyists, and friends. They are almost always dependent on others. One of Reeher's interviewers describes the feeling "of being pulled in a million different directions time wise." [47] The pace is sluggish at times, but it quickens as the session proceeds. And when adjournment is in sight, the pace becomes frenetic. It is almost impossible during the last few days to even tackle the legislation that is moving through one house or the other. Each day is uncertain and frustrating, at least in some respect. Anyone who prefers routine and nine-to-five office work would be mightily uncomfortable in a legislature (if by chance they got there in the first place). On the basis of his interviews, Reeher recaps the negative feelings legislators have: "being pressured, powerlessness over the inability to achieve desired goals, frustration over partisanship, and pique due to repetitive speeches and predictable political dynamics." [48]

Brown had little trouble figuring out anything, let alone how to adapt to the California Assembly. He got a shaky start when he opposed Jesse Unruh, who was running for reelection as speaker. He voted against him because Unruh had supported the incumbent whom Brown had challenged and beaten in the primary election. Unruh punished him but later decided that the best way to handle Willie was to make him an ally. Not only did Brown emerge from the doghouse, but he had Unruh as a friend and patron as he made his way up the leadership ladder. He learned as he went along, first as chair of the assembly's Ways and Means Committee and then as an unsuccessful candidate for speaker against Leo McCarthy.[49] In his adaptation to legislative life, Brown learned how to restrain his arrogance and channel his intelligence, drive, flexibility, and interpersonal skills to win and hold top leadership longer than anyone else had done in California history. Becoming speaker is a pretty sure sign of effective adaptation in a legislative body.

Loftus had some of the same qualities as Brown, but without the Californian's constant need for the spotlight. Loftus too was self-confident and assertive, with a good strategic sense. He had more patience than Brown and was an enthusiastic teacher and an avid learner. He was able to climb the leadership ladder early in his career and managed to hold the top spot in the Wisconsin Assembly for a number of years. His adaptation could hardly have been more effective.

Keyserling neither sought nor attained leadership. That was not her thing. In view of her initial sense of inadequacy, it was an accomplishment for her to stand for election to the legislature in the first place. She too managed to adapt to legislative life—at least for a number of years. Although

Keyserling hesitated to engage in discussion or debate on a par with her colleagues, she did participate as a team player for the Crazy Caucus, a group of reform-minded members in the South Carolina House, and taking notes, doing research, working hard, and helping to build consensus. She too adapted, in her way and not the way of Brown or Loftus.

The legislature is both demanding and tolerant. The time and workload required can be overwhelming, but members can range widely in just how much they do and how they do it. The legislature is an ecumenical institution; it has a place for a Brown, for a Keyserling, for a Loftus, and for just about anybody else who gets elected to it.

Legislators like different things about legislative life. Brown enjoyed working the back rooms and making deals (in fact, after he left the assembly he wanted to be remembered as the best deal maker ever). The risk, excitement, and exercise of power had great appeal for him. Loftus was more attracted to the opportunities to learn from experience and teach his colleagues. He liked to forge compromises and make the Wisconsin Assembly work, taking pride in being part of the system of representative democracy. Keyserling's chief likes in the South Carolina legislature were the issues in which she engaged—education, day care, the environment, women's rights, and political reform. Her chief satisfaction came from a sense of policy accomplishment and defending, as she saw it, the "public interest" against "special interests."

In serving, legislators have different objectives. Some are crystal clear about their ambitions for higher office; others want to achieve status and influence within the legislature itself. Some enjoy demonstrating their expertise in committee or on the floor; others prefer to use their political skills behind the scenes. Some like to engage in a good fight; others would prefer to achieve consensus before taking a vote. Most are also advocates for values they hold, policies they espouse, and interests they represent.

In pursuing their objectives, legislators employ different styles of adaptation, depending upon their personalities and preferences. No legislators employ a single style exclusively, but for most of them one or two of the following dominate their behavior.

Ombudsmen. Former New Jersey legislator Gordon McInnes describes the majority of his colleagues as ombudsmen, that is, local public officials rather than lawmakers. New Jersey legislators spend relatively little time in Trenton, but much more time in their districts with constituents. They pride themselves on helping constituents with their problems. Such a style is very acceptable in the legislature and very welcome in the district.

Politicos. These legislators are especially sensitive to and absorbed by the political aspects of their jobs. They delight in the challenges of getting a bill passed or one defeated. They are adept at strategizing. They like to take risks. Politicos appreciate the "game" aspects of legislative politics. Legislative party leaders usually behave according to this style.

Socializers. A number of members focus on and enjoy most the social relationships in legislative life. These members like getting along with their colleagues on both sides of the aisle. They bring people together and help reduce tension. They are first and foremost people persons. They resemble those legislators Ralph Wright characterizes as "backbenchers" in the Vermont House.[50]

Outsiders. A few members in every legislative body adopt a distant or critical style. They may be Republicans or Democrats, but they play on no particular team. They pride themselves on their independence. Their special contribution is to question how the process works, the degree to which the business is getting done, and whether their colleagues are behaving with integrity. A member of the Vermont House, Madeleine Kunin felt like an outsider. As a woman, she was uncomfortable in a male-dominated culture and power structure. Yet her outsider status gave her, she thought, "an uncluttered view of right and wrong." Identifying as someone outside the system, she found it difficult but by no means impossible to work within the power structure to get what she wanted and at the same time oppose the structure when she disagreed with it.[51] William Schluter, throughout a lengthy career in the New Jersey Legislature, stood apart and questioned the leadership process, campaign finance system, power of lobbyists, and legislative ethics. Schluter's style did not win him popularity among his colleagues; yet he had a following outside the legislature, in the media, and among reformers around the state. He also had, most would concede, a successful tenure in the legislature. Elsewhere, copies of Schluter also thrive. John Marty, a veteran member of the Minnesota Senate, acts as a critic of the system, a gadfly, and a proponent of reform. He too commands attention.

Policy Entrepreneurs. These are the legislators Wright refers to as "issues people." [52] They are the advocates who want to make improvements in one or several domains of public policy. Virtually every legislator sponsors legislation, but not all of them can be stylistically classified as policy entrepreneurs. Frequently, those who chair particular standing committees take on an entrepreneurial style in their jurisdiction. But many other legislators also mainly advocate for one policy or another, or for multiple policies.

John McDonough of Massachusetts exemplifies the single-domain advocate who sees things through a clear policy lens:

> My chief passion, for thirteen years in the Massachusetts House of Representatives . . . has been health: public health, health care access, health care quality, health care cost control. It is often noted that access, quality, and costs are the three legs of the health care stool, and we are advised in crafting policy proposals to "pick any two" because you can't have all three. Sometimes you can. Improving child immunization rates, for example, improves quality and access and lowers costs. Reducing medical errors—an epidemic in U.S. medical practice—improves quality and reduces costs without harming access. Those victories, though, tend to be rare. Most of the time, we try to improve one or two legs without doing heavy damage to the third. [53]

An example of entrepreneurship across domains is provided by Sandy Rosenberg, who keeps a diary of his experience in the Maryland General Assembly. The entry for January 11, 2007, focuses on issues near and dear to Rosenberg's heart. He notes at the outset that, after sponsoring the embryonic stem cell research bill (which "will touch more lives than anything else I've done or will do"), other endeavors would pale by comparison. Then, he notes having written a friend: "I don't recall ever being as excited for the start of a legislative session as I am for this one. So many interesting issues that I'm working on." [54]

The policy entrepreneurs, as well as others who sponsor legislation, want to get bills passed. In order to do this, they need the votes of their colleagues—which, in turn, requires that they maintain cordial relationships with their colleagues and a willingness to accommodate them. Kunin reflects on how the legislative process was by nature collegial, each member with an equal vote: "Just as I did not know whom I would need next, they would not know when they would need me," she writes. [55]

Legislators who have lawmaking as one of their goals have to rely on one another. That is why *reciprocity* is an almost universal norm in legislative bodies. "The way you treat a colleague," legislators believe, "is the way you can expect that colleague to treat you." Thus, to succeed as a lawmaker, one has to deal cordially with people who hold different views and even to respect views that are opposed to one's own. When he was in the New Mexico Legislature, Bruce King (who later served as governor) quickly learned how to get a bill through the house:

> I saw that it was important to remain always congenial . . . and I tried to make as many friends as I could.

One-on-one was the best approach to colleagues for King. He would approach a colleague, explain his position, give the colleague all the facts, and identify the problem the bill was addressing. "I know that even if, for any reason, he couldn't vote for my bill," King writes, "maybe next time he would." [56]

It would seem that anyone who can manage to be elected and reelected can prove himself or herself in the legislature. That is because in the legislature there is a role for virtually everyone. The senate and house are essentially welcoming bodies. Every member has a constituency and a vote; every constituency matters and every vote is needed.

Why Legislators Leave

Some years ago, I ran into Fred Risser at a conference in Florida. At that time, Risser was in his forty-second or forty-third year of service in the Wisconsin Legislature. I admire people who commit themselves to public service, and especially for such a long period. I had known Fred for years and, jokingly, I said to him: "Fred, when are the voters in Wisconsin going to wake up, pass term limits, and get rid of the likes of you?" Risser looked me straight in the eye and replied: "Alan, I, myself, favor term limits." "You do?" I questioned. "Yes," he replied, "a limit of fifty years and not one year more." Risser was putting me on, of course, and I have told this story frequently, wondering if Risser would keep his "vow." There is no need to wonder any longer. In January 2007, at the age of seventy-nine, Fred Risser celebrated his fiftieth year, making him the nation's longest-serving legislator. "When I started out in the Legislature," Risser said, "I had no intention of serving this long." [57] Risser was undecided as to whether he would run still again the following year. But at some point he will leave. They all do. Some leave involuntarily and some voluntarily; some leave after a short duration and some after a longer one; but only a few stay on longer than twenty or thirty years, let alone fifty.

Those who lose elections, leave. Others retire because they are in districts they cannot win. Some exit when they face opponents they cannot beat. In just about every election, an experienced legislator is defeated for one reason or another. Ralph Wright of Vermont was one of them. Yet not many incumbents fail to be reelected—perhaps 5, 10, or 15 percent depending on the state and the year (with a higher percentage being forced out after decennial redistricting). These legislators would have preferred to stay; they exit involuntarily.

Those legislators who are from the fifteen legislatures where term limits are in effect also have to leave after six, eight, or twelve years depending on the law in each state. A number of these term-limited legislators run for seats in the other house, but most seek public office outside the legislature or have to return to private life. Brown would have liked to serve as speaker of the California Assembly as long as he could. But a six-year term limit forced him to leave, and leave a year early if he wanted to continue in public office by running for mayor of San Francisco.

Other involuntary departures are caused by ill health, which makes it difficult to continue in office, and death, which makes it even more difficult.

Some legislators go voluntarily. On the basis of his interviews in Connecticut, Maine, and New York, Reeher explains the decision to exit by a "convergence of several related personal, professional, and political factors." [58] One set of such factors involves political opportunities—inside and outside the legislature. Voluntary departers include members who have a chance of winning higher office—moving up from the state house to the state senate, running for a congressional seat, or contesting statewide office. Voluntary departers also include members whose opportunities for influence within the chamber are blocked.

A number of lawmakers leave when they feel that they have gotten whatever they could from their experience in the legislature. For some the departure time comes after ten years or so. For Madeleine Kunin the time came midway through her third term in the Vermont House: "I had proven I could do the toughest job in the House; I felt I had learned what it had to teach me." Furthermore, she was concerned that if she stayed too long she would become a professional legislator and part of a structure that she preferred to keep at some distance. She felt she was ready to run for higher office.[59]

More legislators exit in order to move up than exit simply to move out. Loftus was one of the former. He left to run for governor of Wisconsin. But he also felt that it was time to go, in order to make room for his Democratic colleagues on the assembly leadership ladder. New Jersey's John Paul Doyle once said that he intended to remain in the legislature until he was elected (and served as) speaker, or until he knew he couldn't be elected speaker. Other legislators give it up when they too run up against a political wall. They may feel especially frustrated as members of the minority party, or they may be on the outs with their own party's leadership. McDonough of Massachusetts left largely because he wound up on the wrong side of Speaker Thomas Finneran and was unlikely to be able to get much done in the domain of health policy, to which he had committed himself. Marshal Harris of Florida, who exercised enormous influence as chair of the House Appropriations Committee, decided to retire, he announced, because he wanted to spend more time with his family and watch his daughter grow up. It should be noted, however, that he announced his retirement after he lost a bid for the speakership, running against Don Tucker, a powerful incumbent. It was clear that Harris had no chance of being reappointed by the speaker as chair of appropriations and would likely have to work extra hard to get out of the doghouse.

Internal political reasons for retirement run the gamut. They usually lead to frustration and sometimes even more negative feelings on the parts of members. Keyserling lost all of her taste for serving in the South Carolina House after the Republicans gained the majority. In her view, civility had given way to confrontation. Many of her Crazy Caucus colleagues had already left, depriving her of the support system she treasured. Add to this the toll of an ulcer, high blood pressure, and the fact that the GOP was targeting her seat, and she had no difficulty deciding to retire from the fray.

Bulger observed that in Massachusetts "the life of a new legislator is rarely a happy lot." The specific agonies vary among members, but transition is at the core of suffering that impatient new members undergo. They have to deal with processes that delay the best of intentions and require constant consensus-building and compromise. For some new members, according to Bulger, "the learning curve seemed to be made of barbed wire," wounding them or even leaving permanent scars.[60] Many of these members exited after a relatively brief stint.

Equally important to the political are personal factors that impel departure. Financial concerns weigh heavily on some, and especially on those whose children are approaching college age; substantial expenses await them. In states like New Hampshire, where the salary is negligible, few people can afford to remain in the legislature very long. Some legislators feel that they cannot pursue two careers at once and decide to give up their legislative profession and return to their outside one. Frank Smallwood, for instance, ran for the Vermont Senate while he was on sabbatical leave from Dartmouth College. In his memoirs, he describes his attempt to reconcile his two jobs after his sabbatical ended:

> Every day became a blur of conflicting demands: meeting classes, grading student papers, preparing lectures, serving on college committees, following up constituency chores, studying bills, answering letters, giving speeches, appearing on radio shows, meanwhile with the telephone ringing, ringing, ringing all day long.[61]

Years ago, Edward A. Shils, in a brilliant essay on the sources of strain on the legislator, noted the hazard of a career neglected. If a legislator is in the professions or business and decides to return full time, "he will have to make up the distance which his contemporaries have gained on him." Young men and women, whose professional or business careers hold particular promise, feel the strain intensely. Paul Sarbanes, a legislator in Maryland from 1967 through 1970 who went on to the U.S. House and U.S. Senate, is an example. Sarbanes tried to continue the practice of law while serving in the Maryland General Assembly, but he could not help feeling that he was doing neither job as well as he should. Moreover, he sensed that his lawyer colleagues were getting way ahead of him, working full time, developing their skills, and advancing their legal careers. A person with two occupations has trouble competing with a person practicing only one. It was so frustrating that Sarbanes decided to risk his career running against an incumbent congressman, a veteran and committee chairman, so that he would end up with only a single job—either law or politics, whichever it turned out to be.[62] Along with the political and policy frustrations, the financial sacrifices, and the professional anxieties are the strains that are produced more directly by disruptions in family life. Occasionally, such strains are the proximate cause of a legislator's retirement. More often, they work with other factors to cut short careers in the legislature.

On Balance

Despite the stresses and strains of legislative life and compelling reasons for getting out earlier rather than later, not many members leave of their own volition. Very few leave because they are dissatisfied with the job. Most incumbents run again and again for a significant period of time. When asked in the nationwide 2002 State Legislative Survey whether they planned to run for reelection, 84 percent of the legislators replied that they "definitely" or "probably" would do so. What would they do after leaving the senate or house? Only 26.8 percent said that they would return to their nonpolitical careers. Apparently, the rest intended to continue in politics, along one path or another.

Nearly all of those serving in the legislature like the job, although perhaps not exactly for the same reasons. Brown certainly enjoyed the power, the excitement, and the collegiality. He recognized that it was necessary for him to be a listener, a diplomat, a deal maker, and a warrior, as well as a person who colleagues could count on.[63] The attraction for Loftus was forging compromises and making the place work. For Keyserling it was ideas, issues, and accomplishments. After fifty years in legislative harness, Fred Risser summed up: "It's probably one of the most frustrating activities one can get involved in, but that stimulates the adrenaline."[64] Meaningful work, learning, power, excitement, risk, and a sense of achievement all play a role. Perhaps as much as anything else, legislators enjoy the friendships they make with colleagues. Years later, when asked what they miss most, they refer to the collegiality of the legislature—despite partisanship, despite conflict, friendships are forged.

In his interviews in Connecticut, Maine, and New York, Reeher asked members to indicate their satisfaction with the legislature on a nine-point scale, with "9" indicating the highest degree of satisfaction. Ninety-one percent of the respondents selected "6" or above, including 50 percent who selected "8" or "9." [65] On balance, then, legislators are quite satisfied with their experience in the legislature. That is why they choose to pursue the careers they have chosen.

However much satisfaction legislators derive from their jobs, the questions we conclude with here concern whether these are the people who deserve to hold such jobs. How should legislators be rated: The way they are portrayed by the media? The way the public perceives them? Or the way constituents regard the legislators who represent their own districts? What about Keyserling, Loftus, and Brown? Certainly, these are able individuals who wanted to accomplish something for their states, their constituents, and the public. Are they unique or are they representative? My impression is that they are unusual, but not that unusual. Many legislators have similar motivational sets, and most wind up giving the public more than its money's worth.

This is not to deny the existence of corrupt, self-serving, and incompetent legislators. My impression, however, is that they are a small minority (who, it should be pointed out, are not chosen by other legislators, but rather are elected and reelected by constituents in their districts). On the whole, we get pretty decent people to represent us.

Notes

1. The chapter's references to Brown are from James Richardson, *Willie Brown* (Berkeley: University of California Press), 1996; references to Keyserling are from Harriet Keyserling, *Against the Tide: One Woman's Political Struggle* (Columbia: University of South Carolina Press), 1998; and references to Loftus are from Tom Loftus, *The Art of Legislative Politics* (Washington, D.C.: CQ Press, 1994).

2. Other memoirs also deserve mention and are well worth reading: Frank Smallwood, *Free and Independent* (Brattleboro, Vt.: Stephen Greene, 1978); John E. McDonough, *Experiencing Politics: A Legislator's Stories of Government and Health Care* (Berkeley: University of California, 2000); William M. Bulger, *While the Music Lasts: My Life in Politics* (Boston: Houghton Mifflin, 1996); and Ralph Wright, *Inside the Statehouse* (Washington, D.C.: CQ Press, 2005). Smallwood and Wright recount their experiences in the Vermont legislature, twenty-five years apart. Smallwood served only a single two-year term, while Wright was a member for sixteen years. Willie Brown's *Basic Brown: My Life and Our Times* (New York: Simon and Schuster, 2008) complements Richardson's biography. Other worthwhile biographies are Taylor Pensoneau, *Powerhouse: Arrington from Illinois* (Baltimore: American Literary Press, 2006) and Richard Hyatt, *Mr. Speaker: The Biography of Tom Murphy* (Macon: Mercer University Press, 1999).

3. Richardson, *Willie Brown,* xii.

4. This description is by Richard Riley, the former governor of South Carolina, in his forward to Keyserling, *Against the Tide,* xii.

5. Harold D. Lasswell, *Politics: Who Gets What, When, and How* (New York: Peter Smith, 1950) and *Psychopathology and Politics* (Chicago: University of Chicago Press, 1930).

6. James D. Barber, *The Lawmakers* (New Haven: Yale University Press, 1965), 217–233.

7. Richardson, *Willie Brown,* 35.

8. Madeleine M. Kunin, *Living a Political Life* (New York: Vintage, 1994), 123.

9. Bulger, *While the Music Lasts,* 323.

10. Wright, *Inside the Statehouse.*

11. Gary Moncrief, Peverill Squire, and Malcolm Jewell, *Who Runs for the Legislature?* (Upper Saddle River, N.J.: Prentice Hall, 2001), 34–35.

12. Mordecai Lee, "Political-Administrative Relations in State Government: A Legislative Perspective," *International Journal of Public Administration* 29 (2006): 1029.

13. Moncrief et al., *Who Runs for the Legislature?,* 34–35.

14. The term limits study was conducted by the National Conference of State Legislatures (NCSL), the Council of State Governments (CSG), and the State Legislative Leaders Foundation (SLLF). Also participating were fourteen legislative scholars. The results are reported in Jennifer Drage Bowser, Kean S. Chi, and Thomas H. Little, *Coping with Term Limits* (Denver:

NCSL, August 2006); Karl T. Kurtz, Bruce Cain, and Richard G. Niemi, eds., *Institutional Change in American Politics: The Case of Term Limits* (Ann Arbor: University of Michigan Press, 2007); and Rick Farmer, Christopher Z. Mooney, Richard J. Powell, and John C. Green, eds., *Legislating without Experience: Case Studies in State Legislative Term Limits* (Lanham, Md.: Lexington Books, 2007). This survey will be drawn on in this and later chapters and referred to as the 2002 State Legislative Survey. A four-page questionnaire was mailed to 7,430 legislators in February 2002. Responses were received from 2,982 legislators, or 40.1 percent.

15. Alan Ehrenhalt, *The United States of Ambition* (New York: Random House, 1991), 135.

16. Grant Reeher, *First Person Political* (New York: New York University Press, 2006), 38.

17. Ibid., 35.

18. McDonough, *Experiencing Politics,* 33–34.

19. "Legislative Fun Facts," *New Jersey Monthly* (April 2003): 85.

20. Joseph A. Schlesinger, *Ambition and Politics: Political Careers in the United States* (Chicago: University of Chicago Press, 1966), 27.

21. Moncrief et al., *Who Runs for the Legislature?,* 40–44.

22. Reeher, *First Person Political,* 46.

23. Wright, *Inside the Statehouse,* 1.

24. Ehrenhalt, *The United States of Ambition,* 17, 19.

25. Reeher, *First Person Political,* 32. Lee Hamilton, a former member of the U.S. House, has spent the better part of his life among politicians. Although aware of their shortcomings, he believes that most are well-intentioned, "trying to do what they perceive to be in the best interests of their communities and the nation." "Comments on Congress," October 19, 2007.

26. See Reeher, *First Person Political,* 42.

27. Bulger, *While the Music Lasts,* 316.

28. The fact that New Jersey legislators have district offices encourages constituency service.

29. Wright, *Inside the Statehouse,* 1.

30. Schlesinger, *Ambition and Politics.*

31. The most prominent contemporary example of party change is that of Michael Bloomberg, a Democrat who converted to Republican in order to win a nomination for mayor of New York City. After several years in office, Bloomberg switched once again, becoming an Independent.

32. Joseph I. Lieberman, "Guidelines for Initiating Legislation and Understanding Its Scope," in *Perspectives of a State Legislature,* ed. Clyde D. McKee Jr. (Hartford, Ct.: Trinity College, 1978), 55–56.

33. Peverill Squire and Keith E. Hamm, *101 Chambers: Congress, State Legislatures, and the Future of Legislative Studies* (Columbus: Ohio State University Press, 2005), 50.

34. This survey of legislators in Maryland, Minnesota, Ohio, Vermont, and Washington will be referred to in this and subsequent chapters as the "Five-State Survey." It is drawn from Alan Rosenthal, *Heavy Lifting: The Job of the American Legislature* (Washington, D.C.: CQ Press, 2004). The data can be found on pages 19–27.

35. Loftus, *The Art of Legislative Politics,* 7.

36. Reeher, *First Person Political,* 34.

37. Richardson, *Willie Brown,* 95.

38. See Daniel Elazar, *American Federalism: A View From the States,* 2nd ed. (New York: Crowell, 1972).

39. Legislatures normally do not meet on weekends until the session is approaching its constitutional deadline. Therefore, a legislature that is restricted to, say, sixty *calendar* days will spend less time in session on lawmaking than a legislature that is restricted to sixty *legislative* days.

40. Karl T. Kurtz, Gary Moncrief, Richard G. Niemi, and Lynda W. Powell, "Full-Time, Part-Time, and Real Time: Explaining State Legislators' Perceptions of Time on the Job," *State Politics and Public Policy Quarterly 6* (Fall 2006), 326–327.

41. Reeher, *First Person Political,* 88.

42. Squire and Hamm, *101 Chambers,* 134.

43. Tom O'Neill, *One to a Customer: The Democratic Downsides of Dual Office Holding* (Trenton: New Jersey Policy Perspective, 2006).

44. Reeher, *First Person Political,* 91.

45. Smallwood, *Free and Independent,* 9–10.

46. Reeher, *First Person Political,* 83–85.

47. Ibid., 80.

48. Ibid., 78.

49. Brown, *Basic Brown,* 89–90, 116–124.

50. Wright, *Inside the Statehouse,* 98–104.

51. Kunin, *Living a Political Life,* 123, 136.

52. Wright, *Inside the Statehouse,* 98–104.

53. McDonough, *Experiencing Politics,* 319.

54. Diary of Del. Sandy Rosenberg, January 11, 2007.

55. Kunin, *Living a Political Life*, 135–136.

56. Bruce King, *Cowboy in the Roundhouse* (Santa Fe, N.M.: Sunstone Press, 1998).

57. Quoted by Ryan Foley, Associated Press, January 2007.

58. Reeher, *First Person Political*, 111.

59. Kunin, *Living a Political Life*, 142.

60. Bulger, *While the Music Lasts*, 57.

61. Smallwood, *Free and Independent*, 222.

62. Edward A. Shils, "Resentments and Hostilities of Legislators: Sources, Objects, Consequences," in *Legislative Behavior*, ed. John C. Wahlke and Heinz Eulau (New York: Free Press, 1959), 348–349.

63. Brown, *Basic Brown*, 24–25.

64. Quoted by Ryan Foley, Associated Press, January 2007.

65. Reeher, *First Person Political*, 70.

3

Rooted in Their Districts

LYNDA W. POWELL, Richard G. Niemi, and Michael Smith open their chapter on constituents and interest representation in a book on term limits with the statement: "Representation is what legislatures are all about."[1] It is certainly what legislators are *much* about. That was beautifully demonstrated to me some years ago, when I accepted an invitation to address new members of the Washington Legislature who were attending an orientation at a conference center in Seattle. I arrived in time for the opening session—a dinner for the new legislators. After the meal, as an ice-breaking exercise, about forty legislators who had just been elected were asked by a facilitator to give brief descriptions of the districts they represented. Each had a district with about one hundred thousand people. Some districts were predominantly Republican, others predominantly Democratic, and others more equally balanced; some, like Seattle and Tacoma, were urban, while others were suburban and rural; some were in the western area of the state, lying roughly along or near I-95, others were in the more sparsely populated eastern area; some districts were generally more well-to-do, while others were needier. Despite the diversity, anyone who listened to these new legislators would have been impressed by their knowledge of and feeling for the districts they represented. Each spoke with pride and affection, almost as if they were real-estate agents trying to sell their new colleagues houses in the districts where they lived. Although I had long appreciated how legislators are tied to their constituencies, as a result of this session I truly understood just how strongly legislators are attached to their districts.

Their attachment results essentially from three factors. The first is *identification* with the district, that is, being "one of them" and being "at one with them." As Michael A. Smith writes in his penetrating look at legislators and their constituencies, "The successful representative must fit the district."[2] Most often the nature of the district and the personal traits and politics of the legislator coincide. The fact that many legislators have lived in their districts for quite some time—usually twenty years or longer—helps. But even relative newcomers take on a district's identity quickly. If they have political aspirations and/or hold elective office before running for the legislature, identification is a virtual requirement. Identification smoothes the path for affect—approval, liking, loyalty.

The second factor that accounts for their district orientation relates to the *representational role requirement.* Every citizen is aware that legislators have a responsibility to represent their districts. Legislators accept such a role as a major requirement of the office to which they have been elected. They feel they have to be concerned with the needs of their districts as well as those of their state. In the 2002 State Legislative Survey legislators were asked whether they felt they should be primarily concerned with the needs of their district or with those of the state as a whole. About 62 percent of the respondents chose points 3, 4, and 5 at the middle of a seven-point scale, while 17 percent chose points 1 and 2, indicating a primary concern with their district, and 21 percent chose points 6 and 7, indicating a primary concern with the state. Most of these legislators understandably felt that they had to balance the two.

The third factor that accounts for their district orientation has to do with *electoral necessity.* If legislators do not please voters in their district, they had better start looking for another line of work. One means of pleasing voters, members believe, is through advocacy and service, and there is evidence to support their belief that it pays off with votes.

Thus, for legislators, an orientation toward and concern for their districts comes naturally. From the perspective of the individual representative, "It is what I ought to do, what I want to do, and what I have to do." Legislators could hardly have any stronger incentive for how they do their job.

What Their Districts Are Like

In every state but one people are represented by one member of the senate and one (or sometimes two or more) members of the house (or assembly, as it is sometimes called). In Nebraska, with its unicameral legislature, a single senator represents each district. Senates are divided into districts that range in total members from sixty-seven in Minnesota to twenty in Alaska, while houses are divided into districts that range from four hundred in New Hampshire to forty in Alaska. In most instances the boundaries of senate and house districts are not coterminous. But in Arizona, Idaho, New Jersey, North Dakota, South Dakota, and Washington, senate and house districts are identical. In these six states the house is comprised of two-member districts, with the same lines for both senate and house units. In New Hampshire and Vermont multimember districts exist together with single and/or two-member districts.

According to the U.S. Constitution, as interpreted by federal and state courts, within each state both senate and house districts must be equal in population. The number of people in any district will depend on two factors: the size of the state population and the number of members in the senate and in the house. For example, California's population is roughly thirty-four million. Dividing the total population into forty senate districts results in almost 850,000 people per district. Dividing the total into eighty assembly districts results in approximately 425,000 people per district.

Table 3-1 shows the number of seats and the district population in each of the fifty state senates and houses. Districts vary greatly, with large states tending to have more people in each district and small states tending to have fewer.

The largest districts are in California, followed by Arizona, Florida, Illinois, Michigan, New Jersey, New York, Ohio, and Texas. The smallest districts are in Alaska, Montana, New Hampshire, North Dakota, Rhode Island, Vermont, and Wyoming.

The size of a legislator's district is of enormous importance. Imagine the difference between representing house districts in Ohio, which has about 115,000 constituents, and in Vermont, which has about 4,000. It is difficult in the former to campaign personally house to house, but it is very doable in the latter. Ralph Wright, former speaker of the Vermont House, recalls a visit with William Bulger, president of the Massachusetts Senate. After hearing that Wright had a district (at the time) with only 3,700 constituents, Bulger, who had almost fifty times as many constituents, remarked: "My God, I could take that many to lunch."[3]

Table 3-1 Legislative Districts

State	Senates		Houses	
	Seats	Dist. pop.	Seats	Dist. pop.
Alabama	35	127,060	105	42,353
Alaska	20	31,347	40	15,673
Arizona	30	171,021	60	171,021[a]
Arkansas	35	76,383	100	26,734
California	40	846,791	80	423,396
Colorado	35	122,893	65	66,173
Connecticut	36	94,599	151	22,553
Delaware	21	37,314	41	19,112
Florida	40	399,559	120	133,186
Georgia	56	146,187	180	45,480
Hawaii	25	48,461	51	23,756
Idaho	35	36,970	70	36,970[a]
Illinois	59	210,496	118	105,248
Indiana	50	121,610	100	60,805
Iowa	50	58,526	100	29,263
Kansas	40	67,210	125	21,507
Kentucky	38	106,362	100	40,418
Louisiana	39	114,589	105	42,562
Maine	35	36,426	151	8,443
Maryland	47	112,691	141	37,564
Massachusetts	40	158,727	160	39,682
Michigan	38	261,538	110	90,349
Minnesota	67	73,425	134	36,713
Mississippi	52	54,705	122	23,317
Missouri	34	164,565	163	34,326
Montana	50	18,044	100	9,022
Nebraska	49	34,924	NA[b]	
Nevada	21	95,155	42	47,578
New Hampshire	24	51,491	400	3,089
New Jersey	40	210,359	80	210,359[a]
New Mexico	42	43,311	70	25,986
New York	61	311,089	150	126,510
North Carolina	50	160,986	120	67,078
North Dakota	49	13,106	98	13,106[a]
Ohio	33	344,035	99	114,678
Oklahoma	48	71,889	101	34,165

(Table continues)

Table 3-1 (continued)

State	Senates		Houses	
	Seats	Dist. pop.	Seats	Dist. pop.
Oregon	30	114,047	60	57,023
Pennsylvania	50	245,621	203	60,498
Rhode Island	50	20,966	100	10,483
South Carolina	46	87,218	124	32,355
South Dakota	35	21,567	70	21,567[a]
Tennessee	33	172,403	99	57,468
Texas	31	672,639	150	139,012
Utah	29	77,006	75	29,776
Vermont	30	20,294	150	4,059
Virginia	40	176,963	100	70,785
Washington	49	120,288	98	120,288[a]
West Virginia	34	53,187	100	18,083
Wisconsin	33	162,536	99	54,179
Wyoming	30	16,459	60	8,230
U.S. Congress	100	NA	435	645,632

Source: National Conference of State Legislatures. Reported in Alan Rosenthal, *Republic on Trial* (Washington, D.C.: CQ Press, 2003), 98–99.

Note: District size is calculated by dividing the number of seats into the total 2000 population. District sizes are for single-member districts in states with mixed district types.

[a] Two-member districts.
[b] Unicameral legislature.

In large states such as California, Florida, New Jersey, New York, Pennsylvania, and Texas, legislators rely heavily on staff to help them on constituency matters. Offices in their districts do constituent service year-round, which amounts in large part to trying to help citizens who are having problems with governmental agencies. Nine states provide district offices for all members and thirteen others provide funding for legislators' district-service operations. In the smaller states, where they still have "citizen-legislator" status, members of the senate and house lead very different constituency-related lives. They can get to know a large proportion of their constituents and interact with them face to face.

The topography, as well as the population, of a district also counts. Urban districts are more geographically concentrated, with people spread out vertically in high-rise buildings, while rural districts are more geographically dispersed, with people arranged horizontally. One set of estimates of intrastate variation shows that California districts range from about 18 square miles to 28,991 square miles, New York's from 1 to 4,731 square miles, and Colorado's from 6 to 12,916 square miles.[4]

The larger the territory, the more difficult it is for representatives to get around and meet personally with constituents. Take Rep. Rosie Berger of Wyoming. She only has a little over eight thousand people in her district, but they are scattered over such a wide area that she drives over twenty thousand miles a year just doing constituent service.[5] One of Alaska's senate districts encompasses over 240,000 square miles, making it about the size of Texas. In order to get around the district, its senator has to travel by car, plane, and ferry. Travel, particularly in bad weather, takes quite a while. To visit every town in the district on a single trip would require that the senator spend more than three months away from home.[6]

Geography can make life difficult. Representing a Colorado district divided by the Rocky Mountains, the island of Lanai and part of the island of Maui in Hawaii, and a number of islands in and around Penobscot Bay off the coast of Maine is challenging even for the most intrepid traveler among legislators. And where districts are compact, as in large cities like New York, it is not always clear sailing. Legislators often are barred from access to their constituents by locked doors and security in apartment buildings.

Serving Their District's Interests

Whether they were born and raised in their district or migrated from elsewhere, legislators work assiduously to serve the interests of their constituency and constituents.[7] Service entails just about everything, from the symbolic "being one of them" to the very practical "bringing home the bacon." Constituents have to feel that their legislator is truly their representative, that he or she identifies with their needs and problems. Legislators must not only be available to their constituents, they must also reach out and invite constituents in. For John E. McDonough in Massachusetts, as well as for legislators elsewhere, the requirements are "arduous, draining, time consuming, and relentless."[8] Representatives have to communicate with empathy and in a way that shows that they understand the pressures that constituents undergo in their lives.

They Provide Access and Connection

Nowhere else do people have the access that state legislators afford them. Few constituents can get time with the governor, with department heads, or with bureaucrats in the executive branches. Unless they are on trial themselves, their access to the judiciary is severely limited. But legislators understand that a large part of their job is constituency service, part of which includes providing access and connection.

The Five-State Survey of Maryland, Minnesota, Ohio, Vermont, and Washington offers evidence of how important legislators regard staying in touch with constituents. "Above all else," said one Maryland lawmaker in response to a question, "answer your constituents' mail and phone calls first." When asked to rate the importance of communicating with constituents, legislators in the survey overwhelmingly agreed it was "very important." Another Maryland legislator volunteered, "I wish constituents contacted me more often. I am constantly trying to find more ways to contact them." The 2002 State Legislative Survey revealed the same emphasis. Respondents said that they spent more time keeping in touch with constituents than anything else. Some legislators send letters of congratulations to families celebrating a child's high school graduation or of condolence to those mourning the loss of a parent. An increasing number have Internet sites, to which they refer constituents. In Ohio and Washington, for instance, they make use of newsletters. If legislators represent more suburban or rural areas, they may be able to write a column in a weekly newspaper that circulates locally.

However they are able to manage it, legislators try to stay in touch with people in their districts. They do much of this through communications from their capitol offices. They will meet with constituents who visit them there or see them at interest group–sponsored receptions held in the capitol. But most often their face-to-face contact occurs when they are back home in their district, either during the interim period between legislative sessions or over a long weekend when the legislature is in session.

In states where legislators maintain offices in their districts, one or more staff members will be responsible for local operations. Occasionally people visit the district office; more frequently they call. Some legislators make themselves available on a regular schedule, others meet with constituents by appointment. In most states, however, legislators do not have district offices as such. They operate from their law or business offices or out of their homes when they are back in the district. If they have personal staff in the capital, as in Ohio, constituency work is done by them.

When home, legislators make the rounds. They host or attend town hall meetings; they speak at breakfasts, lunches, and dinners of service clubs like the Kiwanis and Elks, League of Women Voters, senior citizens, businesses, schools, and other organizations in the district; they visit with constituents at churches and in supermarkets, wherever and whenever they are approached. Whether grocery shopping, dining out, or walking the dog, they are on duty.[9]

A former New Jersey legislator, who represented a very competitive district and was facing a tough race for reelection, had to spend about nine out of ten evenings at one local function or another. Even on days when the legislature had been meeting in Trenton, he got home for evenings with various groups. Generally speaking, according to the Five-State Survey, members spent three or four nights a week out, both when the legislature was in session and in the interim.

Unlike physicians, who have to be visited at their offices by appointment, legislators do make house calls. They go practically anywhere they are invited. It is a large part of their job of maintaining contact and offering constituents access they get nowhere else.

They Inform Constituents

First and foremost, legislators inform their constituents about themselves. They are constantly on display, presenting themselves to people in their districts. Just how they do so depends largely on who they are and what their constituency is like.[10] Willie Brown seemed flamboyant, politically astute, and confident in his San Francisco district. Tom Loftus came across as a product of Sun Prairie in Wisconsin. And Harriet Keyserling surely appeared to be caring, concerned, and conciliatory in Beaufort, South Carolina. Allowing for some tweaking here and a tuck there, what constituents see in their representatives is essentially what they get.

Much of the information legislators provide pertains to what they are dealing with at the capitol. In the Five-State Survey about 80 percent of the legislators thought it was very important for them to educate their constituents about issues in the legislature. One house member in Ohio even said: "As a new legislator I hope to teach my constituents about the votes of their political leaders and encourage them to become more active in the political process and proactive on issues that affect them." A majority surveyed also thought that they ought to educate constituents on the system of representative democracy, although they probably had different ideas of what that would entail. It might involve activities such as a nationwide program sponsored by the National Conference of State Legislatures (NCSL). In this program legislators are encouraged to visit schools in their districts and discuss representative democracy and the legislature with students. For example, California assemblywoman Betty Karnette, who taught for over thirty years, regularly visits schools, where she engages students through role-playing and mock committee hearings.[11]

It should be noted that in addition to what individual members do by way of education, legislatures collectively have expanded their educational outreach functions enormously in recent years. They always performed public information functions and distributed information on request. Now they reach out proactively. Over half the states now offer legislative programming on television, like C-SPAN in Washington, D.C. Some have gavel-to-gavel coverage. TVW in the state of Washington offers a variety of programming. The station's slogan, "Dare to be boring," probably is descriptive of how regular people would regard most of the programming that is aired. Legislatures today have Web sites that provide information to the public, and fifteen states have online coverage (Webcasts). Takers may be few, but legislative information is available to anyone who wants it. The supply far exceeds the demand, but informing the public is part of the representational responsibility, which the legislature is trying to fulfill.

They Provide Comfort to Constituents

When he served in the West Virginia Legislature, Joe Manchin (who later was elected governor) recounted a telephone call he received from a constituent who complained about a barking dog who was disturbing her and other residents in the neighborhood. The woman went on for a while, and when she appeared to be done Manchin asked her, "Ma'am, I appreciate your problem. What would you like me to do about it?" The woman replied, "I don't want you to do anything; I just want you to listen." Many constituents want just that—an ear. Better still, a sympathetic ear. They usually get it and even more.

Constituents receive acknowledgment from those who represent them. In the district this comes in the form of legislators showing up at events and meeting and complimenting the individuals and community groups involved. In the capitol building acknowledgment is an ongoing legislative enterprise. Between floor sessions, caucuses, and committee meetings, legislators will go from one place to the next to meet and greet individual constituents and delegations. Collective and more formal acknowledgment of constituents goes on in the senate and house chambers before every daily session.

Following the call to order, the prayer or devotional exercise, and the pledge of allegiance, and before the calendar of legislative business is addressed on the floor, a senate or a house normally will recognize visitors in the gallery or near the podium. The Ohio Senate, for instance, has no gallery, so visitors are seated on both sides and at the rear of the chamber. During one session, the Ohio Senate welcomed the Graham High School wrestling team, which had just won the division wrestling championship. The senator who represented the district introduced the seventeen young men on the team. "I congratulate you," she said, "as a mama who had two wrestlers." At another session, in St. Paul, the University of Minnesota at Duluth women's ice hockey team was applauded by the members assembled in the senate chamber, while in recess. It had won the National Collegiate

Athletic Association (NCAA) Division I women's hockey championship. Since the team's players had to be in class, they were not able to be there to watch the Minnesota Senate and House pass resolutions commending them, so the team coach and university administrators stood in for the players being honored. On another day in the legislature, members of the University of Maryland Terrapins basketball team were honored for their success in the NCAA tournament. They were commended in a resolution passed by the Maryland Senate for being a "source of pride" for the state. Earlier in that same legislative session the house recognized a group of citizens from Allegheny County. A delegate from Western Maryland introduced the visitors, who stood in the gallery while legislators rose at their desks on the floor and applauded. A week later the Snow Hill Eagles boys' basketball team was commended for its 22-5 record, and team members had their picture taken with the speaker.

In each of these states hundreds and hundreds of resolutions are passed at each legislative session to acknowledge youngsters and adults alike.[12] In a small state like Vermont about two hundred resolutions are passed at each session, similar to J.R.S. 49, in which Sen. Gerry Gossens congratulated a high school field-hockey team. The resolution gave a capsule description of the Mount Abraham Eagles' championship game against the team's rivals from Champlain Valley Union High School. Mentioning the entire team by name in one "Whereas" clause and the coaching staff in another, the resolution concluded with the Vermont General Assembly's congratulations.

The period before the work of the daily session begins is usually set aide for the explicit recognition of constituents. Resolutions, kind words, a standing round of applause, a photograph taken at the podium with the presiding officer—all are manifestations of the bond that exists between the represented and their representatives.

They Provide Assistance to Individuals

At the simplest level legislators respond to requests for information. One constituent asks where she should go to replace a lost driver's license. Another inquires about residence requirements for voting. Many questions come from elementary and middle school students who need information about the state's flag, symbols, and political jurisdictions.

It can be more complicated than that. McDonough describes the job by applying a string of metaphors, including "social worker, preacher, negotiator, salesman/saleswoman, coach, street worker." He especially likes the metaphor "plumber," since the legislator fixes problems and tries to improve systems.[13] Normally, however, the most difficult constituent problems that legislators handle fall under the rubric of "casework."

If constituents are looking for employment, legislators try to be of assistance. They are especially helpful to constituents who are seeking appointments to nonpaying positions on state boards, commissions, and authorities. Frequently, such appointments are made by the governor and it is up to legislators to state the case for the men and women they are sponsoring. (In return for appointments, of course, governors may seek a legislator's help on an issue the executive is pushing.) Legislators also assist others who are looking for employment in state government or even elsewhere.

Job acquisition is a relatively small part of a legislator's casework load. Most of it relates to helping individual constituents with problems they encounter regarding welfare benefits, health and hospital insurance, unemployment compensation, nursing home care, driver's licenses, taxes—almost anything under the sun. Even when an issue does not fall within the jurisdiction of the state legislature, legislators offer to help. Speaker Seth Hammett of the Alabama House tells a story about a constituent who called and complained about the problem his wife was having with her Social Security benefits. Speaker Hammett responded that Social Security was the federal government's responsibility and not something with which the state legislature dealt. The constituent continued, however, and the speaker repeated that there was nothing he could do about Social Security benefits. The constituent then asked, rhetorically: "If you can't help me, why did we elect you?" This registered with the speaker, who quickly answered, "What is your wife's Social Security number?"

How much casework do legislators do? More than in the past, especially in legislatures that are essentially full-time. Research conducted some years ago by Malcolm Jewell shows that constituency service loomed large in California, Massachusetts, Ohio, and Texas, but less so in Indiana, Kentucky, and Tennessee, and hardly at all in Colorado and North Carolina.[14] Casework has increased since then. On the 2002 State Legislative Survey, legislators were asked how much time they spent helping constituents concerning problems with government. On a five-point scale, 42 percent responded at the highest point—"a great deal"—and another 32 percent chose the next highest point in the scale. Legislators surveyed recently in Maryland, Minnesota, Ohio, Vermont, and Washington attested to the importance of casework. On a scale of 1 (not important) to 5 (very important) overall they rated its importance at 4.46, with little variation among the states. In these states 50 percent of the legislators responding to the survey handle ten or more cases a week year-round—that is, almost five hundred cases a year (with some constituents represented by more than a single case). Legislators in Vermont predictably work on fewer cases than do those in Ohio, since their districts are much smaller. Generally, the larger the district, the more cases. Legislatures that provide staff to help members also handle more cases than legislatures where members have no help at all.

Whatever the caseload, legislators try to be as helpful as possible. In some instances that means putting a constituent in touch with the executive agency that can respond to the matter. In others that means interceding with an executive agency on behalf of the constituent, increasing the chances that the requester will receive a timely and satisfactory response. Occasionally, legislators go whole-hog for constituents. Jim Townsend, who was majority leader in the Oklahoma House, recalled a complaint that he received from a constituent. The grass on the median strip in the state road in front of the constituent's home was overgrown and needed mowing. Townsend called his contact at the executive department of highways, who said the problem would be addressed right away. Two weeks later the constituent called his representative back, reporting that nothing had been done, and the grass continued to grow. Townsend did not even bother calling the department again. He just put his own rider mower in his pickup truck, drove to the constituent's neighborhood, and mowed the median strip himself.

Because of the service orientation of their representatives, constituents not only receive help; more important, perhaps, they get the feeling of being helped. And it works wonders. As Massachusetts representative Peter

Koutoujian puts it: "Constituents want you to try to help them. They don't expect the world."[15] Legislators themselves derive satisfaction and a sense of efficacy from helping people out and solving a problem or two. Finally, the attention legislators pay to casework builds political support; a favor may be returned with a vote. And votes are seldom far from the minds of most legislators.

They Acquire Resources for the Constituency

In addition to communicating and assisting constituents personally, legislators work to advance the interests of their district collectively. Most significantly in this respect is the work they do securing for their districts the greatest possible amount of state aid—especially school aid—and projects. They spend less time making sure the district gets its share than they do helping out constituents with problems. But half of those questioned in the 2002 State Legislative Survey said they spent "a great deal" of time or almost that. Legislators responding to the Five-State Survey consider getting local aid formulas that produce dollars for their districts to be as important as getting projects for people and groups in their constituencies. Overall, they rank its importance at 3.65 (on a scale of 1 to 5), roughly the same in Maryland, Minnesota, Ohio, and Vermont, but slightly lower in Washington.

In Vermont Sen. Cheryl Rivers, the chair of the Finance Committee, discussed with fiscal staff revision of Act 60, the school-aid formula, and the variety of very technical indexes that could be used to allocate funds to towns for their schools. The staff had employed different models and produced numerous computer runs. Amidst the technical comparisons, however, Rivers did not ignore one thing: how her own constituency would fare under successive options. "It's unfair to my little town," she interjected. "They're going to be mad." That is because her constituents felt the state was "sending all the money north," and her district was further south.

Similarly, in the midst of managing the legislative process in the Maryland House, Speaker Cas Taylor turned his attention to a bill that would appropriate additional money for Allegheny County schools—that is, schools in his district. He had worked with local school boards in fashioning the bill. The new money would be included in the governor's supplemental budget bill, and Taylor would make sure of it. In addition, he would ask the governor to issue a press release that would notify his constituents that the district was benefiting. Although the schools had asked for more, the speaker managed to get them about $5 million in additional funding, by no means a bad day's work for a legislator trying to serve his district.

Budget deliberations in Minnesota reveal just how seriously legislators regard aid for their districts. Majority party members in the senate, for example, worked assiduously to promote the educational finance interests of their districts. One computer run after another was brought to their attention as they spoke in favor of "fairness" to their districts. One Democratic-Farmer-Labor (DFL) senator, relating how education was suffering in his district, felt so strongly that he almost burst into tears while meeting with the majority leader. During consideration by the Tax Committee of the omnibus K–12 financial bill, another senator complained, "I have five school districts and they don't think it's equal at all." Some DFLers did better than others for their districts. Lawrence Pogemiller was one of them. As chair of the Education Committee for eight years, he had provided aggressive leadership and managed to protect the interests of his Minneapolis district, while his suburban DFL colleagues fared less well.

Bringing home the bacon—otherwise known as pork, earmarks, member items, turkeys, or simply pet projects, depending on the particular state—is also on the serving-the-district agenda of legislators. Projects range from the prominent (construction of courthouses) to the paltry (funds for boys' choirs and high school bands). In some states legislatures routinely allocate a certain amount of the budget for members to appropriate to their districts. Each legislative body organizes the distribution of pork among members and their districts in a somewhat different way. Illinois had a "member initiative spending program" that was part of a larger infrastructure development plan for roads, schools, and transit. Under member initiative spending, the Democratic and Republican Party caucuses in the senate and house decided how funds would be distributed throughout the state.[16] New York also exemplifies a well-developed system for the allocation of "member items." The legislature normally sets aside about $200 million—$85 million for the senate, $85 million for the assembly, and $30 million for the governor. These sums are divided up within the two houses between the legislative party leaders, who in turn distribute their allotment to members largely on the basis of political need. Incumbents who are threatened electorally tend to get more projects for their districts.

In other states securing pork requires justification in a formal process. For example, in Maryland the process of constructing the capital budget—which includes local projects—commands the undivided attention of legislators, who feel strongly about bringing something home. It is up to legislative leaders to figure out how to divvy up the limited amount of funding for capital projects. Speaker Taylor wanted a one-time expenditure for his district, Allegheny County, included in the capital budget. The subcommittee chair handling the capital budget was concerned: "My only problem is that I open the door to twenty-three other counties," he said. As the process continued, requests were whittled down. At a hearing of the Senate Budget and Taxation Committee, at which constituent groups were advocating for their projects, Sen. Barbara Hoffman, the chair, questioned: "How much do you need for Healthy Neighborhoods?" When she was told $2 million, Hoffman responded: "You've got to be kidding. How about $1 million?" That amount would have to do. Other requests were eliminated. All told, members of the Maryland Senate and House had asked for $39.1 million for projects such as museums, recreation centers, theaters, hospitals, and so forth. The capital budget finally included less than half of what was requested, amounting to $18.8 million for legislators' bond bills.

In many places, serving the districts' interests is more of a free-for-all. Take Minnesota, for instance. On the one hand, a minority party freshman senator, Michele Bachmann, offered an amendment in committee that would have provided $18 million to pay for a four-lane bridge over the St. Croix River. She was not able to get her amendment voted on in committee or later on the senate floor. Meanwhile, majority party members had their own problems, because Gov. Jesse Ventura had taken a position against adding local projects to an emergency bonding bill. Already included in the bill were funds for the University of Minnesota, flood hazard mitigation, conservation, digital television conversion, and wastewater treatment, totaling $213.5 million. But the DFL anticipated a rash of amendments for local projects that would never survive a conference committee. Members of the

DFL caucus were asked by their majority leader, Roger Moe, to stick together and be disciplined. "What do we do about amendments on local projects when they come up?" asked one senator. "What about the balance between metro and rural?" questioned another. DFL members were committed to getting as much as they could for their individual districts, and they were competing for a limited pie. Understandably, the caucus discussion of local projects became pretty contentious.

Legislatures have come under intense criticism because of their budgetary practices in appropriating funds for political reasons rather than according to merit. The money, critics insist, should be distributed by formula or by a decisional process lodged in the administrative agencies of the executive branch. Appropriations should not be made by individual members, or by party leaders, or for political reasons, but strictly on the substantive merits. Critics also challenge the process because it is closed to the public, and even to rank-and-file legislators, in some states. In New York, for instance, grants were once listed individually in the state budget, where they were open to scrutiny. But in 1999, after Gov. George Pataki line-item vetoed many requests by lawmakers, six thousand or so items were gathered by the legislature in a lump sum, thus making it difficult for the governor to get rid of them.[17]

The media, especially the *New York Times*, periodically publish stories on the waste involved in pork-barrel spending. Actually, the amounts of monies legislatures allocate in this manner are extremely small portions of the total state budget. Those grants played up by the media tend to look foolish at best and fraudulent at worst. In New York, for example, grants have been made to private hunting clubs and to clubhouses of fraternal organizations. Most, however, go to well-known institutions and worthwhile causes, such as cancer and AIDS research, Little Leagues, town halls, and fire departments. In New York $5,000 went to educate Russian Americans about voting and $2,500 to repair a broken boiler in a church. A good portion of the grant funds was designed to restore cuts in the budget made by Governor Pataki.[18] Keith L. T. Wright, an assembly Democrat from New York City, pointed out that he and the speaker, Sheldon Silver, had given millions to a biological research institute at City College, which was in the assemblyman's district. "This center is going to help find the cure for cancer, for Alzheimer's, for diabetes," Wright said. "But all we hear about is money being given to the cheese museum." [19]

They Sponsor Local Bills

Constituency service involves a multiplicity of legislative activities. A proposal that would financially assist people who have high levels of radium in their well waters was of special help to residents of Pasadena, Maryland. A bill specifying that a county transfer station could not be built within two miles of Bowie State University was of special benefit to the African American institution, which maintained that an industrial site ought to be found for a station where garbage would be taken in and compacted before being shipped off. The senate president, in defense of his district, pushed legislation that would block construction of a supermarket and a strip mall.

In some states local jurisdictions depend on the legislature for decisions that in other states could be made by local authorities. Massachusetts is a state in which local governing bodies have to seek authority from the state house in Boston. The large majority of bills Massachusetts legislators sponsor on behalf of localities apply only to specific jurisdictions. A bill related to city services in Somerville, a department of public works in Topsfield, borrowing money for road improvements in Brewster, enforcing delinquent service fees in Taunton, regulating tax deferrals in Princeton—all are examples of local legislation.

They Go Even Further

McDonough suggests that constituency service is limited only by the willingness of the representative to take on local tasks. Every Saturday morning, a Massachusetts colleague of McDonough's helped constituents unload newspapers and bottles from their cars for recycling in Saugus. That constituted constituency service. As for McDonough himself, he describes the laborious efforts he made to resolve differences between the Eggleston Square community in his Boston district and a local street gang and of his work to develop an economic development master plan for the area. [20]

Expressing Their District's Views

Serving their district's interests is relatively straightforward for legislators. The other part of representation—expressing their district's views—is more difficult for them to figure out and more difficult to do.[21] What views exist and whose views ought to be expressed? At what level of specificity are such views? And how do constituency views square with constituency interests? What role should the intensity, organization, and affiliation of district views play in the representative's decision? What about the representative's own views? All of these questions confound the notion of representation as the simple expression of constituency views. There is nothing simple about it.

How Legislators Find Out Where People Stand

For some constituents it is easy for their representatives to discover their views. These people come forward with ideas for legislation. A few legislators encourage constituents to propose bills that they can introduce. California senator Joe Simitian, for example, started a "There Oughtta Be a Law" contest in which constituents could submit ideas for legislation. In the four years since he started the contest, Simitian received over five hundred ideas, thirteen of which he turned into bills. Eight of these were signed into law.[22]

Most legislators welcome ideas for bills that constituents bring them. Richard Bagger of New Jersey acknowledged that a substantial proportion of bills he introduced during his career in the legislature came from people in his district. Massachusetts goes as far as any state, by constitutionally encouraging constituent submissions. The "right of free petition" ensures that legislators will introduce bills "by request" for constituents who have ideas to promote. Many such bills receive no support and expire early in the legislative process. But other constituent proposals are welcomed by legislators who are happy to sponsor them, and some make it all the way through.

There is no question in a representative's mind as to where people who come forward with ideas for legislation stand. But these individuals are very few in number. What representatives would like to know is where most people in the district, and voters in particular, stand on the issues that come before the legislature and on which the representative must vote. Such issues include the tens or even hundreds of bills that legislators vote on in their committees and the hundreds and even thousands of bills that come to the floor of the senate and house.

How do legislators find out where people stand on particular issues? They hear from constituents and are constantly meeting with them. If there is a local press, they pay attention to it. On a number of issues they already have a sense of where people stand, because of previous experience. Rarely do legislators poll their district. Rather, they rely on information that individuals and groups furnish them. In the Five-State Survey legislators were asked to rate the importance of eight possible sources of information in helping them figure out where their constituents stood on different issues. Political supporters in the district rank highest in each of the five states. Friends and associates rank next, except in Ohio. Positions taken by organized groups and by political leaders in the district are virtually tied for third and fourth ranking. Information from lobbyists ranks lower in importance.

Do Constituents Have Views on Issues Before the Legislature?

Legislators feel that on most issues they hear from too few constituents. They think that if they learned directly from constituents more about their views they could better represent their district. They surely do not want to lose votes and possibly an election because they strayed from where their constituents stood on one issue or another.

However, as Hanna F. Pitkin notes in her brilliant theoretical work on representation, a constituency does not have an opinion on every topic. A representative thus cannot reflect what is not there to be reflected.[23] Similarly, in his study of voting in Congress, John W. Kingdon observes that on many matters that reach the voting stage constituents have neither expressed an opinion nor held one.[24] In his memoir McDonough tells of his engagement in campaign finance reform, which was being promoted by Common Cause. During the long process in the legislature, and with all the furor going on, McDonough writes, "I never had a single call or letter from a constituent commenting on my votes, my role, or the issue."[25] It is difficult, if not impossible, then, for representatives to express the "people's will." The fact is, most often there is no such will. It did not take long for Ralph Wright to realize "that most people back home didn't have a clue as to what the legislature was doing 'up in Montpelier,' and a whole lot didn't much care."[26]

Why should we expect constituents to care about or have views on most issues over which legislatures deliberate? Most people have little interest in politics or public policy. They have other matters on their minds and/or their agendas. Only a few issues engage their attention and arouse some concern, but not many. Indeed, not many issues before the legislature have any consequence for individuals back home. That is because the large majority of bills in the legislative process have to do with narrow and technical matters, and are only of concern to specialized publics and organized interest groups. They are matters on which legislators, as well as constituents, have no position, no knowledge, and little or no interest.

Several years ago, one Florida legislator pointed out that there was virtually no opinion in her district on 95 percent of the issues about which she had to vote. She recalled that one of her votes affected the disposition of the Florida state stamp on a beer can. Why should constituents have an opinion on such a subject? Certainly it cannot be their civic duty to have such an opinion. "It is rare," the Florida legislator commented, "that I have a sense of really what my district feels on any issue, except the most major questions."[27] While the "beer can" issues are many, the major questions—relating to taxes, abortion, gay rights, and the like—are few.

As part of the Five-State Survey, lawmakers in Maryland, Minnesota, Ohio, Vermont, and Washington were asked to take into account all the bills on which they had to cast a vote during a particular biennium. On what percentage of them, respondents were asked to estimate, did a substantial number of their constituents have an opinion? All told, 74 percent thought their constituents had an opinion on about 10 percent or fewer. Of those, 48 percent perceived constituents' opinions on 5 percent or fewer. Only 26 percent thought their constituents had opinions on 25 percent or more of the issues. Legislators in Maryland and Minnesota reported slightly less by way of constituency opinion and those in Ohio somewhat more. But for the most part, as far as constituency opinion is concerned, legislators are on their own.

Even if constituents held opinions, their representatives might not have a sense of a "district will." The opinions of some constituents may be on one side, the opinions of some constituents may be on the other side. Supporters and opponents might balance out, leaving the representative in a quandary as far as "district will" was concerned. The opinion, therefore, that counts is that which approaches a mandate for one side or the other, or at least gives one a very visible edge. Legislators in the Five-State Survey, therefore, were asked on how many bills that they voted on during the past two years did their constituency have a clear position (i.e., a large number of constituents were on one side while substantially fewer were on the opposite side). Of the five-state total, 49 percent saw a clear constituency position on five or fewer bills over a two-year period. Roughly two out of three respondents in Ohio and Vermont (but only one out of three in Washington) reported five or fewer bills with clear constituency positions. Of the five-state total, 72 percent saw a clear constituency position on ten or fewer bills over the two-year period, while only 17 percent felt their districts had a clear position on twenty bills or more.

In every session of the legislature, a number of issues arise in which constituents do have views. On some of these issues legislators perceive that their district leans in one direction or the other. But on the overwhelming majority of issues on which legislators vote, not to mention the many amendments to bills, they seldom have much of an inkling of where their constituents stand. In these cases the constituency, as such, is neutralized and other factors come into play as far as legislators' decisions are concerned.

Why Legislators Tend to Be Trustees Rather than Delegates

No discussion of representation would be complete without reference to the classic dichotomy between "delegate" on the one hand and "trustee" on the other. In her book on representation Pitkin posits a continuum, ranging from a "mandate" theory of representation, where legislators assume delegate roles, to an "independence" theory, where they assume trustee roles. At the mandate/delegate end of the continuum, the representative acts on explicit instructions from constituents. Here the representative as delegate is an agent of the constituency, a tool or instrument by which the constituency acts. Further along the continuum, the representative exercises some discretion, but is required to consult on controversial issues and then do as the constituency wishes, or else resign. Toward the middle of the continuum a representative acts as he or she thinks constituents would want, unless they give instructions to the contrary, which the representative must obey. Proceeding further toward the independence/trustee position, the representative acts in the way that he or she thinks is in the interests of constituents, unless constituents give instructions to the contrary, which then have to be obeyed. Near the independence/trustee position, the representative must do as he or she thinks best, except insofar as the representative is bound by campaign promises. At the very end of the continuum the representative, once elected, is entirely free to use his or her own judgment as trustee, no matter what he or she promised or what the constituents want.[28]

Political scientists have been exploring the delegate-trustee distinction for almost fifty years. In 1962 John C. Wahlke and his associates analyzed the representational role orientations of legislators in California, New Jersey, Ohio, and Tennessee. On the basis of responses to an open-ended survey question, which was later coded, the investigation found that the trustee role predominated in each of the legislatures. More recently a survey of Minnesota legislators found that 85 percent viewed their role mainly as that of trustee, while only one out of ten saw their role primarily as that of delegate. An Ohio study produced somewhat different results. Only 13 percent reported a delegate orientation, while 47 percent reported the trustee orientation. But 40 percent were classified as "politicos," because they insisted that both the delegate and trustee orientations were important to them.[29] Apparently, these politicos saw their role as a mixture of expressing constituency views and using their own informed judgment, depending on the issue.

There are a number of reasons why the trustee orientation is more widely held than the delegate orientation. First is the philosophical justification that is expounded by British statesman Edmund Burke in his speech to the electors of Bristol in 1774:

Their [constituents'] wishes ought to have great weight with him; their opinions high respect; their business unremitted attention. It is his duty to sacrifice his repose, his pleasures, his satisfactions, to theirs—and above all, ever, and in all cases, to prefer their interest to his own. But his unbiased opinion, his mature judgment, his enlightened conscience, he ought not to sacrifice to you.... Your representative owes you, not his industry only, but his judgment; and he betrays, instead of serving you, if he sacrifices it to your opinion.

The representative extolled by Burke is a free agent, left unfettered to do his work in the legislature. Burke, in fact, did not think that the act of representing even required that the represented be consulted. If the interests of the constituency are objective and unattached to individual constituents, as Burke believed, it is possible for the representative to promote the interests of constituents without consulting their wishes. The representative simply has to know what is in the constituents' best interests.

Second, a rationale for the Burkean position is the belief that representatives not only have better judgment but also greater knowledge about the issues and the process. Legislators are exposed to more information and a different perspective than their constituents. Moreover, they have to deal with the details of legislation, which requires day-to-day decision making that cannot be directed by the district. The third reason is that the very nature of the constituency and constituents' views precludes a delegate role on the overwhelming majority of issues. If constituents have views with respect to only a few of the many decisions the legislature is called upon to make, then legislators cannot look to their districts for instructions, for no instructions exist. They become trustees, if only by default.

The Five-State Survey posed two questions that bear on the delegate-trustee choice, under conditions where constituency opinion is assumed actually to exist. Legislators were asked: "If a constituency position on a bill were to come into conflict with your own views or judgments, which would generally prevail when you cast your vote?" They were provided a continuum with "vote constituency position" at the left end and "vote according to own judgment" at the right. The values 1, 2, 3, 4, and 5 ran from left to right. Thus, 1 accorded with voting the constituency position, 5 accorded with voting according to one's own judgment, and 3 was square in the middle.

Figure 3-1 Constituency Position versus Legislator's Own View or Judgment: Legislators from Five-State Survey

Vote constituency position	1	2	3	4	5	Vote according to own judgment
	6%	14%	21%	44%	15%	

Source: Data compiled by author.

The results are shown in Figure 3-1. The distribution of responses corresponds with the Pitkin formulation mentioned above and the delegate/trustee questions that customarily have been asked in other studies. The modal response is at point 4, toward the own-judgment end of the continuum. Of the total legislators surveyed, 59 percent opt for their own judgment, points 4 and 5, while only 20 percent select the constituency position, points 1 and 2. The other 21 percent are right in the middle, at point 3. The mean score for all legislators is 3.47.

Responses by state vary depending mainly on district size. In Ohio, with large districts, legislators come closer to saying they vote their own judgment (3.73). In Vermont, with tiny districts, legislators come closest to saying they vote their constituency's position (3.20). The larger the district, the likelier it is to be more heterogeneous; the more heterogeneous, the likelier it is to have conflicting views. The smaller the district, the greater the pressure legislators feel to express people's views. As might be expected, members of the senate (whose terms in Minnesota, Ohio, and Washington are longer than those of representatives) tend to vote their own judgment more than members of the house. That may be because the pressure of elections is a little less intense for them or because they tend to have held office longer. Years of service work in the same direction, with veterans feeling freer than juniors to vote according to their own judgment.

The 2002 State Legislative Survey put the question somewhat differently, but with similar results. Legislators were asked: "When there is a conflict between what you feel is best and what you think the people in your district want, do you think you should follow your own conscience or follow what the people in your district want?" A seven-point scale ranged from "always district" to "always conscience." At the two points at the district end were 13.2 percent of the respondents, while at the two points at the conscience end were 34.4 percent. At the three points in the middle of the scale were 52.3 percent, who essentially were responding "it depends."

How Often Do Constituency and Conscience Clash?

When legislators being asked to vote one way or another explain that they are voting their constituency or voting their conscience, their leaders and colleagues give them a pass. Constituency or conscience are more compelling justifications for a vote than anything else. As Rep. Peter J. Koutoujian advised newly elected members to the Massachusetts legislature, "You will never be burned for voting your district or conscience." What he meant is that the senate or house leadership would not impose sanctions if members deserted their party because of their district or their principles.

Constituency or conscience trump all else. But what if they conflict? McDonough argues that the popular view of "an irreconcilable clash between the duties to represent constituents and to be true to one's conscience" is misleading.[30] The popular view, the research of Kingdon on Congress suggests, is way off base. Lawmakers rarely vote against the intense feelings of any significant group of constituents, let alone against an intense majority of them. If a representative perceives a constituency opinion on any given issue, the probability is great that he or she would vote for that position, according to Kingdon.[31] In the case of legislators it would seem either that constituency and conscience are in alignment or, in those instances where they are not, constituency usually wins out.

The first question, then, is how often do a representative's constituency views and a representative's own views come into conflict? As McDonough and Kingdon attest, the answer to this question is "not often." Let us look at a number of issues on which constituents are likely to hold views and the constituency is likely to have a position. These are hot-button issues—capital punishment, abortion, taxes, gun control, gambling, and gay rights. In Maryland, Minnesota, Ohio, Vermont, and Washington all of these issues, with the exception of gambling, were high on one of the five states' lawmaking agendas. Legislators were asked with respect to each of these six issues: (1) whether their constituents had a predominant view; and (2) whether their own views were basically the same or substantially different from those of their constituents. The responses are shown in Table 3-2. Of initial interest is the middle column of the table, which indicates that—as perceived by legislators—no overall constituency view exists in some districts even on these extremely salient issues. The fact that 42 percent perceive no predominant constituency view on gambling is probably because gambling has not become a political issue in places, or perhaps because the district is evenly divided on this issue.

By contrast, as Table 3-2 also shows, predominant views on abortion, gun control, and taxes exist in about nine out of ten districts. In the case of taxes there are predominant views in nineteen out of twenty districts. The first column reports percentages where the representative's own views and constituency views (as perceived by the legislator) are basically the same. The third column represents percentages where the representative's own views and constituency views are different. The ratio of same-to-different views range from about 12:1 in the case of taxes to about 3:1 in the case of gambling. In short, in most districts and on the salient issues representatives and most of their constituents agree. In only a small minority of districts (ranging from 7 percent with respect to taxes to 16 percent with respect to gambling and 15 percent with respect to capital punishment) does disagreement exist. These are the places where conscience and constituency come into conflict. All told, in the five states where legislators were surveyed the clash of conscience and constituency does not appear to be a widespread problem. Of the total responding on these six issues, 58 percent reported no conflicts to all, another 23 percent had a conflict on one of the issues, 13 percent on two, and only 5 percent on three or more.

Why is there such a high rate of agreement between representatives' own views and those of their constituencies? In some cases the representative has adapted to his or her constituency and taken on the dominant views on major issues. This is especially likely if the representative's own position is not strongly held. In most cases, however, the representative and the constituency truly agree. After all, he or she is one of them. Moreover, many districts in practically every state tend to be relatively safe for one party or the other. When representatives perceive their constituency, at least on the dimension of public policy, they tend to perceive mainly

Table 3-2 Correspondence of Constituency and Legislator Views

| | Percentage of legislators reporting | | |
Issue	Own views and constituency views are basically the same	No known predominant constituency view	Own views and constituency views are different
Capital punishment	56%	29%	15%
Abortion	75	14	11
Taxes	87	6	7
Gun control	78	12	10
Gambling	42	42	16
Gay rights	66	20	14

Source: Data compiled by author.

their supporters—Democrats generally see the Democratic base and Republicans the Republican base. The likelihood is that on major issues Democratic legislators agree with their supporters and Republican legislators agree with theirs.[32]

There are, of course, one or two issues on which legislators feel torn between conscience on the one hand and constituency on the other. Practically every legislator will have such an experience etched in his or her memory. Tom Loftus of Wisconsin, for example, stood firm on gambling. "This was un-Wisconsin, un-Lutheran, un-Progressive," he wrote, "and I didn't care if I was unenlightened and unrepresentative about what the voters wanted."[33] On issues that weigh less heavily on one's conscience, the vote is likely to hue to the constituency line. McDonough writes about his choice between trolleys, which were supported by two-thirds of his constituents, and buses, which were supported by only one-third, on a public transportation line called Arborway. "To me," he writes, "it was a choice between vanilla and chocolate ice cream, not one of principle, and I respected the expressed view of my constituents on the matter, whatever my personal feelings."[34] Trolleys versus buses for McDonough did not assume the standing of a woman's right to choose on abortion or civil rights, where his own views would prevail (if his constituents' views were different from his own, which given his district, they were not likely to be).

Table 3-3 How Legislators Would Probably Vote if Their Views and Constituency Views Were in Conflict

	Percentage would probably vote		
Issue	Own view	Constituency view	Don't know
Capital punishment	71%	19%	10%
Abortion	82	13	5
Taxes	48	40	12
Gun control	65	27	8
Gambling	46	39	15
Gay rights	71	20	9

Source: Data compiled by author.

What Happens When They Clash?

The incidence of the legislator's conscience clashing with the legislator's constituency is not high, but where it does the outcome depends on the issue. For each legislator there are probably a limited number of issues where conscience would trump constituency. Otherwise, the legislator would follow the dominant constituent view. Legislators responding to the Five-State Survey were asked, with regard to each of the six issues mentioned above, how they would likely vote if their own views and those of their constituency were to come into conflict. The responses of the total number of legislators are presented in Table 3-3. As a matter of principle, from which legislators are least likely to deviate, nothing compares to one's position on abortion. Six times as many would vote their own views. Capital punishment and gay rights show almost as many would stick to their own views, not their constituency's. On gun control more than twice as many would reject the constituency position, if their own views differed.

Taxes and gambling represent somewhat different kinds of issues for legislators. On taxes representatives can go either way. Here, a constituency mandate for lower taxes or against tax increases is probably evident to most politicians. Legislators fear political consequences if they reject such a mandate. McDonough relates an entertaining story on the subject. Massachusetts House Speaker George Keverian was trying to line up eighty-one votes in favor of a tax package. He reached out to Sal DiMasi (who years later became speaker), then recuperating at his home after suffering a heart attack. Keverian asked him if he would make a special trip from his home in Boston to the state house to vote for the tax package. "You don't understand, George," DiMasi said. "I had a heart attack, not a lobotomy."[35]

Electorally Connected

On the overwhelming number of cases on which legislators have to act, no constituency views really exist. On issues where they do exist, they may be evenly divided with no preponderance for one position or the other. Where a preponderance does exist, chances are that the legislator and constituency see eye to eye. In those few cases where conscience and constituency clash, legislators follow conscience on more value-laden issues and split between constituency and conscience on more bread-and-butter ones. Does all this mean that as far as public policy is concerned, constituency doesn't matter much? The answer is "yes," on the one hand, but "no," on the other.

On most issues that a legislature considers, constituency is not a major factor. Only those constituents who are organized in groups care about a number of issues, while fewer constituents care about others. Nor does the resolution of most issues that are decided by a legislature affect constituency to any substantial extent. Nevertheless, the district remains the bottom line for just about every legislator. A Washington legislator put it succinctly: "I always ask what is better for most people in my district." In effect, legislators calculate, consciously or otherwise, how their decisions would help or hurt their districts and their constituents (and particularly those constituents who are not firmly positioned in the opposition camp). Connected to that calculation is another: how their decisions would help or hurt *them* in their districts and with their constituents.

Even when the constituency has no apparent views, the legislators will ask, explicitly or implicitly, "Where would my constituency stand, if it were to take a position?" He or she would also ask, "If I vote this way, will it hurt my constituents and will it hurt me with my constituents?" In other words, "Will I lose votes?" As Richard F. Fenno points out, "there is no way that the act of representing can be separated from the act of getting elected."[36] The next election ensures that a constituency orientation is part of the legislative process, even though constituents themselves may be unconcerned. Yes, legislators feel that it is their job to be of help to their districts and their constituents. Yes, they get gratification from serving district needs. Yes, most of them see eye to eye with their constituents on major issues. But the forthcoming election is what nails it all down. Legislators cannot be sure of what issues will arise and what will become of concern to constituents at that next election. Thus, the next election is ever in mind. Richard A. Posner, among others, does not regard representatives as mere agents of voters. Nevertheless, he recognizes that "the electoral process does tend to align the representatives' interests with those of the voters—to keep the representatives on a tether, though a long one."[37]

"The thought of reelection may not occur to a first-term legislator within the first five minutes after winning the election," opines a Michigan lawmaker, "but I would not count on that." Although a few legislators who have held their seats for some years do not worry about reelection, most legislators do. Even if they come from relatively safe districts, the next election is never completely out of their mind. The closer it gets, the more legislators bear it in mind.

If a consensus on an issue exists, it is easy for legislators to act. But on major issues seldom does such a consensus exist, at least at a level of specificity that provides direction for lawmaking. Legislators operate mostly on matters where consensus doesn't apply. Under such conditions, the political task of lawmakers is damage control, as much as anything else. They want to minimize fallout that might occur back home because of any issues on which they and their constituents may not see eye to eye. Legislators deal in electoral margins or increments. They are never certain how many people unhappy about their stand on an issue would be significant electorally. Nor do they want to find out. Retaliation by an interest group, resulting in a loss of support, is always possible. Reprisal by the voters more generally, because of a legislator's behavior on a particular issue, is more remote. But there can be danger out there.

Legislators are particularly sensitive to any consensus that exists among their constituents, what they perceive to be district "mandates." These are few and far between and vary by district; yet a few, like not raising taxes, are almost universal. When they do exist, representatives usually—but by no measure always—have a pretty good idea of what they prescribe. Or more accurately, what they proscribe. That is because mandates tend to translate into *don'ts* rather than *do's* for the legislator: "don't vote to increase income taxes," "don't vote for gun control," "don't vote for needle exchange." On some issues mandates are overwhelming; according to a member of the Florida House, "You learn it from so many people in so many different walks of life that it is clear."

Occasionally, legislators feel pressure from their party caucus and party leaders or from the governor to defy a constituency mandate and risk alienating voters back home. Or their conviction runs counter to their constituents. When they face a choice between constituency and conscience or party, several courses of action arise. First, they vote their constituency, and thereby do not jeopardize support in the next election. If it is a legislative party matter, their leaders may not need them to achieve a majority and let them off a vote. Second, they try to duck taking a clear stand. Their party leaders, if in the majority, may help them by scheduling votes that will allow them to cast an "aye" vote on one and a "nay" on the other. Or third, they may simply bite the bullet, vote against their constituency, and try to explain their position to people back home.

The nearer the next election, the more difficult it is to defy one's constituency. A graphic illustration of the importance of the proximity of the election is the New Jersey Legislature's vote on the state budget in 2005. Acting governor Richard Codey proposed cutting the state's property tax rebate program in order to balance the budget. Members of the Democratic-controlled senate, who did not face election until 2007, went along with the cut in tax rebates. But members of the Democratic-controlled assembly, who were on the ballot in just a few months, opposed cuts in the rebate program. Assembly members did not want to give opposing candidates any grist for their campaign mills.

However risky it may be, there are times when legislators stick with principle, policy judgment, or party to the displeasure of their constituency. McDonough writes about several of his Democratic colleagues, who represented Republican districts but cast repeated votes to increase taxes and cut spending, "fully understanding that their actions placed their careers in dire jeopardy." Their explanations were that their consciences dictated their actions, regardless of the political cost. They paid the price soon after when they were defeated for reelection.[38]

A wrong move may cost a legislator his or her seat, as it did Cas Taylor, speaker of the House of Delegates in Maryland. A Democrat from a conservative Western Maryland district, he supported a gun-control initiative of Democratic governor Parris Glendening. Later, he tried to recoup political ground at home by sponsoring a gun-safety education bill and working with the National Rifle Association to get it passed. Nevertheless, Taylor was targeted by the Republican Party and defeated in a close race in the 2002 election. No one expected that the speaker would lose his election, but he did. His vote on guns certainly contributed to his defeat.

Vermont illustrates the broader costs that may be incurred when conscience confronts constituency. In December 1999 the Vermont Supreme Court, in the case of *Baker v. State of Vermont,* issued a ruling that required the legislature to either legalize gay marriage or create a "parallel institution," a domestic partnership.[39] The chief justice's opinion required that the legislature act; the legislature had little choice. In 2000 a civil unions bill providing for domestic partnership worked its way through the Vermont legislature. The question of whether legislators should follow their conscience or heed the views of constituents became central to the deliberations that took place. Polls showed that a slight majority of Vermonters opposed the proposal, while legislators favoring civil unions argued that they would have to vote according to the dictates of their conscience. The legislature finally passed a civil unions law.

A number of legislators knew that their votes in favor of civil unions put their careers in jeopardy. These included the speaker, who understood that his speakership was imperiled by the issue, and legislators who were already feeling the anger of opponents. These legislators believed that the work they did on this bill was, in the words of one journalist, "their finest hour." Subsequently, seven senators and twenty-nine representatives who supported the law retired or were defeated in the election of 2002.

Legislators tend to tread carefully, but they aren't always sure of how an issue will play out in their districts. Usually, they are reluctant to vote themselves salary increases, no matter how justified they believe them to be. (Many states have established independent salary commissions, or some other processes, by which legislative pay is determined, thus reducing the political risk to legislators who can receive raises without paying for them.) However, the Pennsylvania legislature voted raises in 2005, just before adjourning for the summer. Members were convinced that they deserved the increase—but they were not prepared for the reaction. After four months of bombardment by the press and the public, the legislature repealed the pay raise, by a whopping 50-0 vote in the senate and a just-as-whopping 197-1 vote in the house. It was too late, however. In the May 2006 primary elections, because of their votes on the salary bill, seventeen legislators, including the senate president pro tem, lost their seats. Their constituents had the last word, and it was not a friendly one.

District Blocks

Legislatures are constitutionally parochial. In each of the ninety-nine legislative bodies in the fifty states, the local district is the basic building block for the state legislature. Members seldom range far from their districts. They live in their districts, have affection for their constituents and constituencies, serve them, promote their interests, and depend upon them for political survival.

Their overall orientation is toward their districts. Yet when it comes to matters of public policy and just how they make laws at the capitol, their constituencies give them considerable leeway. On the large majority of issues they are not restricted by constituency mandates, although they may be limited by the concentrated demands of constituency groups. However free they may actually be, they normally take into account where their district is and where district groups line up on issues. They also anticipate where their district and where district groups are likely to be, if they vote one way or another. Years ago Kingdon demonstrated that representatives' constituencies are very much on their minds as they make their decisions and are extremely important to what they decide.[40] It is not at all different in state legislatures today, where similar parochialism prevails.

Notes

1. Lynda W. Powell, Richard G. Niemi, and Michael Smith, "Constituent Attention and Interest Representation," in *Institutional Change in American Politics: The Case of Term Limits*, ed. Karl T. Kurtz, Bruce Cain, and Richard G. Niemi (Ann Arbor: University of Michigan Press, 2007), 38.

2. Michael A. Smith, *Bringing Representation Home: State Legislators Among Their Constituencies* (Columbia: University of Missouri Press, 2003), 199.

3. Ralph Wright, *All Politics Is Personal* (Manchester Center, Vt.: Marshall Jones Company, 1996), 20.

4. Anthony Gierzynski, "Elections to the State Legislature," in *Encyclopedia of the American Legislative System*, ed. Joel H. Silbey (New York: Scribner's, 1994), 441.

5. Jane Carroll Andrade, "Keeping in Touch," *State Legislatures* (February 2006): 30.

6. Peverill Squire and Keith E. Hamm, *101 Chambers: Congress, State Legislatures, and the Future of Legislative Studies* (Columbus: Ohio State University Press, 2005), 60.

7. This section draws on Alan Rosenthal, *Heavy Lifting: The Job of the American Legislature* (Washington, D.C.: CQ Press, 2004), 23–34.

8. John E. McDonough, *Experiencing Politics: A Legislator's Stories of Government and Health Care* (Berkeley: University of California Press, 2000), 163.

9. Andrade, "Keeping in Touch," 30–31.

10. See Richard F. Fenno Jr., *Home Style: House Members in Their Districts* (Boston: Little Brown, 1978), 54–135.

11. Andrade, "Keeping in Touch," 31.

12. Some states are trying to limit the number of personal and congratulatory resolutions introduced. In Georgia, house members are permitted a limited number of drafted resolutions; after that they have to pay the costs. In Massachusetts, house members have to type their own resolutions. In North Dakota a commendatory resolution is allowed only if the achievement has brought national attention or recognition. American Society of Clerks and Secretaries, *Inside the Legislative Process* (Denver: National Conference of State Legislatures, October 2005), 3/126–128.

13. McDonough, *Experiencing Politics*, 59.

14. Malcolm E. Jewell, *Representation in State Legislatures* (Lexington: University Press of Kentucky, 1982).

15. At the Massachusetts institute for new legislators, University of Massachusetts, Amherst, December 12, 2000.

16. Michael C. Herron and Brett A. Theodos, "Government Redistribution in the Shadow of Legislative Elections: A Study of the Illinois Member Initiative Grants Program," *Legislative Studies Quarterly* 29 (May 2004): 288, 291.

17. On taking office Gov. Eliot Spitzer proposed that member items be listed in the budget individually. Senate and assembly leaders signaled their support for his proposal. (*New York Times,* January 5, 2007.) At about the same time, the New Jersey Legislature also moved to identify what it referred to as Christmas-tree items in the budget.

18. *New York Times,* November 28, 2006.

19. Ibid., January 22, 2007.

20. McDonough, *Experiencing Politics,* 46–48.

21. This section draws on Rosenthal, *Heavy Lifting,* 35–56.

22. Andrade, "Keeping in Touch," 29.

23. Hanna F. Pitkin, *The Concept of Representation* (Berkeley: University of California Press, 1967), 147.

24. John W. Kingdon, *Congressmen's Voting Decisions* (New York: Harper and Row, 1973), 69.

25. McDonough, *Experiencing Politics,* 195.

26. Wright, *All Politics Is Personal,* 159.

27. Quoted in Alan Rosenthal, *The Decline of Representative Democracy* (Washington, D.C.: CQ Press, 1998), 20.

28. Pitkin, *The Concept of Representation,* 125, 145–146. See also Jane Mansbridge, "Rethinking Representation," *American Political Science Review* 97 (November 2003): 515–528.

29. John C. Wahlke et al., *The Legislative System* (New York: Wiley, 1962), 267–286; Royce Hanson, *Tribune of the People* (Minnesota: University of Minnesota Press, 1989), 232; and Samuel C. Patterson, "Legislative Politics in Ohio," in *Ohio Politics,* ed. Alexander P. Lamis (Kent: Kent State University Press, 1994), 24.

30. McDonough, *Experiencing Politics,* 312.

31. Kingdon, *Congressmen's Voting Decisions,* 30, 41.

32. In his work on Congress, Kingdon finds that representatives perceive a district opinion among those elites that are part of their electoral support coalition. *Congressmen's Voting Decisions,* 32, 34.

33. Tom Loftus, *The Art of Legislative Politics* (Washington, D.C.: CQ Press, 1994), 153.
34. McDonough, *Experiencing Politics,* 161–162.
35. Ibid., 142.
36. Fenno, *Home Style,* 233.
37. Richard A. Posner, *Law, Pragmatism, and Democracy* (Cambridge: Harvard University Press, 2003), 167.
38. McDonough, *Experiencing Politics,* 156–157.
39. This account is based on David Moats, *Civil Wars: A Battle Cry for Gay Marriage* (New York: Harcourt, 2004), 241.
40. Kingdon, *Congressmen's Voting Decisions,* 31.

4

Legislative Parties and Elections

LEGISLATORS LIVE FROM ELECTION TO ELECTION. So do legislatures. In five states—Alabama, Louisiana, Maryland, Mississippi, and North Dakota—both senators and representatives have the luxury of four-year terms. In forty-four states house members run every two years. In eleven of them senators also run every two years. In thirty-three, plus Nebraska, senators have four-year terms. There is always an election ahead, and individual members, political parties, and the legislature itself have to take it into account.

What's at Stake in Elections

Elections not only are frequent but they are focal, especially for legislators who experience them close-up. They are important for others, too, who also have a stake in their outcome. Everyone who is involved wants to win. In politics, as in sports, "winning may not be everything," as Jesse Unruh, one-time speaker of the California Legislature, put it, "but losing is nothing." Winning means even more in politics than in sports. In sports, if you don't win, another game or another season lies ahead. In legislative politics, if you don't win you have to look for another line of work (or an alternative means of doing public service). If your political party doesn't win, it is relegated to minority status, at least until the next election. Unruh has opined here as well: "Being in the majority isn't everything, but being in the minority is nothing." The alternatives for contestants in legislative elections leave no doubt as to which is the preferred one.

A lot is at stake for individual legislators. They want to retain power. With-out it, they cannot promote the values, policies, and interests in which they believe. Moreover, they have dedicated time and other resources to their leg-islative careers and passed up opportunities outside. At each election their chosen careers are squarely on the line. Although they are generally strong, their egos do not take well to losing. Many defeated politicians bounce back, redeeming themselves with an election victory after a loss. They suffer little permanent damage. But those who exit political life by virtue of electoral defeat have trouble adjusting. It is not pleasant to be rejected, especially by those one has spent a career trying to serve.

Political parties have high stakes in legislative elections. They want to control the legislative branch by achieving majorities in the senate and house. Unless some of their members defect, majority status allows a party to allocate personnel among standing committees and set the agenda for the conduct of business. Normally, the majority party shapes the major policies that the chamber enacts. The minority party may force the majority to make concessions, but rarely can it achieve significant policy results on its own. The majority party, furthermore, generally has an advantage in the forthcoming election on the fund-raising front. It is usually easier to maintain a majority than to achieve one.

Interest groups also have a stake in legislative elections. Any group wants its allies and friends to win seats in the legislature. That is the surest way to protect and advance the group's interests. Persuading legislators who already agree with a group's agenda is much more manageable than convincing ones who have no interest group alignment at all. For the most part, interest groups support legislators from both parties, but some groups tend to prefer candidates of one party rather than the other; for example, small-business owners favor Republicans and teachers favor Democrats.

Because the stakes are high and the stakeholders many, campaigns for election to the legislature are critical. It should not come as a surprise that in legislative campaigns combat is intense, money is raised and spent, and attacks are frequent; nor that among legislators themselves partisan behavior is the norm and incivility appears to be on the rise.

How Incumbents Face Elections

Put yourself in a legislator's shoes. Why risk a loss? As a legislator, you will do what you have to do in order to win. It would be irresponsible on your part not to. You would be letting down your family, friends, supporters, party, and interest group allies. You would be letting down yourself.

Objectively speaking, many legislators would not seem to have much to worry about. That is because most districts at the state legislative level (as well as at the congressional level) are relatively safe for one party or another ("safe" meaning that the district was won by 55 percent or more of the vote in the prior election). Depending on the state, generally from two out of five to four out of five legislative districts can be categorized as safe. In California, for instance, as of 2006 almost every district could be classified as safe. In New Jersey four out of five are predominantly Democratic or predominantly Republican. By contrast, in Iowa many more districts are up for grabs.

Why are so many districts safe? Political pundits attribute the situation to redistricting processes that draw district lines, or "gerrymander," districts to the advantage of either the Democrats or the Republicans. Redistricting certainly plays a part, but of even greater weight are more natural tendencies of ideological sorting on a geographical basis. Democrats are inclined to live close to one another (often in cities and inner suburbs), as do Republicans to other Republicans (often in rural areas and outer suburbs). Increasingly, as Bill Bishop demonstrates in a demographic analysis, people choose to live near people like themselves—in political as well as other respects. In 1976, for example, Americans tended to live, work, or worship with people who supported a different party than their own. Only 26 percent of the country's voters lived in counties that had landslide elections for president that year. By 1992, however, 37.7 percent lived in landslide counties; by 2000 the proportion was 45.3 percent; and by 2004 as many as 48.3 percent of Americans lived in places where one or the other candidate for president won big.[1] To some extent, as well, districts are safe because of the advantages of incumbency—at least in times when voters feel things are going well and have no urge to "throw the rascals out."

Indeed, as the 2002 State Legislative Survey shows, the safety of some incumbents is attested to by the fact that one-third are unopposed in general elections and two-thirds are unopposed in primary elections. These incumbents do not have to make a strenuous effort in order to win. The one-third without opposition from the other party have clear sailing, at least in the general election, while others endure the rigors of a campaign for reelection.

In his study of legislators in Connecticut, New York, and Vermont, Grant Reeher tried to get at incumbents' sense of their own electoral vulnerability. Half selected "relatively safe" as a response describing their districts, another third chose "somewhat competitive" as a description, and only 12 percent selected "very competitive."[2] A much earlier study of legislators demonstrated that nearly all of them felt unsafe, despite being in districts where their party enjoyed 55–45 percent or even 60–40 percent margins. Whatever the nature of their districts, most incumbents do not take victory for granted.

Incumbent legislators are not impressed by statistics regarding their past electoral success rates. They feel vulnerable. Nothing is certain in politics. Lightning can always strike, and does occasionally. It is the lightning that legislators remember, not the statistical probabilities. They have seen colleagues relax their efforts and subsequently lose their seats. They have seen incumbents swept out by a national tide, an unpopular candidate at the top of their ticket, or a scandal that suddenly catches fire. They have seen colleagues lose after being pummeled by the press. They have seen seemingly entrenched legislators go down in defeat because they cast a vote that upset their constituency or caused a key group to mobilize against them. They have witnessed successful primary challenges to incumbents by members of their own party who attacked them from the right or the left. All of these add up to relatively few cases, but they are the ones that stick in a legislator's mind.

Because they feel vulnerable, most incumbents find it safest to "run scared." This means that they bar no holds in their campaign. They raise as much money as they conveniently can. They may not really need it, but still, campaign funds are a *sine qua non* of contemporary elections. Moreover, money has multiple uses. In many states legislators can use campaign accounts to pay for district offices and other expenses relating to representation.[3] John E. McDonough maintained that most of his colleagues in Massachusetts raised as much as they needed for the current cycle, and no more. But some, who are particularly ambitious, "use their position to extract campaign donations from everyone in sight." They want to have funds for a future run for higher office or to hand out to colleagues and amass credit and influence within the legislature. Most important, they want to have sufficient money to discourage individuals from challenging them.[4]

Several years ago, a Wisconsin legislator complained to me that she did not have an opponent in her bid for reelection. This surprised me; it had been my impression that it was the dream of every elective politician to run without opposition. So I asked her what bothered her about not having an opponent. "If I don't have an opponent," she answered, "I really can't raise money for a campaign. If I don't raise enough money, I will not succeed in discouraging opponents from running in the future." The objective, it seems, is to raise enough money to frighten off serious opponents but still have a weak opponent so that campaign contributions continue to come in.

Incumbents, moreover, cannot pick and choose when they will and when they won't raise money. They cannot stop because they have an easy race, then start again when they have a tough one. Raising money for a political campaign, it has been said, is like milking a cow. If one stops milking the cow, it dries up. If one stops raising campaign funds, contributors fall out of the habit of giving. The fund-raising machine has to be revved up again, and that is not easy to do.

Finally, money is raised to be spent. Direct mail is costly, as is radio. Even costlier is television. Few candidates can know just how many mailings or radio advertisements are sufficient or just how many votes can be gained per dollar increments. Few candidates can be sure that the opposition will not make an expensive radio or television assault during the final weeks of the campaign, an assault that will have to be countered rapidly. If the funds that are raised for a campaign are not spent, they can be used in the next election or can be contributed to the campaigns of colleagues who face serious threats. Despite the reasons for vigorous fund-raising, as we shall see below, in most places not a lot of money is raised or spent on most campaigns for the legislature.

Running means more than raising and spending funds. It means paying substantial attention to one's constituents, constituent groups, and the constituency as a whole. It also means trying to avoid exposure on issues that will divide one's base, mobilize opposition voters, provide an opponent with the text for a thirty-second radio advertisement, or risk the loss of independent voters. All of this constitutes the democratic connection between representatives and their districts.

How Political Parties Face Elections

About 90 percent of the nation's congressional districts and perhaps two-thirds of its legislative districts are largely Democratic or largely Republican; they are not very competitive at all. Yet the United States is closely divided in partisan terms. On political maps about half the states appear blue (Democratic) and half red (Republican). The 2000 and 2004 presidential elections were hotly contested, and recently the U.S. Senate and the U.S. House have been closely divided.

At the state legislative level Democrats dominated for decades until a Republican resurgence occurred in the 1990s, both in Congress and the states. Actually, Republicans had been gaining seats in state legislatures since the 1960s. Before then, Democrats held 95 percent of the legislative seats in the South. Since then Republicans made great gains in the southern states. In 1994 they won control of the house in South Carolina and North Carolina and the senate in Florida. In 1995 the Tennessee Senate and in 1996 the Florida House and Texas Senate fell to the Republicans. In the years thereafter the Virginia Senate (1998), Virginia House (1999), South Carolina Senate (2001), Georgia Senate (2002), Texas House (2002), Georgia House (2004), and Mississippi Senate (2007) all came under Republican control.[5] The Republican upsurge in the South led to the balancing of control by the two political parties in the legislatures of the fifty states. Twenty-five years of party control are shown in Table 4-1.

After the 2004 elections the nation was about as balanced as it could be in terms of party membership in and control of state legislatures. Out of 7,382 legislators, of whom 7,316 were members of one or the other major party, 3,663 were Democrats and 3,642 Republicans.[6] In total only twenty-one seats—or 0.3 percent of the 7,316—separated the two parties. Of the ninety-eight senates and houses organized on a partisan basis (excluding Nebraska's nonpartisan unicameral) forty-seven were controlled by Democrats, forty-nine by Republicans, and two were tied, very close to partisan parity. Of the forty-nine legislatures (again excluding Nebraska), Democrats controlled nineteen, Republicans twenty, and control was split in ten.

Of the eighty-eight chambers being contested in 2006, about twenty could have gone either way. Largely because of national issues and the un-

Table 4-1 Party Control of the State Legislatures, 1982–2006

	Partisan control, by number of states		
Year	Democratic	Republican	Split[a]
1982	34	10	5
1984	26	11	12
1986	28	9	12
1988	29	8	12
1990	30	6	13
1992	25	8	16
1994	18	19	12
1996	20	18	11
1998	19	17	13
2000	18	17	14
2002	16	21	12
2004	19	20	10
2006	22	15	12

Source: Data from *The Book of the States,* published annually by the Council of State Governments.

[a] Ties are counted as split control.

popularity of President George W. Bush, Democrats made significant gains in Congress and the states in this election. They took control of the U.S. Senate and U.S. House and increased their governorships by six. They picked up ten legislative chambers (while one moved from Democratic to a tie and one from a tie to Republican). They gained 325 legislative seats nationwide, and for the first time in twenty-five years suffered no net loss in the South but gained nineteen seats. In the legislative elections held the following year—in Louisiana, Mississippi, New Jersey, and Virginia (the so-called odd-year elections)—Democrats continued to do well. They retained their majorities in five of the eight chambers in contest, and they picked up majorities in two others. The Republicans had to be satisfied with the gains they made, although short of a majority, in the Louisiana House.

Overall, the Democrats appear to have the lead in the states, at least for a while. They are solidly in control in seven states: Alabama, Arkansas, Hawaii, Maryland, Massachusetts, Rhode Island, and West Virginia. By contrast, the Republicans are entrenched in only three states: Idaho, Utah, and Wyoming. Even New Hampshire, which had been solidly Republican, fell to the Democrats in 2006. New York has been divided for years, with a Democratic assembly and a Republican senate. Indeed, the senate had been Republican for over forty years. But in a special election to fill a vacancy the Democrats picked up a seat, leaving Republicans with a majority of only one. The rest of the states are competitive or somewhat competitive, with either party able to win a majority over the course of one or two election cycles.

The incentives for political parties are quite different in competitive and noncompetitive states. In the latter, their role—and especially their electoral role—is likely to be a lesser one. But where control is up for grabs, the two parties' stakes are high and their involvement substantial.

Legislators and Their Parties

Political parties provide much of the glue that holds the governmental system together. In a constitutional arrangement that disperses power, parties allow for greater centralization than would otherwise happen.[7] They hold things together, insofar as systems rooted in federalism and the separation of powers can be held together. This is because parties, unlike other groups, perform four major functions: first, they serve to give many Americans political identity and a group with which to affiliate; second, they serve as policy promoters with agendas of their own; third, they serve as campaign organizations, which recruit candidates and help them get elected; and fourth, they serve as governing bodies, assigning personnel and making public policy.

Parties as Identity Groups

Despite the increase in the number of Americans who regard themselves as independents (and the ability of this group to determine the outcome of close elections), the large majority identify as either Democrats or Republicans. In the 1960s and 1970s eight out of ten persons did so; since then the number has declined, but still six or seven out of ten affiliate or identify with one party or the other. And of the one-third or so who consider themselves independents, a number lean toward the Democrats or toward the Republicans.

These partisan identifiers represent different constituencies. Generally speaking, Democrats and Republicans differ by geography (urban, inner suburban, outer suburban, and rural), church-going, race, and—to some extent—occupation and income. The two parties have differing ideological constituencies as well. Data from the 2002 State Legislative Survey show a sharp contrast between Democrats and Republicans. When asked to characterize the political views of primary voters in their districts, Republican legislators characterized them: 93.0 percent conservative, 6.2 percent moderate, and 0.8 percent liberal. Democratic legislators characterized them: 59.0 percent liberal, 28.2 percent moderate, and 12.8 percent conservative. They also have differing group constituencies, district by district. Respondents in the 2002 State Legislative Survey were asked whether each of twelve groups in their district were "strong supporters" or not. In every group, as Table 4-2 indicates, the disparities between group support for Democratic and Republican legislators are substantial. The strongest Democratic supporters are the labor unions, teachers, African Americans, women, environmentalists, and pro-choice. The strongest Republican supporters are business, tax relief, gun owners, pro-life, and the Christian Coalition. Clearly, then, the two parties have different demographic, ideological, and group bases.

People who identify as Democrats also act differently than people who identify as Republicans. The former vote for Democratic candidates, the latter vote for Republican candidates. Just examine voting behavior in the 2004 presidential election. Nine out of ten people who identified as Republicans voted for George W. Bush; almost the same percentage who identified as Democrats voted for John Kerry. A similar pattern was evidenced in the 2000 race between Bush and Al Gore. The presidential election is a highly visible affair. Voters have access to as much information as they can digest about the candidates' records, positions, performance, personalities, and even their private lives. However much they actually want, Americans wind up with more information in a presidential election than in any other. Nonetheless, the partisan identification of the candidates has more influence on voting choice of partisan identifiers than any other factor. If party is important in a presidential election, which is a high-visibility, high-information contest, it stands to reason that it is even more important in legislative elections, which are low-visibility, low-information contests. As Gerald C. Wright and Jon Winburn explain: "The information costs of legislators'

Table 4-2 Group Support for Democrats and Republicans

Group	Respondents saying they are strong supporters		
	Democrats	Republicans	Difference in support[a]
Labor unions	75.5	9.1	+ 66.4
Teachers	83.7	32.4	+ 51.3
African Americans	39.2	2.7	+ 36.5
Women	52.1	16.2	+ 35.9
Environmentalists	49.6	13.8	+ 35.8
Pro-choice	48.5	13.3	+ 35.2
Latinos	18.1	3.7	+ 14.4
Business	42.2	90.9	− 48.7
Tax relief	9.3	56.8	− 47.5
Gun owners	27.6	70.9	− 43.3
Pro-life	17.9	58.6	− 40.7
Christian Coalition	5.6	39.8	− 34.2

Source: 2002 State Legislative Survey.

[a] A (+) indicates a difference of support in the Democratic direction; a (−) indicates a difference in support in the Republican direction.

behavior is high so many citizens rationally use party as a shortcut in making electoral choices."[8] People are busy with nonpolitical affairs, so they are happy to rely on cues. Thus, the party designation of the legislative candidate is the single most important piece of information a voter can have.[9]

Parties as Policy Promoters

Parties not only act as voting cues for their constituencies, they also offer their constituents a significant choice. In the 1950s and 1960s the two political parties were generally regarded as Tweedledum and Tweedledee—that is, with little difference between them. One reason for their likeness was that, at the congressional level, Democrats ranged from northern liberals to southern conservatives and Republicans included both moderates and conservatives. It was thought, at least by many observers, that the public had little to choose between. The ideological lines were somewhat blurred, and a prestigious committee of the American Political Science Association issued a report titled "Toward a More Responsible Two-Party System." Alan Ehren-halt, describing the situation, writes, "If you look back to that time, you find most experts proclaiming that the cure for legislative failure was more par-tisanship, not less."[10]

The situation is very different today. At the congressional level, many for-mer southern Democrats have been replaced by southern Republicans, while throughout the country the ranks of Republican moderates have thinned considerably. The congressional parties are much more polarized than they used to be. National patterns have manifested themselves in the states, albeit in different ways and to a lesser extent. Americans have a real choice and, consequently, they too are becoming more polarized and "bet-ter able to discern differences between parties and to rate one party posi-tively and the other negatively."[11]

Democratic and Republican identifiers see things differently. The CBS/New York Times survey periodically asks Americans whether they think there are important differences between Democrats and Republicans. Re-cently three out of four respondents have been answering "yes" to the ques-tion, the largest percentage since 1980. At about the same time the Pew Research Center for the People and the Press has been finding that Republi-cans and Democrats have become more polarized than they had been in earlier years.

Most issues that come before the legislature do not distinguish between the parties, but a few do. The role and size of government, the amount of spending, the incidence of regulation, targets of taxation, and a number of social issues find Democrats tending in one direction and Republicans in the other. Their constituencies, including the loose constellation of interest groups attributed to each (as shown in Table 4-2, p. 118), follow their general direction.[12] Not only do the parties disagree over some of the big issues of politics, but they disagree on the means of reaching common goals in the lawmaking process. For example, in dealing with poverty, Democrats would call for more job training and social assistance programs, while Republicans prefer more spending on economic development to attract new businesses.[13]

The two major parties not only reflect division in the nation and states; they also promote division as they represent different people and different groups. Analysis by Gerald C. Wright and Brian F. Schaffner, for instance, shows that the parties, in vying for electoral advantage, adopt positions on emerging issues to bring in new voters. They package these new positions with their existing issue stands. By bundling diverse issues, the parties "produce the ideological two-dimensional space as a by-product of their efforts to win office." In their analysis, the authors demonstrate how the nonpartisan Nebraska legislature differs. They conclude that nonpartisanship "undermines the possibilities for popular control of government." [14]

Thus, party policy agendas both reflect and encourage disagreement in the nation and in the states. The electorate is offered a choice and their partisanship is further fueled. "The divisions that partisans reflect and invent," Russell Muirhead reminds us, "are natural in democracy." It is the parties, bound by shared beliefs and interests, that "make the political world turn." [15]

Parties as Organizations

Party organizations vary significantly from state to state. In the South and throughout most of the West, state parties were never very strong. They are probably somewhat stronger today, especially with the rise of two-party systems in the southern states, where Republican parties emerged and where the few Democratic organizations that existed were lethargic and had to shape up. The emergence during the past twenty years of the Republicans in Florida and elsewhere attests to the new vitality of party organizations.

In states such as Connecticut, Illinois, Indiana, Michigan, Ohio, Minnesota, New Jersey, New York, and Pennsylvania, local and state parties have been strong for some time. But since World War II a weakening has occurred as a result of a number of factors. First, urban political bosses no longer have the control they once had, although they still are prominent features of the landscape in a number of states. Second, the reapportionment decisions of the U.S. Supreme Court in the 1960s broke down county party control of urban delegations to the legislature. Third, the expansion of state government positions covered by civil service reduced—but by no means eliminated—the amount of patronage available. Fourth, the nominating processes were transformed in most states, going from conventions to primaries and from closed to open primaries. Insurgencies against candidates endorsed by the party leaders grew in number and in the incidence of success. Fifth, the nature of campaigns changed with the rise of an officeholder class and candidate-centered efforts.

Years after political party organizations went into decline, there are signs of resurgence. For example, in New Jersey county parties continue to play a role organizationally and have renewed clout in the legislature. Democratic organizations in Camden, Essex, Hudson, and Middlesex and Republican organizations in Atlantic, Morris, Ocean, and Somerset exercise influence over what goes on governmentally.

Despite the resilience of some state and local party organizations, no longer do these agencies control election campaigns for legislative seats. Such campaigns are in the hands of candidates themselves and/or under the control of the legislative parties and legislative party leaders. The role of legislative parties used to be that of governing in the capitol, largely exclusive of campaigning on the ground throughout the state. Nowadays, governing and campaigning to a large extend are fused.

Parties as Governing Bodies

Out of the ninety-nine legislative chambers across the nation, only one—Nebraska's unicameral—is not organized and operated along party lines. Through their control of legislative bodies the Democratic and Republican Parties—whichever has the majority in a chamber—manage to govern. "Governing" by the legislature involves making law (which will be discussed in detail in chapters 9, 10, and 11), including appropriating funds through the budget act. To a lesser extent, "governing" involves the oversight of executive departments and agencies and their implementation of legislatively enacted policies. Legislative governance by the parties—with the majority party having major responsibility—consists of many activities, including organizing the legislature, appointing committees, scheduling legislation, getting the necessary votes, and negotiating with the other chamber and the governor. How all of this is done will be detailed in subsequent chapters on organization, leadership, and policymaking. The subject needs only brief mention here.

The majority party normally selects one of its members for the top position in each chamber—the speaker in the house and the president, president pro tem, or occasionally the majority leaders in the senate. The majority party—through its leadership or their designees—decides on the structure of the committee system in the chamber and appointments to each of the standing committees. The majority party also can exercise control over which bills get referred to each committee and whether and when the bills that come out get on the calendar for floor consideration. It may also determine if and how bills may be amended.

The majority party caucus is the centerpiece of legislative party influence. Active caucuses exist in four-fifths of the legislative chambers. The caucus meets frequently or regularly, nominates candidates for chamber office, gets feedback from members, sets the agenda, reviews the daily or weekly calendar, builds consensus within the party, and decides on and executes strategy. Finally, through its leaders, the majority party of each chamber negotiates its agenda with the other chamber and with the governor.

Governing and Campaigning. The above-mentioned roles in governance have traditionally been performed by the majority party. But in the past twenty-five to thirty years, the majority party (as well as the minority party) in the legislature has taken on still another role as part of its governing job—the role of campaign organization as a means of achieving governmental power. Governing and campaigning go on simultaneously, continuously, and coordinately in contemporary legislatures. As Allan J. Cigler and Burdett A. Loomis have written regarding national politics, "The distinction between the politics of elections and the politics of the policy-making is blurring."[16]

What is happening at the national level is also happening in the states. The campaign role of legislative parties and legislative party leaders began in California in the 1960s when Jesse Unruh was speaker of the assembly. He was the first presiding officer to raise campaign funds for members of his caucus in order to maintain majority status for the Democrats. Unruh coined the phrase that has since become an axiom: "Money is the mother's milk of politics." Assembly members quickly came to expect Unruh and subsequent leaders to fund-raise for them. When Speaker Leo McCarthy neglected the job because he was raising funds for his own campaign for a U.S. Senate seat, Democratic caucus members expressed their displeasure by trying to unseat him as speaker. Willie Brown, who followed McCarthy in the speaker's chair, heeded the lesson. He became known for, among other things, his success in fund-raising. Since then, leadership and/or caucus political action committees developed in Illinois, Michigan, New Jersey, New York, Washington, Wisconsin, and thereafter in about every state where parties are at all competitive.[17]

The legislative leadership and caucus role in campaigns has replaced the one that used to be played by local political parties. In most states, if that role ever existed, by the 1990s it had evaporated. Moreover, without the legislative party management of campaigns, the governor would play a much larger part raising money and allocating it to candidates, at least those in the governor's party. The governor would be likely to have a greater say over who ran, who got elected, and how they operated once in office.

The rationale for legislative parties as fund-raisers is accepted by most legislative leaders. Finances are critical in many campaigns, particularly the most competitive ones. Control of a legislative body may hinge on the outcome of ten, fifteen, or twenty races. Therefore, all members of the legislative party benefit if those seats that are targeted can be won. Whether the mechanism is the legislative leadership PAC or the legislative party PAC, leaders are the ones who do best at soliciting contributions from interest groups, lobbyists, and others. Fund-raisers are hosted by legislative leaders. Interest groups, their lobbyists, and others buy tickets and attend. Most of those who have legislative agendas can be counted on to pony up. Even in a state like Vermont, with its citizen legislature and amateur politics, legislative leaders take it upon themselves to help fund campaigns. Ralph Wright brought modern legislative fund-raising to Vermont. "By my second year at the podium," he writes, "I had established an annual event called the 'Speakers Soiree'." It was held in the middle of a week in February and timed "to take advantage not only of good attendance but of the period when most bills had already been introduced but not acted on."[18]

Legislative leaders also have the principal say as to which candidates receive money that they and their legislative parties have raised. Most of the money goes to the parties' incumbents and challengers in targeted districts, for example, those districts that are closely contested. It is on these battlefields that control of the senate and house gets determined.

Leadership and caucus PACs have come under heavy criticism from some legislators and many people who are upset with the campaign finance system. Individual incumbents sometimes find it more difficult to raise money for their own campaign, because their leaders get first dibs on the available funds. Incumbents who are not in competitive races also receive little or nothing of the amounts that leaders raise for their members. Instead, money goes where it will have the greater payoff—close races. Reformers, who tend to be wary of both money and power, feel that leaders use the funds they amass to exercise undue influence over members. They also believe that leaders give preference to those who give to them. In most legislative bodies it is not difficult for a leader to prevent a bill from advancing to the floor and thus carry the water for a group that is on the defensive.

Despite criticisms, the leadership/legislative party fund-raising and fund-dispensing system has been retained most everywhere, largely for the following reasons.

First, it tends to maximize the amount of money collected. In New Jersey, for example, party entities comprised 59 percent of total contributions in the assembly elections of 2005, with legislative leadership committees contributing most of the money to candidates.[19] That is because contribution limits were higher for these party entities than for individual candidates. It is also because contributors find it more difficult to say no to requests from leaders than to requests from individual candidates. In Michigan too the legislative party dominates campaign finance. In 2006 caucus committees raised and spent more money in competitive elections than the candidates themselves. In addition, they helped direct funds from other sources to the targeted races.[20]

Second, the ways in which leaders allocate money to candidates tend to benefit the legislative party. Candidates who have no real chance of winning get little or no support from the leaders, as do candidates who have no real chance of losing. Candidates in competitive, targeted races are the ones who receive support. The money goes where it can make a difference in terms of winning or losing. Without leadership and legislative party PACs to channel contributions, the distribution of monies would be less efficient. Many more dollars would be "wasted" on candidates who either did not need it or could not benefit from it. More money certainly would have gone to safe incumbents, instead of to serious challengers.

Third, legislative leaders and party caucuses can, and do, balance out the monies expended directly by interest groups on behalf of individual candidates. Such expenditures could make a real difference in a close race, especially if they were made in the final days. Steve Sviggum, the Republican speaker of the Minnesota House, raised $2.4 million for his caucus in 2005–2006. His view is that if the caucus were not involved, as it was, special interests like labor, business, and teachers would largely determine whose campaigns got support and, perhaps, whose campaigns would be successful.[21]

The popular conception is that legislative campaigns have become enormously expensive. Take the special election in 2007 to fill a senate vacancy in New York. By election day the Republican and Democratic candidates had raised over $5 million, breaking a state record in 2002 of $4.7 million. The month that the campaign was waged, spending ran to about $200,000 a day—mainly for radio and television commercials.[22] For each party, this election was critical. Republicans had controlled the seat for many years, but their margins were being whittled away election after election. If the Democrats could win this election, they could have pulled within a few seats of the majority. It was little wonder, then, that so much was being spent.

In other large states campaigns can become expensive, especially when the margins in the senate or house are close and either side has a chance to take the seat. In New Jersey competitive races can run to $2 million or more. But in districts that are relatively safe for one party or another, the costs are much lower. Take Illinois in the elections of 2002. The average campaign expenditure of winners was $808,793 in the targeted senate districts (of which there were nine), but only $125,847 in the nontargeted senate districts. In house races the average campaign expenditure of winners in targeted districts (of which there were eleven) was $680,417, in nontargeted districts $152,473.[23]

Where there are relatively few competitive districts, as in Massachusetts, campaign costs are not high at all. In the 2004 elections the average for the senate was $93,370 and for the house $31,432. This was a large increase over 2002, because several well-funded challengers took on incumbent senators.[24] In the smaller states, the costs are considerably lower. For thirty-five senate seats in Maine, expenditures were in low five figures; for 151 house seats expenditures rarely exceeded $10,000.[25] In Vermont Wright never spent more than a few hundred dollars on a race. When the Republicans finally targeted him, they spent the grand total of $14,000 to retire him from the speakership and the legislature.

Campaigns and the Legislative Process. The campaign that formerly was run by constituency parties and individual candidates *outside* the legislature now is run largely by the legislative leadership and legislative party *inside* the legislature. Alan Greenblatt describes the new system in which the candidate is more an "instrument of party purpose" than an independent actor:

> The brief heyday of the entrepreneurial candidate is drawing to a close. A new era of party control—not the old-fashioned machine but a different kind—is starting to emerge.[26]

Sure winners and sure losers still run their own campaigns, but increasingly the campaigns for the targeted seats come front and center in the operations of the legislature. Almost every aspect of the legislature touches on the campaign, not only for a few months in the fall every other year, but for the entire biennium leading up to election day. While fund-raising appears to be the most visible campaign activity of the legislative party, it is by no means the only one.

Legislative leaders and parties recruit candidates to run. They work with local party leaders in efforts to find people who fit the district well and have a good chance of winning. Where races are costly and may require hundreds of thousands of dollars, candidates who (in addition to other qualifications) have their own money to stake are especially appealing. Legislative leaders also participate in the hiring of consultants and pollsters and in developing overall campaign themes and strategies, which are then modified from district to district. They allocate field staff and technical assistance as well.

Many of the people who work on key legislative races are members of the professional staff of the legislature itself. They are not the nonpartisan professionals who comprise legislative reference, research, and bill drafting units. Rather, they are the partisan professionals who are employed by legislative leaders and party caucuses. In much earlier times, these legislative staffers conducted some of their campaign activities within the state house itself, and even when they went into the field they remained on the legislative payroll. That system led to legal challenges in a number of states, including New York, New Jersey, Washington, and Wisconsin. So nowadays the campaign activities by any members of the legislative staff have to be done outside of the statehouse and off the state payroll. Partisan staffers may volunteer to work on a campaign, but when they do so they take time off and either volunteer their services to a campaign or go onto a party or candidate payroll. A former partisan professional in New Jersey once remarked, "We do nothing *on* the campaign, but everything *for* the campaign." What he meant was that the partisan staff has the incentive to help its members retain or win control, just as the legislative party itself does.

Thus far, we have described campaign activities *per se* that legislative leaders and parties perform. In addition, the legislative process itself has become part of the election campaign. This is because the majority party, which controls the machinery of the chamber, tries to use the legislative process to advantage its members electorally, while the minority does what it can to disadvantage majority party members. Each party, of course, espouses issues and takes positions that it hopes will win votes in key districts. Each tries to maneuver the other into an unfavorable stance. The minority will offer amendments designed to force majority members to cast unpopular votes; the majority will use procedural methods to fend off such amendments.

Although the minority party is at a disadvantage in such campaign activities, over the course of time its posture can have electoral effects. That has certainly been the case with the Republicans in the South. Before the 1990s, Republicans were weak minorities in southern legislatures. But as the Republicans gained strength, they became more combative in the legislature as well as in the campaign. They tried, with some success, to achieve benefits by using amendments to create issues that would favor their candidates in upcoming elections.[27]

The majority party has more resources at its disposal. It normally makes an effort to shore up those members who are running in competitive districts. They receive committee assignments that will benefit them in their races. An assignment may be made to the appropriations committee, which affords a better chance to provide projects for their district. Or they may get a seat on one of the committees that has jurisdiction over economic matters, which affords them a better chance of raising campaign funds from business groups. These committees are known as "juice" committees in California.

Majority party incumbents also are favored with popular bills to sponsor, so that they receive media coverage that would not otherwise be available to them. If the governor is of the same party, they may be deputized to carry one of his or her initiatives and to be pictured with the governor at the bill-signing. In order to assist them in their districts, the leadership awards them a larger share of the pork that is distributed in the budget. In Illinois, for example, the legislature has had a member-initiative program to deliver infrastructure grants totaling about $1.5 billion to communities in the state. According to an analysis of the distribution of such grants, districts that were politically safe received a smaller share of the pie than did districts that were electorally pivotal.[28]

Threatened incumbents will also be let off the hook by the leader of the majority party, in order to help them avoid taking a stand on an issue that will cost them votes in the district. For example, if the majority party is advocating legislation that will raise taxes, and if it can get enough votes to pass it, incumbents with tough races will be allowed, or even encouraged, by leaders to vote against the legislative party. Their votes are not required for passage, but their reelection may be required for their party to retain control of the chamber.

Just as the majority party works to protect its threatened members, it also works to weaken minority party members whom it targets in the forthcoming election. These are minority party members who can be beaten at the polls. Consequently, targeted members of the minority party have a tough time getting preferred committee assignments. They may have trouble getting their bills heard in committee, reported out, and passed on the floor. Because their electoral prospects would not be affected by legislative maneuvering, minority party members from safe districts tend to suffer much less political discrimination.

As part of the electoral campaign in the legislature itself, the two party groups constantly position themselves to take advantage. Thrust and parry is the order many days during the session. Each party cherry-picks issues that will have voter appeal and each, insofar as possible, tries to avoid being on the wrong side of an issue with swing voters. Each points a finger at the other, casting blame on the one hand and trying to avoid it on the other.

Consequences of Taking the Campaign into the Legislature. It should come as no surprise that legislatures have become more partisan, certainly in those states where the two parties are competitive. Even where parties have not traditionally been strong, as in the western states, partisan politics is pervasive in legislative bodies. Such politics, legislators and observers agree, has led to a decline in collegiality and even in civility in legislative bodies. Legislators themselves are upset by what has happened to the atmosphere, but do not know what can be done to remedy the situation.

Civility suffers especially because election campaigns are conducted within the legislature itself, by legislative parties and leaders.[29] The campaign today is a continuous one, so members have little respite. They remain in a campaign mode. Legislators who are targeted, along with their caucus colleagues, cannot be expected to have warm feelings toward other colleagues who are attempting to get them defeated. Given battlefield conditions, it is the exception rather than the rule to conduct friendly, even civil, relationships with people who are shooting at you. How can legislators who faced blistering attacks from leaders and members of the opposition party put the combative nature of the campaign behind them if they are reelected and return to the legislature?

As long as the legislature is an electoral—as well as lawmaking—battleground, civility will be strained. Legislators tend to believe that, because of the contentious atmosphere, it has become difficult to build consensus and avoid gridlock. Yet consensus—that is, 50 percent plus one or better—does get built on most issues. The principal effect of incivility is on the legislature itself and how it appears to the public. The legislature as an institution normally has little public support. Incivility, as reported in the media or reflected in campaigns, only makes the legislature's image worse.

Yet diminished civility within legislatures reflects a number of potent forces, not the least of which is the assimilation by legislatures of electoral campaigns. In some states attempts have been made to bring legislators together—in retreat settings or on other occasions. But these palliatives alone cannot redress the contending forces that are at work in a divided political system.

Legislative Redistricting

The political role of the legislature extends beyond the campaigns that are conducted every two or four years. It usually includes redistricting, a process that occurs every ten years, after the release of population figures from

the decennial census of the United States. Both the U.S. House of Representatives and all ninety-nine state legislative bodies are redistricted in order to
reflect population growth, decline, and shifts in accordance with the principal standard of the process—"one person, one vote"—that was enunciated
in cases decided by the U.S. Supreme Court in the 1960s. The first major
case was *Baker v. Carr* (1962), in which the Court ruled that redistricting
was a "justiciable" matter, that is, that the subject was within the jurisdiction
of the courts. The second major case was *Reynolds v. Sims* (1964), in which
the Court ruled that both chambers of state legislatures must be apportioned on the basis of population.

At the federal level the U.S. Senate is unaffected, because the U.S. Constitution provides that each state, however large or small its population, is entitled to two senators. The size of the U.S. House is determined by statute.
The law currently provides for 435 members, who are apportioned among
the fifty states depending on population. With 280 million people, according to the 2000 census, and 435 House seats, each representative must come
from a district of 645,000 or so people. California has almost 10 percent of
the nation's total population and consequently receives about 10 percent
of the total U.S. House seats. Each state, even if the population is under
645,000 (as in Wyoming), receives at least one seat in the U.S. House.

Redistricting in the states runs along similar lines. The number of senators and representatives are established constitutionally or statutorily state
by state. In each state, senate districts that are required to have equal populations per senator and house districts are also required to have equal populations per representative.[30] Over the course of the decade, however, the
population within a state shifts. Some districts gain more, some gain less,
and some lose. By the end of the decade districts drawn earlier no longer are
equal in population. Therefore, it is necessary to redraw district lines in
order to equalize the population for senate and house districts.[31]

Who Does It

Traditionally, the tasks of congressional redistricting (that is, the redrawing
of the lines of U.S. House districts) and that of legislative redistricting (that
is, the redrawing of the lines of state senate and house districts) have been
done by state legislatures. Over the years, however, a number of legislatures

ceded redistricting authority to independent commissions; others had the authority taken away from them and given to commissions as a result of ballot initiatives passed by the electorate.

Currently, thirty-eight legislatures along with their governors still are responsible for legislative redistricting. The process in these states resembles the regular order of lawmaking: a redistricting plan, introduced as a bill, must pass both chambers in identical form and be signed by the governor in order to become law. As one might imagine, enactment requires considerable negotiation, because individual members, the four legislative parties, and the governor all have different ideas of what a good plan should be. Five of these states, where legislatures do the job, have backup procedures that authorize boards or commissions to do the redistricting if the legislature is unable to adopt a plan.

In the other twelve states (Alaska, Arizona, Arkansas, Colorado, Hawaii, Idaho, Missouri, Montana, New Jersey, Ohio, Pennsylvania, and Washington) redistricting is done by a board or commission, not by the legislature. Such agencies may be partisan or nonpartisan in composition.[32] In New Jersey, for instance, a legislative redistricting commission has been in operation since the 1970s. It consists of ten members, five Democrats and five Republicans, who are appointed by state and legislative party leaders. These ten members have thirty days to adopt a redistricting plan. If they are deadlocked and fail to do so, the chief justice of the New Jersey Supreme Court appoints an eleventh member as chair and tie-breaker. The process in New Jersey is highly political, but the tie-breaker (whose vote has been decisive in the four redistrictings since the commission's establishment) has the ability to shape the outcome. By contrast, the Iowa system is designed to be nonpolitical. A legislative staff agency is authorized to draw the districts, with the injunction to keep county lines and political jurisdictions intact, wherever possible. More important, the staff agency cannot make use of voting information or an incumbent's residence in drawing districts. Staff are not allowed to use data as to where Democrats and where Republicans reside or whether incumbents will wind up with many or few of their former constituents and supporters. The Iowa General Assembly gets to vote on the staff plan but cannot modify it.

State courts also play a critical role in the legislative redistricting process (as federal courts play in the congressional process). If the legislature or commission in a state cannot agree on a plan, the court normally will develop a plan on its own, appointing a special redistricting panel to do the drafting. For instance, in the 2001 redistricting in Minnesota, the legislature (with a Democratic senate and a Republican house) could not agree on a plan. The Minnesota Supreme Court named a special panel to do the job. Even if the legislature or a commission agree and enact a plan, it may be challenged in court. If a plan appears to disadvantage one party, normally that party will find or contrive constitutional or statutory grounds on which to base its case. If a plan appears to disadvantage certain groups, such as Hispanics or African Americans, an appeal is also likely to be made to the judiciary. The courts may uphold the plan, or parts of it; they may require the redistricting authority to draft a different plan; or they may undertake redistricting themselves.

Redistricting has to conform to certain legal standards. The single absolute standard is population. Over the years, the courts have established that legislative districts for the state senate and state house must be substantially equal in population (with about a 5 percent deviation from absolute equality allowable).[33] In the 1980s the U.S. Voting Rights Act was interpreted by the U.S. Department of Justice and the federal courts to require majority/minority districts wherever possible. In the 1990s redistricting this led to the creation of districts with minority populations large enough to elect an African American or a Hispanic representative. The courts changed course in the 1990s, ruling that, while racial factors may be used in redistricting, they cannot be the sole or the predominant standard.

Other than population, redistricting standards in most states are left undefined or loosely defined by constitution and statute. Several standards are sometimes statutorily specified, and more often are referred to in discussions of desirable practice. Among the foremost such standards is "compactness," which requires that districts not be far-flung, wandering across the state, but insofar as possible be shaped like a square or rectangle. "Contiguity," another standard, requires that individual districts be of one piece and not separated by bodies of water or other obstacles. "Community of interests" applies primarily to county and municipal boundaries (and not partisan, political ones), emphasizing that these jurisdictions be kept intact within legislative districts rather than divided among a number of different districts. "Continuity" refers to the popular composition of the district from one decade to the next. Insofar as possible, and allowing for shifts in population, people ought to remain in the same district that they had been in previously rather than be placed in a new and unfamiliar one.

A recently articulated standard is "competitiveness," which requires that a plan ensure that districts be as equal as possible in partisan composition. Arizona, which established by ballot initiative in 2000 an independent redistricting commission, has also enacted a set of explicit standards, of which electoral competition is a principal one. This standard has special appeal today, because in 2001–2002 the protection of incumbents assumed such prominence in the redistricting of Congress and many state legislatures. As a result, for instance, in California's 2004 election not one of 120 state legislative districts changed party control. In other states, as well, the number of seats that were considered safe for each party has been on the rise recently.

Although "competitiveness" is thought by many to be a worthy goal[34] it may be difficult to achieve, at least in most places and in many cases. That is because of a natural congregation by people into dominant-party districts, with Democrats tending to live near Democrats and Republicans near Republicans. Redistricting does not create such tendencies; it reinforces them. "When you get right down to it, a large element of non-competitiveness we're seeing in America is social sorting," says Bruce Cain, a University of California political scientist. "People are moving into areas with people like themselves."[35]

How It Is Done and for Whom

Redistricting is at best a remote concern of Americans. People may have some idea of the process and the political shenanigans involved; but that is as far as it goes. Redistricting is a game for insiders. They are the ones who have considerable stakes in what happens every ten years.

- Political parties seek to gain seats in the legislature, wherever they can. This entails drawing districts to maximize their partisan votes and minimize the votes of the opposition party.
- Political leaders within a state desire to maintain or enlarge their clout in the legislature and, perhaps, eliminate incumbents who oppose or threaten them.

- Incumbents do not want to lose any of their electoral base and strive to increase that base with partisan voters.
- Potential challengers want the opposite of what incumbents want. They would like to see part of an incumbent's base taken away, so their chances as challengers improve.
- Municipal officials testify as to the importance of keeping their jurisdiction intact and not divided among two or more districts, thereby assuring their community greater influence vis-à-vis the legislator who represents them.
- Ethnic and racial groups would like to ensure the election of one of their own, particularly if this can be accomplished without any sacrifice of partisan advantage.
- Interest groups that are loosely allied with one party or the other or with an incumbent want that party and that individual protected.

The principal players in the redistricting process are the legislative parties and legislator incumbents. Their strategies overlap but are not identical. The party's aim is to carve out districts that maximize the party's representation in the senate and house in relation to the party's overall vote in the state. Maximization can be accomplished by means of gerrymandering, which entails drawing district lines in order to maximize the votes of one's own party and minimize the votes of the other party. Gerrymandering can only be accomplished when the legislature and governor have authority to enact a plan and when one party has sole control.

If the senate and house are Democratic, for example, but the governor is Republican, the governor will veto a plan that advantages Democrats and disadvantages Republicans in the legislature. Unless the Democrats have a veto-proof majority in each chamber, the governor's veto will stand and, unless there is a backup provision for redistricting by commission, the courts will have to settle the issue. If, however, both chambers—along with the office of governor—are in the hands of the same party, the opportunity for drawing a plan to benefit that party exists. Over the years, these conditions have permitted a number of political gerrymanders that overrepresented one party at the expense of the other.

Take a simplified, hypothetical example of redistricting. Assume a state where Democrats control both chambers and both branches. The total population is four hundred thousand, and the legislative body being redistricted has four members. The four members would have equal populations in their districts—one hundred thousand per district.

To effectively gerrymander, Democrats would have to know voting patterns town by town and precinct by precinct. Databases by local level for voting in statewide and national elections exist, so the distribution of votes by partisan behavior can be calculated. The campaign software currently available allows the legislators, staff, and consultants who produce maps to know just where to draw the lines in order to maximize their party's votes.

In the hypothetical presented above, two hundred thousand people have a history of voting Democratic and two hundred thousand have a history of voting Republican. Under a "fair" redistricting two Democrats and two Republicans would be elected to the legislative body. The lines, however, can be drawn to produce different results in partisan terms. Even though the two parties tie in their total statewide vote, two hundred thousand to two hundred thousand, the Democrats succeed in winning three out of the four seats at stake. They win Districts 1, 3, and 4 each by comfortable margins of 60–40 percent. They lose only District 2, but by the wide margin of 20–80 percent. What enables them to win three out of four seats is their ability to "pack" so many Republicans into a single district where their votes are wasted. Democrats wasted an equal number of votes but spread over three districts—only 9,999 votes per district. With 50 percent of the statewide vote, the Democrats manage to win 75 percent of the legislative seats. All this is attributable to the way in which they packed Republicans into one district, neutralizing many of their votes, while spreading Democrats around and making solid use of their votes.

District	Democrats	Republicans	Total
1	60,000	40,000	100,000
2	20,000	80,000	100,000
3	60,000	40,000	100,000
4	60,000	40,000	100,000
Totals	200,000	200,000	400,000

Gerrymandering for partisan purposes is neither unconstitutional nor illegal, according to the courts. Political factors, such as where incumbents reside, can be taken into account in the drawing of district lines.

The other primary players in the redistricting game are incumbent legislators. If incumbents are in the majority party and that party has control, the interests of these members most likely will be protected. In order to benefit the legislative party as a whole, some members may have to give up some of their voters in order to maximize their party's advantage. Nevertheless, these members will still have a comfortable margin in their districts when the redistricting dust has settled. By contrast, some members of the minority are likely to be targeted for defeat in a majority-controlled process.

When government is divided, neither party will have the ability through redistricting to gain seats at the expense of the others. Under such conditions, each party's efforts turn to making its incumbents somewhat safer. The results, at least marginally, are more relatively safe districts and fewer competitive ones. Bipartisan commissions may produce similar results to those of divided government, protecting the status quo. If they are not mandated or choose not to insist on a standard of district competitiveness, they may produce plans that tend to advantage incumbents. However, even a bipartisan commission can produce a map that favors one party over the other, as the New Jersey commission in 2001 demonstrated when it gave the Democrats what they wanted.

In the 1990s race and ethnicity were important factors, but they receded from prominence in the next decade. In the last cycle of redistricting, partisan gerrymandering and bipartisan incumbent protection dominated. One analyst calculated that in the 2001 redistricting twenty-seven states experienced either Democratic or Republican gerrymandering of one type or another. Of the other twenty-three states, seventeen adopted bipartisan incumbent protection plans while outcomes were neutral, following no pattern in the six remaining states.[36]

The results of 2001 spurred efforts to take redistricting authority away from legislatures, and even out of partisan politics. The Iowa and Arizona redistricting processes served as the principal models for those who advocated reform. A ballot initiative campaign to establish a panel of retired judges to do the job was led by Gov. Arnold Schwarzenegger in California. It failed. Another initiative took place in Ohio, which also failed. The reform movement continues. But it may have lost some steam when the 2006 elections for the U.S. House and for state legislatures demonstrated that despite the many noncompetitive districts, there were enough competitive ones for voters to throw out the governing party and install a new majority in state legislatures and the Congress.

Notes

1. Bill Bishop, *The Big Sort: The Clustering of Like-Minded America Is Tearing Us Apart* (Boston: Houghton Mifflin, 2008).
2. The remaining 7 percent selected "other." Grant Reeher, *First Person Political* (New York: New York University Press, 2006), 98–99.
3. In many instances nowadays legislators draw on their campaign accounts for trips they take to participate in the activities and attend the events of their national associations, such as the National Conference of State Legislatures.
4. John E. McDonough, *Experiencing Politics: A Legislator's Stories of Government and Health Care* (Berkeley: University of California Press, 2000), 181.
5. "Scheming Magnolias," *Governing* (November 2007), 24.
6. The remaining legislators included all forty-nine members of Nebraska's unicameral legislatures, who run without party labels, and seventeen members from other states, who were classified as "Independents" or "Progressives."
7. For their role at the federal level, in Congress, see *The Legislative Branch*, ed. Paul J. Quirk and Sarah A. Binder (New York: Oxford University Press, 2005).
8. Gerald C. Wright and Jon Winburn, "Patterns of Constituency-Legislator Policy Congruence in the States," paper presented at the Second Annual Conference on State Politics and Policy, University of Wisconsin–Milwaukee, May 24–25, 2002.
9. Party designation may be less important in the case of gubernatorial elections, where information is relatively abundant. Many of those who are elected governor appear to buck the partisan odds. For example, Democratic governors were elected in twelve states that Bush had won in 2004 (including nine by margins of ten points or over) and Republican gover-

nors were elected in nine states that Kerry had won (including seven by margins of ten points or over). See Josh Goodman, "Against the Grain," *Governing* (October 2006), 38. See also Louis Jacobson, "List of Popular Govs Is Full of Surprises," *Stateline.org,* November 15, 2007.

10. Alan Ehrenhalt, "Theory of Partisan Relativity," *Governing* (March 2006), 9–10. See also Bishop, *The Big Sort,* 221–303.

11. Russell Muirhead, "A Defense of Party Spirit," *Perspectives on Politics* 4 (December 2006): 714.

12. E. E. Schattschneider, *The Semi-Sovereign People* (New York: Holt, Rinehart and Winston, 1960), 57.

13. Wes Clarke, "Divided Government and Budget Conflict in the U.S. States," *Legislative Studies Quarterly* 28 (February 1998): 9.

14. Gerald C. Wright and Brian F. Schaffner, "The Influence of Party: Evidence from State Legislatures," *American Political Science Review* 96 (June 2002): 377. The authors demonstrate how the nonpartisan Nebraska legislature differs, concluding that nonpartisanship undermines popular control of government.

15. Muirhead, "A Defense of Party Spirit," 723.

16. Allan J. Cigler and Burdett A. Loomis, eds., *Interest Group Politics,* 6th ed. (Washington, D.C.: CQ Press, 2002), 382.

17. See Anthony Gierzynski, *Legislative Party Campaign Committees in the American States* (Lexington: University Press of Kentucky, 1992).

18. Ralph Wright, *Inside the Statehouse* (Washington, D.C.: CQ Press, 2005), 153.

19. New Jersey Election Law Enforcement Commission, "The 2005 Assembly Elections: New Trends on the Horizon?" (Trenton: The Commission, September 2006), 18–20.

20. Alan Greenblatt, "Wired to Win," *Governing* (October 2006), 26.

21. Steve Sviggum, in interview with Minnesota Civic Caucus, February 15, 2007.

22. *New York Times,* February 6, 2007.

23. Christopher Z. Mooney and Tim Storey, "The Illinois General Assembly, 1992–2003," paper prepared for Joint Project on Term Limits (August 16, 2004).

24. Figures furnished by the Massachusetts General Court, June 2006.

25. Thad Kousser, *Term Limits and the Dismantling of State Legislative Professionalism* (New York: Cambridge University Press, 2005), 46.

26. Greenblatt, "Wired to Win," 28.

27. Thad E. Hall, "Change in Legislative Support for the Governor's Program over Time," *Legislative Studies Quarterly* 27 (February 2002): 119–120.

28. Michael C. Herron and Brett A. Theodos, "Government Redistribution in the Shadow of Legislative Elections: A Story of the Illinois Member Initiative Grants Program," *Legislative Studies Quarterly* 29 (May 2004): 288, 289, 291.

29. This section draws on Alan Rosenthal, "Civility or Civil War in Legislatures: Is There an In-Between?" *Spectrum: The Journal of State Government* (Spring 2005): 22–24.

30. If some of the districts are single-member and others multimember, as in New Hampshire and Vermont, the ratio of legislators to people will be the same for both types. For example, in Vermont a single-member house district would have one legislator representing 4,059 constituents, while a two-member house district would have two legislators representing 8,118 constituents.

31. The population of senate and house districts, state by state, is shown in Table 3-1, pp. 75–76.

32. Ronald E. Weber, "State Legislative Redistricting in 2003–2004," *Book of the States 2005,* vol. 37 (Lexington: Council of State Governments, 2005), 120.

33. Federal courts permit zero deviation for congressional seats. See also Bishop, *The Big Sort.*

34. For a dissenting view see Thomas L. Brunell, *Redistricting and Representation* (New York: Routledge, 2008). We will return to "competitiveness" in chapter 12.

35. Quoted in Alan Greenblatt, "Real Power," *Governing* (June 2006), 48.

36. Michael P. McDonald, "A Comparative Analysis of Redistricting Institutions in the United States, 2001–02," *State Politics and Policy Quarterly* 4 (Winter 2004): 386–388. See also Weber, "State Legislative Redistricting in 2003–2004," 116.

5

Interest Groups and Lobbying

DEMOCRATIC POLITICAL THEORISTS emphasize the role and responsibilities of individuals in the political system. Citizens are expected to attend to and understand the issues, keep track of how people in office are performing, advocate not only for their own interests but for that of the public as well, and hold those who govern accountable for their decisions. E. E. Schattschneider, however, demurs: "The public is far too sensible to attempt to play the preposterous role assigned to it by the theorists," he writes.[1] People are too busy with their jobs, families, and leisure activities, not to mention all the other distractions of life. They delegate to others the business of representing them in the American political system.

We have already discussed two of the three principal channels for representation. The first is by means of legislators whom citizens elect to office to respond to their needs and express their views. The second is by means of their affiliation, whether stronger or weaker, with the Democratic or Republican Party. In a general sense, people are represented by legislators from their party, even if these legislators are not from their district. The third principal channel, which will be discussed in this chapter, is interest groups—groups in which people have membership or loose affiliation.

A proliferation of groups at the national and state levels offers people representation and also a way to be involved in politics. According to Allan J. Cigler and Mark Joslyn, such involvement, particularly if it is in a wide variety of groups, tends to breed tolerance and feelings of trust and efficacy—in other words, orientations considered supportive of democratic processes.[2] Such benefits are indirect. More directly, interest groups play a critical role by *organizing, representing,* and *advocating* for publics who hold diverse values and interests.

140

Although most Americans belong to at least one or more interest group, the overwhelming number of them are relatively inactive as far as their membership goes—just as they are inactive as far as other forms of political participation go. Whether they actively participate or not, however, their values, interests, and views get represented. Even nonmembers who share a group's values, interests, or views get represented.

The Nature of Groups

Most of the thousands of interest groups in existence are not politically involved. That still leaves a tremendous number, including many in each state, that are politically active. Some of these tend to be aligned with the Democratic Party, others with the Republican Party, but the largest number cover their bets as far as partisan alignments are concerned.

Groups can be categorized along various lines. Virginia Gray and David Lowery distinguish among three types: membership groups, associations, and institutions. Membership groups are comprised of individuals; included here are labor unions and cause or ideological groups, whose members are individuals. Such groups account for 23 percent of all registered lobbying organizations in the states. Associations are comprised of other organizations; included here are business, professional, and governmental organizations, which have individual members. Such groups account for 30 percent of all registrations. Institutions have no members; included here are corporations and universities. Such groups account for 46 percent of all registrations.[3]

Another distinction is between interest groups that are registered in only one or in multiple states. Examples of the former include Binions's Horseshoe Hotel and Casino in Nevada; the Golden Age Fisheries in Alaska; the Memorial Medical Center, Inc., in Georgia; and Wattkins-Shepard Trucking in Montana. Examples of multistate organizations include Anheuser-Busch Companies, Inc., and AT&T, which are registered in forty-nine states; the Bankers Association, in forty-eight states; and the AFL-CIO, Association of Realtors, and the National Federation of Independent Business (NFIB), each registered in forty-seven states.[4] Still another distinction is between interest groups whose members have a direct economic stake in policy and whose members don't.[5] Perhaps the simplest categorization would sort interest groups according to the following orientations: professional, occupational, labor, business, or cause/advocacy/ideological (the latter of which are also known as citizen groups).

No matter how they are characterized, the numbers of interest groups in the states, as well as in the nation, have increased enormously since World War II. Business groups have multiplied and cause groups have proliferated. Cigler and Joslyn illustrate the interest group rise by noting the growth of the animal rights movement in the past twenty-five years. Traditional animal protection organizations were already in place when groups such as People for Ethical Treatment of Animals (PETA), Progressive Animal Welfare Society, Committee to Abolish Sport Hunting, and the Animal Rights Network arrived on the scene. It is estimated that currently four hundred animal rights organizations exist, with approximately ten million members.[6]

Why do groups organize and get involved with government, and particularly with state legislatures? They do so because they have interests to advance and/or protect by means of lawmaking processes. Singly, people with identical interests might not carry much weight in state houses, but collectively these people with identical interests add up to a political force with which legislatures must reckon. They cannot ignore people who are banded together in order to express their constitutional right to seek a "redress of grievances" from lawmakers.

Interest group agendas with respect to state legislatures and legislation include the following:

- Law or regulation that advances group views within a policy domain, gives it an advantage over the competition, or furnishes protection from others.
- Opposition to law or regulation that threatens group views within a policy domain, puts it at a disadvantage vis-à-vis the competition, or removes its protection.
- Additional funding, through tax reductions or budget additions.
- Opposition to tax increases and budget reductions that affect the group.

Interest Group Issues

Practically all of the major issues that legislatures act on find interest groups heavily involved. Abortion, gay rights, gun control, education, health care, and the environment are among the major issues on group agendas. But other issues, which are much less visible and affect fewer people, also are of great concern to one or several interest groups. Perhaps one-quarter to one-third or so of the bills introduced in a state legislature relate to what are often called special-interest issues. Such proposals have relatively narrow effects beyond the groups that are fighting for and fighting against them. For every group looking for some policy or some advantage, there is another group opposing that policy or resisting being taken advantage of.

There is no way for groups to ignore the legislature entirely; its impact on interests large and small is too great. Corporations and associations can be affected by many of the bills that are introduced. A public utility company, such as gas and electric, is impacted by almost anything government does. It is a big taxpayer, so a change in tax policy can be critical. Environmental legislation—water, air emissions, solid and hazardous waste—has important ramifications for its operations and balance sheet. To illustrate how any type of group is affected by government, take the situation of the nation's cemeteries and crematoriums. They have been challenged by those who question whether buried bodies could contaminate underground water or if cremation could be a source of toxic air pollutants. The umbrella groups representing the interests of crematoriums are concerned because some states had environmental laws that lumped crematoriums together with other incinerators; to them, that did not make sense. The issue for cemeteries and/or funeral directors was that, just as cremation was becoming popular, it began to be threatened by antipollution laws. And the laws differed significantly from state to state, making the situation more complex.

Take as another example the real-estate industry. It is under pressure from discount brokers who make use of the Internet. Associations of realtors are trying to have laws enacted that require agents to provide a minimum level of services, which discount brokers, who charge less than 6 percent on the sale of a house, cannot afford to do.[7] The food industry is still another example. Through the National Restaurant Association and its twenty state organizations, it is pushing "commonsense consumption" laws that prevent lawsuits seeking personal injury damages related to obesity to be filed against restaurants.[8]

Often one group is battling another over turf. In what has become known as "Eye Wars," optometrists have been trying to gain the legal authority to conduct certain procedures that fall within the jurisdiction of ophthalmologists. The latter opposed the former every step of the way. In Maine the major struggle was "Fish Wars." Lobstermen and trawler fishermen have been competing over what they catch in the water. Until 2007 lobsters accidentally caught in nets could not be sold. In that session of the legislature the so-called "ground fishermen" tried to get the law changed so that they could land some of the lobsters caught by mistake. The lobstermen, however, insisted that no one encroach on their turf (or is it surf?). In the words of the president of the Maine Lobstermen's Association: "They [the ground fishermen] ruined their fishery totally. Now they're looking to us to bail them out, and it's just not going to happen.... There are 6,400 lobstermen that will go nuts if they even consider it."[9]

Takeda, a Japanese-owned pharmaceutical company based in Deerfield, Illinois, is a member of the Pharmaceutical Research and Manufacturing Association (PhRMA) and can rely on it for representation. But it also has its own government affairs managers to advance the company's agenda. Takeda has the following legislative concerns: (1) antimarketing, gift disclosure, and prescriber data bills; (2) price controls and mandatory discount programs; (3) importation/counterfeiting; (4) Medicaid reform; (5) health care reform; (6) state pharmacy assistance programs; (7) direct-to-consumer advertising; (8) disclosure of clinical trials; and (9) tort reform. Like other pharmaceutical companies—such as Johnson and Johnson, Merck, Pfizer, Novartis, and Bristol-Myers Squibb—Takeda finds itself on the defensive. During recent years many bills were filed in state legislatures to reduce drug prices, require pharmaceutical manufacturers to disclose marketing expenses, and restrict the commercial use of physician participation data. Other bills would regulate industry sales representatives, require the publication of clinical-trial information, and restrict advertising.[10]

Another perspective on interest group agendas is from that of a single state legislature facing diverse issues. The Massachusetts legislature during 2005–2006 found the usual large number of groups trying to advance their interests legislatively. During that session the Massachusetts Medical Society was promoting medical malpractice reform, which would eliminate "joint and several liability" and reduce the cap on "pain and suffering" payments. A proposal to create a Massachusetts Transit Fund, in order to expand commuter rail service, had as proponents a coalition of the state's construction industry and labor, along with environmental groups. Pharmacists backed a bill that would give them greater autonomy in managing patients' therapies and drug treatments. Interior designers sought autonomous status vis-à-vis architects, to whom they were subordinate. Libraries advocated a measure that would match grants to public libraries with state money. School committees and school superintendents wanted all supervisors to be taken out of the union, while school nurses wanted to be put in the same union as teachers rather than being grouped into a union with janitors. The horse- and dog-racing industries pushed a bill to authorize the location of slot machines at the four state racetracks, in an effort to increase revenues.

Meanwhile, the Massachusetts Association of Realtors was trying to defeat a number of land-use bills and an affordable housing transfer tax on Martha's Vineyard and Nantucket. The realtors were also supporting legislation to control the dumping by methamphetamine laboratory operators of toxic waste down drains or in yards (which lowered the value of impacted properties and neighborhoods). They were also behind legislation to expedite the permitting process and to promote uniform wetland and septic system codes.

The agenda of the Massachusetts Senior Action Council was just as ambitious. The council was promoting the extension of a "first refill" provision under Medicare Part D, full funding of the Prescription Advantage program, passage of a nurse-staffing bill, legislation for funding home care and housing vouchers, support for the personal care and attendant industry, and restoration of dental and eyeglass coverage under the Massachusetts health program. In addition, the council was trying to advance a constitutional amendment guaranteeing adequate and affordable health care.

The above constitute a small sample of the many items proposed (and opposed) by organized interests in Massachusetts. The situation in other states is not very different.

Just as important as legislation *per se* is the competition that takes place among groups striving to obtain funding for their programs in the state budget. The 2006 budget session in Massachusetts is illustrative. Anti–domestic violence advocates wanted a 69 percent increase over what the governor had proposed. The Phobic United Foundation sought additional money for the homebound. The Metropolitan Council for Education Opportunity, which sends city students to suburban schools, wanted to close a $15 million gap in its budget. The Massachusetts Immigration and Refugee Advocacy Coalition asked the legislature for more than the governor included in his budget. After-school programs required additional funds, as did teen pregnancy prevention programs. Groups advocating for the blind, homeless, deaf, mentally ill, and disabled also argued that they merited additional state aid for their programs. These represented only a few of hundreds of claims on the state budget by Massachusetts groups.[11]

Interest Group Resources

Virtually every interest group, just like every individual, has access to the legislature. That is to say, someone will listen to the case it makes and, most likely, someone will be willing to introduce a bill that it wants enacted into law. But whether its cause will be zealously promoted is another matter, and whether or not a group has a good chance of success on one or several issues depends on a number of factors: the issue and its environment, the group itself and its resources, the composition of the legislature, and the lobbyists and their strategies.

The Issue and Its Environment. Of great importance is the nature of the issue and the arguments the group can make in support of its position for or against it. Some issues have more appeal than others and are relatively easy for legislators to back. Penalties for drunk driving are an example. As will be shown in later chapters, almost every issue in the lawmaking process is debated in terms of its merits. The merits of a case are not the only matters that count, but count they do. Usually, however, both sides can make a persuasive case on the merits, although some cases are easier to make than others. When an interest group is making a claim on the state budget for resources, the situation is different. Here, a number of groups with worthy claims are competing for limited resources. The question is which claims get preference. If no organized group opposes another group's issue proposal, expression of the merits is one-sided. If no strong case is made in the negative and no oppositional resources are brought to bear, the results are predictable.

The Group and Its Resources. Some groups are advantaged in terms of their ability to get what they want in the legislature, but not necessarily because they are wealthy and contribute to legislators' campaigns. Perhaps more important than anything else is the size of the group—that is, the number of members it has. As Schattschneider pointed out years ago, "The political system is broadly equalitarian, *numbers* are important in politics."[12] Large membership groups rarely are ignored by legislatures. Such groups exist on both sides of the abortion, gay marriage, and gun control issues. Depending upon the particular state, one side may be much larger than the other. But the primary resource of these groups is their membership base.

Not only the size of a group's membership, but also its dispersal counts. A membership concentrated in a few legislative districts has less political clout than a membership spread in legislative districts across the state. State employees are located in the capital and large cities of the state. The influence of their unions is enormous in those districts where their members live, but much less elsewhere. By contrast, teachers associations have members teaching, living, and voting in every legislative district of the state. Their influence may not be overwhelming in any single district, but it is still substantial locally, and it reaches everywhere.

The cohesion of a group matters. If its members themselves do not buy into a group's position, the legislature is unlikely to be very impressed. Associations often have a difficult time agreeing on issues that divide their memberships. An association of businesses, for instance, may find large businesses and small businesses opposed to one another on an issue. Under such circumstances an association will not be able to take a position, and its individual members, both large and small, will have to lobby on their own.

Along with cohesion, a group's intensity counts. One of the primary resources of many advocacy groups is intensity. The positions these groups take are based on principle, from which they do not budge and with which they claim the high ground in the struggle. The intensity of environmental groups, among other things, has led to their success in putting business interests on the defensive.[13] The National Rifle Association, along with other gun-owner groups in many states, is also known for the passion with which members relate to politics. Members believe strongly in their right to bear arms and will vote against those who threaten that right, no matter what their positions may be on other major issues. Relatively few groups are endowed with memberships that are so devoted to their cause. When legislators are aware that concentrations of group members in their districts will support the group's position in the voting booth, they try as best they can not to oppose that position.

A group's standing in the state makes a difference. Large corporations are taken seriously because of their relevance to the state's economic well-being. They are especially important as employers of the state (and district) workforce. Pharmaceuticals in New Jersey, oil in Texas, electronics in California, and dairy in Wisconsin are examples of industries that legislatures cannot afford to ignore. The value they bring to the state's economy ensures that the legislative inclination will be to help them out if at all possible (as it usually is). Massachusetts is one of a number of states promoting development in biotechnology, so it is not surprising that the legislature has looked favorably on legislation and appropriations in this area. In 2006 it enacted a major economic stimulus bill, which included $80 million for investment in the life sciences and technology. Indeed, because of his assistance to the industry, Senate President Robert Travaglini received a "legislator of the year" award from the Biotechnology Industry Organization. Professional football, baseball, and basketball teams also have standing in the states where they play. Legislatures usually are willing to subsidize them because of their fan base and the prestige they bring to the state. If major league teams threaten to leave, legislatures respond with a package to keep them. Other groups also have standing with the public, mainly because of the issues they represent. Their clout may not run deep, but it does help move their cases forward in the legislature.

Money cannot be overlooked when it comes to a group's resources vis-à-vis the legislature. Money enables the group to involve itself in campaign politics, in particular by contributing to legislative leaders and legislative members. Later in this chapter, I shall discuss why groups contribute and what their contributions get them in the lawmaking process. For now, no one is likely to object to the assertion that money does matter. Even if an interest group does not make campaign contributions, money enhances its organizational capacity. It buys information systems, grassroots mobilization capacity, and skilled staff and lobbyists.

The Composition of the Legislature. Years ago, Schattschneider pointed out that the success of interest groups was due less to the "pressure" exerted by these groups than to the fact that they shared beliefs with members of the legislature.[14] His observation is just as correct today. At the broadest level, many interest groups are allied with political parties. Their objectives and their constituencies overlap. They are typically tied to one another on issues and they work to get their political friends elected to office. When Democrats control the legislature, state employees and labor are better positioned to gain more or lose less. When Republicans control the legislature, business is generally better off. Nothing is guaranteed, of course, but the difference between a legislature controlled by one party and not the other can be substantial for an interest group.

At a more specific level, probably the best representation for an interest group is to have group members serving in the legislature. Associations of teachers expect teacher-legislators to favor their cause because their views on education have been shaped in the classroom, like those of other teachers. Associations of trial attorneys expect lawyer-legislators to defend their interests, because attorneys inside the legislature are likely to agree on issues related to their profession with attorneys outside the legislature. Alabama in recent years has had a large percentage of legislators who were working teachers, retired teachers, or members of the families of teachers. This certainly helped the cause of the state education association. Of 104 legislators in Utah, twenty-two are also real-estate brokers, one of whom is the former president of the National Association of Realtors.[15] It is not surprising that the Utah Legislature is friendly to real-estate interests. Together, Republican control and realtor membership ensure that the industry's interests will be regarded positively.

Lobbyists and Their Strategies. It is not sufficient to add up the arguments, group resources, and allies in the legislature. The campaign on the ground—issue by issue, bill by bill—is what counts. That campaign depends initially on the policymaking context: whether niche or policy community, referring to the scope of interest group involvement; whether it is symbolic, distributive, or redistributive in nature; and whether it involves public confrontation or not.[16]

Lobbying strategy depends also on whether it is offensive or defensive in nature. Insofar as much of lobbying is on behalf of business interests, most campaigns are designed to defeat or water down bills averse to business. Business for the most part wants to be left alone. A defensive position is an easier one to play, since a bill moving forward has to overcome a series of hurdles along the way—committee, caucus, and floor of one house and committee, caucus, and floor of the other house. Anywhere along the line, the defense has a good shot at a bill. There are, in the words of a Colorado lobbyist, "a hundred ways to kill a bill and only one way to pass one." The strategic considerations in a lobbying campaign "for" or "against" are numerous, complicated, and continuously challenging. But strategy, and its implementation, makes a big difference. This is where the art of lobbying and the skill of lobbyists come into the picture.

Lobbyists and Their Jobs

The newspaper press tends to play up both the number and influence of lobbyists registered in state capitols. Everywhere more lobbyists are registered than legislators are elected. The *New York Times,* by way of illustration, informs its readers of these ratios. In Albany, with its 384 registered lobbyists, legislators are outnumbered eighteen to one. In California, Florida, Illinois, and Ohio the ratio is ten to one. On average in the fifty states there are five lobbyists to one legislator.[17] Given the numbers, it would seem that legislators have little chance. But not all lobbyists are equal. The number of registered lobbyists in a state depends on several factors, not the least of which are the size of the state and its economy. Also relevant are lobbyist registration laws. When they are broad they apply to more individuals, when narrow they apply to fewer individuals. In any case, most of those who are registered do relatively little lobbying.

In terms of their influence, lobbyists are portrayed by the media and perceived by the public to exercise virtual control over lawmaking in the states. The stereotypical lobbyist still is Artie Samish, who from the 1930s through the 1950s was reputed to be "the secret boss of California." A 1949 *Collier's Magazine* cover immortalized Samish as a lobbyist by picturing him holding a ventriloquist's dummy labeled "Mr. Legislature." Sitting there, with the dummy on his lap, Samish is pulling its strings. In the magazine's story, Gov. Earl Warren is quoted: "On matters that affect his clients, Artie unquestionably has more power than the governor."[18]

It may have been that Governor Warren had little interest in the issues that affected Samish's clients. He probably had bigger fish to fry. Still, the influence of Artie Samish in the California Legislature was indisputable. No lobbyist today wields anything like his clout, but lobbyists are still very much part of the lawmaking process.

Their power has declined from the days of Samish, their methods have been refashioned, but their image has gotten worse. Samish himself was an independent or contract lobbyist, a so-called "gun for hire." These lobbyists operate singly or in firms and represent a number of clients, sometimes as many as a hundred or more. These are the lobbyists that most people think of when the subject arises. They account for about 15–20 percent of lobbyists at the state level.[19] There are also in-house lobbyists, who represent only one client. They work on the governmental relations staffs of state and national associations, labor unions, and companies of various types. They also are employed by a wide range of advocacy groups that have legislative agendas. They constitute the large majority of registered lobbyists in the state capital.

It is difficult to imagine any issue in the lawmaking process that is not lobbied by someone or other. It is the job of contract and/or in-house lobbyists to make the case for or against legislation, to work with legislators who are especially friendly to their issue, and to try to persuade others to go along. Their objective, for the most part, is to satisfy the client who retains them or the organization that employs them, at the same time trying to work out arrangements with which legislators can live, and live at low political risk. Cause lobbyists play a different game. They have to please their members in order to keep them as members, and this entails greater stridency, confrontation in the legislature, and less concern for the political comfort of legislators. On a large number of issues lobbyists and legislators work toward the same goals and employ common strategies to reach them.

This is not, by any means, because legislators are handmaidens of certain interest groups (although some may be). Rather, it is because advocates for the environment, transportation, health, and other issues—legislators and lobbyists both—are natural allies in their advocacy of public policy. In fact, in the dealings that take place between legislators and lobbyists, legislators are almost always the dominant partners. Legislators need lobbyists, lobbyists need legislators; but when push comes to shove, lobbyists are needier than legislators.

The modes of lobbying differ greatly, depending largely on the client or organization and the types of issues involved. Most of the issues lobbied in state capitals are mainly economic in nature, with different interests having conflicting stakes. Businesses struggle over economic advantage, occupational groups dispute over which has jurisdiction in a particular area. On such issues contract lobbyists and representatives of business and occupational associations predominate.

The effectiveness of lobbyists also depends on the merits of their case, the strength of their client's or organization's membership and political support, and the standing of the lobbyists themselves in the legislative community. Most of the fights in which these lobbyists engage are well below the public's radar. It is difficult, if not impossible, to discern just where "*a* public interest" let alone "*the* public interest" might lie.

Some of the issues are broader, and some far broader, in nature. Education policy, environmental policy, transportation policy, and other major policy questions are constantly being decided. On some issues many people are being affected, as on abortion, guns, gay rights, and so forth. On these issues, the modes of lobbying are unlike the modes on narrower, economic issues. Membership organizations and advocacy groups are involved. Contract lobbyists, the prototypical denizens of state house halls, are less likely to be featured in the struggles that take place. The issues, the causes, and their advocates take center stage. Political support, at least by way of financial contributions, and lobbyist standing and relationships are of relatively little importance. The substance and politics of the issue loom larger.

Economic and turf disputes are contested primarily by inside strategies and lobbyists who are accustomed to the "inside game." Policy issues in dispute tend to be debated within various domains, by organizations and lobbyists who specialize within each domain. Social, or so-called "hot-button" issues, arouse advocacy or cause groups who engage mainly in an "outside game," relying on grassroots members, the media, and the public. The modes and games of lobbying have to be distinguished, if one is to understand how lawmaking proceeds in a state legislature.

Establishing Trust and Credibility

Any lobbyist will tell you how important relationships are in the legislative process. That is because people are dealing with one another constantly. They have to rely on one another for information and support. In order to establish a relationship with legislators, lobbyists must be considered trustworthy. Trust is the *sine qua non* of lobbyists' dealings with legislators. In the legislative process, members decide on the basis of information furnished them by lobbyists. There is little or no time for verification. Things move quickly. Moreover, the narrower and more technical the issue, the more important the relationship and the more critical the trust. Legislators cannot afford to be misled and lobbyists cannot afford to mislead them. The building of trust is mainly a one-way street, since legislators are less compelled to win the trust of lobbyists than vice versa.

First, trust depends on lobbyists being trustful. This requires that they inform legislators not only of the benefits of supporting a proposal, but also of the drawbacks. If a legislator's support might prove costly in political terms, the lobbyist is obliged to issue a warning. Second, trust is contingent on the reliability of the lobbyist. Can the lobbyist be depended upon for assistance at critical times? Or is the lobbyist a fair-weather friend, and not much more? Third, trust is based on whether a lobbyist keeps his or her word to legislators. A broken promise undermines a trusting relationship. Finally, the building of trust requires predictable behavior on the part of lobbyists. This means that lobbyists should not take legislators by surprise, or blindside them, but be careful to prepare them in advance for shifts in direction.

The vast majority of lobbyists do not betray the trust that they develop with legislators. They cannot afford to. If a lobbyist misleads a legislator or breaks his or her word, that lobbyist will become *persona non grata*. The abused legislator will spread the word and other legislators will heed it. The lobbyist in question will lose friends and the information he or she provides will be discounted. Lobbyists are probably among the most trustworthy people in politics. Their livelihood depends on it.

Relationships that are established on a foundation of trust are best developed on the job and over time. The experience that a legislator has with a lobbyist under battlefield conditions has the greatest impact. If the two have worked together for a while, their trusting relationship has been tested and forged. There is no substitute for actual dealings in the process or proof of trustworthiness.

One reason that ex-legislators are recruited as lobbyists by firms and organizations is that they already have developed relationships within the legislature. Not only do they have access to their former colleagues but, more important, they have proved their trustworthiness in the trenches with them. Unless they have earned a solid reputation in the legislature, they are not likely to be invited into the lobbying community. If they were considered untrustworthy legislators by their former colleagues, they will start off being considered untrustworthy lobbyists by those they have to lobby.

The substitute—albeit a poor one—for having had dealings with one another is socializing with one another. Trust can be established on a personal basis, not only on a work basis. Lobbyists tend to be outgoing individuals with skills for relating to people. As described by Vermont's former speaker, Ralph Wright: "Lobbyists learn to be extremely friendly people endowed with a generosity not often found even in one's church."[20] Lobbyists try assiduously to get as much face time as possible from legislators. It is not to press specific issues on them, but rather to build a relationship and, perhaps, even develop a friendship.

In earlier days, socializing among legislators and lobbyists was far more salient than it is today. Legislators and lobbyists dined together, traveled on junkets together, attended sporting events together, played golf together, and occasionally rented houses and roomed together in the capital city. Lobbyists picked up the tab for all of the meals and entertainment that buttressed the building of relationships. No longer is socializing as prominent a technique; no longer is entertainment the glue making it all possible. Thanks to changed social habits, stringent ethics laws, an intrusive state house press corps, public distemper, and legislator caution, capital cultures have changed radically.[21]

In most states, gifts (including food and drink) are either prohibited or limited, or must be disclosed publicly. Whether required by law or not, many legislators go cold turkey and accept nothing. They do not want to risk the appearance of being influenced by lobbyists' largesse. Nowadays, the social occasions for lobbyists to mix with legislators are pretty much confined to charity events and fund-raisers for legislative campaigns. Fewer opportunities exist for lobbyists to get the quality time required for relationship-building.

Without social opportunities, relationship-building depends almost entirely on the experience lobbyists and legislators share working with one another. Such experience is especially brief in legislatures where members' terms are limited by constitution or statute. With a six-, eight-, or even twelve-year limit, legislators turn over regularly. Lobbyists continuously encounter new members with whom they have to start from scratch, proving themselves and their trustworthiness.

Being Part of a Legislator's Political Support

Lobbyists, and the interests they represent, can score points by enlisting in a legislator's political support group. Legislators have a warm spot in their hearts for those who help them where and when they need help.

First, lobbyists and interest groups *enlist* candidates for legislative office. In a number of states—particularly several states in the South—business groups, trial lawyers, and teachers try to recruit candidates from their ranks who share their views on a number of specific issues. Legislators who are recruited to office in this manner do not have to be persuaded. They already agree, at least on some matters, with the groups and individuals who first recruited them and now lobby them. They are advocates; that is simply where they stand.

Second, lobbyists and interest groups *endow* candidates. That is, they provide group endorsements, funding, and sometimes campaign workers. Endorsements probably have little influence on how people vote, but candidates seek them and groups give them. Only a few groups are able to furnish campaign volunteers, teachers being one of them. Volunteers are appreciated and help forge a connection between legislators and the parent groups.

No doubt, the most widespread and important assistance lobbyists and interest groups provide is campaign funds. Money has to be raised. In the states where politics is less professionalized and districts are small, it doesn't take much to run. Family, friends, and partisan supporters are able to endow many of the candidates. But even in these states, competitive races cost more and require funding from groups and organizations, which comprise the special interests that deal session after session with the legislature. Not all interest groups contribute, but many do. This is reflected by the fact that almost twelve thousand PACs exist in the states and contribute to political campaigns.[22] In the larger states, with more professionalized legislatures, there does not appear to be any substitute for interest group money.

Interest groups have come to see the campaign as a principal avenue to influence in the legislature. This is because the campaign, as indicated in chapter 4, is now intertwined with lawmaking. As Allan J. Cigler and Burdett A. Loomis point out, the distinction between the politics of governing and policymaking is blurring. The ties between the two have been strengthened because of the idea of the "permanent campaign."[23] The boundaries between electoral campaigns and lobbying strategies are less defined than they used to be. In this environment, lobbyists play a critical role. They steer money from their PACs or clients to candidates. Some contract lobbyists raise and bundle money for candidates. Their work does not go unappreciated. Florida's senate president, Jim King, explained how the system works:

> You can't serve and run a campaign without money. The choice is to spend your own, or rely on other people to go out and help, and in that regard the lobbyist who can control a lot of PACs usually stands in good favor.[24]

Not only do interest groups contribute to legislative candidates and parties, but they also spend money on their own during campaigns to elect people they favor. Independent expenditures are now a feature of election campaigns in many states and are focused on districts where the races are close. In Minnesota, for example, during the 2006 election, Education Minnesota (a teachers' interest group) spent $2.9 million; the American Federation of State, County, and Municipal Employees (AFSCME) spent $1.9 million; and the casinos spent $1.12 million.[25]

Third, lobbyists *enable* legislators by directing assistance toward their efforts as representatives and lawmakers. For example, a constituent may have a problem with a service or product provided by the company a lobbyist represents; the constituent complains to her legislator about it. The lobbyist happily gets his company to handle the constituent's problem. Lobbyists for telephone, cable, gas, and electricity are ready and willing to ensure constituent-customers better service, if legislators intervene on their behalf. Constituents appreciate what their representatives do for them and representatives, in turn, appreciate what lobbyists do for them in helping constituents. The lobbyists will also invite legislators to association or company events or to industrial plants, where they can address or meet with voters in their districts. In addition, lobbyists will assist on issues and bills that are of no special concern to their clients but are of special concern to the legislator. They may be able to furnish the legislator with information, identify others who may be enlisted in the legislator's cause, or actually join forces in attempts to enact or kill a piece of legislation.

Fourth, lobbyists are allies in the lawmaking process, side by side with legislators, with whom they share interests and objectives. They decide on strategy and tactics together. In cooperation, they manage bills they favor or try to derail those they oppose. They count votes, compare their counts, and figure out just how to get the number they need. All of this is central in the lawmaking process, to which we shall return in chapters 9, 10, and 11, where interest groups and lobbyists play important roles.

Making the Case

Most of what lobbyists do is rather straightforward. They make a case for their employer's or their client's position. They argue the merits of a proposal, if they are playing offense, and the demerits of a proposal, if they are playing defense. Whenever legislators are asked about the role of lobbyists, they inevitably reply that what lobbyists do is provide information. They are not mistaken in their perception. Conveying information is the main job of lobbyists. Despite the media's emphasis on money as the explanatory factor in lawmaking ("Follow the money," the reader or viewer is told), information, including its packaging and its transmission, is the lobbyist's stock-in-trade.

"However important money may be . . . ," write Cigler and Loomis, "useful information is usually worth more."[26] Lobbyists are not the only people in the information business, but they are major presenters. They summarize, synthesize, and package in order to make their client's case as persuasive as possible.[27] They frame issues to their client's advantage, relating them whenever possible to the legislator's constituency. They also try to frame them so that it is not a zero-sum game in which one side loses if the other wins. The strategy is to disarm one's opponents at the outset so no battle needs to be fought. There are no losers in the best of all possible lobbyist worlds.[28]

The merits lobbyists argue are both substantive and political. Substantively, reference is to whether enactment of a bill will help or hurt people, a group, the economy, the state; whether other states do it; whether it is a high risk or a low risk; whether it is fair or unfair; whether it costs a little or a lot; and so forth. Experts and analysts support the substantive case lobbyists make. Politically, reference is to whether enactment will win or lose votes in the state and in the legislator's district. Do people favor it or do they oppose it? Do they even care? "It can't hurt you," is the reassurance lobbyists want to be able to give.

At just about every point in the process, the merits or demerits are being discussed. They are certainly what lobbyists stress in one-on-one conversations with legislators in the halls of the capitol, in an office, or back in the district. This is what they communicate to legislative leaders and committee chairs. It is the substance of their testimony in committee. It is also what they talk about with members of the legislative staff.

On some issues many members have already made up their minds. They are familiar with the issue. It has been around for some time and legislators have commitments and a record on it. But some issues in the lawmaking process are new to members; they have no predispositions in one direction or the other. In such instances the merits will weigh more heavily than otherwise. And whether or not the balancing of information on one side against information on the other is decisive, the information is necessary in the process. Just about every legislator wants to be able to justify his or her position. Whatever the various reasons for a decision might be, justification is made on the basis of a merit-based argument.

Determining and Executing Strategy

Lobbyists, like legislators, are constantly deriving strategies and changing them as the need arises. If their interests coincide, lobbyists and legislators may strategize jointly. They are in it together and are seeking the same objective—passage or defeat of a bill or, more likely, a compromise that tilts in their direction.

If a lobbyist has a bill in play, probably the first question he or she will ask is, "Who is for it and who is against it?" An initial strategy is to put together a coalition advocating for the same position. If that coalition appears stronger than an opposing coalition, then the lobbyist is off to a good start. Perhaps the most imposing coalition is one made up of unlikely allies—such as business and labor or environmentalists and manufacturers. Such a coalition will impress any legislator and help allay whatever doubts he or she may have about a measure.

Along with interest group partners, lobbyists quickly identify their legislator allies. These are the people that they are sure to enlist. They need these legislators to lobby their legislator colleagues in an effort to round up votes. Along with several other techniques, this one falls within the category of "indirect lobbying." A study by Richard L. Hall and Alan Deardorff explores how lobbyists lobby their allies, not to change their minds but to mobilize them in pursuit of common objectives.[29] Anyone who observes the legislature at close hand can see lawmakers trying to convince their colleagues—in one another's offices, on the telephone, or in the chamber—to vote their way. Lobbyists work the same way, but probably with less effect than legislators themselves. Lobbyists and legislators start out as allies in advocacy or opposition on many issues before the legislature, and it is easy for them to coordinate their strategies and efforts.

If lobbyists are backing a bill, they must decide which legislator to ask to be a sponsor. Normally, they would choose a member of the majority party, and ideally they would recruit a member of the leadership team to take on sponsorship. They could obtain no better sponsor than the chair of the standing committee to which the bill is being referred. Occasionally, a bill can be drafted so that it falls within the jurisdiction of a chosen committee. Lobbyists usually focus their efforts on the chair and members of the committee with jurisdiction over their issues. With the chair on one's side, the effort usually runs smoothly. But if the chair is undecided or hostile, the opposition's chances are substantially bettered. Opponents also focus on the standing committee, trying to kill or at least water down the bill at the outset.

Strategy for proponents involves a determination of which chamber should move the bill first. Sometimes it is helpful to have the senate pass a measure before the house; sometimes the reverse is preferred. Often proponents settle for the chamber where they have the most support in the hope that their side will gather momentum as their bill proceeds.

Strategy for opponents involves a determination of whether a bill should be fought head on or whether amendments ought to be offered to weaken it or substitute another approach for dealing with the problem. If opponents are certain of the votes to defeat a measure, they are not likely to settle for less. Otherwise, the likelihood is that the opposition will try to modify or undermine the proposal. Both proponents and opponents in their strategizing have to decide what compromises they would be willing to make and what amendments they would be willing to accept. What are they willing to live with? Their decisions depend upon how many votes they think they have and how many more they think they can get if they do X, Y, or Z. Strategizing continues and strategies change constantly, depending upon where legislators stand and where they seem to be moving.

At the outset, however, lobbyists ordinarily do what they can to avoid conflict wherever possible. They will try to ask for things to which no one is likely to object. They may ask for less than they want, if that will keep opposition from arising.[30] And they will attempt to work things out in advance with other concerned interest groups.

A major part of devising and executing strategy is spent by lobbyists rounding up votes and counting them. Depending on the issue, rounding up votes can require quite a lot of man (or woman) power. Certainly in the large states and on high-stakes issues, contract lobbyists are hired to target certain members. One lobbyist may be taken on to lobby only the Democrats, another only the Republicans; or one may lobby only the senate, another the house. A woman lobbyist may be assigned women legislators, an African American lobbyist to African American legislators. A former Florida speaker and senate president, who currently is lobbying, explained how interest groups targeted legislators: "If they knew that I might be close to one person they'd . . . hire me just to lobby one guy," he said. "It's almost man-to-man now."[31] In New York the governor, the speaker of the assembly, and the majority leader of the senate are critical on major economic issues. According to one analysis, companies have found that they can make a more effective case when their lobbyist has ties to the official being lobbied. It has, therefore, become the practice for large companies to hire separate lobbying firms, each with special access to one of the top three officials. Some call this "stool lobbying," or hiring a separate firm for each of state government's three legs.[32]

In collaboration with their legislator allies, lobbyists face the task of persuading legislators to support their case. Some legislators already have staked out positions, others have predispositions one way or the other, and the votes of a number are up for grabs. The narrower and less important the issue, the likelier that most legislators will be open to persuasion. The broader and more important the issue, the likelier that most legislators will have their minds made up earlier on. But even on these issues lobbyists play a critical role, because part of their job is to redefine the issue or get legislators to focus on a different aspect of it. On the big-ticket issues, the influence of lobbyists is exercised at the margins. As Beth L. Leech et al. point out (with regard to lobbying Congress), legislators are so constrained by their political parties, their constituencies, and their own well-entrenched policy preferences, "it is unlikely that a lobbyist could change a legislator's political beliefs simply by talking with the legislator, supplying information, or donating campaign funds."[33] Lobbyists do not try to change the legislator's position. Instead, they try to focus the legislator's attention on something that will help, not hurt, the lobbyist's cause. Amendments and details are where lobbyists make their largest contributions.

Counting the votes helps determine the strategy and tactics pursued. As Hall and Deardorff write: "Lobbyists are well-situated to provide head counts, identify the undecided or wavering legislators and determine the nature of those legislators' concerns, to which the group's legislative allies might speak in trying to win over waverers."[34] After the votes are tallied in the senate, the house, or both chambers, the job may be over for the moment. The bill may have been defeated, in which case both sides can rest until the next legislative session. If enacted, the proponents will turn toward the executive branch to make sure their bill is not vetoed, while the opponents have a last chance to defeat it by winning the governor over to their side.

Mobilizing Grassroots

Grassroots lobbying can be defined as "the identification, recruitment, and mobilization of constituent-based political strength capable of influencing political decisions."[35] Grassroots constitute one element of an increasingly important "outside game," a form of indirect lobbying that now supplements the "inside game" of direct lobbying.

Some issues are narrowly based and/or technical; some affect interest groups who have no grassroots capacity. These issues ordinarily are lobbied the old-fashioned way. But many other issues are fought on both fronts, with grassroots (or "grass tips" or "key contacts," where relatively few constituents are involved) and direct lobbying working in combination. Interest group members testify before standing committees, fan out and visit individual legislators in their offices, rally on the state house steps, and hold demonstrations near the capitol.

Varieties of grassroots lobbying are illustrated by events during the 2006 session of the Massachusetts legislature.[36] The National Association of Social Workers held its Lobbying Day at the statehouse in March. The association had medical malpractice, parole for drug offenders, and in-state tuition rates for unauthorized immigrants on their agenda. On Residents' Day on Beacon Hill, also in March, physicians rallied in support of bills on booster-seat requirements, primary seat-belt enforcement, school nutrition, physical education, and early education. That same month the Coalition of New American Voters turned out 2,500 people to protest proposed federal legislation. Outside the statehouse in April about forty people, along with four greyhounds, were opposing slot machines at horse and dog tracks. Inside about twenty-five people waited at the door of the speaker's office, chanting "Save our jobs" (by authorizing slots at the four Massachusetts racetracks). That same month more than two hundred people, many using wheelchairs and walkers, rallied to support a bill that would help the state's personal care–attendant workers. After a bill that would make wearing helmets optional had passed the senate, but had not yet been voted on by the house, three hundred motorcyclists circled the state house to make their point. During debate by the senate on a primary seat-belt law, families of car-crash victims sat in the gallery and held up pictures of the killed and injured. In June environmental activists held a rally on the Boston Common across the street from the statehouse in support of legislation that would add Massachusetts to states that had joined the Regional Greenhouse Gas Initiative.

Economic interests are at some disadvantage when it comes to grassroots, since they do not have individual members. But many corporations and large businesses try to develop a grassroots capacity, enlisting employees and their families, suppliers, and even customers. Many others hire consultants to round up grassroots, or convey the appearance of grassroots, for specific-issue campaigns in the legislature. By contrast, groups with membership bases—and especially advocates of a cause—go to the grassroots well frequently.

Groups with financial resources, which dominate the pool of campaign contributions, seldom have much grassroots capacity. Groups that can mobilize their memberships often have little in the way of disposable financial resources. Some groups—notably labor and teachers—have both money and numbers. Grassroots are an invaluable resource for an interest group. But there are limits as to how often grassroots can be mobilized.[37] There are also risks that overly aggressive grassroots campaigns can annoy legislators and thus boomerang.

Media and Public Relations

Media and public relations approaches, like grassroots, are intended to impress lawmakers with a particular position. This approach is the most indirect one. It is designed in part to project issues favorably to the public and win people over. Most important, its objective is to give the impression that the public supports a group's position, whether it actually does or not. With enough media and advertising committed by an interest group, legislators may be more inclined to relent and seek a settlement acceptable to the group. The techniques that fall within this area include newsletters, position papers, brochures, news releases, press conferences, television and radio interviews, editorial board meetings, and advertising of all types.

Interest groups that play an outside game rely on the media to carry their message. Often the media attention comes without cost. But a well-endowed group will buy media in order to communicate both its substantive and political messages as widely as possible. In the 2006 session in

Massachusetts, the Health Care for All coalition sponsored radio advertisements urging support of a health care plan requiring employees to provide insurance for workers or pay a payroll tax into a state fund. Business groups in the state also conducted an advertising campaign warning that a payroll tax would hinder economic growth. The Massachusetts budget that year impelled various groups to advertise. A coalition of antismoking advocates undertook an ad campaign in newspapers and on the radio statewide to restore the state's Tobacco Control Program. Involved were Tobacco Free Mass and the American Cancer Society. The Massachusetts Teachers Association wanted more money for schools than Gov. Mitt Romney had proposed in his budget and bought sixty-second radio spots in Boston and selected communities, thirty-second television spots in the Boston and Springfield markets, and a thirty-second ad on cable statewide.[38]

California is well ahead of the curve when it comes to public relations and advertising campaigns intended to influence lawmaking. Firms that once specialized in corporate public relations not too long ago turned to political PR. Corporations became their main clients. Generating public support increasingly became integrated into selling a corporation's issues to the legislature. What used to be done exclusively in the back rooms began to be done in the front rooms as well, with regular people attending—if not as equal participants, then as audience members that might be roused by candidates at election time.

"Advocacy advertising" or "issue advocacy" is also part of the scene in the large states and for the wealthier interest groups. Teachers in a number of states use advocacy advertising as part of general and longer-term campaigns to shape public and legislators' perceptions of teachers and public education. For example, the New Jersey Education Association has engaged in a "Pride in Public Education" advertising campaign since 1994, which is believed to be effective in giving the public and lawmakers a more positive orientation toward teachers in the schools.

The Direct Legislative Process

Interest groups can expand their campaigns beyond appeal to their grassroots or the public at large. In almost half the states they can initiate legislation by collecting the required number of signatures and putting their proposal on the ballot for the voters to decide. The initiative bypasses the legislature, except where it is indirect, as in Massachusetts. Here the legislature can prevent an initiative, with the requisite number of signatures, from making it to the ballot.

Initiatives run the gamut—from a coalition of animal rights groups trying to ban dog racing by law to various groups trying to ban same-sex marriage by constitutional amendment. In 2006, for example, seventy-seven measures were initiated in eighteen states, the largest number since 1996. Most of these initiatives are promoted by interest groups of one type or another, many by business groups, but a good number by advocacy groups. An analysis by Todd Donovan et al. of fifty-four California initiatives from 1986 to 1996, showed that the following groups had proposed and campaigned for ballot propositions: taxpayers (five); labor (four); lawyers (three); industry (three); education (two); business (two); insurance (two); consumers (two); public interest (two); environmentalists (two); welfare (one); suicide prevention (one); sports fishers (one); law enforcement (one); and several corporations.[39]

The effectiveness of bypassing the legislature and going directly to the voters is demonstrated by the California Teachers Association (CTA). The group's goal in its sponsorship of Proposition 98 in 1988 was to make sure that school funding kept increasing at no less a rate than the cost of living and enrollment. CTA's proposal, which passed narrowly, in effect required that at least 40 percent of the state's general fund be devoted to public schools and community colleges. The CTA became a champion of direct democracy, because it served the group's interests. Between 2000 and 2004, as Joe Mathews points out, the teachers association spent more than twice as much on ballot campaigns as on candidate campaigns and lobbying.[40]

Perhaps even more important than the election itself is the leverage afforded a group that threatens to go to the ballot. In California, when the teachers threatened a ballot initiative to increase per-pupil spending, Gov. Gray Davis responded by adding $1.8 billion for education to his already large budget request. "Every single Democratic constituency group threatened ballot initiatives against him," according to the governor's chief of staff.[41] Proponents of charter schools in California began circulating petitions to qualify an initiative for the ballot, but indicated that they would withdraw it if the legislature passed acceptable legislation. The legislature responded satisfactorily and the petitions were withdrawn.[42] In Massachusetts, Common Cause's threat of an initiative resulted in the legislature's coming up with a proposal of its own.[43] And the Health Care for All coalition's application of initiative pressure provided an important incentive for the Massachusetts legislature to take on the problem of health insurance.

Money in the Lawmaking Process

Money is perceived to be the main determinant of whether legislation passes or fails. Many people believe that campaign contributions buy votes, or at least enough votes on enough issues. Some years ago, a statewide survey in New Jersey asked respondents what percentage of legislators in Trenton sold out for campaign contributions and the like. Two-thirds of those responding said that anywhere from 50 percent to 100 percent sold out.[44] Whatever the prevailing belief about the overwhelming influence of money in the process, it is simply not the case that money trumps everything else.

Many people contribute to parties and candidates, expecting nothing in return. Candidates themselves contribute personally to their campaigns. They also solicit and receive contributions from family, friends, and partisan supporters. No *quid pro quo* is involved in these transactions. Everyone can appreciate that in such instances contributors are giving to candidates who they believe will do a good job and with whom they share ideas. Such money changing hands arouses little or no suspicion that legislators are being bought.

People's suspicions are aroused, however, when organized groups contribute. Not all interest groups make campaign contributions through political action committees or otherwise; most don't, but still many do. They recognize, as indeed they should, that campaign support means a lot to legislators. Before legislators can serve their constituents, the public, and the state, they have to be elected. Where there's an election, there's the possibility of losing. Therefore even those in relatively safe districts seek support. Interest groups with individual members may be able to deliver voters to a candidate, but most organized groups—and, in particular, corporations, businesses, and professions—cannot deliver votes. But they can deliver dollars; and they do so, to the best of their ability, for a number of reasons.

First, interest groups contribute to get like-minded candidates elected and legislators who side with them on a range of issues reelected. In such cases, the legislator's vote does not follow the money, the money follows the vote. The particular group and the individual legislators happen to be on the same side. It is natural, then, to try to get policy friends and allies elected to office. This is probably why most contributions are made.[45]

Second, campaign contributions are intended to make natural friends friendlier. By this, I mean that contributions may spur one's allies to take on a more active role on an issue that is important to the group. Instead of simply voting in accordance with a group's position, a beneficiary legislator may feel obliged to take a leadership role, managing the issue and persuading his or her colleagues to cast their votes the same way.

Third, on occasion, contributions are intended not so much to elect friends as to defeat enemies. This rarely occurs, but if a group's enemies are vulnerable, it may be the case. Most often, however, enemies are tough to beat and, therefore, seldom targeted. Interest groups do not expend their limited resources on long shots, especially if they risk alienating incumbent legislators.

Fourth, groups may contribute to legislators who oppose them and who are secure in their seats. The objective here is not to convert them, but to soften them up. Opponents may not vote with the contributing group, but they may not be as vocal or energetic as otherwise in opposing the group's position. The intention is to dissuade legislators from mobilizing their colleagues in opposition.

Fifth, lobbyists usually explain that all they hope to get in return for a campaign contribution is access—that is, the opportunity to make their case with a legislator. No doubt, they are looking for "preferred" access. They want to move to the head of the line, so they can see a legislator on quick notice and have their telephone calls and emails returned quickly.

Sixth, beyond preferred access, they are looking for the benefit of the doubt. If they have no objections to a measure and if there is no downside, legislators might be willing to support interest groups that support them. Why shouldn't they?

Seventh, interest groups give to political campaigns not only for purposes of advancing their positions, but also for defensive reasons. Their competitors may be attending fund-raisers and making contributions. To stay even with the competition, it is best to give as others do.

Eighth, giving is important, particularly if legislators believe a group ought to do so. Not every group is expected to provide funding. Environmental groups, consumer groups, and civil rights groups are among those not expected to set up PACs. Business and professional groups, however, are different. If an interest group is expected to participate monetarily, what will happen if it doesn't? Will it lose legislator friends? Will it lose issues in the process? Few groups are willing to increase the uncertainty of their position in an already uncertain lawmaking process. Why risk losing friends in the legislature? The worst situation may be one in which a group has stopped contributing to candidates, after having been a regular player in the campaign finance system. It is not worth jeopardizing a group's agenda, when all that is required is a certain level of giving. Just as in a poker game, where each player has to ante up before receiving a hand, in lawmaking interest groups (some, but not all) believe that it is best to contribute to campaigns in order to enhance their chances of not losing in the legislature.

Whatever the objectives of interest groups, the bottom-line question is: What do interest groups get in return for the money they give legislative candidates? Insiders acknowledge that much of a lobbyist's influence is based on "how much money you raised and how big a friend you are."[46] Yet many lobbyists believe that campaign contributions are not one of the major weapons in their arsenal. Instead, they think that meeting personally with legislators, being part of coalitions, and having grassroots capacity are their most effective weapons.[47]

Interest group contributions probably guarantee access, although just about anyone can get an audience with his or her representative. Political support does provide quicker, easier, and better access. Money, however, is not the only commodity that opens doors more readily. A good lobbyist can do the same thing, and broad coalitions and large membership groups rarely have trouble getting heard when they want to be heard. But, as the discussion of group objectives indicates, access is only one payoff sought by interests that contribute. Access is at the margins of the lawmaking process, which is not to say that the margins are unimportant. That is what political science research indicates. Money seldom determines how legislators vote, but, according to Anthony J. Nownes, "it may affect their behavior on the margins. . . ."[48]

As Frank Sorouf argues: "The nature of influence in a legislative body involves much more than final role call votes. [Interest groups] exert influence at other stages in the legislative process—in initiatives not taken, in committee amendments, or in special rules affecting floor consideration."[49] In the legislative process most of what happens is in the stages of deliberation and negotiation. A legislator on the receiving end of a contribution may vote "no" but not lead the opposition against a measure. A legislator also on the receiving end, who is a proponent, not only will vote "aye" but also round up votes for passage of a bill.

The intensity, although not the direction, of a legislator's behavior may be affected by campaign contributions. Along these lines, according to Gray and Lowery, PAC contributions do not change votes, but rather "buy time and attention." Legislators inclined to support an interest group's position might use their time on other matters, but campaign support induces them to make a greater effort on the group's behalf. Legislators want to help their political friends and find many ways to do so. They can provide lobbyists with strategic information, refer them to colleagues who will be more positively inclined to their cause, and help them mediate disputes.[50] In all of these so-called "marginal behaviors," money may not be the sole factor or even the main one. Political support often is based on more than campaign contributions. For instance, the importance of lobbyists' reputations and relationships cannot be discounted.

On issues that are salient and visible, affect broad policy, involve ideology or principle, or divide the political parties, campaign contributions *per se* count for little. Too many other influences are more important. Take the health care package enacted by the Massachusetts legislature in 2006. Rep. Eric Turkington no doubt was on target explaining, "It's nothing about money." Campaign contributions certainly did not drive that process, not even in the details of the complex legislation. The advocacy groups who did not contribute to campaigns did more to shape the outcome than the business groups that contributed regularly. John E. McDonough, the executive director of the coalition of advocacy groups Health Care for All, was asked how his organization could compete with the business lobby that was trying to defeat a payroll tax. McDonough replied, tongue in cheek: "bake sales."[51] But Health Care for All did more than compete. It drove the issue, despite its absence from the fund-raising arena.

Political scientists who study Congress generally conclude that party, ideology, and state or district trump money. "All things being equal," writes Gary C. Jacobson, "members of Congress favor interests that help finance their campaigns. But all things are rarely equal."[52] Yet other congressional researchers find that campaign contributions do make a difference in roll-call voting under certain conditions: when the visibility of the issue is low; when the issue is narrow, specialized, or technical; when the issue is non-partisan or nonideological; when the public is indifferent, divided, or ignorant; and when no opposition exists.[53]

Many issues in a state legislature would meet one or several of the conditions specified above. Probably one-quarter to half or more of the bills introduced can be labeled as "special interest" legislation, and additional bills have special provisions that are of concern to one group or another. These are the issues where the decisions of legislators are most likely to be affected by money. A campaign contribution can make the difference where there is no obvious public interest and no discernable constituency interest, where the legislator's own values and beliefs do not come into play, and where the legislator's party has no position. Along these lines, the research of Justin Buchler and Matthew Jarvis demonstrates that "the less visible and salient a vote is, the greater the effect money has." These researchers explain that on highly visible and important votes, legislators cannot afford to sell their votes because of the danger of suffering electorally as a consequence.

On issues of little salience, campaign contributions may be linked to access, and access gives lobbyists time to talk to legislators and convince them to vote in their favor.[54] Alternatively, legislators (as shown in chapter 3) look to their political supporters for cues. Thus, on issues where nothing else is operative, they would likely pay more attention to the arguments made by contributors than by their opponents.

When other factors are not operative, campaign support is likely to count more. But only if a meritorious argument accompanies such support. Under similar circumstances, factors other than the monetary contribution might be ones swaying a legislator. Personal experience, the advice of a colleague on the standing committee to which a bill is referred, or a relationship with an individual lobbyist may affect one's vote.

Who Has How Much Power

Cigler and Loomis are among the leading scholars on the subject of interest groups at the national level. In their judgment it is difficult, if not impossible, to answer the question "Who has how much power?" They conclude that "The politics of organized interests is messy, frustrating, and fully integrated into our system of checks and balances. In that sense, there are few permanent victories and even fewer unassailable generalizations." In the end, they write, organized interests have their say on almost all issues. Yet they do not dominate the lawmaking process in Congress.[55] The same can be said for interest groups and lawmaking in the states.

A Case of Merchants and Merchandise

A single instance, of course, proves nothing. But well worth examining is a case in which the New Jersey Retail Merchants Association (NJRMA) sought, by means of law, to remedy a problem faced by some of its members a number of years ago. We can learn a lot about lobbying, interest groups, and the legislative process by reviewing just what happened here.[56]

NJRMA is an interest group with over two thousand retailer members. Its president was Melanie Willoughby, who commanded great respect as a lobbyist in New Jersey. One of her association's member companies was concerned that its cosmetic products were illegally ending up in flea markets around the state. A bill, requested by the New Jersey Food Council, had already been introduced. It would prohibit flea markets from selling baby food and nonprescription drugs that were subject to federal expiration-date requirements. Willoughby got the original bill amended to include cosmetics, and NJRMA became the principal lobbying force behind senate and assembly bills.

Willoughby argued in favor of the bill, as follows. Products that had been damaged or whose shelf life had expired were being sold at flea markets. Her retail members, however, were being asked to exchange items or refund money for defective items that had not been sold in their stores. Flea markets, it was suggested, had become a major outlet for the sale of merchandise like batteries, shampoo, cosmetics, or over-the-counter drugs that had been stolen from retailers. Some of these stolen products being sold at flea markets, if applied to the body or taken internally, posed a risk to consumers. No one testified against the bill, nor did any group oppose it in committee or on the floor of the senate and the assembly, where it passed by votes of 34-0 and 76-1. The governor signed it into law shortly thereafter.

If the test is success, then Willoughby and NJRMA certainly passed. Their bill was enacted. What should be apparent to the reader, however, is that there was no opposition. One might have expected flea market merchants to fight a bill that targeted them with regulations. What this case illustrates—at least to this point—is the following:

- An interest group that has standing in the state and an apparently meritorious case will find legislators willing to sponsor legislation that it is proposing.
- When no opposition arises, legislators and the legislature—on the basis of the merits as presented—will support an interest group (that is, if no budgetary or financial costs are incurred).
- Trust is an important component of the process. Willoughby trusts her members to identify problems and needs. Legislator sponsors trust NJRMA and Willoughby. Members of the legislature trust their colleagues, who sponsored the bill, and the committee that reviewed it.

The legislative process was not over, however. Shortly after the bill was signed, and only then, did the flea market merchants learn of the law's existence. They had not been organized as an interest group and had no lobbyist to monitor the legislature's actions. They simply did not know what had been going on. When they found out, the merchants reacted quickly. They called the offices of legislators around the state, including that of the speaker of the assembly, who had a large flea market in his own district. The *Asbury Park Press* took up the cause of the flea markets, portrayed the new law as anticompetitive, a restraint of trade, and orchestrated by special-interest groups.

The flea market vendors took action. They were pledged financial assistance by the owners of flea market properties. They hired a veteran lobbyist, Barry Lefkowitz, to get the law changed. Lefkowitz organized the vendors into a trade association; launched a campaign to educate the media and public; framed the issue as big business versus small, independent sellers; started a grassroots campaign; and hired an attorney to file a lawsuit against NJRMA for defamation and slander in publicly accusing flea market vendors of being thieves.

Vendors explained that the goods they were selling had not been stolen but purchased from liquidation sales held by large chain stores. NJRMA's consumer safety/quality assurance argument was challenged. Given the furor, the two legislator sponsors regretted having introduced the original bill. They sought to change the law they had gotten passed; and they did so by requiring all retailers, not only flea markets, to provide proof of purchase and by prohibiting the sale of expired over-the-counter drugs and baby food formulas by all retailers. The new bill, replacing the existing law, sailed through the legislature and was signed by the governor. The flea market merchants wound up giving the retail merchants a taste of their own medicine, regardless of whether it had expired or not.

One of Yogi Berra's frequently cited observations about life, "It's not over till it's over," doesn't really apply to the lawmaking process. Here, it is *never* over, not even after a law has gone into effect. It can always be repealed, amended, or superseded. Lawmaking is an ongoing process, and advocates and interest groups continue to struggle over what they believe is best for themselves and for the public.

The flea market vendors' reaction was late, yet still in time. Their efforts and the legislature's action suggest additional points about interest groups and lobbying:

- Interest groups require some presence at the capitol, in order to monitor legislation and identify that which might adversely affect them.
- Legislators do not welcome surprises; they prefer that opposition surfaces early.
- Most issues, especially those dealing with interest groups, have two sides and legislators try to be fair and work for balanced solutions.
- The merits of the case always play a part in the process; almost always there are merits on both sides.
- Weaker groups can prevail against stronger ones, depending on circumstances.
- On narrower, less salient, and low-visibility issues, legislators and their staffs do little analysis of their own but depend on opposing interests to make their case.
- No one is completely shut out, although depending on the situation, certain groups have an advantage.
- Opposition and conflict usually ensure that the process is "reasonably" fair (although it may never be "perfectly" fair, whatever that might mean).

The Power of Lobbyists

When the media accuse lobbyists of wielding enormous power, seldom is a denial heard. It is in the interest of lobbyists to be perceived by their clients and/or employers as being able to get done whatever needs to be done. So lobbyists are happy to admit to power. Some lobbyists have more power than others and in some states lobbyists seem to be more powerful than in others. Term limits may have enhanced the power of lobbyists in the fifteen states where legislators come and go more rapidly. Most observers in these states think that lobbyists have gained some power, because novice legislators have to rely more heavily on them for knowledge. However, the job in these places may be more difficult for lobbyists, because relationships have to be established with successive cohorts of legislators who are replacing those who have been termed out.[57]

Independent or contract lobbyists rely on their reputations and relationships, as well as their strategic skills and knowledge of the legislature and its members. They are most effective when the issues are such that values, constituencies, parties, and voters are not in play. On more significant issues, other factors weigh more heavily. But even here, lobbyists land punches—not haymakers, perhaps, but body blows in the clinches—they are the ones who help work out the details involved in compromises among interest groups.

Reputation and relationships, if not skill and knowledge, are of somewhat less importance to in-house lobbyists. Their employers—known in the lobbying trade as "principals"—count more than they do. Whereas legislators are more likely to attach a name to independent lobbyists, they are more likely to attach an organization's name to in-house lobbyists. The latter's influence is highly derivative—depending on the political, economic, and social significance of the organization they are representing and whose issue is in question.

The Power of Groups

The real questions to ask relate to the power of interest groups. Which groups have power? How much? These questions are easier to ask than to answer. As Sarah McCally Morehouse and Malcolm E. Jewell point out, any kind of measurement is virtually impossible. Not all groups are active on the same issues or in the same domains. Some groups get involved in many issues, others in only a few. Some groups are "potential" and do not have to act unless threatened. In any case, political circumstances change over time, benefiting the objectives of some groups while impeding the objectives of others. Finally, some groups are mainly defensive, trying to protect themselves, while others are on the offensive, trying to enact policies in a legislative system that confers an advantage to the defense.[58]

Despite difficulties, Clive S. Thomas and Ronald J. Hrebenar conducted a study that ranked interest groups in the fifty states. The rankings were done by observers in each state, so some variation in the standards used has to be expected. Teacher organizations, business organizations, utilities, attorneys, labor, doctors, insurance, manufacturers, health care, and bankers generally ranked in the top ten, while environmentalists and senior citizens ranked lower.[59]

Such a ranking suggests groups that tend to be regulated, including business and the professions, are continuously involved in the lawmaking processes at state capitols. Other groups—such as oil, tobacco, and pharmaceuticals—however visible nationally are not very visible in most of the states. Groups with limited goals, such as Mothers Against Drunk Driving, ordinarily are not perceived as powerful because of the narrow and focused nature of their efforts.

Not all interest groups are equal to one another, but generally they are competing in different domains. None dominate, none prevail on every issue they contest, and none are ascendant everywhere or for very long. Just how well each of them does, state by state, hinges on a number of factors:

1. *Group resources,* or its wherewithal to do the job. First, the *composition* of the group, that is the size of its membership and its dispersion across the state. If a member base can be mobilized for grassroots action, the group has a considerable advantage. Second, the group's *cohesion.* How unified are its members on the group's political objectives? Can the members be mobilized for grassroots issue activity and for election campaigns? Third, whether the group is part of a broader *coalition.* The breadth and strength of groups in combination matter a great deal. Fourth, a group's *conviction,* which relates to the intensity

of members' beliefs and their zealousness in pursuing group goals. Fifth, the *case* that the group makes on behalf of its legislative objectives. Sixth, the *cash* a group has at its disposal to fund lobbyists and grassroots as well as to contribute to political campaigns.[60]

2. *Group standing,* or how the group is regarded in the state. Only select groups have high standing with the public. Teachers are among them, and firefighters and nurses. Other groups, in particular business ones, have high standing with governmental elites, including legislators, because of their role in the economy and their ability to provide employment. How the group is regarded by the media is of particular importance. Citizen groups have a great advantage in being able to gain positive attention in the press, especially when they provide journalists with a David and Goliath–type of story.

3. *Group skill,* in terms of conducting direct and indirect lobbying, also weighs into the balance.

4. *Governmental control and representation* matter. When the Republicans control the legislature, business interests tend to breathe easier. When the Democrats control the legislature, organized labor and environmentalists feel more comfortable.[61] If a group has dependable allies within the legislature, especially legislators who also belong to the group, it is at a distinct advantage. Whether they are members or not, legislators ally with certain groups because of similar beliefs and mutual agreement on the issues. When allied, lobbyists and legislators work in tandem. The lobbyists provide information, analysis, justification, and intelligence, the legislators buttonhole their colleagues for votes. This is why most lobbyists tend to lobby their allies a lot—not to change their minds, but to assist them in achieving common objectives.[62]

5. *Circumstances* make a difference. The mood of the nation or state at the time can work in favor of or against a group's agenda. The state of the economy certainly affects how much a group can depend on getting from the budget. The timing involved in moving an issue along during the legislative session cannot be overlooked. Success may also hinge on what else is on the legislature's agenda.

6. *The nature of the issue* is as important as anything else. The disposition of an issue that is visible and important to many is by no means

the same as that of an issue that is below the radar and of concern to only a few people. If the public and its elected officials mobilize, even the strongest and wealthiest interest groups have to settle for much less than they want and think they deserve. As a Michigan lobbyist put it, "If the people are united on something, they get it. We have to get out of the way."[63] The lower the salience and visibility of an issue, the greater the influence of interest groups.

If an interest group's legislative objectives require an appropriation of state funds, the dynamic changes. Different groups and different causes compete for limited resources. Much lobbying occurs over budgets and taxes, normally resulting in incremental changes, rarely in big winnings or big losses for any group.

A group with little or no opposition is way ahead. If a group has an "issue niche," in which no other organized interests are active, it will have a great advantage.[64] Having the ground for themselves, because no one else has staked out a claim, is worth a lot in what is normally a struggle between and among groups. And having easily achievable objectives—that is, not asking for much—raises a group's batting average.[65]

When a group is unopposed and there is no direct cost to taxpayers, as has been suggested by the flea market merchants' case, the legislature's inclination is to say "yes." Legislators want to be of help, and the political rationale for doing so is compelling. It is explained by Mordecai Lee, a former member of the Wisconsin Legislature. In his estimation it is less campaign contributions than potential grassroots impact, even by small groups in large districts. On low-salience issues, if a legislator supports the group, then constituent members of the group will become active supporters of the legislator in the next election. Other voters would feel unaffected. If the legislator has opposed the position of the group, then constituent members of that group would actively support the legislator's opponent in the next election. Lee concludes:

> A small number of disgruntled constituents can have an inordinate impact of "poisoning the well" through the friends-and-neighbors effect. Yet, a comparable increase in active support from the rank-and-file citizens for supposedly standing up to a specific interest group, would not likely occur.[66]

The political logic of saying "yes" rather than "no" is inescapable.

Yet there are risks here. Suppose no opposing interest exists? The argument is made that it doesn't hurt anyone but helps a particular interest. If it is not a zero-sum game in which someone has to lose if someone else wins, why not? Many issues are probably uncontested. They are invisible to the public and to almost all the legislators.[67] Nonetheless, indulging a group may indirectly do damage to the broader, unorganized, unconcerned public. It is easy to imagine business interests seeking legislators to help them increase profits, although at the expense of consumers. Business certainly ought to be able to do so, but on such an issue it would be necessary to hear from consumers as well as business.

Where conflict exists, the issue is joined. The two sides may not be equal, but legislators are more likely to try to work out an equitable solution. With only one side, legislators can be negligent. They have too many major issues to settle, too many conflicts to resolve—so they don't look for more. It is not that an interest group dominates. None really does. It is just that, while one unopposed group may benefit, an unorganized public may pay the price. The price may not be high, but it is a price nevertheless.

The Legislature Decides

Interest groups are ubiquitous. The system has been called one of "hyper pluralism." Legislatures are certainly attentive to whatever interests come before them, but to say that interest groups dominate and legislatures simply obey would be way off the mark. Legislators themselves feel the power of special interests has been exaggerated in the media and by the public. In the 2002 Term Limits Survey of legislators throughout the nation, on a scale ranging from 1 (least influential) to 7 (most influential), only 12 percent of the respondents rated interest groups as either 6 or 7. On visible and salient issues, too many other factors are operating for any group to prevail without significant outside support. Legislators are the ones who decide. On less visible and less salient issues, groups often check and balance one another. On the narrowest and least visible issues, interest groups are likelier to get their way. But the losses others suffer tend to be small or to be absorbed by the community at large. Interest groups serve as channels of representation, as an integral part of a larger system—a governmental one that adjudicates disputes and allocates resources in a highly pluralistic society.

Notes

1. E. E. Schattschneider, *The Semi-Sovereign People* (New York: Holt, Rinehart and Winston, 1960), 134.

2. By contrast, involvement in a group that has members of similar backgrounds and viewpoints will promote quite different orientations. Allan J. Cigler and Mark Joslyn, "Groups, Social Capital, and Democratic Orientations," in *Interest Group Politics,* ed. Allan J. Cigler and Burdett A. Loomis, 6th ed. (Washington, D.C.: CQ Press, 2002), 41–42, 44, 46.

3. Virginia Gray and David Lowery, "Interest Representation in the States," in *American State and Local Politics: Directions for the 21st Century,* ed. Ronald B. Weber and Paul Brace (Chatham, N.J.: Chatham House, 1999), 245–246.

4. Jennifer Wolak, Adam J. Newmark, Todd McNoldy, David Lowery, and Virginia Gray, "Much of Politics Is Still Local: Multi-State Lobbying in State Interest Communities," *Legislative Studies Quarterly* 27 (November 2002): 540, 541, 550.

5. Paul J. Quirk and Sarah A. Binder, eds., *The Legislative Branch* (New York: Oxford University Press, 2005), 292.

6. Cigler and Joslyn, "Groups, Social Capital, and Democratic Orientations," 32.

7. Alan Greenblatt, "Real Power," *Governing* (June 2006), 48.

8. *New York Times,* July 7, 2005.

9. *New York Times,* February 28, 2007.

10. Information provided author by National Conference of State Legislatures.

11. Report by Massachusetts State House News Service during 2006 session.

12. Schattschneider, *The Semi-Sovereign People,* 119.

13. Jeffrey M. Berry, "Interest Groups and Gridlock," in *Interest Group Politics,* 6th ed., ed. Alan J. Cigler and Burdett A. Loomis (Washington, D.C.: CQ Press, 2002), 339–340.

14. Schattschneider, *The Semi-Sovereign People,* 43.

15. Greenblatt, "Real Power," 46.

16. Richard A. Smith, "Interest Group Influence in the U.S. Congress," *Legislative Studies Quarterly* 20 (February 1995): 114.

17. *New York Times,* January 24, 2006.

18. Karen Getman, "Artie Samish," *California Journal* (November 1999): 43.

19. Gray and Lowery, "Interest Representation in the States," 257.

20. Ralph Wright, *Inside the Statehouse* (Washington, D.C.: CQ Press, 2005), 143.

21. Alan Rosenthal, "The Effects of Legislative Ethics Law," in *Public Ethics and Governance: Standards and Practices in Comparative Perspective,* ed. Denis Saint-Martin and Fred Thompson (Oxford: Elsevier, 2006), 155–177.

22. Gray and Lowery, "Interest Representation in the States," 258.

23. Allan J. Cigler and Burdett A. Loomis, "Always Involved, Rarely Central," in Cigler and Loomis, *Interest Group Politics,* 382.

24. Lucy Morgan, "Money World," *St. Petersburg Times,* March 7, 2004.

25. Rep. Steve Sviggum, Civic Caucus, Minnesota, February 15, 2007.

26. Cigler and Loomis, "Always Involved, Rarely Central," 390.

27. Richard L. Hall and Alan Deardorff, "Lobbying as Legislative Subsidy," draft manuscript dated May 2, 2005.

28. Experienced lobbyists are well aware that legislators would prefer, if at all possible, not to anger either side in a dispute among interest groups.

29. Hall and Deardorff, "Lobbying as Legislative Subsidy."

30. Anthony J. Nownes, *Total Lobbying* (New York: Cambridge University Press, 2006), 206–207.

31. Malory Horne, quoted in Morgan, "Money World."

32. *New York Times,* May 15, 2005.

33. Beth L. Leech et al., "Organized Interests and Issue Definition in Policy Debates," in Cigler and Loomis, *Interest Group Politics,* 280.

34. Hall and Deardorff, "Lobbying as Legislative Subsidy."

35. Kenneth M. Goldstein, *Interest Groups, Lobbying, and Participation in America* (New York: Cambridge University Press, 1999).

36. These examples have been reported by the Massachusetts State House News Service.

37. Nownes, *Total Lobbying,* 92; also 74–80.

38. Massachusetts State House News Service, January–April 2006.

39. Todd Donovan, Shaun Bowler, David McCuan, and Ken Fernandez, "Contending Players and Strategies: Opposition Advantages in Initiative Campaigns," in *Citizens as Legislators: Direct Democracy in the United States,* ed. Shaun Bowler, Todd Donovan, and Caroline J. Tolbert (Columbus: Ohio State University Press, 1998), 101–103.

40. Joe Mathews, *The People's Machine: Arnold Schwarzenegger and the Rise of Blockbuster Democracy* (New York: Public Affairs, 2006), 90.

41. Ibid.

42. Elizabeth Gerber, *The Populist Paradox* (Princeton: Princeton University Press, 1999), 24.

43. John E. McDonough, *Experiencing Politics: A Legislator's Stories of Government and Health Care* (Berkeley: University of California Press, 2000).

44. One-third of New Jerseyans, in response to another question, thought that 50 percent or more of the legislators took bribes. Alan Rosenthal, *Drawing the Line: Legislative Ethics in the States* (Lincoln: University of Nebraska Press, 1996), 43, 117–118.

45. Hall and Deardorff, "Lobbying as Legislative Subsidy."

46. John French, a Florida lobbyist, as quoted by Lucy Morgan, "Money World."

47. Nownes, *Total Lobbying*, 81, 90–92.

48. Ibid., 80.

49. Quoted in Smith, "Interest Group Influence in the U.S. Congress," 95.

50. Legislators have many opportunities, besides voting, to be helpful or harmful to interest groups. Only a few of the ways legislators can behave are mentioned here.

51. Massachusetts State House News Service, March 1, 2006.

52. Gary C. Jacobson, "Modern Campaigns and Representation," in *The Legislative Branch*, ed. Quirk and Binder, 120.

53. See the review of research results in Smith, "Interest Group Influence in the U.S. Congress," 94–95.

54. Justin Buchler and Matthew Jarvis, "Reassessing the Impact of Campaign Contributions on Legislative Roll Call Votes: Electoral Danger and Issue Salience" (unpublished paper, no date), 21.

55. Cigler and Loomis, "Always Involved, Rarely Central," 390. See also Andrew McFarland, *Neopluralism: The Evolution of Political Process Theory* (Lawrence: University Press of Kansas, 2004).

56. The case, "Lobbying: A Case of Merchants and Merchandise," was written by Jennifer Crea and Alan Rosenthal (unpublished paper, May 2001).

57. Jennifer Drage Bowser, Keon S. Chi, and Thomas H. Little, *A Practical Guide to Term Limits: Final Report of the Joint Project on Term Limits* (Denver: National Conference of State Legislatures, July 2006), 10–11. See also Christopher Z. Mooney, "Lobbyists and Interest Groups," in *Institutional Change in American Politics: The Case of Term Limits,* ed. Karl T. Kurtz, Bruce Cain, and Richard G. Niemi (Ann Arbor: University of Michigan Press, 2007), 119–133.

58. Sarah McCally Morehouse and Malcolm E. Jewell, *State Politics, Parties, and Policy,* 2nd ed. (Lanham, M.D.: Rowan and Littlefield, 2003), 68.

59. Ronald J. Hrebenar, *Interest Group Politics* (Armonk, N.Y.: M. E. Sharpe, 1997).

60. In their study of congressional lobbying, Baumgartner and his colleagues found that group resources had no significant correlation with positive policy outcomes. Frank Baumgartner, Jeffrey Berry, Marie Hojhacki,

David Kimball, and Beth Leech, manuscript titled "Lobbying, Advocacy, and Democracy," 24.

61. Baumgartner et al., in "Lobbying, Advocacy, and Democracy," cite as most important in congressional lobbying the degree of support the group already has among policymakers.

62. Hall and Deardorff, "Lobbying as Legislative Subsidy."

63. Quoted in Gray and Lowery, "Interest Representation in the States," 265.

64. Frank R. Baumgartner and Beth L. Leech, "Interest Niches and Policy Bandwagons: Patterns of Interest Group Involvement in National Politics," *The Journal of Politics* 63 (November 2001): 1202.

65. Nownes, *Total Lobbying*, 95–100.

66. Mordecai Lee, "Political-Administrative Relations in State Government: A Legislative Perspective," *International Journal of Public Administration* 29 (2006): 1030.

67. Baumgartner and Leech, "Interest Niches and Policy Bandwagons," 1206.

6

On Legislative Terrain

LEGISLATURES ARE THE FIELDS on which legislators, constituencies, political parties, and interest groups wage contest. There are many features of legislative terrain, some that have already been mentioned, and others either too specific or too minor to be dealt with here. Among the most important features, which are the subject of this chapter, are the following. First, the professionalism and/or professionalization of legislators and legislative bodies. Here, the emphasis is on whether members are considered, and whether they consider themselves, to be amateurs or professionals and whether legislatures have more or less capacity to do their jobs. Second, organizational structure. The terms members serve and their turnover make a difference. So do the size and basic structure of the legislature. Probably as important as anything else organizationally, as far as lawmaking is concerned, are the standing committee systems by means of which labor is divided, specialization encouraged, and influence delegated. Third, the legislative culture and the ethical standards under which members operate. These factors are of increasing importance, not only to the process but also to how legislators and legislatures are regarded by the public at large.

Professionalism

Fifty years ago, only a few state legislatures could be thought of as professional bodies with full-time, professional members.[1] Practically all legislatures could be characterized as amateurish, with part-time citizen legislators as members. Political scientist Alexander Heard described the legislature of the mid-twentieth century as poorly organized; technically ill-equipped;

functioning with inadequate time, staff, and space; and operating with outmoded procedures and committee systems. "State legislatures," he summarized in a plea for reform, "may be our most extreme examples of institutional lag."[2]

Legislative Reform

In the 1960s the situation began to change and by the 1980s many legislatures had been transformed; nearly all felt the effects of a legislative modernization wave that had swept across the nation. Had it not been for generational change in members and the shift of representation away from rural to suburban areas, both of which resulted from the reapportionment decisions of the judiciary and the subsequent redistricting, legislative modernization might not have happened. The movement itself was a loosely articulated campaign involving legislative leaders, legislators, legislative staff, academics, and citizens. The legislative models the reformers had in mind were the U.S. Congress and the California Legislature, both of which possessed substantial institutional capacity.

Jesse Unruh, the speaker of the California Assembly, was the principal catalyst for legislative modernization, first in his home state and then in the rest of the country. He managed to increase the power of the legislature shortly after he became speaker; then in 1966 he spearheaded the drive to have Proposition 1A adopted by his state's voters. Its adoption led to a full-time legislature, with higher salaries and larger staffs. What happened initially in California spread elsewhere, as state legislatures began building the capacity (or the wherewithal) necessary to do the jobs of representing, lawmaking, and balancing the power of the executive.

Space had to be expanded, so that more room and additional facilities would be available for committees and individual members.

Sessions had to be structured in order to provide more time and more flexible time for lawmaking. In 1969 legislatures met annually in only half the states and biennially in the other half. By 1985, after the reform movement had pretty much run its course, they were meeting annually in forty-three states. Constitutional limitations that had restricted the length of regular sessions or the time legislatures could spend working in the interim period were removed in a number of states. Although legislatures have more time, as of 2008 a few states still meet biennially and sessions are still limited by constitutions in twenty-eight states and by statute in five others. Only twelve states have no limits whatsoever.

The *structure* of legislatures also needed streamlining in the view of the reformers. The size of houses in Connecticut, Ohio, Vermont, Massachusetts, and Rhode Island was reduced in order to achieve greater efficiency. Unicameralism was another structural feature that appealed to reformers, but that structural change went nowhere. Outside of Nebraska, which became unicameral in 1934, no other state has chosen to abolish one of its chambers.

Increasing legislator *salaries* was another feature of the modernization movement. It was believed that able people would not choose to serve, even on a part-time basis, if they had to make too much of a financial sacrifice. The problem was that in almost half the states circa 1970 compensation was set in the state constitution and could only be changed by a constitutional amendment, which required a public referendum. By the end of the twentieth century, however, only five state constitutions set salaries. Compensation in most places has risen over the years.

Staffing provided the single greatest boost to legislative capacity. Probably as much as anything else, professional staffing is the linchpin of the professional legislature. In its 1971 manifesto, which evaluated legislatures in all fifty states, the Citizens Conference on State Legislatures (CCSL) advocated the strengthening of staff support in thirty-eight states, committee staffing in thirty, staff for legislative leaders in thirty, and staff for rank and filers in thirty-three. Staff seemed to be the panacea for what ailed legislatures.[3] Until the 1960s professional staffs were small and removed from the hurly-burly of the legislature processes. But from 1968 to 1974, staffs grew by more than 100 percent.

Legislative Staffing

From 1979 to 1988 permanent staff in the fifty states increased from 16,930 to 24,555, or by approximately 50 percent. It grew by more than 10 percent from 1988 to 1996, to 27,822. After that staffing in state legislatures

Table 6-1 Size of State Legislative Permanent Staffs, 1979, 1988, 1996, 2003

State	1979	1988	1996	2003
Alabama	200	339	316	422
Alaska	116	251	237	307
Arizona	280	323	472	631
Arkansas	230	250	292	339
California	1,760	2,865	2,506	2,334
Colorado	173	189	213	209
Connecticut	225	400	446	393
Delaware	32	49	58	84
Florida	1,095	1,581	1,896	1,650
Georgia	275	466	511	603
Hawaii	150	151	256	170
Idaho	55	51	61	75
Illinois	984	1,066	969	905
Indiana	138	171	183	304
Iowa	93	163	180	172
Kansas	126	117	121	100
Kentucky	135	216	317	386
Louisiana	327	360	419	688
Maine	46	138	133	156
Maryland	328	447	505	850
Massachusetts	595	782	850	935
Michigan	1,047	1,287	1,359	1,153
Minnesota	420	602	638	602
Mississippi	130	124	132	150
Missouri	212	368	476	321
Montana	108	128	119	122
Nebraska	182	199	202	217
Nevada	85	115	170	230
New Hampshire	84	120	139	165
New Jersey	492	780	1,465	1,206
New Mexico	40	49	49	145
New York	1,600	3,580	3,461	3,077
North Carolina	90	118	168	290
North Dakota	26	31	31	32
Ohio	390	524	552	505
Oklahoma	101	171	260	302
Oregon	173	288	240	181

(Table continues)

Table 6-1 (continued)

State	1979	1988	1996	2003
Pennsylvania	1,430	1,984	2,682	2,947
Rhode Island	81	153	216	297
South Carolina	146	251	269	247
South Dakota	75	67	60	56
Tennessee	270	175	213	253
Texas	986	1,460	1,964	1,745
Utah	71	86	111	108
Vermont	34	34	35	52
Virginia	306	191	468	410
Washington	370	582	535	561
West Virginia	124	126	158	195
Wisconsin	476	568	691	756
Wyoming	18	19	18	29
Fifty state totals	16,930	24,555	27,822	28,067

Source: National Conference of State Legislatures, November 2003.

plateaued at 28,067 (or 34,903, if session-only staff is added to the permanent staff). The sizes of the staffs by state are shown in Table 6-1. The largest staffs are in New York, Pennsylvania, California, Texas, Florida, New Jersey, and Michigan, with one thousand to three thousand employees. The ratio of staffers to legislators is about twenty-one to one in California, sixteen to one in New York, and twelve to one in New Jersey. The smallest staffs are in Wyoming, North Dakota, Vermont, South Dakota, Idaho, and Delaware, with fewer than one hundred professionals employed. The ratio of staffers to legislators in Wyoming, Vermont, and North Dakota is 0.2 to 1.

Staffing patterns differ among the states. In every legislative chamber administrative staffs—including the clerk of the house, secretary of the senate, sergeant at arms, recording clerks, and doorkeepers—are responsible for the day-to-day functioning of the body. The house clerk and the senate secretary work directly for the presiding officers and are charged with administrative and housekeeping duties as well as the management of floor sessions. Beyond these staffs are the nonpartisan and partisan staffs. Generally, the smaller states with less professionalized legislatures depend on nonpartisan

Figure 6-1 The Partisan Composition of Legislative Staffs

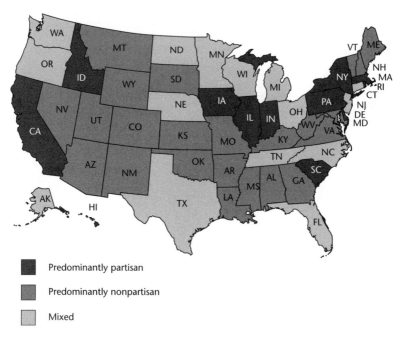

■ Predominantly partisan

■ Predominantly nonpartisan

□ Mixed

Source: National Conference of State Legislatures, November 2003.

Note: NCSL classifies New Jersey as "predominantly partisan," but it is more balanced.

staffs organized into legislative councils or legislative service agencies. Normally these staffs are centralized, with personnel having responsibility for bill-drafting, research, budget and fiscal analysis, and committee support. As Figure 6-1 shows, twenty-three legislatures are staffed entirely or predominantly on a nonpartisan basis. The largest states are not among them. Partisan staffing predominates in twelve states, including California, Illinois, Massachusetts, New York, and Pennsylvania. In these places Democratic and Republican professionals in each house are responsible for staffing committees and individual members, as well as handling research, communications, and constituency service tasks. The remaining fifteen states have mixed patterns, with partisan or caucus staffs sharing duties with centralized, nonpartisan agencies. Florida, Michigan, Minnesota, and New Jersey are examples here.

The major change in staffing since the 1980s has been the increasing role and influence of partisan staff. Connecticut, Florida, Minnesota, North Carolina, Texas, Washington, Wisconsin, New Jersey, and South Carolina all have witnessed the surge of Democratic and Republican staff serving members of their respective parties. This has led naturally to the expansion of partisan staffing. In turn, such staffing has resulted in more partisan stakes in issues and more of a division in legislative bodies along partisan lines. The relationship between partisan staffing and partisanship is a reciprocal one. Overall, the influence of partisan staff has been on the rise, while that of nonpartisan staff has not changed much. In a survey of legislative staff directors conducted by the National Conference of State Legislatures, 54 percent said that while the influence of partisan staff had increased, only 3 percent thought it had decreased, and 43 percent said it had stayed the same. The influence of nonpartisan staff had increased, according to 21 percent, decreased according to 23 percent, and stayed the same according to 56 percent.[4]

Professional and Citizen Bodies

While virtually all legislatures have become more professionalized, thanks to the capacity-building that took place from the 1960s to the 1980s,[5] some legislatures are clearly more professional than others. In recent years, political scientists have developed a series of measures of legislative professionalism, and have classified the states accordingly.[6] Generally, these measures have included items reflecting both organizational and individual capacity. On the organizational side, the more days in session and the larger the staff, the more professional the legislature is said to be. On the individual side, the higher the salaries of members, the more professional the legislature is said to be.[7]

Both the capacity of the institution and the characteristics of members contribute to the professionalism of legislatures. Professional, rather than amateur, legislators help professionalize the legislature. Institutions with substantial capacity encourage members to spend more time at the job and thus become more professional. Thus, the building of institutional capacity, which was designed in part to benefit members with better tools, also encouraged career politicians. That may not have been the intention, but by providing for annual sessions, offices, secretarial assistance, and professional staff, and by increasing salaries and benefits, modernization established conditions in which career legislators could thrive.

Since the 1960s the time demands on legislators have increased everywhere. Within any legislative body, some members put in more time, others less. Even in relatively nonprofessional legislatures, some members spend almost full time on their jobs. Still, as expected, full-time legislators are more likely to be found in the more professional legislatures. In places like California, New York, Pennsylvania, Wisconsin, Massachusetts, Illinois, and Michigan, most members spend virtually full time on their legislative jobs. By contrast, in the smaller states, such as Wyoming, North Dakota, and New Hampshire, members have dual employment. They spend roughly one-quarter to one-half time on their legislative duties (unless they are leaders, who normally spend more), and the rest of their working time on outside employment.

The overall trend has been for legislators in both the more- and the less-professional legislatures to spend greater amounts of time on their public jobs and less on their private ones. But unlike the U.S. Congress, no state legislature—not even California—precludes a member from earning outside income. From time to time, discussion takes place within a state to make the legislature full time, usually with the hope that eliminating outside employment will also remove the appearance of conflicts of interest by members. At the same time, in some places the discussion is about making the legislature less full time and more of a citizen body. An effort is underway in Michigan to make the legislature part time by amending the state constitution to limit time in session and reduce salaries. Gov. Arnold Schwarzenegger of California also favors more of a citizen legislature. Recognizing that a number of members of the legislature, especially those chairing committees, are gainfully occupied, he believes that too many other members sponsor bills because they have little else to do. As for them, Schwarzenegger suggests: "It's better if they just go and take care of business and then go back to work, whatever they do."[8] In other words, in the governor's opinion, they should spend more time at home.

Professional legislators can be defined not only by the amount of time they spend on their legislative duties, but also by their motivations to pursue careers in politics. Professionals normally want to remain in legislative office, or to move on to higher office. The rates of voluntary retirement from the legislature tend to be low in professionalized bodies, but considerably higher in citizen legislatures where the majority of members plan on only limited stints in politics before returning to outside careers. Over the years, in both professional and citizen legislatures careers in politics have appealed to large numbers of people. In just about every legislative body a hard core of careerists exists, and in the more professional bodies only a few members want to leave politics for other endeavors, if they can hang on.

Term Limits

Term limits have changed the opportunity structure for legislators, without necessarily changing the incentive system. Between 1990 and 2000, a total of twenty-one states adopted constitutional amendments or statutes limiting the number of terms legislators could serve in one or both houses of the legislature.[9] In nineteen of these states, electorates, who were essentially unhappy with their legislature and legislators, adopted term limits in referendums. In Utah the legislature preempted a referendum by passing its own version. In Louisiana, which does not have ballot initiatives, the legislature succumbed to public opinion and enacted term limits on its own. Since their adoption term limits have been struck down by state supreme courts in Massachusetts, Oregon, Washington, and Wyoming and been repealed by legislatures in Idaho and Utah. As of the beginning of 2008 term limits had taken effect in fourteen states and were due to have an impact in Nevada in 2010. The states and the most salient term-limits provisions are shown in Table 6-2. The limits of legislators' terms range from six in the California, Maine, and Michigan Houses to twelve in the Oklahoma, Louisiana, and Nevada Houses and Senates. In two-thirds of the chambers members are limited to eight years. Lifetime limits, which apply to both chambers in California, Arkansas, Michigan, Missouri, and Nevada, mean that individuals can serve terms in each body, but only once. They cannot sit out an election and then serve again. In Oklahoma individuals are entitled to a total of twelve years, either in one chamber or the

Table 6-2 State Legislative Term Limits

State	Year of impact	Year adopted	Lifetime or consecutive service	Limit in house (years)	Limit in senate (years)
California	1996	1990	Lifetime	6	8
Maine	1996	1993	Consecutive	8	8
Arkansas	1998	1992	Lifetime	6	8
Colorado	1998	1990	Consecutive	8	8
Michigan	1998	1992	Lifetime	6	8
Arizona	2000	1992	Consecutive	8	8
Florida	2000	1992	Consecutive	8	8
Missouri	2000	1992	Lifetime	8	8
Montana	2000	1992	Consecutive	8	8
Ohio	2000	1992	Consecutive	8	8
South Dakota	2000	1992	Consecutive	8	8
Oklahoma	2004	1990	Lifetime	12 (total)	12 (total)
Nebraska	2006	2000	Consecutive	n/a	8
Louisiana	2007	1995	Consecutive	12	12
Nevada	2010	1996	Lifetime	12	12

Source: Adapted from Thad Kousser, *Term Limits and the Dismantling of State Legislative Professionalism* (Cambridge: Cambridge University Press, 2004), 12.

other or a combination. The limits in Maine, Colorado, Arizona, Florida, Montana, Ohio, South Dakota, Nebraska, and Louisiana are more lenient. Legislators whose terms expire can wait a specified period and then serve again. They just cannot serve consecutive terms in the same house.

In non-term-limited legislatures members have an easier time pursuing careers in public office. They may opt to run for a congressional seat and the full-time service that goes with it, or for statewide elected office and ascend the ladder to the governorship. They can wait for an opportunity to arise, remaining in the legislature until one does and as long as they can win reelection. In legislatures with lifetime limits, careers in the legislature tend to be finite, ranging from no longer than twelve years in Oklahoma to no longer than twenty-four years in Nevada. Generally speaking, term limits have not deterred individuals with political experience and political ambition from running for the legislature, no matter how uncertain the future. They simply get to the legislature and then start worrying about where they can go next.

Legislative Turnover

Even if incentives are not terribly different as a result of term limits, the turnover of members in each legislative chamber is. Turnover rates depend, at least in part, on the frequency of elections. Legislators in forty-five houses and twelve senates run for two-year terms. Legislators in five houses and thirty-eight senates run for four-year terms. (In Illinois and New Jersey, senators have one two-year and two four-year terms, in order to accommodate redistricting schedules.)

In the 1960s turnover was relatively high for both senates and houses, but it diminished in the 1970s and 1980s, only to increase slightly in the 1990s. Trends in legislator turnover are shown in Figure 6-2. By 2003 turnover nationally had inched up to 26.3 percent and from 2000–2006, according to Gary Moncrief, averaged 22 percent in senates and 25 percent in houses. Turnover rates in the ten house chambers where term limits had gone into effect increased by an average of 11.5 percent from 1991–2000, as compared to 1981–1990. Right after term limits take effect, turnover is extremely high. For example, term limits in Louisiana impacted incumbent legislators in 2007. Almost half were termed out. The result was that a majority of members in the 2008 Louisiana House were freshmen. After term limits have gone into effect, turnover rates tend to decline and stabilize. But they are still higher than in non-term-limited states. During 1991–2000, turnover in houses was 30.8 percent in term-limited states, as compared to 22.3 percent in non-term-limited states. In senates it was 25.9 percent in the term-limited states and 22.3 percent in the non-term-limited states.[10]

If we look at the houses alone, during 1991–2000, of the eight-highest turnover legislatures (ranging from 34 to 51 percent), five are in term-limited states (Arizona, California, Maine, South Dakota, and Montana). New Hampshire's turnover is traditionally high and has not changed much, while Maryland's high turnover reflects the four-year term of house members. During the same period, the lowest turnover in houses, ranging from 11 to 18 percent, occurred in four of the more professionalized legislatures (New York, Pennsylvania, Texas, and Wisconsin), as well as four others (Delaware, Indiana, Tennessee, and Virginia).[11]

Figure 6-2 Membership Turnover, 1960s–2006 (in percentages)

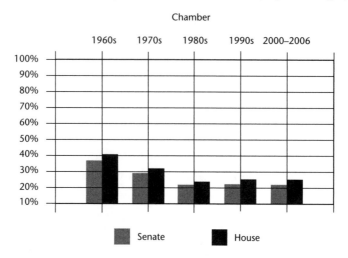

Chamber

Senate   House

Source: Gary F. Moncrief, Richard G. Niemi, and Lynda W. Powell, "Time, Term Limits and Turnover: Trends in Membership Stability in U.S. State Legislatures," *Legislative Studies Quarterly 29* (August 2004): 366.

Note: Data for 2000–2006 provided by Gary Moncrief.

Higher turnover has resulted in fewer experienced members in term-limited states. When senators leave, they are likely to be replaced by house members. This is because the senate is considered a step up politically, while the house is a step down. The 2002 State Legislative Survey, for instance, found that 27.7 percent of house members said that they would run for the senate after their service in the house ended, while only 4 percent of senate members were interested in running for the house. So inexperience is more of a problem for houses than for senates. Very few term-limited house members have many years under their belts at any given time. Colorado is an example. Of the sixty-five members of the house, by 2003–2004 only eight had six or more years of experience, as compared to twenty-three in 1993–1994, before term limits took effect.[12]

How Legislatures Rank Professionally

On the basis of a combination of institutional and individual elements, legislatures can be classed roughly into categories of professionalism. Peverill

Table 6-3 State Legislative Professionalism

Most professional		↔	Least professional	
California	Arizona	Missouri	Rhode Island	Maine
New York	Alaska	Iowa	Virginia	Montana
Wisconsin	Hawaii	Minnesota	Louisiana	Alabama
Massachusetts	Florida	Nebraska	Kansas	Utah
Michigan	Colorado	Oregon	West Virginia	South Dakota
Pennsylvania	Texas	Delaware	South Carolina	Wyoming
Ohio	North Carolina	Kentucky	Georgia	North Dakota
Illinois	Washington	Vermont	Tennessee	New Hampshire
New Jersey	Maryland	Idaho	New Mexico	
	Connecticut	Nevada	Mississippi	
	Oklahoma		Arkansas	
			Indiana	

Source: Peverill Squire, "Measuring State Legislative Professionalism," *State Politics and Policy Quarterly* 7 (Summer 2007): 211–227.

Squire has used legislator pay, number of days in session, and staff per legislator (as compared to the same characteristics for Congress) to score the fifty legislatures on professionalism. Instead of reporting scores or rankings, here the states are grouped in Table 6-3 on a continuum from most to least professional. The most professional legislatures, as would be expected, are in the larger states, with California, New York, and Wisconsin at the top. The next most professional grouping includes a variety of states, including Florida, Colorado, Texas, Maryland, and Connecticut. At the other end of the continuum are New Hampshire, North Dakota, Wyoming, and several others. Another dozen states are positioned next to the least professional extreme.

Organization

Legislatures throughout the states appear to be essentially alike—they constitute one of the three major branches of government, they provide representation to citizens and groups, and they make laws. But they differ in how they do all this organizationally.

Not all of these institutions are officially called "legislature." Twenty-seven are, but nineteen others are titled "general assembly," two "legislative assembly," and two "general court." Except for one, every state has a bicameral legislature. Each has a senate, forty-one have a "house of representatives," four an "assembly," one a "general assembly," and three a "house of delegates."

House and Senate

Nebraska takes great pride in its unicameral system. It is unique among the American states, although in the eighteenth century Georgia, Pennsylvania, and Vermont also had unicameral legislatures. Nebraska holds itself out as a model for other states but is unlike its counterparts in a number of key respects. The legislature is nonpartisan, and its members run for seats without Democratic or Republican designations. It is a relatively small body, with only forty-nine members. And perhaps as important as anything else, the system is highly individualistic, with a tradition of weak leadership.

Unicameral legislatures have been considered by other states, and not too long ago in California. The arguments in favor of one rather than two chambers keep cropping up. First, unicameralism would allow the state to economize by eliminating elected legislators and saving on salaries. Second, it would enable legislation to be considered more expeditiously and result in fewer bills being introduced and even fewer being lost between one chamber and the other. Third, it would fix responsibility on a single chamber, which would eliminate the buck-passing in which the two chambers sometimes indulge.

Finally, proponents argue, no longer do the two chambers provide different perspectives. Before the "one-man, one-vote" ruling of the U.S. Supreme Court, legislatures, and especially senates, were malapportioned. While houses tended to represent people, if inaccurately, senates tended to represent geographical units, such as counties. The system in the states then resembled the system at the national level, where the U.S. Senate represents the states. With reapportionment reform, both chambers in the states today represent people and not geography. Thus, a system of dual representation is no longer necessary.

Two houses may no longer be required for effective representation, but bicameralism serves other purposes. It probably retards the pace and volume of lawmaking, at least to some extent. That was one of James Madison's justifications for a bicameral Congress, as stated in *Federalist* No. 62. It was understood that it would be more difficult to reach consensus within each chamber and between the two than in one chamber alone. This would appear to be the case in contemporary legislatures. Yet the opposite has been suggested; that is, when both chambers are originators, as well as vetoers, it is possible that a bicameral structure will actively produce more, rather than fewer, laws.[13]

Houses and senates, despite representing similar populations, are very different from one another. Houses are larger than senates, normally with two or three times as many members. Usually house districts are smaller than senate districts. The cultures of the two bodies are very different. As described by the biographer of an Illinois Senate leader, the two chambers resemble communities on opposite sides of the train tracks. The senate is in the section of town with big homes. The house is in the section with smaller homes, and cannot match the "genteel image" and "aristocratic tenor" of the senate.[14] The leaders and the members of the two chambers differ in their agendas, and the chambers adhere to different norms and rules. Most important, in practically every state the senate and house are rivals and, on occasion, even adversaries. Take Georgia, for example. The competition between the two bodies is regarded as "natural" and "inborn." It intensifies when the speaker of the house and the president of the senate (in this case, lieutenant governor of the state) do not get along. Tom Murphy, the speaker, and Zell Miller, the lieutenant governor, had one of the longest and most public feuds in capitol history, thereby keeping the house and senate at loggerheads.[15] Indeed, the divide between the chambers may be greater than that between the parties. There is no question whatsoever that senate and house, regardless of party, look at the same issues through different lenses. It is hardly surprising that they come to different conclusions.

It is almost impossible to think of senates and houses that are in sync with one another. In California, Florida, Ohio, Georgia, Minnesota, and Maryland, for example, the two chambers operate on separate tracks. They seldom get together, except to resolve differences and to negotiate over senate bills stalled in the house and house bills stalled in the senate.

Massachusetts nicely illustrates the difference two chambers make. Here, Democrats have large majorities in both. All committees, other than Ways and Means, are organized jointly, with senators and representatives hearing and deciding on bills together. Joint committees are designed to facilitate building senate and house concurrence early in the process. And on many issues, no doubt they do. But on big-ticket items the two chambers seem to follow separate paths. Divergent initiatives have to be reconciled in a conference committee or included in or amended onto omnibus bills like the budget. Each chamber has its institutional ego and jockeys to prevail over the other. The two presiding officers, even if from the same area of the state and the same ethnic background, tend to be rivals.

Two houses make it more difficult for consensus to be built, and encourage contrasting perspectives, additional study and deliberation, and further compromise. Both substantively and politically, bicameralism would appear to improve the legislation that does get enacted. At the same time, it frustrates advocates who can amass support in one house but not the other, and it disadvantages legislation that gets caught up in interchamber rivalry. Whether a legislature has one chamber of two does matter. On the one hand, those who are inclined to want more bills passed and more laws enacted probably would benefit with the hurdles in one chamber only. On the other hand, those who want to put obstacles in the way of enactment and stress more by way of deliberation, negotiation, and consensus-building are probably better off under the status quo.

Size

The size of legislative bodies varies considerably among the fifty states. Senate and house memberships, as well as total numbers of legislators per state, are shown in Table 6-4. At one extreme, ten states have senates with 50 or more members, with Minnesota's 67-member senate the largest, New York's 62 members second, and Illinois' 59 third. At the other extreme, the smallest senates are in Alaska with 20 members, Delaware and Nevada with 21, and New Hampshire with 24. In every state the house is larger than the senate—two or three times the size or more. The largest house by far is the 400-member body in New Hampshire. Following it are eight houses with 150 or more members, led by Pennsylvania with 203, Georgia with 180, and Massachusetts with 160. At the smaller end of the house continuum are Alaska's 40 members, Delaware's 41 members, Nevada's 42, and Hawaii's 51. Overall, then, the most

Table 6-4 Size of Legislatures, Number of Members

State	Senate seats	House seats	Total
Alabama	35	105	140
Alaska	20	40	60
Arizona	30	60	90
Arkansas	35	100	135
California	40	80	120
Colorado	35	65	100
Connecticut	36	151	187
Delaware	21	41	62
Florida	40	120	160
Georgia	56	180	236
Hawaii	25	51	76
Idaho	35	70	105
Illinois	59	118	177
Indiana	50	100	150
Iowa	50	100	150
Kansas	40	125	165
Kentucky	38	100	138
Louisiana	39	105	144
Maine	35	151	186
Maryland	47	141	188
Massachusetts	40	160	200
Michigan	38	110	148
Minnesota	67	134	201
Mississippi	52	122	174
Missouri	34	163	197
Montana	50	100	150
Nebraska	49	NA	49
Nevada	21	42	63
New Hampshire	24	400	424
New Jersey	40	80	120
New Mexico	42	70	112
New York	62	150	212
North Carolina	50	120	170
North Dakota	49	98	147
Ohio	33	99	132
Oklahoma	48	101	149
Oregon	30	60	90
Pennsylvania	50	203	253

(Table continues)

Table 6-4 (continued)

State	Senates	Houses	Total
Rhode Island	50	100	150
South Carolina	46	124	170
South Dakota	35	70	105
Tennessee	33	99	132
Texas	31	150	181
Utah	29	75	104
Vermont	30	150	180
Virginia	40	100	140
Washington	49	98	147
West Virginia	34	100	134
Wisconsin	33	99	132
Wyoming	30	60	90

legislators are found in New Hampshire with 424, Pennsylvania with 253, Georgia with 236, New York with 211, and Minnesota with 201. The fewest are found in Alaska with 60, Delaware with 62, and Nevada with 63.

Over the past half century, the trend has been to reduce the size of legislatures, in an effort to streamline operations and reduce costs. Reformers and citizens alike have supported reductions in size, while most incumbent legislators, fearful of losing their seats, have opposed them. It is impossible to specify an optimum size for a legislative body, but larger ones appear to have advantages over smaller ones. The main advantage is having more members to do the work of the legislature. In just about every legislative body labor is divided, largely according to the interests members have and the assignments they take. First, and of utmost importance everywhere, labor is divided between the majority and minority parties. Especially in competitive states and more so in houses than senates, majority party roles are the critical ones. Second, labor is divided into leadership and rank-and-file roles, with elected leaders and members of leadership teams having special responsibilities. Third, labor is divided among standing committees, each of which has broader or narrower subject-matter jurisdiction.

Every legislative body has multiple tasks. The larger the membership of the body, the more people available to do the work. Take as a hypothetical example a relatively small legislative body, one with forty members. (There are thirty-one senates and one house that are as small or smaller.) Assume that the legislature is organized along party lines, that the parties matter, and that the majority party has twenty-four members. Assume also that roughly half the members of any legislative body are hard working and skilled, while the other half are not qualified for leadership roles. That would mean that in the legislative body under examination here, only twelve members would be available for the most challenging tasks. A few of them would have to be in top leadership positions, leaving the remainder to be distributed among the majority party ranks on the standing committees. Thus, only eight or nine members would be available for six or more standing committees with responsibility for revenue and appropriations, education, health, human services, judiciary, corrections, economic matters, and the like. These members would have to be spread exceedingly thin. If we take as an example a large legislative body, with 120 members (seventeen houses have 120 or more members), then the availability of members for leadership and specialization is much greater. Assume that the majority party has seventy members and that half of them are outstanding legislators. That leaves thirty-five members, of whom four or five will have party leadership positions and another thirty will be spread among the committees to take the lead on the study, deliberation, and negotiation of many policy issues. In a large legislature, there is simply more labor, and more skilled labor to be divided among a myriad of tasks that have to be accomplished.

Size has other consequences as well. Generally speaking, large bodies are more tightly organized, mainly because they have to be if things are to get done. Small bodies generally are more loosely organized and more collegial, with individuals acting autonomously, relying less on party or committee leadership. State senates, which are on the small side, are very different organizations from state houses, which are on the large side. From the point of view of an individual member, the smaller the better. In a small body, a member can have close relationships with each of his or her colleagues and has to win over only a manageable number of them in order to obtain the majority needed for passing a bill (or defeating one). The individual legislator under such circumstances has greater influence than the individual in a larger, more tightly organized body.

Committees

A senate or a house conducts its business, which mainly relates to the screening of bills and the making of laws, through various structures. One such structure is the legislative leadership or leadership team on the majority side and, of lesser significance, leadership on the minority side. Leadership will be discussed at length in chapter 7. Another structure is the conference committee system (if one exists) that is charged with resolving differences between bills passed by the two houses. Still another is the floor of the senate or the house, where the entire membership votes on second and third readings of bills and on conference committee reports. Floor sessions and conference committees will be touched on in chapters on lawmaking. Caucuses contribute still another structure, and an increasingly important one in many states. Nearly every chamber has active party caucuses. The exceptions are both the houses in Arkansas, Mississippi, Texas, and Louisiana, and the senates in Alabama and South Carolina. Majority party caucuses often have the last say as to what gets to the floor and what gets passed.

For now, we intend to examine the committee systems in legislatures. In every state except Connecticut, Maine, and Massachusetts, senates and houses have their own separate committee structures. In a few places senate and house committees are separate, but the budget or appropriations committees are joint. That is, both senators and representatives are members of the same committees. In Connecticut, Maine, and Massachusetts, the standing committees are joint senate–house units (although in Massachusetts budget and appropriations are handled by separate committees in each house). Otherwise, it is standard for the senate and house each to have its own committee system, with each committee having its own jurisdictional area. Sometimes the senate and house committees duplicate one another in jurisdictions, with judiciary, education, higher education, revenue, appropriations, and other committees having parallel responsibilities in the house and senate. Sometimes the jurisdictions are drawn differently for committees in the two bodies.

The structure varies by the number of committees in each chamber. Senates in Delaware, Georgia, Mississippi, Missouri, and New York have twenty-five or more standing committees. By contrast, senates in Alaska,

Maryland, Nevada, New Mexico, and Oregon have fewer than ten. On the house side, twenty-five or more standing committees exist in California, Delaware, Georgia, Illinois, Minnesota, Mississippi, Missouri, New York, North Carolina, Oklahoma, Pennsylvania, Texas, and Wisconsin. The Missouri House has forty-two. By contrast, only Alaska and Maryland have fewer than ten. The number of members on each committee depends on three factors: first, the number of committees; second, the number of legislators in the body; and third, the number of committee assignments for each legislator. On average, legislators have about three assignments each, although in twenty-five chambers they have only one or two.[16] Senators normally have three, four, or five assignments each, while house members usually have two or three. The size of standing committees varies enormously among chambers, with thirty or so members on Maryland's house committees but only five on most of New Jersey's committees.

With a large number of committees, more members can be awarded leadership positions as chairs. In some places every returning majority party member has a chair, which often entitles the legislator to additional compensation. A large number of committees also allows for a greater division of legislator labor and greater specialization. A relatively small number of committees tends to ensure that each legislator will be on a committee that has a substantial workload, and not on one that has only a few bills referred to it. In Maryland, for example, all four senate and six house committees have important jurisdictions and sizeable workloads. In other states a number of committees are "letterhead" committees only, with little to do. Legislators prefer not to be assigned to them.

Ralph Wright, the former speaker of the Vermont House, describes the prestige-ranking of the fourteen standing committees in his chamber. At the top were the appropriations and tax committees, then came health and welfare, natural resources, education, and several others. The least prestigious and least appealing assignments were to municipal elections, agriculture, and fish and wildlife. The latter, according to Wright, "was dreaded by all but those few native-Vermonter members who appeared each snowy morning wearing their fishing license on their caps-with-earmuffs." For the rest of the legislators, an assignment to the Fish and Wildlife Committee "was equal to boarding a ship to Devil's Island." Even worse, if that were possible, was the

General and Military Committee, referred to as the "landfill" committee—a dumping ground for members who didn't get along with their colleagues or with the house leadership.[17]

A relatively small number of committees generally leads to a more equitable division of labor. While fewer leadership appointments are available (unless the standing committees are further divided into subcommittees, which is sometimes the case), workloads for each committee tend to be about the same and the prestige-rankings among committees narrower. Fewer committees normally mean more members per committee, and the larger the committee in membership, the more reflective it can be of the chamber membership at large. Other things being equal, the more reflective of the chamber, the more likely its recommendations will prevail on the floor.

State legislatures differ widely in how their committees are organized. The two chambers differ, and often the number and jurisdictions of committees change when partisan control switches or when new leaders take charge. There are many reasons for differences—too many, as one political scientist writes, "for any single theoretical explanation of committee organization to explain all committee organization."[18] The only sure thing is, "As an army marches on its stomach, so a legislature stands on its committees."[19] It is in the committee that much of the substantive study, analysis, and deliberation of the legislature takes place. It is here that bills are reviewed, citizens heard, budgets examined, appropriations determined, policies proposed—and along the way programs and agencies get some oversight.

Members themselves recognize the importance of working on a committee. In the 2002 State Legislative Survey, legislators were asked to indicate how important they felt their work on a committee was—ranging from 5 or 4 ("very important") to 0 or 1 ("not very important"). Nearly four out of five legislators rated the committee aspect of their job as "very important." Only three out of five rated listening to debate on the floor of similar consequence.

Just how significant committees are varies among legislative bodies. In an exploration years ago, Wayne L. Francis made a distinction between legislatures with committee-oriented decision making and with party-oriented decision making. Where committees are weak, he found, the leadership pursues its objectives through the party caucus. In many states both the caucus and committee shared decision-making power.[20] A similar distinction remains useful today.

Relatively weak committee systems persist in some states. Illinois is an example. Here, standing committees do little by way of screening of bills, and their recommendations carry little weight with nonmembers. Leadership on the committees changes frequently. Party leaders and party caucuses exert control.[21] By contrast, in most states committees are the key agencies in the lawmaking process. On major issues, such as the budget and gubernatorial policy priorities, legislative leaders negotiate the parameters, but committees still hash over the details. Bruce E. Cain and Thad Kousser describe the committees that existed in California as not quite as powerful or as specialized as those in the U.S. Congress, but still "the primary policy-making venues in Sacramento." They write, "Committees make themselves central to the process by examining legislation, screening out unpopular bills, altering others, and framing the debate through their analyses of anything they allow to progress to the next stage."[22]

It is at committee hearings that sponsors, the witnesses for and against a bill, and neutral experts testify. The arguments are made, data presented, and questions of legislators addressed. Nowhere are the merits more forcefully presented than in budget hearings, where advocacy groups, among others, compete for limited dollars. For example, in New Jersey's 2007–2008 budget hearings, about seventy-five groups testified. Ranging from the Cancer Institute of New Jersey and the Friends of the Monmouth Battlefield to the Association of Mental Health Agencies and the Anti-Poverty Network of New Jersey, each group pleaded the importance of its cause and why it required a particular level of funding.

If the committee system is strong, most of the work is done before the bill reaches the caucus or gets to the floor. Committees screen some bills and craft others. Here is where much of the deliberation over issues takes place, especially that over policy considerations (but also political considerations, if the committee wants to succeed).[23] The joint committees in Massachusetts, for instance, play a large role in shaping what comes out. In 2005–2006 about fifty bills on identity theft were introduced and referred to the Consumer Protection and Professional Licensure Committee. Consumer groups, business, hospitals, and financial institutions were all involved. The committee referred the problem to a subcommittee, which it formed especially for the purpose of coming up with a committee bill. The subcommittee took thirty of the referred bills, worked them over, consulted with the concerned groups, and got them to sign off on legislation it drafted. The committee accepted its subcommittee's work on identity theft and reported out an omnibus bill for the senate and house to consider.[24]

Even a proposal introduced by a legislative leader has to run the committee gauntlet in Massachusetts. Robert Travaglini, the senate president, was a vigorous sponsor of a family leave bill. But he acknowledged to the press that his bill was subject to change in the course of the committee process. "I understand, very rarely do you submit a proposal of a piece of legislation and have it go through the process and it emerges unchanged," he told reporters. "I mean I don't live in a cave. I've been through the exercise hundreds of times and acknowledge that negotiations are part of the process, so I'm willing to leave that up to the discretion of the committees."[25]

If committees have experienced members, if they specialize, and if they work hard, then they tend to have substantial influence. That is because they "develop solid reputations for knowing what they are doing" and thus are deferred to by the chamber.[26] Moreover, the less important a bill to the press, the public, and the legislators themselves, the more controlling a committee recommendation will be. Leonard Lance, a Republican member of the New Jersey Senate, explains how members individually defer to committees. Legislators cannot be experts on everything, but they develop expertise through the committee structure. "I seek the advice of those who serve on the health committee on health care issues," he said. "I seek the advice of those who serve on the insurance committee on insurance issues."[27] If committees are representative of the larger body, recommendations have a better chance of being accepted. And if committees manage to develop consensus on an issue internally, their chances are excellent. Wright comments on committees in the Vermont House, noting that no matter what the issue and however complicated, the first thing legislators would look for on a bill would be the last line—how the committee voted. If a bill reported by a committee had a vote of 11-0, 10-1, 9-2, or even 8-3, it would have very good or good prospects. If a bill emerged with a 7-4 or 6-5 majority, its future on the floor would be precarious because "it would be recognized by the full membership as controversial."[28]

Committees vary in the discretion they have over bills referred to them. In twenty-two chambers committees must hear all bills, although a "hearing" need not be lengthy. The bill has to be scheduled; it cannot be buried by the committee chair. In the other seventy-seven chambers the chair determines whether or not a bill will be heard. Committees are required to report out all bills that are referred to them in eighteen chambers, with a variety of reporting recommendations, including "that it pass," "that it do not pass," "that it be postponed indefinitely," "that it be referred to interim study," and "that it be referred to another committee." Committees in the other eighty-one chambers can let a bill die in committee instead of reporting it to the floor of the legislature.[29]

Ordinarily committees do not report bills with negative recommendations, unless the chamber requires that all bills be reported. Maine, with its joint committees, is an exception. Here all bills are reported out, including almost half with unfavorable reports.[30] The problem in a number of places is that the norm of reciprocity has a strong influence on committee behavior. Committee members tend to defer to bill sponsors and report favorably the large majority of bills that are referred. They are reluctant to alienate colleagues whose votes they will need on other issues. So let the other body kill the bill; then the blame is farther away from home.

Committees have a number of ways in which to effectively bury bills on their own. Only rarely are bills pried out of a committee that is sitting on them. As for bills committees recommend favorably, they can be defeated or amended on the floor of the senate or house. But where the committee system is supported by the leadership and respected by the membership, such occurrences are rare. In Oregon, for instance, committee bills cannot even be amended on the floor, just voted up or down. In the Arkansas House, whenever a bill is amended on the floor, it is referred back to the committee as a new bill. In Maryland, leaders encourage members to support committee recommendations, so only on rare occasions does a committee suffer defeat, or even amendment, on the floor. By overturning or substantially amending on the floor, the chamber is sending a message that the committee did not do its job very well.[31]

Massachusetts, under the leadership of Senate President Travaglini and House Speaker Salvatore DeMasi, is different than most other places. Here anything can happen on the floor, and often does. However representative, expert, and hardworking the committees, it is not uncommon for their products to be rejected or reformed on the floor of the senate or house. In most chambers, by contrast, leaders do not bring an important measure to the floor until they believe they have the votes to pass it.

When one talks about standing committees, primary reference is really to the committee chairs. For all intents and purposes, the chair runs the committee. Some chairs do it more autocratically, some less. Some can count on other members to go along, some have to persuade them to. But the chair is the critical actor at this stage of the lawmaking process. A chair requires member support for what he or she wants to do on the positive side, and can usually negotiate the support necessary. On the negative side, a chair normally can deep-six a bill he or she opposes. Few members will object and even fewer will take on their chair in an all-out fight. The understanding is that if they want their own bills to move, members had better stay on the right side of the chair. The chair's principal and almost universal power is control over the committee agenda.[32] "In the legislature," one member commented, "there aren't that many jobs that are better than being a committee chair...."[33]

The job is not what it used to be in states that have term limits. Chairs in these states are lame ducks from the time of their appointment. They have less experience and higher turnover. So do committee members. Thus, committees no longer are expert in a policy domain; in term-limited states they exhibit a "knowledge deficit."[34] Bruce Cain, Thad Kousser, and Karl T. Kurtz have examined the effects of term limits on committee operations in California. They find that committees in both the senate and assembly screen out fewer bills than they did before term limits were in place. Whereas 26.6 percent of the bills used to fail in assembly committees before term limits, afterward only 18.2 percent failed. And whereas 21.0 percent used to fail in senate committees before, now only 14.8 percent do.[35]

In term-limited legislatures, committee members give little deference to their chairs, who are not likely to have greater experience or expertise than the rank and file. And senators and representatives give little deference to committees that, although they can claim jurisdiction, cannot claim specialized knowledge.[36] Legislators have less confidence in standing committees in California and Colorado; their recommendations are ignored on the floor. A former member in Maine concluded, "committee reports do not mean anything anymore."[37]

While the influence of committees has decreased in term-limited states, that of the majority party caucus has increased. Ohio is an example. Since committees have little substantive expertise, majority party legislators look to the majority party caucus for their cues. Since the caucus examines proposals from a partisan perspective, decisions tend to be made more on a political than a substantive basis. However partisan a legislative body, decisions on most issues in most committees are made mainly on a substantive rather than a political basis. Thus, term limits, by weakening committees, have reinforced the partisan forces in state legislatures, while undermining the nonpartisan ones. This is ironic, because proponents of term limits never would have intended such a consequence.

Ethics

In the 1960s legislators did not have to pay much attention to the propriety of their behavior. Outside of statutes prohibiting bribery and extortion, ethical standards were seldom explicit. Lobbyists wined and dined legislators after a session day and took them on hunting and fishing trips in the periods between sessions. In some states lobbyists had free access to leadership suites, where they could use the telephone and run their operations. None of the members, most of whom earned income from jobs on the outside, thought much about conflicts of interest; they certainly were not concerned about the *appearance* of conflicts of interest. The problem of ethics was not high on the legislature's agenda, mainly because it was not important to the public and did not then have the appeal to the media then that it has today. Legislators as a class were not concerned because they believed that they were doing the right thing and behaving accordingly, even though they suspected that a few of their colleagues might not be.

Raising the Bar

Legislatures characterized by an attitude of "anything goes" are a thing of the past. They have been replaced by legislatures that are under continuous scrutiny and investigation, frequent assault by the media, and cynicism on the part of the public. Legislatures nowadays have to abide by a variety of ethics laws, as well as publicly imposed standards that appear to constantly be on the rise. The event that marked the end of one era and the beginning of another was the Watergate scandal, which led to the resignation of President Richard Nixon, a new wave of investigative journalism, and much less trust of those in office by everyone on the outside.

Reformers inside and outside of legislatures in the states had been pressing for change, at least since the early 1960s. At that time, the California Legislature adopted several ethics provisions in exchange for support from the public on a proposition that provided the state with a full-time, professional legislature. But what mainly precipitated ethics reform in the states was scandal and the media and public's reaction to it. In her analysis of ethics laws throughout the nation, Beth A. Rosenson found that state scandals of varying magnitude largely accounted for the ethics enactments that followed.[38] Such scandals ranged from those in which legislators were indicted and convicted as a result of law-enforcement stings to those in which legislators were punished for failing to disclose benefits or for using their office in some way for private gain. Through the 1980s and 1990s, although scandals were reported widely, very few resulted in indictments or convictions. During that period, only seven legislators were expelled from office by a vote of their colleagues. Although unsubstantiated charges and innuendo have been the basis for much of the unethical behavior attributed to legislators, there can be no denying that legislative cultures have been loose, cozy, and permissive and that a number of legislators—albeit a small minority of all legislators—crossed the line separating the ethical from the unethical.

Legislatures have been responding to the scandals, media attention, editorial condemnation, and public criticism they encountered with the enactment of additional laws governing legislative ethics. Over the years, the following laws have been adopted and now govern legislative ethics in the fifty states.[39]

Training and Related Activities. Whether by statute, rule, or practice, ethics training is now offered in most states and is mandated in thirteen states. The training focuses mainly on compliance with law and regulation, and is designed less to raise the ethics consciousness of members about broad issues than to keep them from getting into trouble on very narrow ones. Advice and counseling are also made available to legislators today, with the same objective in mind—keeping them out of trouble. For the most part, it is up to legislators to seek advice—either a formal opinion rendered by an independent ethics commission or a legislative ethics committee (usually made public) or informal advice (sometimes made public by the member in defense of his or her action).

Revolving Door. To guard against an unethical use of influence, legislatures in twenty-seven states have enacted laws that prevent legislators from employment as lobbyists immediately after leaving the legislature. Six states require legislators to sit it out for two years, nineteen for one year, and two require a brief time until legislators can work as lobbyists in their states.

Nepotism. Twenty states now prohibit nepotism. One of the latest is New Jersey, where several legislators were attacked by the Gannett newspaper chain for having relatives on their district office staffs.

Honorariums. Twenty-three states now ban legislators from being paid for addresses they deliver in connection with their public duties. Thus, they are not permitted to use their offices for personal gain by way of speaking engagements.

Gifts. In 1957 Wisconsin passed the first no-cup-of-coffee law, which prohibited legislators from taking anything of value from lobbyists and their principals. Then in 1974, as part of Proposition 9, California adopted a limitation of $10 that lobbyists could spend on a legislator's meal. Today, gifts are banned in about a dozen states, although exceptions allow lawmakers to attend receptions to which all members of the legislature (or of the senate or house, a delegation, or a committee) are invited. It is interesting, as Robert Enten, a Maryland lobbyist, pointed out to me, that in the old days lobbyists spent $30, $40, or $50 on a meal for one or two legislators, but now they have to spend hundreds of dollars to feed a committee or thousands of dollars to feed the entire legislature.

In Minnesota the gift ban has no major exceptions, and members can eat a meal only if they give a speech, which is referred to as the "sing-for-your-supper" provision. In many states, there are limitations on the dollar amount of gifts legislators can take on a single occasion, or annually per source, or total. Trips have also been curtailed, both because they are regarded as gifts and because of restrictions on permissible travel. Legislators nearly everywhere, however, are exempt from these provisions when they are attending meetings of legislative organizations such as the National Conference of State Legislators, the Council of State Governments, the State Legislative Leaders Foundation, and the American Legislative Exchange Council. In states where gifts are permitted members and/or lobbyists have to disclose the nature and the amount of the benefit.

Occasionally, a gift limitation can have unintended consequences. And exceptions need to be made. In Alaska, for instance, a $250 limit on gifts to lawmakers would have prevented a legislative staffer from donating a kidney to a legislator who was suffering from genetic kidney disease.[40]

Financial Disclosure. Every state except Idaho, Michigan, and Vermont requires legislators to make a public disclosure of their assets and sources of income. The rationale for such a requirement is that citizens ought to be able to judge for themselves whether lawmakers' private interests are affecting their public activities. Information subject to disclosure may include assets, income, transactions, and liabilities. Requirements usually pertain to those in one's immediate family, as well as the legislators themselves.

Conflicts of Interest. States have worked to diminish the possibility that legislators will act on behalf of their own personal, financial interest rather than the interest of the public and/or their constituents. The task is difficult because state legislatures, unlike Congress, are part time and permit members to earn income from employment outside. Even in the virtually full-time legislature, many members earn income in addition to what they receive in public salary. Legislatures have tried to deal with the issue in a number of ways: by financial disclosure, counseling, declarations and recusal by individual members, and limitations on outside employment, such as lobbying or lawyer-legislators appearing before state agencies.

Lobbyists. For a half-century, lobbyists have been regulated by the state. All fifty states require lobbyists to register. Two-thirds of the states prohibit contingency fees, and a few others require disclosure of such fees. In all the states, lobbyists must file disclosure reports, which usually include the expenditures made by them on legislators.

Independent Ethics Commissions. The final important change is the establishment by statute of ethics commissions independent of the legislature, with investigative and enforcement powers. Nearly every state has a joint ethics committee or separate senate and house ethics committees, while in two states the presiding officers appoint a special committee when a complaint is filed. These committees not only render advisory opinions, they also undertake investigations, usually in response to complaints. They also make recommendations to the senate and house regarding the imposition of sanctions on members who have acted unethically. In addition to legislative committees, about twenty states now have independent commissions with jurisdiction over legislative ethics, a few of which not only investigate but can also punish ethics violations by legislators. Usually, however, after an investigation a commission's findings and recommendations are transmitted to the legislature for action.

The Effects of Ethics Law

By enacting ethics laws, legislatures have hoped to pacify the press and public so that they could move on with their broader agendas. They succeeded, at least in the short run. But in the longer term, legislatures and legislators remained targets, not only for the media but also for federal and state prosecutors and for a minority party hoping to topple the majority. A prosecutor can establish himself or herself politically with a successful case. A legislative opponent, or an opposing party, can acquire grist for the campaign mill. The press can publish a story that can revive its diminishing readership. Ethics controversy is not likely to desert the legislative terrain any time soon.

It is questionable, however, whether new ethics law has done much to reduce corruption. There was probably not that much actual corruption during the 1980s, when over fifty legislators were indicted or convicted. Violations continue today, with corrupt activity recently taking place in Wisconsin, Tennessee, Connecticut, New Jersey, and Maryland, among other places. Yet relatively few legislators have been involved. John E. McDonough, a former legislator from Massachusetts, accurately sums up:

> Do we have villains, neanderthals, and scoundrels who find their way into our assemblies? Absolutely. Are their numbers substantial? Absolutely not. And there is one more thing about them: everyone of them was chosen as representative and sent to serve by voters, not by the other members of their respective legislative bodies.[41]

Even Louisiana, one of the last legislative holdouts against sweeping re-form, could not withstand change. In 2008, six weeks into his term as governor, Bobby Jindal persuaded a grudging legislature to enact a number of major ethics laws. Tough financial disclosure, a limitation on gifts, a separate ethics board, and annual ethics training were all put on the books. The culture of the Louisiana Legislature was about to undergo serious change.

New ethics regulation has certainly not eliminated corruption, but it has had a marked impact on legislators and legislatures. Probably the major effect has been a transformation of cultures in most state capitals. Today, as compared to yesteryear, wining and dining is minimal. Take Albany, for example. It is no longer the fun place for legislators that it once was. As reported in the *New York Times* on June 18, 2007, fifteen years ago bars and restaurants were a second home to lawmakers three or four days a week when they were at the capital. Lobbyists then picked up the tab, and legislators were able to live high off the hog. That is no longer the case—in Albany, Sacramento, Tallahassee, Columbus, or Trenton. Legislators and lobbyists are a lot less cozy than they used to be. A number of factors account for the change. New generations of legislators have different tastes and develop different habits. They socialize less and work more. Gift restrictions and gift-disclosure requirements tend to keep lobbyists and legislators socially apart. Members no longer live, as they once did, on the lobbyist's dime. Along with everything else, new standards have been defined, and it is to these stricter standards that legislatures and legislators are being held accountable.

Gray Areas

In the contemporary climate of ethics regulation, legislators have to be wary. A mistake can damage their reputations or even end their political careers. Think of the cross pressures that are normal to the job of legislators—whether in California or New York on the one hand or South Dakota or New Hampshire on the other:

- Many earn income on the outside, so the potential of a conflict of interests always exists.
- Each has to balance state interests against the interests of the constituency.

- All of them have to finance their reelection campaigns, although a relatively small proportion has to raise a lot of money. The latter rely heavily on contributions from interest groups, which have a stake in issues that the legislator will take part in deciding.
- To get things done, legislators ordinarily have to compromise, settling for less than they want or having to go along with something they don't want.
- Those who have tough elections are advised to go negative quickly and attack their opponents.
- Opponents are searching for issues relating to character, with which they can call into question an incumbent's integrity.
- The print press, which normally cues the electronic press, is constantly on the lookout for scandal, which is the preferred grist for the media mill.
- Legislators are fair game, even big game, for state and federal prosecutors. They are always fearful that what they write or what they say will be open to misinterpretation, or worse. More and more legislators seem to be following the advice of Martin (Mahatma) Lomasney, a Boston ward politician, who counseled: "Never write when you can talk; never talk when you can nod."[42] Nowadays, one might add, "Never nod when you can wink."

It is not easy for contemporary legislators to avoid at least the appearance of engaging in unethical behavior. Let us examine the case of David Paterson when he was in the New York Senate (before he ran for lieutenant governor and then replaced Eliot Spitzer as governor). Paterson had been questioned for having asked the assembly speaker, a fellow Democrat, to meet with a representative of a small Harlem hospital in his district that was in need of financial assistance. The hospital's representative, indeed its lobbyist, happened to be Paterson's wife. Over the next few years, moreover, Paterson directed state grants totaling at least $150,000 to the hospital, while his wife held a job there.[43]

Paterson can be criticized for allowing himself to be perceived as acting as he did for personal reasons. He defends himself, however, by claiming that he did not help his wife get a job at the hospital; he had been involved in efforts to help the hospital long before his wife worked there, and the hospital provided vital services to his constituents. "If our entire neighborhood in East Harlem was now deprived of the hospital's services because the legislator who represents them doesn't help them because his wife works there, I think that's unethical," Paterson said.

Many of the situations in which legislators find themselves are not clear-cut at all. It may not be easy to decide what is ethical and what is not. Nonetheless, legislators have to choose. In each of the following hypotheticals—which are based on actual cases—legislators have made a choice. The question is whether what the particular legislator has chosen is ethical or not.

1. A constituent, who is a regular campaign contributor, asks for help from his representative. His firm is having a problem getting a permit for development from the state department of environmental protection. The legislator responds to the constituent by meeting with the agency head and maintaining the need for development in the district and the good work done by the constituent's firm, and also drops mention of the support the legislator has given over the years to agency budget requests.

2. The chair of the Ways and Means Committee has not had any success in helping a constituent resolve an issue regarding his driver's license. Unable to have the matter handled satisfactorily by the Division of Motor Vehicles, the chair informs the director that she would certainly remember the issue when the division's budget requests come before her committee a few weeks later.

3. A legislative leader is angry with what a state house reporter for the leading newspaper in the state has been writing about the lawmaking process in the legislature. To demonstrate his annoyance, the leader refuses to meet with the reporter or provide him with any information on the process.

4. The state government affairs committee is debating a bill to legalize casino gambling in the state. The chair of the committee is invited by Steve Wynn to visit Wynn's casinos in Las Vegas to educate himself and his committee members on the subject. Wynn offers to pay the expenses of the chair. The chair takes the trip at Wynn's expense and reports back to the committee.

5. The chair of the committee on economic matters is invited by the state bankers association to speak at its winter meeting in Palm Beach, Florida. The chair goes to the meeting, along with her husband. Expenses for the two of them are paid by the association.

6. A legislator from a northeastern state attends, at state expense, a three-day meeting of the National Conference of State Legislatures. The meeting is held in San Diego in February. The legislator brings along his spouse, at his personal expense, and the two of them continue, at his expense, to vacation in California for another week before going home.

7. A legislator is meeting with a lobbyist in his statehouse office. The lobbyist is trying to persuade the legislator to vote against a bill that would hurt one of the lobbyist's clients. At a break in the discussion, the legislator invites the lobbyist to attend the legislator's fund-raiser, which is being held in three weeks.

8. A member of the house uses his district office allotment for a three-person staff. The director of the district office, who receives a salary of $60,000, is the legislator's spouse.

9. A member of the senate promises to vote for a bill on deregulation that a lobbyist for a business coalition is promoting. A while later the senator is asked by a lobbyist for an environmental group to oppose the bill. Without notification to the business lobbyist, the senator votes against the bill when it is brought up on the floor.

10. The majority leader is a partner in a law firm and practices law between his legislative duties. A major corporation in the state, which has an interest in a number of issues that are before the legislature, asks the firm to represent it. The majority leader, along with his partner, agrees and they take the corporation on as a client.

11. A member of the senate is employed as a teacher in the public school system of her district. A bill before the senate would raise teachers' salaries at every level. The teacher-legislator casts her vote for the bill.

12. A member of the house sponsored and helped enact legislation that provided special funding for charter schools to lease buildings. A building he owns is leased by a charter school that has received about $440,000 in lease aid from the state over several years.

How Legislators Make "Ethical" Choices

Legislators today are very concerned about the consequences of the choices they make. It is easy to take the wrong path and wind up discredited or worse. Most legislators are alert to the consequences of their behavior. Essentially they are guided by three sets of standards, each of which assumes greater or lesser weight, depending on the individual and the issue.

The first and most imposing set of standards has to do with *compliance.* Legislators know that they must comply with the law, with senate or house rules, and with other regulations. Every legislator who is a candidate for re-election has to be concerned with campaign finance law in his or her state. Such law is extremely complex and requires legal interpretation. Some legislators have campaign-finance attorneys on their campaign staffs. Others have access through their parties to such expertise. Legislators, by statute, must disclose their sources of income. They have to be careful either not to accept gifts from several categories of givers or to report what they are given. Under no circumstances can they, according to statutes in most states, use their official position to seek special treatment for themselves from a state agency. Legislators make the law; they also have to abide by it.

But outside of what is legal and what is illegal lies a more ambiguous area, which may be governed by legislative rules or by legislative codes of ethics. For instance, Senate Rule 75 in Minnesota provides that members should not violate "accepted norms of the Senate," "betray public trust," or "tend to bring the Senate into dishonor or disrepute." What are the accepted norms? What is a betrayal of public trust? What behavior would tend to bring the Senate into dishonor or disrepute? The answers are by no means obvious. Most legislative bodies have similar rules or provisions in their codes of ethics.

When legislators are uncertain as to legality, they have the opportunity of seeking advice from state ethics commissions or legislative ethics committees. Before making a decision or taking action, the savvy legislator will request an advisory opinion in writing or informal counsel from the ethics agency. If the advice is to go ahead, the legislator has authoritative support and can defend his or her action. If the advice is to refrain from certain behavior, such advice ought to be heeded. Legislative staff is available to provide information on whether state law or legislative rules apply and on what would be legal or illegal. Staff also can advise on whether a legislator's action would be unethical.

A number of legislatures today—including California, Connecticut, and Kentucky—offer ethics training, and in most of these places members of the legislature are required to attend. The training usually familiarizes members with the laws and rules that govern their behavior. In Maryland, the legislature goes further. Here, members are required each year to meet with an ethics counsel (who also staffs the joint legislative ethics committee) to receive advice on a confidential, attorney-client basis. The discussion usually begins with a review of the legislator's financial disclosure and concludes with any suggestions that the counsel may deem appropriate.

The second standard relates to *whether a behavior feels right* to the legislator. Does the conduct seem ethical? Does it pass the smell test? As Sen. Preston Smith, the chair of the Senate Ethics Committee in Georgia, counseled members: "Listen to the voice inside of you. That's probably your momma talking to you."[44] Critical here are one's motives, with the test of ethical behavior being whether an individual is acting for the right reasons—that is, with the public interest and not one's private interest uppermost.

Most legislators, like the rest of us, think that they are doing the right thing, and doing it for the right reasons. Even if they benefit as a result, they are likely to sincerely believe that the action they take is good for the constituency, the state, and so forth. Take, for example, a legislator who owns a liquor store. His vote against higher taxes on alcohol benefits his business. Does that make his action a conflict of interest? The legislator also believes that added taxes hurt the industry, retailers, and consumers. The legislator is generally against raising taxes, and his constituency opposes tax increases as well.

It is impossible to decode motivation. Whether the liquor-store-owner legislator is acting for the right or wrong reasons is known only to himself, if known at all. However, the allegation that he actually has a conflict is difficult to sustain as long as legislators without ties to or campaign contributions from the liquor industry also take a similar position. They obviously are voting as they do for reasons other than personal gain, since they have nothing to gain personally. The reasons may be constituency opposition to increased taxes, their own record of opposing tax increases, competition from other states, or some combination of all of these. If these legislators can be influenced by such factors, so can the legislator in question. We may not agree with the legislator's position on the issue, but a strong argument can be made that it is not on its face an unethical one.

The third standard that governs legislative behavior nowadays is that of *appearance.* What does the behavior look like? What do people perceive? What will "reasonable" people think of its rightness or wrongness? Dennis Thompson, a political theorist who for years has directed an ethics program at Harvard University, maintains that "appearance" is and should be an important ethical standard. For Thompson, "appearing to do wrong while doing right is really doing wrong." Officials who do wrong, he writes, erode confidence in the political system, give citizens reasons to act as if government cannot be trusted, and undermine democratic accountability. All citizens have to go by is their perceptions. They cannot assess the motivations of public officials, for the motives are many, mixed, and hidden from public view.[45]

The problem, of course, is that what the public perceives is almost exclusively what the media report. Unless people pay careful attention to government and politics, have direct sources of information, and spend time sorting and evaluating, they have to rely on the media. Nearly everyone does. Therefore, if "appearance" is indeed an ethical standard, that standard is under the control of the editorial judgment of the media. And media judgment, in turn, is made mainly on pragmatic grounds—what is newsworthy and will attract an audience.

This is not to argue that appearance ought to be ignored—only that it cannot really be regarded as an ethical standard. Rather, appearance is a prudential, practical, or political standard. The questions that have to be asked before a legislator acts do not involve right or wrong in any moral sense. They involve right or wrong in a political sense. Let us return to the example of the liquor-store-owner legislator who has to vote on an alcohol-beverage tax increase. The questions to be asked are: Is it politically wise to vote against the tax? How will such a vote be treated in the media? How could it be treated by an opponent in the next election? Where would the constituency be on the issue?

This is not to advocate that the legislator duck the issue by recusing himself. When legislators do not participate because of the appearance of a conflict of interest, their constituents are denied representation. And in a number of states, like New Jersey, when a constitutional majority is required to pass a bill, their abstention actually counts as a "no" vote, whatever their intention. It is difficult to argue that such a choice makes ethical sense.

Appearance, however, has to be taken into account, and it is; but not as an ethical standard as such. Indeed, how things will look and how they will impact politically are more on the minds of legislators than questions of right and wrong. Yet legislators lump the ethical and the political together. One frequently hears a veteran legislator tell a new member that the best ethics test is how their conduct will look on the front page of the newspaper the next day. If it won't look good, the conclusion is not to do it. The implicit reason is not that the conduct will be unethical, but rather that it will hurt politically.

Appearance as a standard indicates that ethics and politics cannot be disentangled, as far as real-life legislators are concerned. These practitioners are not oblivious to right and wrong, but they give greatest weight to whether what they do looks right or wrong to their constituents.

Relatively few matters with which legislatures are concerned are simply black or simply white. The overwhelming number are various shades of gray. Legislators themselves have different views of what is ethical and what is not. Increasingly, however, they risk making choices that can get them into hot water politically and occasionally into boiling water legally. They are targets for the media and for law enforcement; they are well aware of it. Most of them play it safe, but some do not, and either cross the line or come too close to it. These are the legislators that the media will focus on and people will hear about. Meanwhile, the overwhelming number of them get through the wars without stepping on any land mines.

Notes

1. This section draws on Alan Rosenthal, *The Decline of Representative Democracy* (Washington, D.C.: CQ Press, 1998), 49–84.
2. Alexander Heard, ed., *State Legislatures in American Politics* (Englewood Cliffs, N.J.: Prentice-Hall, 1966), 3.
3. See Citizens Conference on State Legislatures, *The Sometime Governments* (New York: Bantam, 1971).

4. Brian Weberg and Karl T. Kurtz, "Legislative Staff," in *Institutional Change in American Politics: The Case of Term Limits,* ed. Karl T. Kurtz, Bruce Cain, and Richard G. Niemi (Ann Arbor: University of Michigan Press, 2007), 96.

5. Peverill Squire and Keith E. Hamm, *101 Chambers: Congress, State Legislatures, and the Future of Legislative Studies* (Columbus: Ohio University Press, 2005), 98.

6. Peverill Squire, "Measuring State Legislative Professionalism," *State Politics and Policy Quarterly* 7 (Summer 2007): 211–227.

7. Peverill Squire, "Legislative Professionalization and Membership Diversity in State Legislatures," *Legislative Studies Quarterly* 17 (February 1992): 70–72. Karl Kurtz, in his index of professionalization, adds to those items employed by Squire the "continuity of service" by legislators, in "The Changing State Legislatures (Lobbyists Beware)," in *Leveraging State Government Relations,* ed. Wesley Pedersen (Washington, D.C.: Public Affairs Council, 1990), 23–32. For a general review of measurements, see Christopher Z. Mooney, "Measuring U.S. State Legislatures Professionalism: An Evaluation of Five Indices," *State and Local Government Review* 26 (Spring 1994): 70–78.

8. Quoted by John Howard on *Statement.com.*

9. See Jennifer Drage Bowser, Keon S. Chi, and Thomas H. Little, *A Practical Guide to Term Limits: Final Report of the Joint Project on Term Limits* (Denver: National Conference of State Legislatures, July 2006), 7.

10. Gary F. Moncrief, Richard G. Niemi, and Lynda W. Powell, "Time, Term Limits and Turnover: Trends in Membership Stability in U.S. State Legislatures," *Legislative Studies Quarterly* 29 (August 2004): 366.

11. Moncrief et al., "Time, Term Limits and Turnover," 364–365.

12. John A. Straayer, "Colorado's Legislative Term Limits," Joint Project on Term Limits (unpublished paper, August 2004).

13. James R. Rogers, "The Impact of Bicameralism on Legislative Production," *Legislative Studies Quarterly* 28 (November 2003): 524.

14. Taylor Pensoneau, *Powerhouse: Arrington from Illinois* (Baltimore: American Literary Press, 2006), 115.

15. Richard Hyatt, *Mr. Speaker: The Biography of Tom Murphy* (Macon: Mercer University Press, 1999), 77–78, 204.

16. American Society of Legislative Clerks and Secretaries, *Inside the Legislative Process* (Denver: National Conference of State Legislatures, October 2005), 4/3.

17. Ralph Wright, *Inside the Statehouse* (Washington, D.C.: CQ Press, 2005), 43–44.

18. James Coleman Battista, "Re-examining Legislative Committee Representativeness in the States," *State Politics and Policy Quarterly* 4 (Summer 2004): 177.

19. Alan Rosenthal, *Legislative Life: People, Politics, and Performance in the States* (New York: Harper and Row, 1981), 188.

20. Wayne L. Francis, "Leadership, Party Caucuses, and Committees in U.S. State Legislatures," *Legislative Studies Quarterly* 10 (May 1985): 249.

21. Christopher Z. Mooney and Tim Storey, "The Illinois General Assembly, 1992–2003," Joint Project on Term Limits (unpublished paper, August 16, 2004).

22. Bruce E. Cain and Thad Kousser, "Adapting to Term Limits: Recent Experiences and New Directions," Joint Project on Term Limits (unpublished paper, July 2004).

23. Bruce Cain and Gerald Wright, "Committees," in *Institutional Changes in American Politics: The Case of Term Limits,* ed. Karl T. Kurtz, Bruce Cain, and Richard G. Niemi (Ann Arbor: University of Michigan Press, 2007), 74–75.

24. Interview with Rep. Vincent Pedone, March 9, 2006.

25. Massachusetts State House News Service, June 8, 2006.

26. Cain and Wright, "Committees," 74–75.

27. Interview with Sen. Leonard Lance, February 19, 2001.

28. Wright, *Inside the Statehouse,* 30–31.

29. American Society of Legislative Clerks and Secretaries, *Inside the Legislative Process,* 4–79, 87, 89–94.

30. Richard Powell and Rich Jones, "Maine," Joint Project on Term Limits (unpublished paper, June 2004).

31. Cain and Wright, "Committees," 75.

32. Francis, "Leadership, Party Caucuses, and Committees in U.S. State Legislatures," 246.

33. Grant Reeher, *First Person Political* (New York: New York University Press, 2006), 120.

34. Bowser et al., *A Practical Guide to Term Limits,* 8.

35. Bruce Cain, Thad Kousser, and Karl T. Kurtz, "California," Joint Project on Term Limits (unpublished paper, 2004).

36. Bowser et al., *A Practical Guide to Term Limits,* 8.

37. Thad Kousser, *Term Limits and the Dismantling of State Legislative Professionalism* (Cambridge: Cambridge University Press, 2005), 45.

38. Beth A. Rosenson, *Shadowlands of Conduct: Ethics and State Politics* (Washington, D.C.: Georgetown University Press, 2005). Willie Brown provides a fascinating account of the FBI sting in California of which he was a prime target. Willie Brown, *Basic Brown* (New York: Simon and Schuster, 2008), 165–197.

39. This section is taken from Alan Rosenthal, "The Effects of Legislative Ethics Law," in *Public Ethics and Governance: Standards and Practices in Comparative Perspective*, ed. Denis Saint-Martin and Fred Thompson (Oxford: Elsevier, 2006), 156–158.

40. *State Net Capitol Report*, February 18, 2008.

41. John McDonough, *Experiencing Politics: A Legislator's Stories of Government and Health Care* (Berkeley: University of California Press, 2000), 317–318.

42. Quoted in McDonough, *Experiencing Politics*, 83.

43. As reported in the *New York Times*, April 30, 2008.

44. Remarks at legislative orientation, Athens, Georgia, December 12, 2004.

45. Dennis F. Thompson, "Paradoxes of Government Ethics," *Public Administration Review* 52 (May–June 1992): 257; see also Rosenthal, *Drawing the Line*, 48–72.

7

The Job of Leadership

No doubt the most difficult job in a legislative body is that of leader—not any leader, but top leader. Tom Loftus, who served eight years as speaker of the assembly in Wisconsin, describes how he felt about the job:

> On some days I was like the teacher in front of the classroom. I was the font of real knowledge, and I decided what we did during the day, including when we took recess. On other days I was like someone in front of the firing squad who is fumbling with his blindfold and last cigarette in order to buy time.[1]

The hope of every leader is to have more days of the former variety than the latter.

Leadership is exercised by many members of a senate or house—by those who chair committees and subcommittees and those who are elected or appointed as party leaders. Rank-and-file members also provide leadership on issues they want to advance or retard. Informal leadership by individuals shifts according to personality, placement, and policy. But formal leadership within a legislative body is stable (at least, relatively so) and titular. Normally, house leadership positions include speaker, majority leader, assistant majority leader, minority leader, and assistant minority leader. Some houses also have a speaker pro tem and whips, and a few go even further in specifying leadership positions. Normally, senate leadership includes the president or president pro tempore, and majority and minority leaders. Sometimes these senate leaders are buttressed by deputy and assistant leaders.

Minority party leadership is entirely different from majority party leadership. The majority is responsible for running the house or senate. It is up to the majority to set the agenda; to respond to the governor's agenda; and to manage staff personnel, facilities, printing, and the like. The minority's role is much more circumscribed. Individual minority members sponsor bills and work to get them passed. Minority committee members do engage in study and deliberation and do craft legislation that the committee takes to the floor. But the minority as a group normally has little say on major agenda items in the senate or house.

The minority leadership has several options: it can collaborate with the majority, and thus have some say in the agenda that is enacted; it can disagree on certain issues, such as the budget, but work in a bipartisan manner on others; or it can engage in partisan warfare, hoping to take a majority of seats in the next election. If the minority collaborates, its members will be able to play a greater role in the process. But it will not be positioning itself to win a majority of seats in an election. If, however, the minority is critical of the majority and refuses to go along, it will have less to say about decision making in the legislature. It will have chosen the path of campaigning to become the majority party. Which option the minority picks depends on the competitiveness of the state and the minority's chances of prevailing at the polls. A small minority party is more likely to be collaborative; a larger minority party is more likely to be confrontational.

When the governor is of the same party as the house or senate minority, the role of minority leader is enhanced. Under these circumstances the governor works with minority party members, as well as with majority party leaders, to move his or her agenda through the legislature. As we shall explore in chapter 8, because of the powerful role of the executive, the legislative minority of the governor's party will have an expanded role—unless the legislative minority party is so small, as it is in Massachusetts, that it can almost be ignored.

In this chapter we shall focus on majority party leadership, the job of which is very different from that of minority party leadership. No other member has nearly the responsibility as the top leader in each chamber. In the house the speaker holds the position as top leader, although in North Dakota the majority leader has the greater say. In the senate the president holds the top post in almost half the states; the president pro tem in almost half (where the lieutenant governor constitutionally also holds the position as president of the senate); and the majority leader holds the position in Minnesota, New York, North Dakota, Washington, and Wisconsin.[2]

Becoming a Leader

John Paul Doyle, a veteran legislator in the New Jersey General Assembly, when asked once how long he intended to stay in office, replied, "Until I become speaker or until I realize that I won't become speaker." Not every legislator aspires to the top leadership position, however. Some don't want to spend the time and effort a leadership job requires; they have other interests and other commitments. Some choose to remain backbenchers, preferring to devote themselves to helping their constituents and constituency rather than to managing a legislative chamber and its agenda. Those who are ardent advocates in particular policy areas prefer to chair committees and shape legislation to which they are strongly committed. Some don't aspire to leadership because they doubt that their colleagues would elect them. But that still leaves quite a few members who from day one hope eventually to run the show.

Any member is eligible to be elected to the top position. All it takes is the votes of one's colleagues, which normally means support from a majority of the majority party caucus. Occasionally a candidate who cannot win a majority in his or her own caucus will gain support from a bipartisan coalition that puts together a majority of votes in the chamber.

What does it take to win a majority? Personality, skill, energy, and work; and perhaps more. Theoretically, anyone can do it. Yet until recently women and African Americans had been shut out of top leadership. This is no longer the case. African Americans, notably Willie Brown of California and Daniel Blue of North Carolina, broke the color bar. And women of all races have made marked gains in leadership positions as they have grown in overall membership. Most recently, in 2008 Karen Bass became the first African American woman to hold the speakership in California.

Experience in legislative office helps. As Woody Allen remarked, showing up is 90 percent of life. Showing up—year after year—counts in legislatures. It enables members to demonstrate their stuff, build reputations, forge relationships, do favors, and win respect and support. This means that more senior members ordinarily have an edge when it comes to top leadership. On average, members in non-term-limited states have eight, nine, or ten years or more under their belts before their selection as speaker or president. In term-limited states, members have four or five years of tenure before their selection, with no one having much of an experiential advantage over anyone else.

In some states legislators typically ascend to top positions through the "chairs." They first chair a committee like ways and means or serve as majority (or minority) leader. These positions enable them to show their skills as lawmakers and also do favors for colleagues, all of which helps them put enough votes together to get elected. Legislators who raise money for the campaigns of others may be several steps ahead when it comes to soliciting their colleagues' votes.

A member's ideology may also count. A conservative caucus may insist on a conservative to lead them, a liberal caucus a liberal. A divided caucus is more likely to settle for someone in the middle. In some states it helps if a candidate for top leadership is from one region or another, one type of district, or one of several counties. Generally the selection of leadership is an inside affair. Ralph Wright of Vermont titled his memoirs, "All politics is personal."[3] Being personally liked is a great advantage.

In a few places outsiders become involved in a leadership contest. Major interest groups—such as labor, teachers, lawyers, and business—work behind the scenes to promote their preferred candidates or to oppose those they dislike. Governors also make their weight felt, blatantly in a few places such as Louisiana and more subtly in other places.

There are no hard and fast rules as to just what counts and just how much it counts. The loadings change from selection to selection and campaign to campaign. But few legislators are drafted into top leadership; the overwhelming majority aspire to the position and run for it. They round up votes one by one, most often from members of their own party, but occasionally they cross the divide and seek support from members of the other party as well. Rounding up votes is a retail business, one in which they have to persuade, promise, and cajole their fellow lawmakers. They will point to their experience in leadership and how they have helped their colleagues. They will describe the ways in which they intend to lead the caucus, the chamber, and the legislature. They may even offer a secondary leadership position or a committee chair in return for support.

The Responsibilities of Leadership

Relatively few top legislative leaders achieve electoral success beyond the office they hold. Not many are elected statewide, although some have made it to the U.S. House of Representatives. One of the reasons for their overall lack of success on the political ladder is that their position as speaker or president commands little positive response. They inevitably get into disputes with the governor. They are targets for the media. They are criticized for what the legislature does or fails to do. Because of their many and diverse responsibilities, they have trouble making friends that last beyond their terms but have no trouble leaving many people disgruntled. Perhaps it is simply not possible to succeed, or appear to succeed, at the job of president of the senate or speaker of the house.

Campaign Manager

Shortly after he became speaker of the assembly in New Jersey, Chuck Hardwick addressed an audience at Princeton University's Woodrow Wilson School. His subject was the speakership and its many responsibilities. Reelecting members was the first responsibility he mentioned. That the reelection of party members—holding onto the majority, and even growing it—came before all the other responsibilities was no accident. Without getting his members reelected, Hardwick would not have to worry about the rest of his responsibilities. He no longer would be speaker.

Today, more than in earlier years, the leaders in the senate and the house tend to be campaign managers as well as legislators. With the demise of the old state parties, legislative leaders and legislative party caucuses started to fill the vacuum. We have discussed the role of the legislative party in chapter 4. For now, suffice it to say that legislative leaders have taken on the tasks of campaign manager in almost two-thirds of the ninety-nine legislative chambers.

The basic campaign task of legislative leaders is to raise and distribute funds. Since the 1960s the costs of competitive races have risen enormously. Campaign fund-raising is becoming more important, partly because of the expanded role of legislative leaders. With its large legislative districts (few of which are any longer competitive), California probably holds fund-raising records for the nation, thanks to the efforts of Jesse Unruh, Willie Brown, David Roberti, and the succession of leaders who followed in their footsteps. Even with six-year term limits for the assembly, the importance of leadership fund-raising in California has not diminished. New speakers are selected and take office early in the second year of a biennium, so that they can be as effective as possible in raising money. The fund-raising prospects of a lame-duck speaker would not be as bright as those of a new speaker with at least a session to go. In other term-limited states as well, the electoral role of top leaders has remained important. This is because, with forced turnover, more vacant seats have to be contested. California is not the only state in which legislative leaders have expanded their campaign-finance role. Illinois, Minnesota, Wisconsin, Florida, and New Jersey also rank high in the professionalism of campaign fund-raising by top legislative leaders.

Consider, for instance, the way it worked in Ohio for several decades under Democrat Vern Riffe.[4] During his speakership, Riffe started caucus fund-raising. The money was in Columbus, held by interest groups and lobbyists with offices there. It was Riffe's idea that one huge fund-raiser would achieve an economy of scale. This fund-raising coincided with the speaker's birthday. At the first birthday party reception he held in 1973, tickets sold for $100, netting a total of $165,000. At his party in 1993, tickets sold for $500, netting around $1.5 million. Because he was pro-business, as well as pro-labor, Riffe managed to attract money that otherwise might have gone to Republicans. "I never had an organization turn me down," he recalled when he was leaving the speakership. Not only did Riffe demonstrate personal political skill in the fund-raising enterprise, but he created the impression that the Republicans could not beat him and had little chance to win a majority in the Ohio House.

Legislative leaders are at an advantage in raising funds. It is more difficult to say no to the speaker or president than to a rank-and-file member. The presiding officer can lend valuable assistance on a bill that an interest group wants passed and can be of even greater help in derailing a bill that an interest group wants killed. No lobbyist or interest group wants to risk the good will of a legislative leader; there is no telling what the consequences might be. So they give when asked, since it is better to be safe than sorry; and anyway, their opponents (or prospective opponents) are giving as well. At the least, they want to keep the playing field level for their team.

Public financing arrangements, which have been adopted in a few states, such as Maine, have affected leadership fund-raising activity. Under Maine's "clean elections" law, a large number of legislators accepted public funding for the 2002 election. As a result, they have been less reliant on their leaders for handouts. In any case, according to one leader, many candidates considered it politically risky to accept money from a leadership PAC. Doing so would make it appear that they were beholden to leadership. Although leaders here are less involved in raising and allocating money, they still are expected to campaign for members.[5]

The campaign manager role extends beyond finance; just how far depends on the particular state and the individual leader. In many states leaders take part in the recruitment of candidates for legislative seats. Informal recruitment activity has been going on for years, but as the struggle for control of the legislature became more competitive, recruitment efforts in competitive districts became organized and intense. Ohio's Riffe exemplifies the practice. He would target six or seven seats that the Democrats could win and then collaborate with county party leaders in a search for candidates. As an inducement, Riffe offered to pay for polling, mailing, and media and provide staff and money for their campaigns. His counterpart in the Ohio Senate—Stanley Aronoff, a Republican—would solicit county chairs, civic leaders, and business and labor leaders for lists of potentials. The top criterion for endorsement by Senate Republicans was viability—could the candidates win? As speaker in Minnesota, Steve Sviggum was heavily involved in recruiting Republican candidates. He drove all over the state, time after time, in order to encourage candidacies. He recalled that one day he left the legislature at 2:30 p.m., drove to Thief River Falls for an 8 p.m. meeting with a prospective candidate, and then drove back to St. Paul, arriving at 5:30 a.m. He was just in time to shower and shave and prepare for the next day at the capitol.[6]

The leader's campaign responsibilities are pursued inside the legislature itself, as well as outside in the state and districts. Incumbents who face challenges from the opposition party are afforded special protection. They are assigned to standing committees that help them in one way or another with the coming election. These incumbents may also benefit by leadership putting their bill introductions on the fast track, so that they can claim credit back home. The leader may also give them a "boutique bill" to sponsor that will gain favorable attention in the district. Speaking engagements, appointments to special commissions, and photo opportunities with the senate president, house speaker, or perhaps the governor are other benefits conferred on their people by leadership.

Minority party incumbents who are targeted by the majority party also receive special treatment by leadership. Minority leaders try to do whatever they can to shore up these members, while leaders of the majority try to increase their vulnerability. In competitive, two-party states, chances are that the committee assignments of targeted minority members are among the least desirable politically and that relatively few of their bills pass. Majority party leadership, insofar as possible, will obstruct their efforts to compile a legislative record on which to run for reelection.

Personnel Director

The presiding officers are responsible, ultimately at least, for the hiring of staff within their chambers. The membership of the body or the caucus usually has a say in the matter, but leaders can shape the professional staff as they choose. Through the legislative budget that they formulate, they determine the number of staff positions and their allocation among legislative agencies. As far as appointments are concerned, they normally play a role in the hiring of the directors of nonpartisan legislative service agencies and the administrative staff of the chamber. Their major involvement, however, is likely to be with the top partisan staff appointments. As a rule, while personnel actions are delegated—to committee chairs, individual lawmakers, and agency directors—the final say resides with the leaders themselves.

The principal personnel responsibility of legislative leaders is assigning members to and naming the chairs of standing committees. In nearly every house, the appointment power resides with the speaker. Only in a few places is the power shared. On the senate side, the formal power to appoint resides with the president in most cases, while it is dispersed in the remainder with a committee on committees or rules committee having the job. Either way, the top senate leader has the principal say. Minority appointments to committees vary. Sometimes the minority leader makes them; sometimes the minority leader recommends appointments to the speaker or president; sometimes the minority and majority leaderships consult; and sometimes the minority simply has to settle for whatever assignments they receive from the majority leadership.

Although leaders use the committee appointments process to help their supporters and advantage those party members who have tough reelections ahead, they operate under a number of constraints. Members' preferences count. Normally, before a legislative session gets underway, lawmakers are asked to list three or four preferences for committee assignments. Leaders usually try to give members one of their preferences, although possibly not the top one. Tenure on a committee also matters. Members who ask to be reappointed ordinarily have their requests granted. Leaders also take seniority into account, and try to balance their committees by geography, gender, and ethnicity.[7] In some places they carefully stack those committees, like appropriations, that are critical to their legislative party's success. They want to be as sure as they can that the votes are there when they need them.

One of the most significant personnel responsibilities of top leaders is the appointment of committee chairs. The person who occupies the chair position is the driving force within each policy domain of the legislature. In about 60 percent of the legislative chambers committee chairs are appointed by the presiding officer. In others, a committee on committees or rules committee decides. In the South Carolina House chairs are elected by members of the committees. In appointing chairs, leaders take into account the legislator's experience on the committee and seniority in the chamber. They also consider balancing region, gender, ethnicity, and perhaps ideology in their slate of appointments. Some of their appointments may constitute payback for a legislator's vote in a leadership race or support for the party's agenda.

Leaders cannot appoint anyone they choose. They have to appoint competent legislators to chair at least the major committees. Otherwise, the chair may lose control of the committee and the leadership may be forced to intervene, or else the work just won't get done. Although the chair may be at fault, the buck does not stop until it gets to the office of the speaker or the president. Legislative leaders have to rely on their committee chairs, who are part of their leadership team. They cannot involve themselves in everything, so they delegate but try to keep informed and possibly maintain control of a few key items. Only on rare occasions will they intervene in a committee's affairs, although more frequently they may bypass a committee that is out of step with them.

Formally or informally, a leadership team is put together. The team can vary in size and composition, with the smallest including only a few legislative party leaders and the largest extending to major committee chairs as well. Individual top leaders feel free to organize their teams as they wish. The larger the team, the more legislators are likely to feel a stake in the agenda and commit themselves to support it.

Organizational Manager

The top leaders of the senate and house are responsible for the overall management of their organizations. They delegate nearly all of the administrative tasks to the secretary of the senate and clerk of the house, who report directly to them. The secretary, the clerk, and their staffs conduct the day-to-day operations when the legislature is in session, and they run a leaner operation during the interim. Joint senate-house operations, such as legislative service agencies that do research and bill drafting, among other tasks, are usually governed by a legislative council or a joint senate-house leadership committee. The presiding officers, or their designees, usually chair these committees.

As organizational managers, the top leaders control, or at least influence, the provision of resources to rank-and-file members. They may be able to offer a member better office space, more equipment and furnishings, or more convenient parking. These are not incidental, as far as legislators are concerned. Their possession, as well as making life more comfortable, can enhance their recipient's status. Although most legislative chambers provide seating on the floor by party, seniority, district, or region, the leaders can—if they choose—determine where individual members sit and who sits next to whom.

Probably the most significant leadership role with respect to management relates to standing committees. Leaders have the strongest voice in deciding on the number of standing committees, their jurisdictions, and the number of members on each. Their decisions usually have to be ratified in the adoption of the rules for each new legislature. The rules overall are largely those the senate president and house speaker want, many of which are readopted session after session.

Traffic Controller

Wright describes the speaker in Vermont as a "traffic cop," who is at "... the very heart and soul of all that occurred in the building." The speaker, according to him, "was the traffic control center for a busy international airport. Nothing could take off or land without at least the knowledge and often the OK from the controlling officer."[8] The traffic-cop metaphor relates to a wide range of activity—leaders steering debate, determining the flow of bills, and scheduling the session.

Imagine presiding over 180 members, as Tom Murphy did for twenty-five years as speaker of the Georgia House. His biographer, Richard Hyatt, describes Murphy at the podium, the floor abuzz with members conversing and students filing into the galleries. Members wander about and pages scurry back and forth. Murphy recognizes the next speaker as one lawmaker finishes talking about a piece of legislation. Meanwhile, he poses for "grip-and-grin photographs" with a stream of visitors. If there is too much noise he swings his gavel. If there is a serious question about a bill, he responds immediately. "Somehow he juggles all these things and still makes a cogent ruling."[9]

When presiding over a session of the senate or house, leaders manage the process by which bills proceed through second and third readings and final passage. They recognize members who want to speak on an issue and determine the order in which they speak. They are usually evenhanded, giving each side its due. They are expected to permit full discussion, but they are also expected to move the body to a decision. They can determine, subject to appeal from the floor, which amendments are germane and which are not. They rely on the secretary of the senate or clerk of the house for parliamentary advice. In presiding at a floor session, leaders have to be fair, but at the same time they have to move the process along.

Not all leaders preside, and none preside all the time. In senates often the lieutenant governor is the one presiding. Sometimes a rank-and-file member takes over. Probably the main value of presiding is that it permits leaders to demonstrate their skills—their knowledge of rules and procedures, their clarity of action and reaction, their decisiveness, and their ability to maintain control without being arbitrary. Just as in the schoolroom, where the teacher at the front of the class is an authority figure, so is the speaker or president on the dais in the house or senate chamber.

Not only do the leaders steer debate, they also steer the bills that get debated. In most states, the leaders are responsible for referring bill introductions to standing committees. In the overwhelming majority of referrals, the process is handled by the secretary of the senate, the clerk of the house or a staff aide on behalf of the presiding officer, or a rules committee. Defined committee jurisdictions and bill topics serve as the criteria for referral. From time to time referrals follow the requests of bill sponsors, who want them referred to a friendly committee. The presiding office might also have leeway, because one committee has broad jurisdiction, committee jurisdictions overlap, or the bill has been drafted so that it can be sent to various places. And if the leadership frowns on a bill, Wright points out, the speaker "could send it to a *black hole committee,* never to be seen again." [10]

Leaders have greater discretion when it comes to calendaring bills. In some places, calendaring may be their principal power—both over members inside and interest groups outside the legislature. This is the case in New Jersey, where the major power of the speaker and the president is keeping a bill from coming to the floor for a vote. In Trenton parlance, this is the power to keep a bill from "being put on the board." In some places bills go directly to the calendar in the order in which standing committees report them. But that does not necessarily mean that they receive consideration on the floor in that order. They may need a go-ahead from the presiding officer or the rules committee. In New York, for instance, even if a bill finds its way onto the calendar, the leaders can "star" it, or assign the bill a designation that prevents it from reaching the floor.

In exercising their calendaring power, leaders cannot ignore the needs of members. Occasionally, a bill arouses emotion and controversy; most lawmakers don't want to vote on such a bill, where a vote would result in more losers than winners. Leaders consider it their job to protect members—at least members of their own party—by keeping such bills from coming up.

Factotum

The archaic word *factotum* applies to a person employed as chief of household to serve the master. The speaker and the president spend a lot of their time and energy serving their masters—the membership of the house and the senate. If they are doing their jobs effectively, they are at the beck and call of their members. Their office doors have to be open—not just during certain hours but essentially at all times.

Georgia's Murphy, for instance, kept his door open. No matter who came first, the speaker would give preference to any house member who stopped by. It was his way of showing respect and making 179 members feel important.[11] When he was majority leader in the Michigan Senate, John Engler went even further in his service to his members. He did not wait for them to come around but scheduled meetings with all of his Republican colleagues to make sure that he met with each caucus member at least once a month.[12] Russ Arrington, as leader in the Illinois Senate, went even further. He sent out his staff to the Springfield watering holes to mingle with Republican senators and report back to him. He wanted to know everything—their concerns, their gripes, what they wanted.[13]

Legislators come to their leaders with problems that run the gamut from the political to the personal. One member wants an appointment to a state board for a constituent and pleads with the leader to intervene with the governor. Another is having marital difficulties and needs a sympathetic ear. At the very least, leaders have to listen and be empathetic. Sometimes, they have to act to help a member address a problem. Wright discusses how far he would go to help his members in the Vermont House: "As long as it wasn't against the law, didn't require that I go to confession, or wouldn't break up my marriage, I did it."[14] Apparently, there wasn't much that Wright would not do, leaving quite a bit that he would. He made telephones in his office available for members when other phones were being used. He made the showers in the speaker's bathroom open to jogger-members who wanted to use them. He put his own money in a slush fund on which members could draw for a short-term loan. Wright was sure to be in the capitol cafeteria in the morning, when members congregated before committee meetings, so that he could find out their concerns. He would keep track of all his colleagues, and would make a special effort to seek out those he hadn't run into during a week or two.

Willie Brown went just as far when he was speaker in the California Assembly. He tried hard to make the experience of being in Sacramento "fun and exciting" for members. That meant that he had to figure out ways to relieve their stress, particularly during the period when the budget was taken up and especially if it took a lot of time and work to resolve. On such occasions Brown would throw a cookout and party for all the members, staffers, and their families on the statehouse lawn.[15]

Flack-Catcher

The leader has a role as flack-catcher, someone who provides cover or takes the heat for members. One way, as mentioned above, is by keeping bills off the floor that might force members to cast politically risky votes. What may appear at first glance as unilateral action most often is a leader's sensitivity to member needs. If someone has to oppose a measure that appears popular with the public or has editorial support in the statewide media, the leader is there for members who need protection. If the legislature has to act on a pay raise for members, the leader is expected to carry the bill and lead the charge.

In Massachusetts, Senate President William Bulger stood between the members and a term-limits proposal being pushed as an initiative. He was publicly criticized (even by some of his own members, who privately approved) for his stand. In Pennsylvania, Senate President Robert Jubilerer was out front on a pay-raise bill, which the legislature passed and later rescinded after a public outcry. Jubilerer paid for his leadership by being defeated in a primary election shortly thereafter. Murphy, who served twenty-two years as speaker of the Georgia House, described his role in this regard: "I give them [the members] all the credit and I take all the blame."

Role Model

Whether the top leaders are conscious of it or not, they serve as role models for members of their chambers. What they say and how they act set the tone. Members take the cues their leaders offer. In the area of legislator ethics, for example, if leaders are serious about their own ethical behavior, members are also more likely to be serious about their own.

I recall a visit I made to Connecticut a number of years ago, where I addressed the members as part of a day of training on legislative ethics for members. The legislature had authorized the training by law. The majority and minority leadership greeted their colleagues at the beginning of the day but left immediately after their welcoming remarks. If the leaders themselves felt other things took precedence over ethics training, why shouldn't the legislators being trained feel likewise? And they probably did, thanks in part to the cues from their leaders.

Members would be well advised to model themselves after Sid Snyder, a veteran member of the Washington Senate.[16] It is worth describing Snyder and the model he presents to his colleagues in some detail. He grew up poor, but borrowed enough money to open a grocery store, Sid's Market, in 1953. Four years before he went into business, he was hired as an elevator operator in the state capitol. He went on to work in the house and senate staffs, serving as secretary of the senate for nearly twenty-one years. In that role, according to Washington governor Gary Locke, "For all practical purposes, Sid Snyder created our state Senate as we know it today."

In 1990, about forty years after his career on the staff of the legislature began, Snyder was appointed to the senate to fill a vacancy. Later that year, he was chosen by his colleagues to be caucus chair. In 1995 he was elected Democratic leader, and since then served both as minority leader and majority leader.

Many legislative leaders, in order to do their jobs, keep members happy, and line up votes on issues, have to be pragmatic. In one or another scuffle, they may lose sight of principle. Not Snyder. His faith in the legislative process, in law and parliamentary rules, and in protection of the right of the minority party was strong enough to raise principle over pragmatism. Thus, in the 1997 session, when he was serving as minority leader, he threatened to resign on a matter about which he felt strongly.

Toward the close of the session, the Republican majority, in order to pass a bill that had failed twice, decided to change the senate rule on reconsideration. Snyder objected to a sudden change in the rules, which were part of a long tradition. After debate, with the majority bowing to expediency and changing the rule, Snyder took the senate floor, made an angry speech criticizing the Republicans, and announced that he had no choice but to resign. He would not serve, he said, unless the rules were respected.

Before he sent his letter of resignation to the governor, Snyder was urged by nearly all of his colleagues—including twenty-three of twenty-six Republicans—to rescind his resignation. "He's the glue that holds this place together . . . like one big tube of Superglue," said Ralph Munroe, the Republican secretary of state at the time. Snyder was persuaded by his colleagues; he reversed his decision and returned to the senate a week after he had announced his resignation. Upon taking the floor, he was greeted with cheers and a standing ovation by his colleagues. Throughout, Snyder's behavior was totally genuine; he had been sincere when he left and he was sincere when he returned.

Strategist

Every lawmaker spends much time strategizing, trying to figure out how to get a bill passed or defeated, or how to shape the budget to serve his or her district. Indeed, many of the moves legislators make involve strategic consideration. Leaders, however, are in the very center of things. They are the chief strategists of the legislature. For them, strategy is a constant, beginning before issues are raised and ending, at least temporarily, only when the senate and house adjourn *sine die*. So many of the sustained conversations leaders have with their colleagues, executive officials, or lobbyists involve planning ahead of one kind or another.

Thinking several steps ahead, having an endgame in mind is part of the leadership job. Among his other attributes as a legislative leader, Michigan's Engler was a consummate strategist. "Engler was a masterful chess player," his biographer writes. "He was always five steps ahead of everyone else." [17] On major issues, especially the budget, the endgame is likely to involve negotiations with the other body and also with the governor. Either way, the strategy in drafting and passing the budget bill (as well as other bills) requires that certain items be set aside and others included, so that the leader's chamber has the ability to trade during the process of settlement. Each side needs to use flexibility and resources in the process. Strategies are always changing, adapting to new circumstances. In the legislature nothing is stable for very long, so leaders have to be quick on their feet. Nothing is entirely out of the question.

One leadership strategy that frequently works in helping legislators reach agreement is keeping members on the floor for long hours. Leaders believe that consensus can emerge out of discomfort. "When the members are grumpy and tired and want the issue to be over," said Speaker Scott Jensen of Wisconsin, "is when a deal can be made." Some legislative leaders will not break for lunch in the belief that hunger will prompt members to move faster. Some leaders take up major bills on Fridays, because the process will move faster when members want to get home for the weekend.

Roger Moe, the former majority leader of the Minnesota Senate, likened his overall strategic task to trying to put together all the pieces of a jigsaw puzzle. Each of his members had a piece, but Moe as leader had the cover of the box with the picture of the assembled puzzle on it. Only he had a chance to fit the pieces together, because only he knew what the final product was supposed to look like. But it was the members' pieces that determined how the assembled puzzle looked. Some legislators are consummate strategists, among them Sheldon Silver, the speaker of the New York Assembly. In the words of Gov. Eliot Spitzer, with whom he had to bargain, Silver "is an enigma, the grandmaster of the chess game of Albany maneuvers."[18]

Consensus Builder

William M. Bulger, a former senate president in Massachusetts, put it this way: "You come into the Senate every day with a wheelbarrow of 33 cats. Your job is to get the wheelbarrow with 17 of those cats to the other side of the chamber." In his memoirs, Bulger describes the job as requiring a great deal of sympathetic listening: listening for points of agreement that can be developed into a base upon which to build and listening for areas of compromise. The leader, according to him, should offer suggestions to keep the process moving. Although the leader is the navigator, Bulger writes:

> ... [T]he end product—whether to support or oppose a bill, or to agree on a viable compromise—is not something that can be inflicted by leadership; it is a consensus resulting from the communal wisdom and goodwill of the membership.[19]

Perhaps the most important job of the leader is to help colleagues work toward and arrive at agreement.[20] "My job is to bring people together," is how Mike Miller, president of the Maryland Senate, characterized his leadership role. His counterpart in the Maryland House, Speaker Mike Busch, described his goal as consensus and his job "to provide the information and build consensus."[21] Moe put it somewhat differently, but his goal was similar: "Get all the passion in the same room. Only a legislative leader has the ability to get three, four, or five disputants together on short notice."

More is involved than getting them together and leaving them to their own devices. The tough part is getting them to resolve their differences, to agree on something. Leaders have to broker deals among people with different interests and conflicting positions. No one was better at this than Willie Brown. Because of the position he held and the skills he exercised, Brown could bring together major stakeholders for a series of meetings in his office and at Frank Fat's restaurant in Sacramento. The culmination of these sessions at Frank Fat's was what became known as the "napkin deal," which led to compromise legislation changing California's liability laws. As described by James Richardson, the speaker's involvement was essential if consensus among conflicting interest groups was to be built:

> As plates of chicken wings and pea pods were shuttled to the tables, the representatives of the warring industries scribbled on legal pads, trying to work out a political truce. They were joined by Democratic State Senator Bill Lockyer and eventually by Willie Brown. The night wore on, and Brown shuttled between the tables, talking with each participant, probing for trouble spots. The talk nearly broke down when the trial lawyers balked over a detail. Are you going to trust me? . . . Are you going to let me deal for you? Brown closed the deal.[22]

The most critical consensus-building task of leaders takes place in the party caucus. Although leaders mediate among all members to work out disputes, their primary efforts are to get members of the caucus together on major issues, and especially on the budget. Often the party caucus is geographically and ideologically diverse. Molding a consensus from such a group is no small feat. It starts with the leaders helping the caucus locate its will on major items. Then, leaders translate that will into a bill or an amendment, which they try to enact into law. Engler was almost always able to pull things together in the caucus, mainly by "taking the common elements in everyone's position and knitting them together into a whole," and then figuring out what compromises were needed to get the final vote.[23] Building consensus in the party caucus entails the development of a broad base of support, which is more than rounding up a majority of votes. Leadership strives to build as much support for a measure as possible—within the caucus, not necessarily between the parties. The objective in most partisan states, at any rate, is to include one's party members in a majority consensus, and not to have to rely on the minority for votes.

Negotiator

Everyone in the legislature negotiates. Leaders, however, are the chief negotiators, the negotiators of last resort, the big-ticket negotiators. When committee negotiations are underway but hit a stumbling bloc, leaders may be called in to help out. When thorny issues cannot be resolved elsewhere, leaders will be invited to sit at the table. Otherwise, leadership strategizing and negotiating normally involve the key issue of the session. That would include the budget, items on the governor's agenda, and a few priorities of the majority party caucus.

A leader will negotiate with rank-and-file members in order to round up votes, but normally one's major negotiations are with the leader of the other chamber and the governor. Whether budgets are formulated by the executive or legislative branch and however much the input of the appropriations or ways and means committees, it is almost certain that top legislative leaders will be the ones negotiating on behalf of their chambers. Because differences invariably exist among the governor's budget, the senate's budget, and the house's budget, in order for a single budget to emerge negotiations have to take place. Realistically, not every member can negotiate. So in effect, majority party caucuses delegate the job to their leader. Especially toward the end of the session, when the two chambers are trying to resolve differences, rank-and-file legislators have to wait for their leaders to come to terms. Leaders go back and forth, checking with the caucus to ensure that they will have support for the settlements they reach.

Massachusetts leaders—House Speaker Salvatore DiMasi and Senate President Robert Travaglini—spent months in 2005–2006 negotiating health insurance with each other and with Gov. Mitt Romney and various stakeholders. Despite their competing pride of authorship, their contrasting negotiating styles, and many difficult issues in dispute, they got the job done. During the final weeks of negotiations, the leaders, along with conferees and staff, worked things out while members spent most of their time in recess.

As negotiators, leaders have to be knowledgeable and skillful. They have to know what their members want and what their caucus needs and also what the other side wants and needs. They have to have a sense of how far they can go and how much they can get, and be able to give as little away as possible. They know they cannot get everything they want; they realize they have to compromise. The question is, what is the bottom line for compromise? New York's Silver has the reputation for being a superb negotiator. One of the assembly's former members, Pete Grannis, describes Speaker Silver's style:

> He waits for things to break his way, not offering anything, just waiting. He'd wait everyone out, and pretty soon, in exasperation, people throw in the towel and make a deal.[24]

In negotiating, patience is the cardinal virtue. Michigan's Engler had it in spades. He would hang on and continue hanging on. He knew the longer he waited, the more others would give. "He was always the last man standing," and thus wound up with deals that were better than he anticipated.[25] Should negotiators fail to agree on a budget by the constitutional deadline or if their disagreement should lead to a shutdown of state services, their negotiations are thought to have failed. But despite the criticism they receive, negotiations continue or resume and settlements are achieved. Or if negotiators come away with less than their members expect, they may lose votes or reputation. Either way, it is a high-stakes game.

Vote Getter

In addition to strategizing, building consensus, and negotiating, leaders have to help round up votes—certainly on major issues and occasionally on less major ones as well.[26] They round up votes one by one. They take repeated counts to figure out how many more members they need to convince. Normally, most majority party members are already with the caucus and the leadership. They are where they are because they believe in the position, are loyal to the party, want to represent their constituency, or just don't want to risk being in the doghouse with their leaders and colleagues. They go along for several of the above-mentioned reasons. Only a few then require a sit-down with the house speaker or senate president.

Leaders can enlist others to help them in the vote-getting endeavor. The governor may be called on, a particular colleague of the member may be enlisted, or an interest group lobbyist may be summoned to appeal for votes. On key issues, and for the last few votes to make a majority, members will be worked in multiple ways. The legislative leader is not only doing his or her personal bit but is orchestrating an allied effort to put a majority together as well.

In writing of his experience in the Massachusetts House, John E. McDonough recalls how George Keverian as speaker and Charles Flaherty as majority leader went about rounding up votes. Keverian owned a set of colored markers with which he kept track of his lobbying efforts. He used one color for his solid "yes" votes, another for his "yes leaners," one color for solid "no" votes, another for "no leaners," still another for "maybes," and one more for those who might take a walk on the vote.[27] The leader has to know which members to approach. Some are at the base of a bill's support, already committed—the solid "yes" members. For example, Wright seldom had to appeal to liberals; they were already on his side. "Whenever we go into counting on issues that were anticipated as being a battle royal," he wrote, "we could merely sit down and check off the members whom we were aware of who would agree with the intent of the bill. They were like money in the bank."[28]

Those in the middle, who are essentially undecided, are the legislators susceptible to leadership persuasion. Not all have to be approached or persuaded, just enough of them to get the necessary majority. "There's an Annapolis axiom," reports Maryland delegate Sandy Rosenberg, "that you don't buy a landslide. That is, don't incur more obligations than needed to get the bill passed."[29] Those members who strongly oppose a measure for reasons of conscience or constituency are usually let off the hook, especially if the needed votes can be found elsewhere.

Occasionally, leaders have to offer inducements in return for a member's vote. The leader may agree to persuade the governor to appoint one of the member's constituents to a state board or commission. Or the leader may persuade the member by putting items in the budget for the member's district. On rare occasions members may be threatened with the loss of a position, benefit, or—more likely—the leader's future favor. But threats are much rarer than inducements in terms of what leaders do to obtain votes. Speaker Murphy, for example, operated on the premise that legislators understand two things: what you can do for them, and what you can do to them. He was far more active in the former regard than the latter.[30]

The main technique that leaders use is simply to ask members for their votes and invoke loyalty to their caucus colleagues. Then they will use whatever arguments they can summon up. Any lawmaker would like to be asked personally by the leader, rather than be taken for granted. So leaders have to know how to ask—differently for different people. Vermont's Wright recalls requesting one of his members for support on a gay rights bill. Their delightful exchange, as recounted by Wright, ran as follows:

"Billy, can I talk to ya for a minute?" I said, as we bumped into each other just outside the Speaker's office. (Billy is a fictitious name.)

"Sure, Mr. Speaker," came the less than enthusiastic reply. Billy sensed he was about to be buttonholed.

"C'mon in the office for a second," I said. He followed like a kid headed for Mother Superior's shed.

"Now, Billy, you know I've been working my ass off trying to get enough votes to pass this gay rights bill and I need your help. I wouldn't ask you but it's going to be an extremely tight vote. What do you say, can I count on you?"

"Geez, Mr. Speaker, I just can't give you a hand on this one," he said. "My district is dead set against me voting for something like this." He was nervous.

"Oh, for Chrissakes, Billy, you know as well as I that by the time the next election comes around no one's going to remember this vote. We're a year and a half from the next time you have to put your name on a ballot," I argued.

"They'll remember this one, Mr. Speaker. I've been getting a lot of mail and calls. This is a tough one." He said it with the confidence of a man winning an argument.

"C'mon, Billy, I really need you on this one," I pleaded.

"Mr. Speaker, you know I'd do anything to help you out if I could but

you know it isn't just my folks back home. Frankly, the bill just isn't right."
That was the killer. He spoke now with the conviction of a used car salesman closing a deal for a lemon with sawdust in the transmission. He repeated this plea.

"It's just not right." Now at his best, his was the voice of an innocent
altar boy. Suddenly my mind flashed back to a rather famous "Tip" O'Neill
tale and I ended the conversation by lashing out at him, paraphrasing the
legendary U.S. House Speaker from Massachusetts:

"Billy, you ass, I don't need you when I'm right. I need you now."

I was up to 66.[31]

Asking a member for a vote is not to be taken lightly: the leader's request
can be rejected. It usually is not, but from time to time legislators turn their
leaders down. McDonough tells how the Massachusetts speaker, George
Keverian, tried to round up the eighty-one votes needed to pass a tax package in the house:

Keverian reached out in late November to Sal DiMasi, a likeable, wise-
cracking attorney and rep from the North End section of Boston. DiMasi
had recently been released from the hospital after suffering a heart attack
and was recuperating at his home, only a five-minute drive from the capitol. Keverian called to ask if he would consider making a special trip to the
State House to vote for the tax package. "You don't understand. George," he
said. "I had a heart attack, not a lobotomy."[32]

Despite exceptional cases and the humor expressed in the stories of
Wright and McDonough, generally speaking leaders are extremely solicitous
of the well-being of their members. They will not strong-arm them for votes
that it might be costly for members to give. Willie Brown, for instance, recalls
that although he exercised tight discipline as California's assembly speaker, "I
never once asked a member to cast a vote that he couldn't live with."[33]

Protector of the Institution

The idea of the legislature as an institution is an abstraction, even to legislators themselves. Identification with the senate, house, or legislature comes
to members relatively quickly. Loyalty to the institution comes at a slower
pace, and concern and responsibility appear later in a member's tenure.

Lawmakers have too much else on their plates to spend much time or energy on institutional concerns. The institutional buck, however, stops with leadership. The house speaker and senate president have to be the ones who put out fires and protect the legislature from attack. If individual members overstep legal or ethical boundaries, leaders figure out what kinds of official inquiry or action their chamber will take. If the media rip into the legislature, the leaders respond on behalf of the senate and house. They are the ones who defend legislative prerogatives in confrontations with the governor or states' rights in disputes with the federal government. They take responsibility for the orientation and continuing education of members, for capitol construction and renovation programs, and for strategies to ameliorate the negative effects of term limits or to deal with a cynical citizenry.

Legislative leaders have yet to figure out just how to represent the senate and house to the public or how to educate citizens as to the workings of the legislature and its functioning in representative democracy. Given all of their other responsibilities, it would appear that they have little left for the task of explaining the legislature to the public. Yet this may be one of their most significant responsibilities as protectors of the institution.

The Question of Power

Given the multiple responsibilities of the speaker of the house and the president of the senate, we would expect that these positions confer power on the incumbents. The top leaders, without doubt, are more powerful than rank-and-file members. They hire and fire staff, appoint members to chair committees, refer and calendar bills, steer the caucus, negotiate, and so forth. All of these functions afford them power.

Leaders acknowledge the power they can wield. Willie Brown referred to himself as the "Ayatollah of the Assembly," Tom Loftus acknowledged the near-dictatorial power that his position conferred, and Ralph Wright recognized that, during the session at least, the speakership made him the most powerful political figure in the state. As much as anyone, legislators see the power of their leaders. In the 2002 State Legislative Survey, legislators in the fifty states were asked to rate the majority party leadership on a scale of 1 to

7, with "1" indicating "no influence" and "7" indicating "dictates policy." Among the respondents, 63 percent of house members and 57 percent of senate members rated the majority party leadership as either "6" or "7." (The ratings probably would have been higher had the question asked about the speaker or president specifically, rather than the majority leadership more generally.) Members, at least, perceive their leaders as having power.

Variations in Power

Not all leaders are equally powerful. In the first place, the power of leadership varies over time. Leaders were a lot stronger thirty or forty years ago than they are today. Before the effects of the legislative modernization movement, leaders in most places had a virtual monopoly of staff and information. They were able to restrict decision making to a few senior members, while the rest of the membership went along. Joe Doria, a New Jersey veteran who had served in the assembly for years and then in the senate, recalled how things used to be: "When I was a freshman [in the 1970s], they treated you like a mushroom. They kept you in the dark and they fed you bullshit." Henry Bellmon, the former governor of Oklahoma, recalls J. D. McCarty, the speaker of the house, with whom he had to work in the 1960s. According to Bellmon, there was no point in dealing with anyone else in the house. McCarty's control was absolute: "Anytime he took the rostrum and pointed his thumbs upwards, the matter under consideration passed with a sizeable majority. Anytime he made the opposite gesture, thumbs down, the measure failed."[34]

Georgia furnishes an example of the dispersion of leadership power over time. The speaker before Tom Murphy, George L. Smith, exerted great control. He did not want a light bulb changed in the house without his knowing it. The first thing every day, the speaker would give his committee chairs their marching orders, and they obediently went along. When Murphy took over as speaker in 1974, things changed. He expected the chairs to run their own committees, which they did. By the end of Murphy's tenure, the house had become more fractious, with more Republicans, more women, and more African Americans. Murphy had to engage and involve various groups and individuals, which he did adeptly in order to deter any challenges to his leadership.[35]

Largely as a result of the capacity-building success of modernization, legislators have wound up with increased staff assistance and information. The rank and file no longer are seated on the sidelines but are expected to participate fully. The times have changed; so has the membership. Whether they serve in professional or citizen legislatures, members today insist on having a piece of the action. Power within the legislative body is more dispersed than it used to be. As Malcolm Jewell and Marcia L. Whicker report, members want to have input into decision making, so leaders have to accommodate them.[36] In the 1990s a survey of three hundred veteran legislators asked about the changing influence of different groups and individuals. Only 24 percent perceived an increase in the influence of legislative leadership, while 47 percent noted a decrease.[37] One empirical indicator of the increasing dispersal of power in legislatures is the enlargement of appropriations committees in the last twenty or so years. Formerly, only a few members served on these critical committees, and power over the budget was held rather tightly. As more members demanded a piece of the action, more were given a say on the budget. And in a few states today every member has a seat on a committee that reviews the budget.

The power of leadership varies not only over time but also by chamber. Power tends to be more dispersed in senates and more concentrated in houses. There are a number of reasons for the contrasting power distributions in the two bodies. The rules ordinarily invest more power in the office of speaker of the house than in that of president or pro tem of the senate. Senate rules committees, or the like, may share in assignments of members to committees and the scheduling of legislation for floor consideration. Houses are larger than senates—two or three times the size, or even more in the extreme case of New Hampshire. In order to get business accomplished on the floor as elsewhere, greater organization and control are required in the larger body. Small legislative bodies are more collegial. Senators, moreover, tend to be more experienced than their counterparts in the house. Many served previously in the house. With their four-year terms, they are somewhat more insulated from political turbulence and tend to rely less on leadership for help in elections. Senates are more individualistic than houses, and this means that senators are less inclined to toe the leadership line.

In addition, the power of leadership varies by state. At one extreme is New York, where both the speaker of the assembly and the majority leader of the senate are perceived by members, the press, and the public to be in a league of their own, with the rank and file almost shut out of the lawmaking process. Leaders are too strong, members are too weak—at least according to some observers.[38] Illinois is another state where leadership is considered to have a tight hold.[39] By contrast, leadership in the Nebraska unicameral is regarded as weak. According to Alan Ehrenhalt, the Nebraska speakership remains one of the weakest of any American legislature. The presiding officer rotates every four years, committee chairs are elected by their committee colleagues, and all bills are taken up on the floor in the order in which they are reported out by committee.[40]

Table 7-1 suggests differences in leadership power among houses in the states and from an earlier period to a later one. The table, constructed by Richard A. Clucas, is based on scores for legislator responses to two questions (one asked in a 1981 survey and the other in a 1995 survey) that are described in the table note. The scores apply to the majority party leadership generally rather than to the top leaders specifically. According to member perceptions, New York, Massachusetts, Rhode Island, and Pennsylvania rank high in perceptions of leadership power in both time periods, while Nevada and Wisconsin rank low. Just about all the other states for which Clucas has data change in ranking from the early to the later year. Membership perceptions afford us an idea—although by no means as precise as the scores might suggest—of how power is distributed among the states. The differences in 1995 between New York and Illinois, Kentucky and Delaware, Vermont and Missouri, or Kansas and Nevada appear to be inconsequential. The differences, however, between New York, Illinois, Massachusetts, and Rhode Island, on the one hand, and Kansas, Nevada, South Dakota, and Maine, on the other, are of greater consequence.

Finally, the power of leadership varies by leader. Individuals differ in how they do their jobs as house speaker or senate president and how they exercise the power at their disposal. The individual makes a huge difference. Unruh of California, for example, made a power center out of whatever job he had in politics. Before Unruh became chair of the assembly Ways and

Table 7-1 The Perceived Power of State House Leaders, 1981 and 1995

	1981		1995	
Ranking	State	Score	State	Score
1	Massachusetts	0.889	New York	0.972
2	Oklahoma	0.833	Illinois	0.947
3	Rhode Island	0.741	Massachusetts	0.935
4	Ohio	0.727	Rhode Island	0.900
5	Missouri	0.656	Kentucky	0.896
6	California	0.050	Delaware	0.895
7	Arizona	0.643	Washington	0.847
8	Hawaii	0.630	Indiana	0.839
9	New York	0.609	North Dakota	0.836
10	Pennsylvania	0.609	Pennsylvania	0.823
11	Iowa	0.519	Hawaii	0.821
12	West Virginia	0.519	Iowa	0.814
13	Michigan	0.478	Alaska	0.808
14	Minnesota	0.464	Maryland	0.803
15	Kansas	0.462	Ohio	0.795
16	Washington	0.455	New Mexico	0.788
17	New Hampshire	0.440	West Virginia	0.764
18	Connecticut	0.424	Arizona	0.758
19	Maine	0.417	Montana	0.757
20	Colorado	0.364	Vermont	0.746
21	Maryland	0.364	Oklahoma	0.743
22	Illinois	0.360	Colorado	0.742
23	Delaware	0.316	Missouri	0.742
24	North Dakota	0.308	New Hampshire	0.717
25	New Jersey	0.250	Oregon	0.707
26	Utah	0.250	Utah	0.696
27	Idaho	0.243	California	0.680
28	Wyoming	0.233	Michigan	0.673
29	New Mexico	0.229	New Jersey	0.655
30	Indiana	0.214	Idaho	0.643
31	Alaska	0.200	Connecticut	0.636
32	South Dakota	0.179	Minnesota	0.623
33	Wisconsin	0.172	Wyoming	0.591
34	Montana	0.162	Wisconsin	0.564
35	Oregon	0.115	Kansas	0.557

(Table continues)

Table 7-1 (continued)

	1981		1995	
Ranking	State	Score	State	Score
36	Vermont	0.087	Nevada	0.550
37	Nevada	0.048	South Dakota	0.531
38	Kentucky	0.037	Maine	0.500

Source: Richard A. Clucas, "Legislative Professionalism and Power of State House Leaders," *State Politics and Policy Quarterly* 7 (Spring 2007): 8.

Note: The scores for 1981 are the percentage of times in each state that lower-chamber members ranked the "Office of Presiding Officers or Majority Leaders" as the most significant place where decisions were made in their chamber. The scores for 1995 are the percentage of times in each state that lower-chamber members identified "Majority Party Leadership" as being the most influential actor in their chamber.

Means Committee, the job was little more than that of lieutenant to the governor. Unruh changed the chairmanship into a bastion of power over money and policy. Before Unruh, the speaker was little more than a mediator between factions. "Unruh turned it into the second most powerful office in the state," according to Bill Boyarsky.[41]

In his memoirs, McDonough discusses dealings with four Massachusetts speakers, "each strikingly different from the other."[42] Each of them had roughly the same power available, but with different personalities, different members with whom to work, and different circumstances. They contrasted dramatically in how they operated. In particularly sharp contrast are Thomas Finneran, under whom McDonough completed his tenure in the house, and Salvatore DiMasi, Finneran's successor. Finneran kept rather tight control, sometimes too tight for his members. But he worked on their behalf and retained their support. After Finneran's leadership, the members wanted to be on a much longer leash. DiMasi obliged; he did not have much choice, if he wanted his colleagues to elect him speaker. He even agreed to allow decisions to be made on the house floor before he had the votes to pass the bills that were brought up. As a result, unlike floor votes in most other chambers, bills are defeated or substantially amended on the floor in the Massachusetts House. The contrast in the senate between Robert Travaglini and his predecessor, Thomas Birmingham, runs along the same lines.

This is not to say that DiMasi and Travaglini are not persuasive—they are. In the opinion of one of the senators, "The speaker and the senate president don't lose when they put the weight of their office behind it."[43] In the 2006 session DiMasi lobbied his house colleagues to vote against a bill authorizing slot machines at race tracks. Travaglini lobbied his senate colleagues to vote for it. The bill passed the senate but not the house. According to DiMasi, the slots vote was one of conscience for members. If so, the conscience of the speaker and his members were in alignment. On other issues, however, the speaker's position did not prevail. He supported the primary seat belt law, which failed by a close vote on the floor. He could not round up the votes to raise the licensed driver's age.

Sal DiMasi quipped about the exalted position of speaker in the Massachusetts House: "It's a good job, except for the members who get in the way." On their part, the members would see it differently: as the speaker getting in *their* way. Both points of view are accurate, to a point. Despite the power that DiMasi and other leaders have at their disposal, they have to tread carefully, because their powers, like those of any legislative leader, are limited.

Among their powers is that of punishing members; but the ultimate punishment is not theirs to dispose. They cannot fire colleagues, who serve at the pleasure of the voters in their districts. However, they can refuse to appoint them to leadership positions or to committees on which they want to serve, and they can remove members from leadership positions they hold. Leaders have broad discretion here, yet they are constrained in how often they use such authority.

If members get out of line, leaders can and do discipline them. That means taking away a position or perks or not bestowing a position or perks. An out-of-the-way office, a relatively remote parking place, an undesirable seat in the chamber, the denial of funds to pay for a trip to a conference out of state—these are among the punishments that leaders hand out. Although they do not appear onerous to the reader, they do affect those who are afflicted. The removal of a committee chair by the leader is probably the most extreme punishment. Sometimes returning members are not reappointed to the committees they have been on or to the chairs they have held. Sometimes leadership discipline involves removing members who are then serving on committees or as chairs. Such punishment is rare. Even the strongest leaders, such as Brown of California and Riffe of Ohio, during the course of their twenty or so years in the speakership, removed only a few committee chairs.

Severe punishment, such as removal from a leadership position, occurs when members go against a position taken by their party caucus. Florida's speakers have from time to time removed members from the leadership team because of their unwillingness to go along with the Republican caucus. In 2001 Speaker Tom Feeney removed Nancy Argenziano and in 2003 Speaker Johnnie Byrd removed Sandra Murman from a leadership council. More recently, in 2007 Speaker Marco Rubio removed two colleagues after they voted against the insurance package that was passed in a special session. The Democratic minority leader defended Rubio's action. "When we take caucus positions on something, we do expect people to support it," said Dan Gelber. "It's a responsibility that comes with leadership."[44]

Preferment, rather than punishment, is the dominant leadership style of dealing with members. Carrots work much better than sticks. That is because leaders need their members as much as members need their leaders. From time to time, they need a member's vote on the floor or in committee and, whether they actually need it or not, they want the member's support in the next election for the house speaker or senate president. Scott Jensen, a speaker in Wisconsin, summarized: "If you punish them today, they'll punish you tomorrow."

The power to steer legislation by referring bills to committee and deciding whether and when they are taken up on the floor is not insignificant. The referral power is not used much, because jurisdictions are spelled out. In a number of legislative bodies, however, leaders have at their disposal committees with broad jurisdictions to which they can refer bills. These are known as "killer" or "graveyard" committees, to which bills slated for burial are sent. If leaders oppose bills reported favorably by standing committees, they usually can, by one means or another, keep them from being considered on the floor. Leadership power to keep something from happening is substantial, and is probably the greatest power at their disposal. But, for the most part, leaders take action that their caucus would approve or does approve. In those cases where the caucus is unconcerned, leaders have great discretion.

Since the transformation of legislative campaigns in state after state, leaders have assumed the job, and also the power, of campaign manager. It is popularly believed that raising and allocating campaign funds affords leaders enormous power over their party colleagues. They can reward their friends with larger allocations and punish their enemies with smaller ones—or with no funding at all, the thinking goes. Here, however, the leaders' hands are tied. Their objectives are to hold their majority, not lose seats, and perhaps even gain a few. They have to allocate money in order to achieve those objectives, which means the competitive, targeted races get the lion's share of what there is to give out. Thus, an enemy of the leader in a targeted district will receive more than a friend of the leader in a safe district. Under such circumstances of competitive politics, leaders cannot afford to settle scores. It is better for them to have a recalcitrant member in their own caucus than an additional member in the opposition caucus. Members in tough districts recognize that they need their leader's help and probably stay in line to get it. But their need to get support from voters in the district outweighs their need to kowtow to their leaders.[45]

Through their roles strategizing, negotiating, building consensus, and getting the votes, leaders certainly appear to be at the head of the parade. But what leaders are doing, except on special occasions, is leading the parade on the route the members want to take. One political scientist, on the basis of interviews with New York lawmakers, expected to hear complaints about the tight grip of leadership. But that was not quite the case, he wrote:

> Though there were such grumblings, much more prevalent was the view that although party leadership ran a tight ship in the legislative battle, the opportunity for input also existed, and that the leadership did respond to the accumulated preferences of its members.[46]

Sheldon Silver, the speaker of the assembly, reinforced a point that few observers of New York state politics appreciate. "Nothing happens here in Albany, in the Assembly," he said, "without the input of rank-and-file legislators."[47]

Legislative leaders are permitted to exercise power only so long as they delegate a good deal of it and follow the wishes of their members with regard to the rest. They can, and do, intervene in the decision-making processes of standing committees, but only from time to time. For the most part, they run with what their committees pass to them. Larry Pogemiller, the majority leader in the Minnesota Senate, resists any assertion that leadership has infringed on the independence of individual members or standing committees. He points out that before becoming majority leader he had chaired twelve conference committees, and not once was he told by top leadership what deal to make or not to make. As top leader himself, he insisted that he never told committee chairs that they had to wait for leadership permission before taking any action in committee.[48]

The committees tend to be the principal policymakers, unless overturned by the majority party caucus. Normally, it is with the caucus membership that the final say resides. DiMasi put it most succinctly when he said with regard to a particular high-profile issue, "Basically we listened to our membership."[49] Wright was surely one of the most assertive speakers Vermont has known, as his memoirs attest. Yet even he was beholden to his colleagues. He writes: "I was captive to my caucus, and that, I believe, is a major reason why I managed to serve five terms . . . they decided their agenda, and I rarely was in disagreement."[50] A majority of the Democrats in his caucus were either liberals or moderates, so Wright was usually in agreement with his colleagues. But if he hadn't been, he would have had either to go along with the majority or abandon the speakership.

On those issues where the caucus is divided, the leader may be able to influence which way a majority goes. But sharp division often means that a measure before the caucus will be tabled unless disagreements can be worked out and a substantial majority of members are on board. If lawmakers are agnostic on an issue, leadership will be given the benefit of the doubt. Here, if anywhere, is where leaders govern. As McDonough writes with respect to the Massachusetts House: "Rank-and-file legislators typically follow their party leadership unless a compelling reason pushes them in a different direction."[51]

Leaders undoubtedly have power. But when drawn upon, it is used at the margins. Leadership power cannot turn around members who, because of conscience or constituency, face the other direction. Leaders, if they hope to remain at the top of the heap, have to please their members—that entails giving them what they want in terms of perks, pork, policy, participation, and power. As dominant a figure as Willie Brown was during his successive terms as speaker in California, he was known in Sacramento as "The Members' Speaker." He did their bidding; he made them happy. So he could always count on a majority of the eighty votes in the assembly to keep him in office. Brown referred to this as "The Rule of 41," a rule he lived by.

Limits on Terms

One of the principal limits on the powers of the top leaders is that there are limits on their terms of office. Brown would have stayed on as speaker were it not for two factors: first, the Democrats lost the majority in the assembly; and second, Brown's assembly career was about to be ended by term limits, which had been adopted by California voters a few years earlier. Another factor that limits the tenure of leaders is defeat at the polls, in a primary or general election. A number of prominent legislative leaders have been targeted and beaten in general or primary elections. Among them are Ralph Wright of Vermont, Tom Murphy of Georgia, Cas Taylor of Maryland, Robert Jubilerer of Pennsylvania, Robert Garten of Indiana, Raymond Sanchez of New Mexico, and John Martin of Maine. Still another way for leaders to exit is by a vote of the members, even when their party retains the majority. Finally, leaders may leave voluntarily, when they decide to move on in politics or go back to private life.

Few lawmakers have long runs in top leadership anymore. In the 1960s and 1970s, it was not uncommon for leaders to hold office for ten, twenty, or twenty-five years. Today, the circulation through leadership chairs is much swifter. The National Conference of State Legislatures tracks leadership change. At the opening of the 2007 legislative session, out of 332 positions (including more than those in top leadership only), 145—or 44 percent—of the leaders were new. Voluntary retirement, term limits, and party change had taken out almost half the nation's legislative leaders.

Term limits have the most drastic effects. The term-limits study found that no leader in a term-limited state had served more than four years in a top leadership post, with the large majority serving only two.[52] In California, for example, since term limits took effect, the average tenure of speakers has been about two years, while that of senate pro tems has been six.

One of the results of diminished tenure is a weakening of the majority party leadership (as well as the weakening of committee chairs), according to the lawmakers responding in the 2002 State Legislative Survey.[53] On the basis of his study of the effects of term limits in Colorado, John A. Straayer explains:

> Leadership is clearly weaker, and that has little to do with the formal authority, which is unchanged, nor with leader personalities and qualities, which do shift. Mostly, it tracks to the immediate lame duck status of leaders . . . they are lame ducks the instant they're selected.[54]

Lame duck status can be crippling. In term-limited states everyone knows exactly when the leader's term will end. For freshmen legislators, there are no long-term consequences for offending a leader.[55] And the possibility of long-term consequences is what mainly keeps members in line.

Much of the power leaders have over members is less about today than about tomorrow. It involves members' expectations of what leaders can do for them or not do for them in the future. Each and every lawmaker will need something—a committee assignment, a bill, a budget item, an appointment for a constituent, or something else. Or maybe all the member wants is recognition. If neither the top leader nor the member has a future in the body, there is little to be expected of what the leader can do. Thus, there is not much reason to follow the leader today, at least not in order to have IOUs for tomorrow.

The power of leaders is limited, not only by constitutional or statutory restrictions on length or service, but also by how long the members want their leaders to serve. A number of legislative bodies, by tradition, restrict top leaders to a term or two. Senates in Alabama, Arkansas, Nevada, New Mexico, North Carolina, Pennsylvania, and Rhode Island restrict the length of terms of their top leaders to four or eight years. By tradition the speakership in Connecticut rotates every four years. In both the senate and house in Massachusetts, the two presiding officers can serve eight years, and in both bodies in North Dakota and Wyoming they are limited to just one session.

Leaders anywhere are never sure bets to go the limit. They can be ousted at any time. Increasingly, leaders are being pressed by members of their own party who want their turns at the top. This encourages incumbent leaders to move on, or risk challenge and possible ouster. During recent decades, many leaders have been pressured to step aside while others have been blindsided by caucus revolts or beaten by bipartisan coalitions. As Steve Sviggum, the former speaker in Minnesota, said: "Friends come and go, but enemies accumulate." [56] A number of leaders have been challenged. Even New York's Silver had to put down a coup, which he did in 2000. Other leaders, however, have been challenged successfully. The ouster of leaders in California, Oklahoma, Massachusetts, Connecticut, Minnesota, New York, Kentucky, North Carolina, and Pennsylvania have surely been noted by leaders elsewhere.

Anything can happen when a legislature organizes. In January 2007 the Tennessee Senate dumped its leader, as one Democrat and seventeen Republicans joined to replace Democrat John Wilder, who had served thirty-six years. The organization of the house went differently in Texas. The Republican speaker, Tom Craddick, who was trying for a third term, had to fight off a challenger in his own party. Craddick prevailed, but his leadership style, which had led to the attempted coup, would probably have to change if he hoped to hang on. Either he would let up, or he would be confronted with greater dissatisfaction within the ranks of his caucus.

Legislative leadership is certainly not what it used to be. Leaders have less time in office to accrue power. The power they have has to be used gingerly. And it is being depleted—as air would be depleted from a slow leak in a tire—because of the leader's expanding responsibilities, the state's increasing demands, and members' growing needs and greater insistence.

Notes

1. Tom Loftus, *The Art of Legislative Politics* (Washington, D.C.: CQ Press, 1994), 47.
2. In the text I shall refer to the top leader in the house as the speaker and the top leader in the senate as the president or president pro tem.
3. Ralph Wright, *All Politics Is Personal* (Manchester Center, Vt.: Marshall Jones Company, 1996).
4. This paragraph draws on Alan Rosenthal, *The Decline of Representative Democracy* (Washington, D.C.: CQ Press, 1998), 181–182; and it also draws on interviews with Riffe in 1995 after his speakership had ended.

5. Richard J. Powell and Rich Jones, "Maine," Joint Project on Term Limits (unpublished paper, 2004).

6. Rep. Steve Sviggum interview with Minnesota Civic Caucus, February 15, 2007.

7. Marvin L. Overby, Thomas A. Kazee, and David W. Prince, "Committee Outliers in State Legislatures," *Legislative Studies Quarterly* 29 (February 2004): 81–107.

8. Ralph Wright, *Inside the Statehouse* (Washington, D.C.: CQ Press, 2005), 26–27.

9. Richard Hyatt, *Mr. Speaker: The Biography of Tom Murphy* (Macon: Mercer State University Press, 1999), 172.

10. Wright, *Inside the Statehouse,* 109.

11. Hyatt, *Mr. Speaker,* 82.

12. Gleaves Whitney, *John Engler: The Man, the Leader, and the Legacy* (Chelsea, Mich.: Sleeping Bear Press, 2002), 94.

13. Taylor Pensoneau, *Powerhouse: Arrington from Illinois* (Baltimore: American Literary Press, 2006), 185.

14. Wright, *All Politics Is Personal,* 24–25.

15. Willie Brown, *Basic Brown* (New York: Simon and Schuster, 2008), 227.

16. This vignette draws on Alan Rosenthal, "More than a Leader," *State Government News* (August 2002): 38.

17. Whitney, *John Engler,* 101.

18. Quoted in *New York Times,* June 20, 2007.

19. William M. Bulger, *While the Music Lasts: My Life in Politics* (Boston: Houghton Mifflin, 1996), 71–72.

20. This section is based on Alan Rosenthal, *Heavy Lifting: The Job of the American Legislature* (Washington, D.C.: CQ Press, 2004), 225.

21. Tom Stuckey, "Master of Consensus," *State Legislatures* (July/August 2007): 29.

22. James Richardson, *Willie Brown* (Berkeley: University of California Press, 1996), 348.

23. Whitney, *John Engler,* 96.

24. Quoted in *New York Times,* June 20, 2007.

25. Whitney, *John Engler,* 98.

26. This section is drawn in part from Rosenthal, *Heavy Lifting,* 226–230.

27. John E. McDonough, *Experiencing Politics: A Legislator's Stories of Government and Health Care* (Berkeley: University of California Press, 2000), 137–138.

28. Wright, *All Politics Is Personal,* 177.

29. Diary of Del. Sandy Rosenberg, March 20, 2001.

30. Hyatt, *Mr. Speaker,* 180.

31. Wright, *All Politics Is Personal,* 25–26.

32. McDonough, *Experiencing Politics,* 142.

33. Brown, *Basic Brown,* 228.

34. Henry Bellmon, *The Life and Times of Henry Bellmon* (Tulsa, Okla.: Council Oak Books, 1992), 203.

35. Hyatt, *Mr. Speaker,* 62, 76, 176.

36. Malcolm Jewell and Marcia L. Whicker, *Legislative Leadership in the American States* (Ann Arbor: University of Michigan Press, 1994), 51.

37. Gary Moncrief, Joel A. Thompson, and Karl T. Kurtz, "The Old Statehouse, It Ain't What It Used to Be," *Legislative Studies Quarterly* 21 (February 1996): 61.

38. See Jeremy M. Greelan and Laura M. Morlton, *The New York State Legislative Process: An Evaluation and Blueprint for Reform* (New York: Brennan Center for Justice, New York University School of Law, July 21, 2004).

39. Christopher Z. Mooney and Tim Storey, "The Illinois General Assembly, 1992–2003," Joint Project on Term Limits (unpublished paper, August 16, 2004).

40. Alan Ehrenhalt, "Uniquely Unicameral," *Governing* (January 2006), 8.

41. Bill Boyarsky, "Jesse Unruh," *California Journal* (November 1999): 47–48. See also Bill Boyarsky, *Big Daddy: Jesse Unruh and the Art of Power Politics* (Berkeley: University of California Press, 2008).

42. McDonough, *Experiencing Politics,* 12.

43. Interview with Sen. Michael Morrissey, May 2006.

44. *Orlando Sentinel,* January 28, 2007.

45. Richard A. Clucas, "Legislative Professionalism and Power of State House Leaders," *State Politics and Policy Quarterly* 7 (Spring 2007): 14.

46. Grant Reeher, *First Person Political* (New York: New York University Press, 2006), 148.

47. *New York Times,* July 22, 2004.

48. Minnesota Civic Caucus interview with Sen. Larry Pogemiller, December 28, 2007.

49. *Boston Globe,* April 28, 2006.

50. Wright, *Inside the Statehouse,* 89.

51. McDonough, *Experiencing Politics,* 225.

52. Jennifer Drage Bowser, Keon S. Chi, and Thomas H. Little, *A Practical Guide to Term Limits: Final Report of the Joint Project on Term Limits* (Denver: National Conference of State Legislatures, July 2006), 7.

53. John M. Carey, Richard G. Niemi, Lynda W. Powell, and Gary F. Moncrief, "The Effects of Term Limits on State Legislatures: A New Survey of the 50 States," *Legislative Studies Quarterly* 31 (February 2006): 125–128.

54. John A. Straayer, "Colorado's Legislative Term Limits," Joint Project on Term Limits (August 2004).

55. Thomas H. Little and Rick Farmer, "Legislative Leadership," in *Institutional Change in American Politics: The Case of Term Limits,* ed. Karl T. Kurtz, Bruce Cain, and Richard G. Niemi (Ann Arbor: University of Michigan Press, 2007), 68.

56. Minnesota Civic Caucus interview with Rep. Steve Sviggum, February 15, 2007.

8

The Governor as "Chief Legislator"

THE FOUNDING FATHERS who drafted the U.S. Constitution devised a devilishly clever system of governance. What they put in place was based on the fear of concentrated power in any one place. Early in the political history of the states, the people's experience with colonial governors, who acted as agents of the English Crown, led to a distrust of the executive. Thus, the framing of state constitutions in the 1776–1787 period began with the weakening of executive power and the granting of power to the legislature and the people. Typically, under the original state constitutions the legislature selected governors, who were limited to one term and had no veto power. Not long after these democratic origins the states began to pull back, reasoning that in a republican form of government the legislative branch had a dangerous tendency to exert control in the service of its own ambition.[1]

The challenge to those who shaped the states and the nation was to prevent the abuse of power, which could result from its concentration. The preventive was a separation-of-powers structure, with three branches of government—legislative, executive, and judicial. This idea of separated powers made its way into the early state constitutions, although it was indefinite and undefined in all of them.[2] The U.S. Constitution specified the separation of powers as no state constitutions had done previously; and thereafter the states generally followed suit.

The plan was that the legislative branch would make law, the executive branch would implement it, and the judicial branch would interpret it. Each branch would have its own perspective and the legislature and the executive would have their own base of representation. The national legislature was closest to the people, given the fact that members of the House of Representatives would have to run for election every two years. Yet each member of the House would represent only a small district and each member of the Senate would represent only one of the states. By contrast, the president, whose selection was more indirect than that of representatives, had a national population to represent and a cosmopolitan rather than local perspective.

The separation-of-powers system, willed to us by our forefathers, also provided for checks and balances. Each branch has the constitutional responsibility to engage in or impact on the operations of the other branches. The executive is involved in legislation, the legislature in administration, and the court decides on matters of constitutionality and legality that govern the other branches. Each branch, in short, has the power to meddle in the affairs of the other.

Take the executive and the legislature. Their powers overlap, as far as lawmaking is concerned. The executive initiates legislation, as do individual legislators. The executive can veto bills that the legislature enacts, and the legislature can override the executive's veto. The legislature has to agree to executive appointments. The executive has discretion as to just how, and how faithfully, laws passed by the legislature are implemented, while the legislature can perform oversight of the executive's administrative performance.

The Sharing of Legislative Powers

One popular view of the separation of powers between the executive and legislative branches is that the legislature makes the laws and the executive administers them. A more accurate view recognizes that both branches are up to their ears in lawmaking. Another popular view is that, as far as lawmaking is concerned, the governor proposes and the legislature disposes. The fact is that both branches propose and both dispose. If, as the saying goes, it takes two to tango, it also takes two to make law.

Agenda Setting

Both the governor and the legislature share in the setting of the agenda for policies and programs that may potentially become law.

State constitutions provide for the initiation of policy by governors. Article V, Section 1, of the New Jersey Constitution is illustrative, stating that: "The Governor shall . . . recommend [to the legislature] such measures as he may deem desirable." Such constitutional provisions give license for special messages, as the need arises, and for the State of the State address in which governors generally put forward their priorities for the legislative session. As a speechwriter for California governor Pete Wilson explained, the State of the State address "is to a governor what a strong serving game is to a good tennis player. It is a chance to put the ball in play and determine the location and movement of his opponent." [3]

Governors have a great advantage in being able to focus—to pick and choose what they will or will not put on their agenda and, consequently, on that of the legislature. If governors concentrate on a limited number of initiatives, chances are that these items will be given top billing by the legislature. If a governor's agenda is both limited and politically astute, and if the governor has drafted proposals after consulting with legislative leaders, the legislature is likely to go along for the most part. But there are no guarantees. Setting the agenda and getting one's way are entirely different. It takes skill, hard work, and compromise on the part of the governor to get favorable results.

When the governor's party holds the majority in the senate and house, governors can establish good records in getting the legislation they want. Gov. Parris Glendening of Maryland had little trouble with a Democratic legislature, even though he upset many members with his leadership style. During the 2001 session, for example, he chose to focus on fifteen administration bills, including collective bargaining for higher-education employees, smart growth, and the outlawing of racial profiling. Just about everything he wanted, he got. Even when government is divided, with one or both houses of the legislature controlled by the party that is not the governor's, governors do pretty well when it comes to achieving their agendas. Zell Miller of Georgia, for instance, was a master at agenda setting. He confined his efforts to one or two major issues. Gov. Ned McWherter of Tennessee also limited the number of issues he asked the legislature to take on. As one legislator commented, "He'll have his package of bills every year, and we always pass them." [4] However, where a governor's agenda is too large and too ambitious, his or her batting average will not be high.

Legislatures have come to expect, even rely on, a gubernatorial agenda. It structures the process for them, at least as much as the process can be structured. Setting their own agenda is a more difficult business for legislatures, because every member has his or her own agenda. Things have to get sorted out in each chamber—by the leaders, in committee, or in the majority party caucus. Often, the two chambers go through the session with different agendas, but they reach agreement on an ad hoc basis. Legislatures have to deal—to some extent, at least—with most of the bills that are introduced, and they certainly have to respond to those that have support outside and inside the body. Governors, by contrast, devote their energies to proposals that they themselves choose (after advice, consultation, and strategic analysis).

For the most part, legislative agendas develop in the course of the legislative process and as member support builds. Sometimes, legislative leaders bring their own policy agendas to their caucus to obtain support. Or they respond to their members' concerns and put together agendas to reflect them. Legislative agendas that shape the process rather than being shaped by it are usually limited, just as are the governor's agendas.

Most governors take on the role of "chief legislator." Harry Hughes of Maryland was one of the exceptions. Hughes believed that it was the legislature's responsibility to exercise leadership in lawmaking, more so than the governor's.[5] Howard Dean of Vermont, during his last years in office, had little of an identifiable agenda but dealt with the legislature on an ad hoc basis.

Budget Formulation

In the large majority of states the governor assembles the most important agenda of all: the one for state spending. It is detailed in the budget and enacted as one or a number of bills. The budget is the only bill introduced in the legislature that must be taken up and enacted every year, as in most states, or biennially, as in several others. The state's budget is where priorities are set, mainly by deciding how revenues are raised and expended and also by introducing new policies. While the legislature, and only the legislature, can actually appropriate funds, governors in most states shape where the money will go and for what it will be used.

"The governor's power to propose budgets," writes Tom Loftus, "is what really gives the governor the tiller when it comes to setting the course of policy."[6] In the budgetary arena, according to a Connecticut analysis, the governor is the "ringmaster." It is with the governor's formulation that the legislature has to work, while "the governor, his policies, and his budget staff are in the center ring." [7] In three-quarters of the states, governors have full responsibility for preparation of the budget. In the other quarter, responsibility is shared with the legislature.[8]

In most states, legislatures have been content to work from the governor's formulation and exert their influence in the process of reviewing the governor's budget. But from time to time legislatures have contested an arrangement that they believe unbalances the relationship. Perhaps the weakest legislature from a budget standpoint is Maryland's. That is because all the legislature can do is cut funds from the governor's budget. According to the Maryland Constitution, it cannot add funds, nor can it switch monies around. This means that it is impossible for the legislature to add or substitute its own priorities and programs as part of its review of the budget. The only recourse available to it is to persuade the governor to include some of its spending priorities in the budget the executive formulates or in a supplemental budget. The Maryland General Assembly is by no means powerless, but it is at a big disadvantage in relation to the governor.

On a number of occasions in the last decade the Maryland legislature deliberated over whether to put a constitutional amendment on the ballot for approval by the voters in a referendum. The amendment would have given the legislature the authority to switch around items and funding, while not exceeding the spending total requested by the governor. Such proposals were opposed by the executive. The legislature failed to enact the amendment, which required a three-fifths majority in each house. It was beaten back by Democratic governors William Donald Schaefer and Parris Glendening and by Republican governor Robert Ehrlich.

The New York Legislature exemplifies those bodies that refuse to allow the governor the advantage that he insists is constitutionally the executive's. The New York Constitution appears to give the governor budget primacy.[9] Redrafted in 1927, the constitution shifted responsibility for the budget from the legislature to the governor. It provided that the legislature could not alter appropriations bills except by striking out an appropriation, reducing it, or adding spending on a separate line. The governor then could veto any legislative additions. In a 1938 revision of the constitution the legislature was prohibited from passing other appropriations until it took final action on the governor's bill. In recent years, New York's governors have used descriptive language in the budget to shape or reshape programs without seeking legislative authorization. The legislature found the practice objectionable. But in 1993, in *New York State Bankers Association v. Wetzler*, the state's judicial branch ruled that although the legislature could change numbers in appropriation bills, it could not alter descriptions of programmatic purposes.

The long-running power struggle between the governor and the legislature in New York had become a battle between the two institutions. According to the governor, negotiated budgets were an unwarranted exercise of legislative power in defiance of the state constitution. According to the legislature, descriptive language did not belong in the governor's budget bill. The conflict came to a head in 2001, when assembly Democrats and senate Republicans joined forces against the Republican governor and passed a bare-bones budget that omitted executive language of purpose and asked that it be submitted as legislation. It was intended to force the governor to negotiate.[10] Two weeks later Gov. George Pataki brought suit, charging that the legislature had "unconstitutionally acted in a way that diminished the executive's power." The governor was challenging the balance that the legislature had to work so hard to achieve.

It was up to the New York courts to referee between the two branches. A justice on the state supreme court—the first level of state courts—ruled that the governor, not the legislature, possessed the authority to alter language in appropriation bills. By the conclusion of 2003, a five-judge panel of the Appellate Division had rendered a similar opinion. According to the New York Constitution, the governor's practice of inserting changes to current law in language accompanying appropriations cannot be altered by the legislature.[11] As 2004 came to a close, the final ruling was handed down by New York's highest court. The ruling affirmed the decision of the lower courts and stated that constitutionally the governor has the sole authority to propose budgets. All the legislature can do is delete or reduce items the governor proposes, although it can add new items on separate lines that are subject to the governor's line-item veto. The legislature's practice, which had been to strike the governor's proposals and replace them with its own, was declared invalid.[12]

Most legislatures have greater authority regarding the governor's budget formulation than Maryland and New York. They not only can eliminate or reduce funds but also add and transfer funds among items. In a number of states, however, the governor does not have sole authority to prepare the budget. The legislature either formulates its own budget or collaborates with the executive in putting one together. One way or another, legislatures have a share of budget-formulation authority in Arizona, Arkansas, Colorado, Florida, New Mexico, North Carolina, Texas, and Utah. Texas has its Legislative Budget Board (LBB), which presents the budget bill while the executive is presenting its budget as a document, not a bill. In Mississippi, as well, the legislature receives two budget proposals—one from the governor and the other from the Legislative Budget Committee (LBC), which is dominated by legislative leaders. In Colorado the governor's budget also plays second fiddle to the budget put together by the legislature's Joint Budget Committee (JBC). Colorado is one of the few states where budget power is tightly held. The Joint Budget Committee consists of three senators and three representatives, four of whom are majority party members and two of whom are minority party members. The committee gets the governor's budget in November, has hearings, and receives state briefings and issue papers. It constructs its own budget document. In Utah and Florida, too, the legislature's budget normally takes precedence over the governor's.

Shaping Policy

The shaping and specification of policy and budgets occurs during the legislative process, as bills go from committee to caucus to the floor in both the senate and house. Although the action takes place on legislative terrain, the governor is a featured player on matters of executive concern.

While the governor's agenda nearly always takes center stage, the plot and script are written by the legislature as well as the executive. Legislatures can ignore gubernatorial proposals, and they do. Take the Democratic Massachusetts legislature responding to Republican governor Mitt Romney during its 2006 session. The legislature refused to roll back the income tax, deregulate the auto insurance industry, or reinstate the death penalty. The legislature can also negotiate with the executive and reach a compromise, and it did so in Massachusetts on a major health insurance package. As we shall see in later chapters, this was a remarkable illustration of power sharing between the senate and the house, the legislature and the governor, and Democrats and Republicans.

There are many more legislative initiatives than gubernatorial initiatives each session. Because of the governor's veto power, the legislature normally is willing to negotiate issues in order to get the governor's assent and signature on an enactment. If the legislature is sure of the votes to override a veto, it has little reason to compromise. But in many instances it would not be able to summon the extraordinary majority needed for an override. In Massachusetts, for example, Romney and the legislature disagreed on a minimum-wage bill, originating with the legislature. Romney proposed changes, but the legislature had enough votes to reject them. On a number of other issues, too, Democrats in the Massachusetts legislature had enough votes to ignore the Republican governor's opposition.

In most states, however, the situation is different. A Democratic-controlled legislature will try to reach a compromise with a Democratic governor. It would be rare under such circumstances that the legislature would attempt to override a gubernatorial veto. A Republican-controlled legislature will try to do the same with a Republican governor. If the legislature is controlled by one party and the executive by the other, chances are that the minority party in the legislature will have enough votes (usually one-third plus one) to uphold the governor's veto. If the legislature is divided, the governor will often have support in one of the chambers.

On the budget, especially, the legislature and the governor will probably negotiate most of the items in disagreement. Even in Massachusetts, a Democratic legislature and a Republican governor had more in common budgetarily than they had differences. On the supplemental budget that passed in June 2006, Romney prefaced the vetoes he cast as follows:

> Many of the provisions which have been brought forward by the legislature are ones which I requested and therefore appreciate. Others are, in some cases, as good as or perhaps better than some of those I put forward. I appreciate these as well.[13]

Elsewhere, too, the senate, the house, and the executive hammer out what the fiscal plan for the state will be. Take New York's 2007–2008 budget. In order to get agreement on a budget, in his first (and only) year in office, Democratic governor Eliot Spitzer had to make several concessions to the Republican-controlled senate. He agreed to restore health care cuts that he had made and consented to adding funds for school aid. He also compromised on property tax relief. The senate gave in to the governor on other items. Spitzer referred to the deals he and the legislature had made as "an intellectual meeting of the minds, across party lines, across regions, that makes tough decisions, and tough decisions that are in line with what I proposed. . . ."[14]

On the big issues, the legislature through its respective leaders and the governor or his or her staff negotiate the major differences. Usually they reach agreement. But legislative leaders are agents of their caucuses or of their chambers. They normally consult as they go along, and by the time the two branches have worked out their differences in the shaping of legislation, rank-and-file legislators are on board. At that point legislators and legislative and executive staff work out the details. For example, in the case of the framework budget agreement among Governor Spitzer, Senate Majority Leader Joseph Bruno, and Speaker Sheldon Silver, it was up to several conference committees of the legislature to hammer out specifics, which they did.[15]

Decision

Governors and legislatures are not always able to arrive at agreement; the legislature can refuse to give the governor anything close to what he or she wants. In such instances the governor can go to the people to get constituents to lobby their legislators on behalf of the gubernatorial initiative. By then, however, it is probably too late. In a state that provides for the initiative process, whereby a proposal can bypass the legislature and go on the ballot for a statewide vote, the governor can lead an initiative campaign. A number of contemporary California governors have gone this route, including Republican governor Arnold Schwarzenegger, who was blocked by a Democratic legislature from getting what he wanted. Then, of course, governors also have recourse, when they fail in the legislature. They can try again, at the next session or after the next legislative elections. Although the legislature is able to say no to a governor, more frequently it takes a gubernatorial initiative and reshapes it to its liking. What emerges as law has the fingerprints of both branches.

The governor can also say no to the legislature by casting a veto. The veto is the governor's weapon, one that most governors would prefer not to use. They would rather have the legislature withhold a bill opposed by the executive, because of the explicit or implicit threat of a veto. Gov. Carroll Campbell of South Carolina, for example, employed the veto early in his administration to establish a dominant position in his relationship with legislators. He wanted to show them that he carried a big stick, and was willing to swing it. Campbell describes how he impressed the legislature and got to the position he was seeking:

> From that point on I haven't had to do that [veto] very often because most of the time if there is something that they are in doubt over what I am going to do, they'll come and ask me. Then it is a much better process because they'll say, "Are you going to veto this?" And I'll say, "Yes, I have to veto it." So they'll say, "Well, what will you take, or what do you want?" When you get into that type of process, it is a much better process, but you have to establish the willingness to veto or to stand up when you think something needs to be done. I do that but I don't try to overdo it; but I've done it quite a bit.[16]

The veto power, which is enjoyed by governors in every state,[17] enables most governors to negotiate from a position of strength. Unless the legislature has the extraordinary majority of votes needed to override a veto, it had better attempt to satisfy the governor's objections. For many governors the veto, whether threatened or used, is a significant part of their governing styles. George Pataki of New York, Janet Napolitano of Arizona, Gary Johnson of New Mexico, and Mitt Romney of Massachusetts made frequent use of their veto power.

The veto is strongest as a gubernatorial weapon during the budget process. Governors in forty-four states have the line-item veto. This enables them to veto sections or items of appropriations bills—ordinarily expenditures added by the legislature—without having to reject the entire bill. (In Maryland, where the legislature cannot add to the executive budget, the governor does not need and does not have a line-item veto.) The line-item veto allows governors to use a scalpel rather than a meat axe, and to reduce an amount or remove a specific activity that they do not want funded. In twenty-six of the states governors can also veto substantive language in appropriations bills.

Usage of the line-item veto varies greatly. In New York, for example, until recently line-item vetoes were rare, since the governor and the two legislative leaders negotiated budgets. From 1983 through 1997, as a matter of fact, New York governors cast no budget vetoes. In 1998 Governor Pataki refused to negotiate a budget with the senate and assembly leaders. Instead, he reviewed the budget the legislature sent to him and cast 1,300 line-item vetoes (and in fifty-five instances vetoed budgetary language as well as appropriations). In 2003, in another executive-legislative confrontation, Pataki vetoed 119 items. In 2006, his last year in office, he blocked $2.9 billion worth of budget items with 202 vetoes.[18]

Some governors have further power, usually in the form of conditional or amendatory vetoes. The conditional veto, as employed in New Jersey, permits the governor to take a piece of legislation and negotiate a change with the legislature without having to start the process afresh. In Massachusetts the governor is able to amend a bill passed by the legislature and the latter can then agree or disagree with the governor's amendments. In Illinois a governor can return a bill to the legislature with specific recommendations for changes and language to amend the bill. If the legislature accepts the revisions by a majority vote in each house, the bill becomes law as amended. Otherwise, it becomes a vetoed bill requiring a three-fifths vote in each house to override. Probably the most extraordinary veto power was possessed by governors in Wisconsin, who had a partial veto at their disposal. It permitted governors to move individual letters from one place in a bill to another, thus changing the meaning of what the legislature intended. It also allowed governors to shift budget funds from one purpose to another. After years of opposition from the legislature, a referendum was approved by the Wisconsin electorate in April 2008 to limit the governor's veto power.[19]

The legislature will have the last word, if it can summon up enough votes to override a gubernatorial veto. Except in Alabama, Arkansas, Indiana, Tennessee, and West Virginia, it takes three-fifths or two-thirds of the members (in most states those elected, but in some states those present) of both houses to override a veto.

Generally speaking, overrides are exceptional. In some places, such as Georgia and New Mexico, they are virtually nonexistent. Nonetheless, some legislatures refuse to take no for an answer and summon up the votes to prevail over the governor. For example, Pataki's 2002 budget vetoes were challenged by the New York Legislature. It overrode practically all of them, restoring the $2.9 billion in spending the governor had cut from the budget bill. In New York a Democratic assembly had to coalesce with a Republican senate to exert legislative will vis-à-vis a Republican governor. That was no mean achievement; it is much simpler when a governor of one party faces a legislature overwhelmingly of the other party, as in Massachusetts. Here, the legislature routinely overrode Romney's vetoes, and on a single day, the house overrode forty vetoes. In 2006 the legislature routinely overrode Romney's budget vetoes, erasing all but 0.8 percent of the cuts the governor had made. In 2007 he vetoed almost $500 million, much of it in earmarks, from the $25.25 billion budget the legislature sent him. The legislature easily overrode Romney on many of the items. Under divided government in Massachusetts the legislature had the last word. Under Romney's successor, Democrat Deval Patrick, the Democratic legislature's stance is different. In other states, where partisan politics are more competitive, legislative overrides are difficult to accomplish.

It depends on the issues and the politics at the time. In Minnesota's 2008 session, for example, Republican governor Tim Pawlenty vetoed a transportation bill passed by the Democratic legislature. The bill would have increased the gas tax to fund road and bridge repairs and the sales tax in the Minneapolis–St. Paul metro area to fund transit projects. The Democratic-Farmer-Labor (DFL) Party picked up six Republican votes in the house and a few in the Senate, overriding Pawlenty for the first time since he took office in 2003.[20]

Why the Governor Has the Upper Hand

The two branches share lawmaking power. Yet for a combination of constitutional, statutory, and political reasons the governor can appropriately be called "chief legislator." No other lawmaker has comparable power.

Unity of Office

In the checks-and-balances system of executive versus legislature, one is better than many. The governor, who is one, has a distinct advantage over the legislature, who are many. The governor is unitary, the legislature bicameral.

The governor is a single elected person, who does not have to share top billing with other elected officials. In Alaska, the smallest legislature—sixty members—each has a say; in New Hampshire, the largest—424 members—each has a say. Either way, it is difficult to figure out just what is being said by the legislature itself.

How governors and legislators make up their minds is totally dissimilar. It is true that governors have to be sensitive to their various constituencies and to the legislature itself in formulating their lawmaking agendas. They have to consult, listen, and modify their plans in light of substantive considerations and political circumstances. Their staffs and department and division heads take part in the process. Governors are rarely free to do exactly what they want—not, at least, if they hope to succeed. However, once governors decide, that is it. Then the task is to move their agenda through the legislature, making whatever adjustments may be required to gain support. In legislatures, by contrast, the central struggle is in persuading coequals in each chamber to agree on policy.[21] Whereas the governor's principal concentration is on getting his or her decisions adopted, the legislature's principal concentration is on fashioning majorities in order to reach decisions. Lawmaking is a cumbersome, arduous, and frustrating process by which legislatures reach consensus. The governor reaches consensus by a much easier path.

The governor's standing vis-à-vis the legislature is also enhanced by the size of his or her constituency. Governors are elected statewide by forty, fifty, sixty, or more times as many voters as elect legislators. Because they represent statewide populations, not district populations, governors can claim statewide mandates. Legislators can do no better than claim local ones.

Anyone who has a doubt about the advantages that flow from gubernatorial oneness ought to consider what lawmaking would be like if the executive were multiheaded instead of unitary. If the multimembered legislature had to deal with a multiheaded executive, the balance of lawmaking power would demonstrably shift away from the governor.

The Bully Pulpit

Because the governor is a single person elected by voters statewide and the legislature is a collection of individuals, each of whom is elected by people in a small part of the state, governors are the ones who command the lion's share of media and public attention that gets devoted to politics and policy. "The cacophony of legislative voices," writes George W. Scott, a former member of the Washington Legislature, "can rarely compete with a governor who can capitalize on his singular visibility in the media." [22] Thad L. Beyle, a political scientist, echoes the observation: "Probably the most significant source of informal power available to governors is their relationships with the public through the media and through other modes of contact." [23] Because the governor speaks with one voice, the governor and not the legislature has a "bully pulpit" at his or her disposal. This affords the governor an elevated and prominent position for expounding administration views and appealing for support for administration policy. Legislators, on the other hand, have no pulpit at all. They have to expound and explain from the trenches, and their voices do not carry far. That is because no one is sufficiently elevated and no one speaks for the entire legislature. At best, the president or president pro tem speaks for the senate—or more likely, the majority party in the senate—and the speaker for the house—or more likely, the majority party in the house. There is no single person to whom the media can turn to obtain the legislative position, for in truth rarely is there such a thing as *the* legislative position. During tugs of war between the two branches, the capitol press corps will go to the legislature, and mainly to the leaders, for reports on the struggle. But it is the governor who the media favors through thick and thin.

Few governors neglect using the pulpit for purposes of advancing their legislative agenda. Not all, of course, are equally adept. But nearly all try to address the public both directly, at local events, and indirectly, through press conferences, photo ops, and accounts in the media. They do so with any one of several objectives in mind:

- to build public support for a measure that the executive and legislative leaders already endorse;
- to build public support and thereby persuade the legislature to back the governor;
- to encourage opposition to a legislative initiative that the governor opposes;
- to go over the head of the legislature, appealing to the public to pressure the legislature into giving the governor's initiative support; and

- to explain to and elicit support from the public for a measure endorsed by both the governor and the legislature.

Although the governor's role in communicating to the public varies, it is most visible when he or she is in conflict with the legislature. Each branch endeavors to win the public over to its side. Governor Campbell of South Carolina was particularly adept at this part of his job. In order to mold public opinion, he traveled around the state holding news conferences, speaking directly to the people, and focusing his office's press operations on his agenda. As a policy advisor to Campbell said, "We had the best message in the state." [24] It can be intimidating for legislators to know that the governor is making his or her case to the public, while they have no real opportunity to rebut it.

Few governors take on the legislature as directly and perhaps as vehemently as have two with celebrity status—Jesse Ventura of Minnesota and Arnold Schwarzenegger of California. When governors combine the visibility of their public office with the fame of their prepolitical careers as professional wrestlers or movie stars, they are in a good position to bully the legislature from the bully pulpit.

Ventura, for example, would verbally abuse legislators, whom he referred to as "gutless cowards." Unable to prevail during difficult budget negotiations, Ventura issued a press release that was typical of his approach:

This process has gone on too long and is now dangerously close to causing a government shutdown. I don't think that the legislature should be playing this game of chicken. It is difficult for me—and I'm sure for the people of Minnesota—to understand why this could not have been done in the five months of the regular session. . . .[25]

As the legislative session was approaching its constitutional end, Ventura on his weekly radio show or elsewhere would vent against the Minnesota Legislature, likening its members to children playing "a game of marbles" or "wanting to take their ball and go home." [26] Even more directly, Ventura went on trips around the state, taking his cause right to the people. Ember Reichgott Junge, a member of the senate at the time, recounts how Governor Ventura, an Independent, addressed a town hall meeting in Wabasha on the subject of unicameralism, a proposal of his that was stalled in the legislature. His plea was passionate:

> "While the legislature has caucuses for Democrats and caucuses for Republicans, I don't have a caucus. I stand alone. But I have you. Don't let me down." Tears started down his cheeks, "Because you're all I got." He paused, as if to compose himself. "I got elected alone and I stand alone." His voice trembled ever so slightly. "I need you. If I don't have you I can't be successful. Thank you very much." The scene was played on the news many times.[27]

Ventura's appeals for a unicameral legislature, however, did not appear to mobilize the public. They certainly did not move the legislature, which stood its ground in opposition.

Republican Schwarzenegger became governor of California in 2003 after Democratic governor Gray Davis was recalled in a special election. The new governor began his tenure employing the outside game of appealing to the public, largely as a backup to the inside game of negotiating with the legislature. Using the bully pulpit was his threat—if the legislature did not give the governor what he wanted, he would go over its head to the people.

Schwarzenegger worked with the legislature; he flattered and cajoled. But at the same time he communicated directly to the people, and this he knew how to do. Joe Mathews writes, in his superb account of Schwarzenegger in office, of his "supernatural ability to get more attention than any other political figure," in an environment where it had become increasingly difficult for anyone to command the public's attention.[28] Despite some success, the governor quickly became frustrated, disappointed with the legislature. "After all the concessions he had made to lawmakers and all the cigars handed out, he still could not get the legislature to address serious issues and pass a budget on time."[29] In going to Californians around the state, his frustration was magnified:

> The legislators are playing games right now in Sacramento. We want action, not games. We want action, not dialogue. We want action, not promises. We want action and not the lies that are up there in Sacramento continuously. You all, all of you, sent me to Sacramento to represent the people of California and to fight for you and I can guarantee you, I am your warrior.[30]

Schwarzenegger was ready to resort to an alternative to representative democracy whereby the California Legislature would be marginalized.

In California, going over the head of the legislature to the people can involve more than words alone. Here, as well as in twenty-five other states, it is possible to ignore the legislature and go to the ballot with a measure, if a sufficient number of signatures are collected on an initiative petition. Under the initiative process, the legislature can be bypassed, a vigorous campaign can be undertaken, and a majority of voters can be persuaded to adopt a measure as either an amendment to the constitution or statutory law. The initiative has become a significant feature of the lawmaking process in Arizona, California, Colorado, Maine, Oregon, and Washington, where legislatures are either forced to take action they might not otherwise take because of the threat of an initiative or are virtually ignored in the making of law. Of the twenty-one states that adopted term limits since 1992, in all but Louisiana this radical change was either enacted by the voters directly or by the legislature under threat that more draconian limits would be put on the ballot and passed by the voters.

However, in California, as in no other place, the initiative has become a favorite tool of governors who are up against a recalcitrant legislature. Governors exploit their pulpit to campaign for initiative measures they favor, to put their own measures on the ballot and get them passed, and to threaten going to the ballot unless the legislature acquiesces to executive demands. Gov. Pete Wilson, a Republican, did an end-run around the California Legislature in 1992 with an initiative to reform welfare and give the governor more power in the budget process. He also ran for statewide office in 1990 and for reelection in 1994 sponsoring several initiatives. Before Schwarzenegger, no California politician had resorted to direct democracy as much as Wilson.[31]

Schwarzenegger carved out a political identity, to accompany his *Terminator* persona, with an after-school programs initiative in November 2002. In the next two years he campaigned for or against twelve measures. After he won the governorship, Schwarzenegger turned to a strategy of pursuing ballot initiatives to give him leverage with the legislature. "It's kind of the carrot-and-stick method," he said. "I like the idea of using the sticks." [32] The Democratic legislature stood fast on a number of issues, however. And the governor went to the ballot in a special election in 2005, which he referred to as the "year of reform." He led a campaign that resulted in four initiative propositions being put to the voters (along with four others that did not involve him). One would have affected teacher tenure, a second would have created a new state spending limit, a third would have taken redistricting authority away from the legislature, and a fourth would have made it more difficult for public employee unions to deduct money from the paychecks of members for political purposes. All four of Schwarzenegger's propositions were rejected by the voters, in the face of the opposition campaign led by the Democratic Party, teachers, nurses, firefighters, and police officers.[33] The voters apparently felt that a special election was unnecessary and the wording of the propositions confusing. They voted along partisan lines, with eight out of ten Democrats opposed and seven or eight out of ten Republicans in favor.[34]

With many more registered Democrats in California than Republicans, the governor came to realize that he would not do well going into battle with the Democratic legislature. A minority party governor, in particular, has to watch his step. Although Schwarzenegger retained the advantages of both official and celebrity status, he realized that he would have to exploit them differently. From then on his relationship with the legislature relied much more on the carrot than the stick.

Party Leadership

As the experience of Schwarzenegger in California illustrates, legislators of the party other than the governor's have no special reason to follow the executive. Indeed, the opposition has an electoral incentive to oppose the governor. At the national level, Morris P. Fiorina points out that "institutional rivalries now are buttressed by partisan rivalry and partisan electoral interest." A legislative majority has every incentive, therefore, to reject gubernatorial initiatives. To accept them is tacitly to support an opposing party candidate's reelection. "Divided control," Fiorina continues, "gives each branch of government an electoral incentive to work for the failure of the branch held by the other." [35]

In roughly half the states control is divided, in that the governor's party does not have majorities in both houses of the legislature. At least one chamber is in the hands of the opposition. Since the 1960s the incidence of divided control has increased from roughly two-fifths to between half and three-fifths of the states, varying with the election.[36] As of 2008 the Democrats controlled the governor and legislature in fourteen states, while the Republicans controlled the two branches in ten states. That left twenty-five (excluding Nebraska with its nonpartisan legislature) divided.[37]

Divided control increases the potential for executive-legislative friction over policy. For example, Democratic governor Janet Napalitano of Arizona has had more than her share of contentious battles with the Republican legislature. "It started out tumultuous," said Ken Bennett, the president of the senate, "and got worse from there." [38] But a governor still can deal with a legislature controlled by the opposition party. It requires doling out favors, compromising, even giving in; and it results in more diluted policy on major issues than might otherwise be the case. Schwarzenegger himself took an entirely different approach to the California Legislature after his initiatives went down in defeat. Having won reelection in 2006, he appointed a Democrat as his chief of staff. He put aside issues that the Democratic legislature and its constituencies would undoubtedly oppose and advanced issues that they could embrace. As an advocate for the environment, he got the legislature to pass legislation requiring cuts in gasoline emissions of 25 percent by 2020 and 80 percent by 2050. The bill got many Democratic votes, but only one from the forty-seven Republicans in the legislature.

Governors do not have to switch parties or transform their agendas to make a record under divided government. In states with divided government a number managed to achieve legislative results during the 2006 session. Six raised the minimum wage, while Massachusetts and Vermont adopted ambitious plans to provide health coverage for the uninsured. One of the key factors was that governors were willing to cross traditional party lines to round up support.[39] In the 2007 session Ted Strickland, Ohio's Democratic governor, got a $52.3 billion budget package through the Republican legislature with near unanimous backing. And Democratic governor Ed Rendell in Pennsylvania managed to work with Republicans in the legislature, even though collaboration did not come easily.

When the governor's party controls both houses of the legislature, there are no guarantees, of course. Gov. Sonny Perdue of Georgia had a Republican legislature but lost on some big issues. Rod Blagojevich had Democratic majorities in the Illinois senate and house but has attacked the legislature repeatedly, trying to mobilize the public instead of consulting or negotiating with legislative leaders. On its part, the Illinois General Assembly, and especially the house under Speaker Michael Madigan, has rejected a number of the governor's main proposals.[40] But normally the sailing is much smoother when the two branches are under the same partisan control. This is because the governor benefits by virtue of being leader of the state Democratic or Republican Party.[41] Party members share a disposition to be loyal to the leader, if they possibly can. As a rule, they share beliefs and interest group supporters. They run on the same ticket in elections, with the gubernatorial candidate or incumbent governor at the top. A governor running for reelection may not have coattails, but an unpopular governor may cost legislators votes. Why do something that might make the governor unpopular? "It is his party," a Georgia legislator said about the governor. Party support is the governor's "ace in the hole," added another Georgia legislator. Whatever their differences with the governor, leadership in the legislature can usually be counted on to go along with him.[42]

When a governor's party is in control, the legislature tends to be somewhat less of a balancer and somewhat more of an enabler. This is the case when the political system is competitive, but in an essentially one-party system, party loyalty to the governor matters less. There is no electoral threat impending that brings the legislature together with the governor. When the minority party becomes a serious challenger, however, the majority closes ranks. Take the case of Georgia. In the early 1980s, the governor and speaker of the house were at odds, each a dominant force within the Democratic Party. By 1994, however, Republicans had gained strength in the legislature and the Democrats could not afford to fight among themselves. "They've got another enemy, so to speak, which is the Republican party," commented one member of the legislature.[43]

"If the governor is of the same party, the Speaker becomes the governor's lieutenant in addition to his or her role as a legislative leader." These are the words of Tom Loftus, a Democratic speaker of the Wisconsin Assembly and friend of Democratic governor Tony Earl. Loftus's *quid pro quo* was that in return for pushing the governor's agenda he wanted projects in the budget for Democratic members to bring back to their districts. Loftus served the governor while brokering the needs of his colleagues.[44] That is how it is usually done. Loftus and other leaders have disputes with governors of their own party, but they try to keep them under wraps so that the opposition cannot reap any benefit. Ohio House Republicans, for instance, wanted to put a provision for a video lottery in the budget, but Republican governor Bob Taft was against it. Legislators wanted to go ahead anyway and were ready to override a Taft veto. Senate president Richard Finan, however, cautioned against splitting with the governor on the issue. "I have to think about the politics," he told the Republican speaker of the house. "I hate to embarrass the governor."

The clout that governors have by virtue of their party-leadership status is by no means constant. It varies with the principals involved and with political circumstances. New Jersey exemplifies the shifting pattern. Generally speaking, divided government in this state has resulted in greater review of gubernatorial proposals by the legislature and more negotiating in order to reach common ground. Under one party's control, by contrast, the governor has traditionally dominated. Majority party leaders in the legislature, out of loyalty and political necessity, would accept the governor's agenda, no matter what the consequences. Governors, moreover, did not see fit to consult with legislative leaders in advance of formulating their agendas. It was their job to decide on a policy and the legislature's job to enact it. Most recently, however, despite Democratic control of both branches of government, the legislature has exerted its independence vis-à-vis Gov. Jon Corzine. It has gone toe-to-toe with him on the 2007 budget, resulting in the closing down of some state operations for almost a week, and it substantially altered the budget he sent over in 2008. It has also carried the ball on legislation for property-tax reform, while the governor did the blocking. This was an unusual reversal of roles, attributable mainly to the Democratic legislative leadership—House Speaker Joseph Roberts and Senate President Richard Codey—and to the fact that the governor was less assertive than had been the norm in New Jersey.

Carrots and Sticks

With the New Jersey Senate split 20-20 in 2002, Democratic governor James McGreevey could not ignore the need for Republican help, especially for his budget. He traveled from one end of the state to the other, bearing gifts of state funding for bond projects and lavishing praise on Republican senators William Gormley in the south and Robert Littell in the north. The governor accompanied Littell in his district on a visit to a dam, where he promised to restore $5 million in funding for its repair. He visited Atlantic City, Gormley's constituency, and offered to make New Jersey's gambling resort the nation's "premier destination" for family vacations, as well as push the senator's plan to streamline casino regulations and provide funds for transportation, boardwalk, and neighborhood improvements. When McGreevey needed a vote for his proposed corporate business tax, he got it from a Republican senator, Walter Kavenaugh, in return for the reappointment of one of his constituents as county prosecutor.[45]

Because of their positions and the resources at their disposal, governors can give individual legislators a lot of what they want—acknowledgment and attention for themselves and benefits for their constituents and district. And little, as well as bigger, things count in politics. Gary Taffett, McGreevey's chief of staff, explains how a legislator's nature works: "People just want that phone call; they want to be in his office." This doesn't require much on the part of the governor. "They're not all big asks." [46]

What governors have to give legislators in order to predispose them to support the administration or to get the last few votes on a big-ticket item varies: a visit by the governor to the legislator's district, an appearance at a fund-raiser for the legislator's campaign, an invitation to the legislator to pose with the governor at a bill-signing. Occasionally, an appointment to a government position for a constituent is necessary. From time to time, the legislator wants a project—something in the budget—that will benefit a community or organization in the district.

Only on the big issues, like the budget, does the governor have to trade something in order to get a vote. But, as McGreevey's efforts indicate, governors are not averse to a deal for a vote here or a vote there. Michael Torpey, a former chief of staff to New Jersey's governor Christine Todd Whitman, explained how he managed to put together majorities on the most important issues: "There wasn't a single big vote I went into that I wasn't negotiating with appointments," he recounted.[47] In New Jersey, at least, legislators are not shy about asking and most governors are not shy about giving. The main thing is governors have what legislators want.

What happens, then, if legislators balk or refuse to go along with the governor? Ned McWherter, a former speaker of the house and governor of Tennessee, answers such a question by telling of his experience as governor trying to get the votes for a gas tax increase—votes not easy to come by. So McWherter invited a certain freshman legislator to his office, explained the program, mentioned that some of the roads would be in the legislator's district, and told him he needed his help in order to fund the program. The legislator, not persuaded, informed the governor that he could not vote for any such tax increase. McWherter continued his efforts but came up short. He could not get the commitments he needed, so he had the freshman legislator come to his office a second time, still without success. Then he had him back a third time, this time to *really* explain things. McWherter recounts:

> When he sat down in front of my desk, I reached in the big drawer in my desk. I pulled out and put on top of my desk a child's toy yellow road grader. I asked the freshman legislator if he knew what it was. He told me that he did. I asked him what it was. He told me that it was a road grader. I held it up and turned it at various angles and told him: "You take a good look at it, Representative. Because if you don't vote for this gas tax bill, it will be the last road grader you see near your district while I am governor." [48]

The governor can provide, and the governor can also deny. Governors do more of the former than the latter, but denial is an ace in the hole.

The governor can withhold attention and turn down invitations to visit. He or she can refuse to give legislators the appointments they want and leave their projects out of the administration's budget formulation. Their denial can manifest itself more aggressively. They can try to have legislative leaders replaced, as Pataki did to Joseph Bruno, the senate majority leader in New York. Or they can go so far as to threaten legislators in their own districts, as Governor Spitzer did in New York. Here, the governor and legislature had disagreed over the appointment of a state comptroller, to replace an incumbent who had resigned because of an ethics problem. The legislature, which had the legal authority to make the interim appointment, refused to abide by the process advocated by the governor. It rejected the nominees of a special panel and instead selected a sitting legislator to become comptroller. Spitzer was furious and began visiting the districts of

Democratic lawmakers to criticize them publicly. "It was, by Albany standards, a shocking breach of etiquette for a sitting governor to lambaste a colleague from his own party in his home district," the New York Times opined.[49] Rarely do governors go to such lengths, but Spitzer did—at least until a sex scandal forced him to resign from office.

The veto is the executive's principal weapon of denial. It is a powerful one. Every legislator who has sponsored and worked for the passage of a particular bill and every legislator who has managed to get an earmark, or project, in a budget bill realizes that the governor can easily thwart the effort. All it takes is the stroke of a gubernatorial pen. Any legislator, consequently, wants to be on the right side of the governor. If that means going along on some of the administration's priority bills, so be it. Usually, no threat of a veto is necessary. The legislator's anticipation of what might happen if he or she crosses the governor is sufficient to deter disloyalty.

Probably no governor has denial power equivalent to that of Maryland's. That is because the Maryland governor can affect legislators where they live—in their districts—with regard to their reelection. While most governors may have their fingers in the decennial legislative redistricting process, the legislature (or an outside commission) is usually responsible for drafting the redistricting plan. Maryland is the only state where the initiative for redistricting is with the governor, not the legislature. Under the state constitution, the governor must submit a redistricting plan to the legislature after the decennial census. If the legislature cannot agree on an alternative plan within forty-five days, the governor's plan becomes law. The governor can draw the lines of every legislator's district, thereby giving each more or fewer voters of their own party, and thus affecting their prospects for reelection.

Gov. Parris Glendening's power to draw lines for legislators' districts during the 2002 redistricting was certainly a fact in the legislative session that year and the previous one. The governor would playfully remind legislators that the contours of their districts were in his hands. On the opening day of the 2001 session he made courtesy calls to the house and senate chambers, carrying with him a rolled-up map that he told members was his redistricting plan. He meant to convey a message, albeit in an amusing way. When legislators visited him in his office, Glendening would intentionally strike a pose as they entered. He would lean over one of two maps, each sitting on an easel. If the visitor was a member of the senate, he would be leaning over a map of senate districts; if the visitor was a member of the house, he would be leaning over a map of house districts. Glendening would look up, smile, and point to the legislator's district on the map. The legislator did not know whether the governor was serious or kidding, or some of both—and did not care to risk finding out.[50] One legislator internalized the governor's message as: "This is no time to annoy him." [51]

How the Balance Teeters

While the governor and legislature share lawmaking powers, with the former usually having the upper hand, just how the executive-legislative game is played varies from time to time and from state to state. It also depends mightily on the players involved.

Over Time

The executive-legislative balance has not been perfectly steady. It has teetered one way or the other since the ratification of the U.S. Constitution. Legislatures started out as the first branch of government (as specified in Article I of the U.S. Constitution), and not until the twentieth century did the executive come into its own, largely as a result of the Progressive movement, which curbed legislative power, and the drive for administrative efficiency, which strengthened governors. Meanwhile, legislatures were becoming increasingly dependent on governors for leadership.

The balance shifted somewhat in the 1965–1980 period. With legislative modernization and capacity building, there came an insistence by legislators that theirs was a coequal branch of government. Since then, however, legislatures have been on a decline vis-à-vis their governors. Thad L. Beyle, a long-time observer of gubernatorial power, has found that between 1960 and 2005 the overall institutional powers of the governors increased. More governors had gained an item veto and their appointment powers edged up. But they declined in their power as party leaders because government was divided more often.[52] While this was happening (and with legislative capacity building having run its course) legislatures' sense of independence eroded. Some confirmation is offered by surveys of state administrators that were conducted in 1978, 1988, 1998, and 2004. They show that the governors' influence over the budget steadily increased until 2004, when it receded somewhat.[53]

Probably the biggest shift in the balance has come in those states that adopted term limits. This is a principal conclusion of the three national legislative organizations and the political scientists who studied the impact of term limits. In all but Ohio, where Governor Bob Taft exerted weak leadership and the tradition of a strong legislature was still intact, influence shifted to the executive branch. In particular, the executive achieved greater control of the budget.[54] The fact was that Taft was a weak governor. When he left office his successor, Ted Strickland, asserted greater executive authority. It was difficult for the term-limited Ohio General Assembly to match him. As political scientist Bill Bunning observed: "You're in the Republican leadership for two terms, maybe speaker for one, and then you're out. You don't have the capacity to take on a skillful governor." The term-limits study found that legislators were of the belief that not only did the influence of governors rise, but also the influence of the executive branch in general rose as well.[55] The three legislative organizations, in a document reporting on the study's findings, sum up: "Perhaps the most significant effect of term limits . . . is the decline of the legislative branch of state government in relation to the executive branch." [56]

A number of term-limited legislatures are in the process of trying to figure out how to maintain or achieve coequality, when institutional memory is gone and legislative leaders are rotating in and out of office. Among the more fascinating attempts is Louisiana, where term limits went into effect with the 2007 elections and where the governor has traditionally controlled the legislature. The legislature appears to want to increase its strength. But it is still too early to tell what success the Louisiana Legislature will have in its efforts to cope with term limits and be independent of the governor.

From State to State

Not all governors are equal. Some states constitutionally, statutorily, and politically favor governors more than do others. Beyle has constructed an index of the institutional powers of the governorship, which gives some idea of differences from state to state.[57] His index of governors' institutional power scores range from a high of 4.1 to a low of 2.7. The institutionally most powerful governors are in Alaska, Illinois, Minnesota, New York, Utah, and West Virginia. The institutionally least powerful are in Alabama, Arizona, Georgia, North Carolina, Rhode Island, and Vermont.[58]

A governor's institutional power, however, is part, but only part, of what counts in the executive-legislative balance. This is best illustrated by the case of Louisiana, where its score of 3.1 on Beyle's index ranks it behind thirty-seven states and tied with four others in terms of gubernatorial power. Yet the political culture in Louisiana is one in which governors, with few exceptions, have dominated the legislature. Louisiana probably has had the strongest governor in the nation. The Louisiana Constitution stipulates that the senate and house elect their presiding officers and that the presiding officers appoint chairs and committee members in their respective bodies. In reality, as journalist John Hill writes, the governor chooses both the president and the speaker.[59] According to Tom Ferrell, a political scientist:

> There is nothing in the formal rules of procedure that grants the governor that kind of power. The legislature has given the governor that power. . . . Louisiana has a strong governorship because it is a culturally strong governorship, not a constitutionally strong one.[60]

One member of the Louisiana House reported that, when he was first elected to the legislature, "I was astonished that there was no separation of powers."

The "cult of the governor" has existed in Louisiana since the time of Huey Long. There are those allied with the governor on an administration team, the majority, and those against the governor on an anti-administration team, the minority. Members of both political parties have incentives to join the administration team, because of what they get in return. As one legislator commented, "In Louisiana, if you're part of the team, you get what you need for your district." He noted that people elected him to get stuff for the district and admitted that it led to dependency on the governor. Another legislator described just how it worked:

> When I was first elected, the governor's staff sat down with me and said, "What do you need for your district?" I said I needed a new student center

at the university in my district. "Well, if you get on our team, we can take care of that," said the governor's aide. I voted right and at the end of the session I had a ground-breaking in my district.[61]

Gov. Mike Foster got rid of House Speaker Hunt Downer in 2001 and several committee chairs who objected to the speaker's ouster. The expectation in Louisiana is that legislative leaders, including committee chairs, are lieutenants of the administration—that they will support the governor's major initiatives right down the line and bury bills the governor opposes. Even during the administration of Kathleen Blanco, who was not one of the state's strongest governors, the house speaker, Joe Salter, took away a legislator's chairmanship because he had worked against the governor's proposal to renew sales taxes paid by businesses on utilities.

Maryland is another state with a strong governor, mainly because of the executive's control of the budget and of legislative redistricting. As far as budget control *per se* is concerned, the governor is strongest in New York, New Jersey, and North Dakota and weakest in Colorado, Mississippi, and Texas.[62] New Jersey takes pride in having what politicos there refer to as the most powerful governor in the nation—perhaps not *the* most powerful, but certainly among the more powerful. This is, in part, because only the governor, and most recently the lieutenant governor, are elected statewide and because of the executive's authority to make appointments. Governors of Connecticut and New York, with few exceptions, have had the upper hand in their dealings with the legislature, as have governors in Georgia.

At the other end of the continuum are places where governors tend to be constitutionally and/or politically weaker than elsewhere. In a few of them the governor is traditionally so constrained that the legislature can lay claim to being the dominant branch of government. Before the onset of term limits, Colorado was one such place. But term limits have weakened the legislature, even in the budget process which it formerly controlled. The Oklahoma legislature used to be strong, but it became weaker in recent years. The office of governor in Arkansas has never been terribly strong, but it is stronger with term limits. Texas is another state where the governor's power is limited. Here, the lieutenant governor, who leads the senate, and the speaker, who leads the house, share power with the chief executive. Cal Jillson, a political scientist, describes the situation governors encounter:

"You're the governor of the state of Texas, your chest swells and if disaster strikes, you get in the helicopter, cameras come and you feel reasonably authoritative. Then the legislature comes back into town, and it's a different story." [63] Fortunately for governors in Texas, the legislature only convenes in Austin every other year, barring a special session in between.

One of the strongest legislatures is the Massachusetts Great and General Court, as it is formally called. Contemporary legislatures in the Bay State, all of which have been under Democratic control, have been hard on their governors, even those of their own party. Michael Dukakis, William Weld, Mitt Romney, and Deval Patrick are all governors who were taught lessons by their legislatures. They learned that they had to accept the legislature's coequality in the making of policy and also had to accept much of what the legislature wanted, if they were to have any success at all with their policy agendas. Governors in Massachusetts tend to be good students, even if they have to struggle with the idea of the legislature as coequal.

From Governor to Governor

Governors vary not only from state to state but also from individual to individual in the power they wield with regard to the legislature. The partisan composition of government is important, as we have discussed above, but also important is how the governor views the legislature—regardless of which party is in control—and how the governor approaches it. The governor, as we have said, has the upper hand—that is, if the governor raises his or her arm.

This explains why some governors manage to be effective legislatively, despite having weak executive systems.[64] Richard Riley, for example, had minimal formal powers as governor of South Carolina, although he furnished strong leadership in policymaking. Florida's governors had been constitutionally constrained by a cabinet system of government, but both Reuben Askew and Bob Graham proved to be relatively strong governors in a weak-governor state. And Jeb Bush demonstrated even greater strength after the state had turned from primarily Democratic to primarily Republican, and after term limits had weakened the legislature. In contrast, a few governors turn out to be weak even though their offices are endowed with substantial authority. David Treen of Louisiana was one of them; he was uncomfortable with the legislative process and not disposed to wield power, as was the norm for governors in his state. Maryland's Harry Hughes was another. He believed that it was the responsibility of the legislature to take the lead in policymaking; and during the Hughes administration the legislature gladly did so. Other Maryland governors—Marvin Mandel, William Donald Schaefer, Parris Glendening, and Martin O'Malley—interpreted their executive role very differently and exercised strong leadership in relation to the legislature.

Some governors start off their relationship with feelings of respect for the legislature. Such feelings are probably the product of their service in the legislature, particularly as legislative leaders. Ned McWherter of Tennessee is a prime example. According to Alan Ehrenhalt, experience in the legislature helps shape one's attitudes toward the legislature later on. McWherter's orientation as governor is attributable to his eighteen years in the Tennessee General Assembly, including fourteen as speaker. By the time he became governor, McWherter "understood the process, the players, the sacrifices he could demand from people, the favors he needed to offer in return, and the issues that were not worth the political risk." [65] He had come to appreciate the legislature and its members.

A respectful gubernatorial attitude usually gets translated into welcoming gubernatorial behavior. According to Governor McWherter's press secretary, the governor was conscious of the fact that legislators "want to be consulted, they want to be informed, and they want to participate." [66] Respectful behavior on the part of the governor amounts to the following: appreciating the needs of legislators as individuals; giving access to legislators, by having an open door policy; consulting with legislative leaders before formulating an agenda, not afterwards; working out disagreements with the legislature, rather than going around the legislature to the public; exhibiting a willingness to compromise; sharing the credit; and not blaming the legislature. Many governors, in addition to McWherter, manage to behave this way.

Some governors, however, do not appear to have much respect for the legislature with which they share governance. A few of them also served previously in the legislature, but their experience failed to shape their attitudes positively. The belief that the legislature is parochial and petty, and its members too self-serving, is held by a number of governors. In New Jersey governors typically have not had high regard for the legislature, although rarely did they show their feelings publicly. Legislators, however, got the message. For someone like Glendening, the Maryland General Assembly was an obstacle to overcome in order to achieve the good policy the governor was advocating.

Few chief executives have been as combative with the legislature as Jesse Ventura. His message to the people of the state was simple: "I'm not one of them." [67] As one Minnesota senator characterized Ventura's attitude: "He has utter disdain for the legislature and utter disdain for us." It was all Ventura, with little room for the legislature. "All I could remember was the Governor announcing the day after the last session that 'I won,'" recalls Ember Reichgott Junge, a legislator at the time. "It wasn't 'we won' or 'Minnesota won.' I guess there's only one winner in a wrestling match." [68]

Contemporary New York governors have not had many nice things to say about the legislature. This may derive partly from the fact that for the past three decades both Republican and Democratic governors have had to deal with a divided legislature—with a Democratic assembly and a Republican senate. Mario Cuomo demonstrated his frustration by once likening legislators to "monkeys." [69] George Pataki took on leaders of both houses throughout his twelve-year tenure. Eliot Spitzer had the most contentious relationship of all. His outspokenness, aggressiveness, and confrontational style in his dealings with the New York Legislature derived from a combination of factors. His combustible personality was one of them. His experience as attorney general battling Wall Street (which he compared to battling the legislature) was another.[70] Focused and rigid, he could not ignore his campaign promise to take on the capitol culture and clean house in Albany. His antilegislative attitude was reinforced by his landslide victory in the 2006 elections, which he interpreted as a mandate. In his 2007 Inaugural Address, with the senate majority leader and assembly speaker on the rostrum behind him, he referred to New York as having slept through the past decade.[71] It was no surprise that Governor Spitzer would not get along with the legislature (although the scandal that ended his brief tenure as governor shocked everyone).

Like Pataki before him, Spitzer threw down the gauntlet in his dealings with the legislature. Pataki had threatened the legislature on many occasions. If the budget was not passed on time, he would shut down state government. He would veto all nonbudget bills until the legislature passed the budget. Pataki did agree to a pay raise for legislators, but only on the condition that their salary be held in escrow until the budget passed. And when the budget did not pass by the deadline date, he tried to withhold legislators' pay, but was prevented from doing so by the courts.[72] Early on, Spitzer told the assembly minority leader that he was a "steamroller" who would roll over anyone who got in his way. When to fill a vacancy the assembly chose one of its own members as comptroller instead of a candidate selected by a panel backed by the governor, Spitzer accused the legislative leaders of "cronyism" and called the legislature's action a "stunning breach of integrity." He also threatened that if the legislature did not pass more of his agenda, including campaign finance reform, he would not approve a legislative pay-raise bill.[73]

After that things only got worse. Spitzer completely alienated the senate Republicans, who held a narrow majority in the chamber. The governor began to work to overthrow that majority by offering several Republican senators jobs in his administration. The rationale was that their districts could be won by Democrats if the incumbents were not running. One Republican accepted a position, and the Democrats succeeded in picking up his senate seat, narrowing the Republican majority to two. Then members of the governor's staff (with or without his knowledge) called on the state police to investigate Majority Leader Joseph Bruno for his use of state aircraft for politically related travel. That was followed by Spitzer's proposal to issue state driver's licenses to illegal immigrants, which was roundly criticized by members of his own party.[74] Governor Spitzer's first year in office was not an auspicious one; but his second year was even worse, when he was forced resign.

Gov. Arnold Schwarzenegger had been encouraged by former Republican governor Pete Wilson to run for governor because "someone who had played *Kindergarten Cop*" in the movies already had the requisite experience to deal with the legislature. Schwarzenegger took the advice to heart. In his account of the Terminator's political rise, Joe Mathews recounts the governor's meeting with a five-year-old girl in a town west of Sacramento. "You are the kindergarten cop!" she squealed as the governor passed, referring to the role he played in a hit movie. "I am the kindergarten cop," Schwarzenegger replied. "And you know something, nothing changed because that's what I am in the capitol still. I have 120 children." The governor was referring to the eighty assembly members and forty senators in the California Legislature.[75]

Probably, the utterance that reverberated most widely was Schwarzenegger's reference to California legislators as "girlie-men," which may have been disrespectful, but still was not mean-spirited. It was part of Schwarzenegger's constant campaign to ingratiate himself with the public and sell the agenda that he was trying to move through the legislature. The advice he received from his handlers was that the public was very antilegislature, "so slapping [the lawmakers] around a bit should be helpful." [76]

Schwarzenegger's strategy for handling the legislature was an extension of who he was and what possibilities were available to him. His was at the pinnacle of his celebrity. Without it, he could not have won the governorship and without it he would have had to adopt a different governing style. He also had available to him California's system of direct democracy, which had enabled him to get established in politics (by promoting an after-school initiative); to get elected (in a recall election that ousted Gov. Gray Davis from office); and to govern (by spearheading several ballot propositions).[77] Schwarzenegger also had confidence in his abilities as a salesman and as a deal maker. Thus, he combined an outside game with an inside one. If he applied enough pressure through the threat of initiatives, he would be able to cut deals with the legislature that were much nearer to his proposals than theirs. In private, he would work at back-room deals; in public, he would campaign as a populist.[78] The strategy worked, at least until Schwarzenegger grew unhappy with half a loaf and decided to go for the whole one.

The strategy that had worked for Schwarzenegger—blending initiative politics with old-style back-room dealing—was resented by a legislature that felt it was being jerked around. John Burton, the president pro tem of the senate, became furious with the governor's appearances before the public. During contentious negotiations over workers' compensation, Burton stormed out of the governor's office, yelling, "Go take it to the people. . . . I don't fucking care. Take it to your fucking people." [79] Shortly thereafter, that was just what the governor did, with a vengeance. He remained convinced that the pressure of initiatives would cause the legislature to cave. But when it didn't, he took his proposals to the people, challenging the Democratic legislature and its interest group allies. The governor was soundly defeated.

It helps a governor with the legislature if the governor is popular with the public. The popularity of Bill Richardson in New Mexico, Brian Schweitzer in Montana, Jodi Rell in Connecticut, Joe Manchin in West Virginia, and Ted Strickland in Ohio gave these governors a leg up with their legislatures. In addition, it usually helps if governors are pragmatic and bipartisan rather than ideological and partisan. Charlie Crist, the Republican governor of Florida, possesses these characteristics. Even though he has a Republican legislature, Crist has conducted what has been called an "olive-branch form of government." [80] He consults regularly not only with Republican legislative leaders but with Democratic leaders as well. According to Kurt Kiser, a lobbyist and former Republican legislator, "That friendly type of personality really serves him well, not only around voters, but in trying to make deals and trying to govern." [81] Crist's approach of laying out broad-based policy goals and then leaving it to the legislature is effective. He invites the legislature to participate, but "he is leading the orchestra." [82] Despite Crist's success, it should be pointed out that his predecessor, Jeb Bush, had a very different approach, but also succeeded in leading the legislature. Bush was partisan and assertive, and the Republican legislature loyal and responsive.

After the defeat of his propositions by the voters of California, Schwarzenegger changed his posture toward the legislature. No longer did he threaten to do an end-run around the legislature. Now it was all about working with the legislature. That meant accommodating the Democrats rather than expecting them to accommodate him. In the tent on the capitol grounds, where he shared cigars and negotiated deals with legislators, he explained to Speaker Fabian Nuñez, "I'm a Republican, but I'm a Hollywood Republican." [83] Thus, according to Joe Cancimilla, a former Democratic assemblyman, what Schwarzenegger has been able to do is to strike deals with Democrats on Democratic issues. "That's really not hard to do," Cancimilla said.[84] However, in doing so, the governor lost support within his own legislative party, giving Democrats additional leverage.

Some governors manage to run roughshod over the legislature, at least for a time. But not many can behave that way for long. The legislature is the other branch of government; it has to be dealt with. As Pete Grannis, a former assemblyman who had a position in Spitzer's administration, told the governor: "The legislature is like your in-laws. You're stuck with them." [85]

From Legislature to Legislature

On less important matters, much of the action takes place almost entirely in the legislative arena, with gubernatorial involvement only when an enacted bill gets to his or her desk. But on the critical issues, governors normally are part of the action, and maybe even the controlling part. The question is, how do legislatures try to deal with governors as coequals in the lawmaking process?

Much depends on whether the legislature has a sense of itself as an institution, independent of and balancing the power of the executive. That, of course, depends on how legislators themselves, and especially their top leaders, see things. Legislative leaders are the ones who deal directly with governors on behalf of their caucuses and their chambers. Just how seriously a legislative leader takes the legislature's responsibility to balance the executive has a large impact on the legislature's role with respect to major policy. With strong, institutional leadership, the legislature will go to the mat; without it, the legislature will back off.

Ralph Wright of Vermont, during his tenure as speaker, was a strong advocate for legislative independence. He writes:

> I had a clear sense of the Founding Fathers' intent regarding the separation of powers between the three branches of government, and I paid careful attention to any endeavor on a governor's part to weaken or abridge the legislative prerogative to make the law. . . . I didn't pursue this philosophy for any reason of self-aggrandizement. I believed, in fact, all that went on in the State House was a matter for the legislature, and the legislature only. It was the Executive Branch's job to enforce what we did; it wasn't their job to tell us what to do. The governors were never in agreement with this type of thinking, as 200 years of history had afforded them entrance into the process to exert great pressures on us.[86]

Democrat Wright describes his relationship with three governors: Democrat Madeleine Kunin, Republican Richard Snelling, and Democrat Howard Dean.[87] Interestingly, the speaker worked far better with the Republican governor than with the two Democrats, mainly because of Wright's appreciation of Snelling's remarkable leadership qualities and the chemistry that existed between the two. What is baffling is how the very partisan Wright could get along so well with a Republican governor. But he has an explanation:

> I not only respected his office, but I respected him, and I believe he felt the same about the office of the Speaker and me. Perhaps more important, I love the man immensely as a human being.[88]

Nevertheless, through the tenure of all three governors, Speaker Wright insisted on the legislature's coequality as a branch of government in Vermont.

Other legislative leaders and their colleagues have managed to stand up to strong and aggressive governors. The *New York Times* constantly refers to the New York Legislature as the most "dysfunctional" such body in the country. Yet the New York Legislature has a lengthy record of standing up for its independence and slugging it out with a succession of governors. The partisan division of the legislature—with the senate controlled by Republicans and the assembly by Democrats—has helped make this possible. And occasionally the governor's own party has lined up, not with the governor, but with its partisan opponents in the other chamber of the legislature. In the words of Senate Majority Leader Bruno:

> Three branches of government, right? If we want to combine them and let the governor orchestrate the whole discussion, direction, agenda, then let's vote to do that, but that is not our Constitution, that is not the government here in New York State.[89]

Across the continent from New York State, the California Legislature, although weakened by term limits and occasionally bypassed by the initiative, has managed to repel a populist assault by Governor Schwarzenegger. The "Governator," as he has become known, ran up against a brick wall. He learned that the legislature is designed to slow things down. "Here in this Capitol, and on the job as governor . . . I think you have to be more patient," he related.[90] The California Legislature, even in its weakened term-limited state, succeeded in putting the governor in his place—that of a coequal, but not a superior. The speaker of the assembly, who had effectively challenged Schwarzenegger, had become, according to *Governing* magazine, the state's main "policy fulcrum," shaping the legislation to the majority party's liking and persuading the governor to go along.[91]

Given the way the separation-of-powers system is set up, it should not be surprising that the executive and legislature come into conflict. Yet on those occasions when the two branches reach an impasse, both the media and the public seem astounded and distressed. Differences between the governor and the legislature over the budget produce the most conflict and occasionally lead to a deadlock that is not broken by the constitutional or statutory deadline date. In 2007, for example, five states started their fiscal year without reaching agreement on a budget.

In Pennsylvania, a budget standoff occurred in 2007 between the Democratic governor, Ed Rendell, and a Republican senate. The governor's agenda was a heavy one, including a statewide ban on smoking, an energy-independence surcharge, a plan to lease the turnpike to private interests, and increased transportation expenditures. The Republican senate had different objectives. Both sides felt strongly about their positions. "This is a test of wills over priorities, and, at heart, philosophies," said G. Terry Madonna, a Pennsylvania political scientist and pollster.[92] Because neither side was willing to blink, no budget could be passed on time, resulting in a partial shutdown of state offices. A day later, however, furloughed public employees could return to their jobs because the governor and the legislature agreed to a deal. Each side got some of what it wanted.

A year earlier, the New Jersey Legislature and the new governor, Jon Corzine, deadlocked for weeks, shutting down part of state government and all of Atlantic City's casino gambling. It was not a case of partisan conflict, since both branches were controlled by Democrats. The stumbling block was a penny increase in the sales tax proposed by Corzine. The assembly, led by Speaker Joseph Roberts, insisted that there were better ways to balance the budget than by means of a sales tax hike. The senate was inclined to go along with the governor, but the assembly held out for an alternative to the administration's plan. Neither side was willing to budge until, after the partial shutdown, the legislature and the governor agreed to a compromise. The governor got his penny increase in the sales tax. The legislature got one-half of a penny of it dedicated to property tax relief. In terms of public relations, it was a costly settlement for the legislature, but it was followed up with a property tax reform package initiated by the legislature and enacted during a special session a year later.

When the legislature is on a collision course with the governor, most people think that it is the legislature that ought to shift direction. The public expects the governor to lead and the legislature to follow. When it happens differently, it is thought to be because of politics or sheer obstructionism. However, the reason is that the legislature has different spending, taxing, and policy preferences—preferences for which it is willing to fight. The legislature seldom looks good in its opposition to the governor, but it is not the legislature's job to look good. Its job is to build majorities—or better still, consensus—for what the legislature deems to be good public policy for the state and its various constituencies.

Notes

1. David Epstein, *The Political Theory of the Federalist* (Chicago: University of Chicago Press, 1984), 132.
2. Peverill Squire and Keith E. Hamm, *101 Chambers: Congress, State Legislatures, and the Future of Legislative Studies* (Columbus: Ohio State University Press, 2005), 39.
3. Quoted in *New York Times*, January 7, 2004.
4. Laura A. van Assendelft, *Governors, Agenda Setting, and Divided Government* (Lanham, Md.: University Press of America, 1997), 89–108.
5. Harry Roe Hughes, *My Unexpected Journey: The Autobiography of Governor Harry Roe Hughes* (Charleston, S.C.: The History Press, 2006).
6. Tom Loftus, *The Art of Legislative Politics* (Washington, D.C.: CQ Press, 1994), 75.
7. Carol Lewis, "Connecticut: Prosperity, Frugality, and Stability," in *Governors, Legislatures, and Budgets*, ed. Edward J. Clynch and Thomas P. Lauth (Westport, Ct.: Greenwood Press, 1991), 41, 46.
8. Thad L. Beyle, "Being Governor," in *The State of the States*, ed. Carl Van Horn, 4th ed. (Washington, D.C.: CQ Press, 2006), 56.
9. These paragraphs are drawn from Alan Rosenthal, *Heavy Lifting: The Job of the American Legislature* (Washington, D.C.: CQ Press, 2004), 204–205.
10. *New York Times*, August 22, 2001.
11. *New York Times*, December 12, 2003.
12. *New York Times*, December 17, 2004.

13. *Boston Globe,* June 25, 2006.

14. *New York Times,* March 28, 2007.

15. *New York Times,* March 28, 2007.

16. Van Assendelft, *Governors, Agenda Setting, and Divided Government,* 180.

17. Until 1995 the governor did not have veto authority in North Carolina, but that was changed by an amendment to the state constitution.

18. *New York Times,* April 13, 2006.

19. Alan Greenblatt, "Observer: Killing Frankenstein," *Governing* (June 2008), 17–18.

20. *State Net Capitol Journal,* March 3, 2008.

21. See John W. Kingdon, *Agendas, Alternatives, and Public Policies,* 2nd ed. (New York: Longman, 2003), 35.

22. George W. Scott, *A Majority of One: Legislative Life* (Seattle: Civitas Press, 2002), 55–58.

23. Thad L. Beyle, "The Governors," in *Politics in the American States,* ed. Virginia Gray, Russell Hanson, and Herbert Jacob, 7th ed. (Washington, D.C.: CQ Press, 1999), 210–211.

24. Van Assendelft, *Governors, Agenda Setting, and Divided Government,* 198.

25. Press release, office of Gov. Jesse Ventura, June 7, 2001.

26. *Minneapolis Star Tribune,* June 2, 2001.

27. Ember Reichgott Junge, unpublished manuscript, 2000.

28. Joe Mathews, *The People's Machine: Arnold Schwarzenegger and the Rise of Blockbuster Democracy* (New York: Public Affairs, 2006), 306.

29. Ibid., 269.

30. Ibid., 257.

31. Ibid., 20.

32. Ibid., 256, 306–310.

33. Daniel Weintraub, "Schwarzenegger Rebuffed," in *State and Local Government, 2007,* ed. Kevin B. Smith (Washington, D.C.: CQ Press, 2007), 23–24.

34. PPIC Statewide Survey, November 2005 (Public Policy Institute of California).

35. Morris P. Fiorina, *Divided Government* (New York: Macmillan, 1992), 87.

36. See Sarah McCally Morehouse and Malcolm E. Jewell, *State Politics, Parties, and Policy,* 2nd ed. (Lanham, Md.: Rowman and Littlefield, 2003), 209.

37. Interestingly, twelve Democrats had become governor in states won by President Bush and nine Republicans had become governor in states won by Senator Kerry in the elections of 2004. See Josh Goodman, "Against the Grain," *Governing* (October 2006), 34.

38. Ibid.

39. *State Net Capitol Journal,* February 5, 2007.

40. Alan Greenblatt, "Observer," *Governing* (September 2007), 18.

41. This section draws on Rosenthal, *Heavy Lifting,* 179–182.

42. Van Assendelft, *Governors, Agenda Setting, and Divided Government,* 74–75.

43. Ibid., 74.

44. Loftus, *The Art of Legislative Politics,* 63–64, 68.

45. *Newark Star-Ledger,* May 26, 2002, and January 13, 2003.

46. Lecture at Eagleton Institute of Politics, Rutgers University, December 4, 2002.

47. Lecture at Eagleton Institute of Politics, Rutgers University, December 5, 2001.

48. Roy Herron and L. H. "Cotton" Ivy, *Tennessee Political Humor* (Knoxville: University of Tennessee Press, 2000), 72.

49. *New York Times,* February 9, 2007.

50. Gov. Parris Glendening interview with author, March 23, 2001.

51. *Baltimore Sun,* March 30, 2001.

52. Thad L. Beyle, "Governors: Elections, Campaign Costs and Powers," in Council of State Governments, *The Book of States,* 37 (Lexington, Ky.: The Council, 2005), 200–201.

53. Nelson C. Dometrius and Deil S. Wright, "Governors, Legislatures, Partisanship, and State Budget Processes," paper prepared for delivery at the State Politics and Policy Conference, Kent, Ohio, April 30–May 1, 2004, and Nelson C. Dometrius and Deil S. Wright, "Comparative Institutional Influences over State Budgets in the New Millenium," paper prepared for delivery at the State Politics and Policy Conference, Michigan State University, 2005.

54. Jennifer Drage Bowser, Keon S. Chi, and Thomas H. Little, *A Practical Guide to Term Limits: Final Report of the Joint Project on Term Limits* (Denver: National Conference of State Legislatures, July 2006), 10; Thad Kousser, *Term Limits and the Dismantling of State Legislative Professionalism* (Cambridge: Cambridge University Press, 2005), 151–176.

55. Lou Jacobson column, October 25, 2007. See also John M. Carey, Richard G. Niemi, Lynda W. Powell, and Gary F. Moncrief, "The Effects of Term Limits on State Legislatures: A New Survey of the 50 States," *Legislative Studies Quarterly* 31 (February 2006): 124–125.

56. Bowser, et al., *A Practical Guide to Term Limits,* 10.

57. Beyle's index is based on (1) whether other state-level officials are separately elected; (2) the tenure potential of governors; (3) governors' power of appointment; (4) governors' control over the budget; (5) governors' veto power; and (6) whether the governor's party controls the legislature. Thad L. Beyle, "The Governors," in *Politics in the American States,* ed. Virginia Gray and Russell L. Hanson, 8th ed. (Washington, D.C.: CQ Press, 2004), 210–218.

58. Beyle, "The Governors," 212–213.

59. This account is based in part on John Hill, "House Flap Gives Rare Real-Life Civics Lesson," *The Advertiser,* March 24, 2004.

60. Quoted in ibid.

61. From a discussion in a meeting at the National Conference of State Legislatures, Denver, June 16–17, 2007.

62. Dometrius and Wright, "Governors, Legislatures, Partisanship and State Budget Processes."

63. *State Net Capitol Journal,* March 19, 2007. For an account of how power is divided in Texas, see Dave McNeely and Jim Henderson, *Bob Bullock: God Bless Texas* (Austin: Clifton and Shirley Caldwell Texas Heritage, 2008).

64. This paragraph is drawn from Rosenthal, *Heavy Lifting,* 184.

65. Alan Ehrenhalt, "The Inside Edge," *Governing* (June 2007), 11.

66. Van Assendelft, *Governors, Agenda Setting, and Divided Government,* 109, 112–122.

67. Virginia Gray and Wyman Spano, "The Irresistible Force Meets the Immovable Object: Minnesota's Moralistic Political Culture Confronts Jesse Ventura," in *Minnesota, Real and Imagined,* ed. Stephen R. Graubard (St. Paul: Minnesota History Society Press, 2000), 194–198; and John E. Brandl, "Policy and Politics in Minnesota," in Gaubard, *Minnesota, Real and Imagined,* 171.

68. Ember Reichgott Junge, unpublished manuscript, 2000.

69. *New York Times,* January 5, 2003.

70. *New York Times,* February 7, 2007.

71. Nick Baumgarten, "The Humbling of Eliot Spitzer," *The New Yorker* (December 10, 2007), 72–85.

72. *New York Times,* January 5, 2005, and January 7, 2005.

73. *New York Times,* February 8 and 9, 2007, and May 1, 2007.

74. Baumgarten, "The Humbling of Eliot Spitzer," 79, 81.

75. Mathews, *The People's Machine,* 58, 270.

76. Ibid., 225, 273.

77. Ibid., 322.

78. Ibid., 285.

79. Ibid., 239, 249.

80. Alexis Simendinger, "The Bellweather Governors," *National Journal* (October 20, 2007): 39.

81. Quoted in Alan Greenblatt, "Golden-Rule Charlie," *Governing* (August 2007), 48.

82. Ibid., 47–48.

83. Jim Carlton, "Working Together," *State Legislatures* (July/August 2007): 37.

84. Greenblatt, "Golden-Rule Charlie," 45.

85. Baumgarten, "The Humbling of Eliot Spitzer," 78.

86. Ralph Wright, *All Politics Is Personal* (Manchester Center, Vt.: Marshall Jones Co., 1996), 117–118.

87. Ralph Wright, *Inside the Statehouse* (Washington, D.C.: CQ Press, 2005), 174–213.

88. Ibid., 184.

89. *New York Times,* May 22, 2007.

90. Weintraub, "Schwarzenegger Rebuffed," 23.

91. Alan Greenblatt, "Policy Fulcrum," *Governing* (November 2007), 40.

92. *State Net Capitol Journal,* July 9, 2007.

9

The Stuff of Law

WHEN PEOPLE THINK OF LEGISLATURES, which for most of us is not very often, they think of them as places where laws are made. At least some of these laws, people realize, affect their lives. So legislatures have consequential business to conduct.

Lawmaking is not a legislature's only business. The legislative job also includes representing constituencies and balancing the power of the executive, as discussed in chapters 3 and 8. They have an advise-and-consent function with respect to gubernatorial appointments. Legislators review administrative rules and regulations before they go into effect, mainly to determine if they conform to law and the legislature's intent in enacting it. They also are responsible for performing oversight—that is, seeing how laws are being administered by the executive branch and how and to what extent they are working to achieve their objectives.

These legislative duties overlap to a considerable degree. Part of the job of representation is expressing constituents' views on public policy—that is, taking into account what policies and programs people back home want. And balancing the power of the executive occurs in the initiation and enactment of policy and budgets. Rule-and-regulation review can be thought of as part of the lawmaking process, in that an administrative agency is working out details that were omitted by the legislature. Oversight also can be considered an extension of lawmaking, especially if review and evaluation lead to the repeal or reformulation of the enacted policy. Or oversight might also be considered to be part of the legislature's job in balancing executive power.

However one looks at the legislature in session at the capitol, making (or not making) law is what it spends most of its time doing. As Mordecai Lee, a former member of the Wisconsin Legislature, puts it: "The raison d'être of a legislative body is to pass laws." [1] Every bill that is introduced can be considered as a proposal for state law, whether the law is broadly focused, as in omnibus legislation extending health care coverage, or narrowly focused, as in legislation renaming a bridge. Whether or not law is policy *per se,* or rather an instrument of policy, is worthy of debate.[2] For the time being, however, we shall use the notion of "lawmaking" and "policymaking" synonymously. Legislative-made law is policy along with administrative regulations, rules, and court decisions. Even though law may be narrow rather than general and affect few people rather than many, it is policy as far as this analysis is concerned.

The Workload

"There ought to be a law" is a familiar expression to many Americans. Virtually any idea can be drafted and introduced as a bill in the legislature. That is the first step in its becoming law and public policy. As we shall see, it is not easy for a bill to go the distance, but as far as square one is concerned, the legislature is a very welcoming place. The number of bills introduced is substantial indeed. Looking at the regular sessions of legislatures in the fifty states during 2006, the number of bills totaled over 100,000. During these legislative sessions, the range in the number of bills introduced, as in indicated by Table 9-1, was enormous—from just over 200 in Wyoming to 17,700 in New York. The numbers of introductions are not comparable from state to state, since practices vary.

States with smaller populations tend to introduce fewer bills. But there are also larger states—Ohio is an example—that are conservative when it comes to the introductions (and passage) of legislation. The number of bills may be increased by the introduction of duplicates, companions, and cross-filed bills. In states such as New York multiple introductions of the same bill are permitted, thus inflating the total number of bills introduced. In states such as Arkansas the budget is not confined to one omnibus bill or even several bills, but is broken down into a few hundred separate measures. In Massachusetts the total is as high as it is because of a constitutional provision, the "right of free petition," that allows any citizen to submit a bill

Table 9-1 Bill Introductions and Enactments, 2006 Regular Session

State	Bills introduced	Bills enacted	State	Bills introduced	Bills enacted
Alabama	1,432	365	Montana[a]	1,441	693
Alaska	308	113	Nebraska	500	135
Arizona	1,453	395	Nevada[a]	1,107	513
Arkansas[a]	3,176	2,325	New Hampshire	1,029	328
California	1,853	632	New Jersey	6,430	237
Colorado	651	440	New Mexico	1,623	112
Connecticut	1,550	206	New York	17,700	750
Delaware	392	214	North Carolina	1,905	264
Florida	2,096	440	North Dakota[a]	944	615
Georgia	1,937	509	Ohio	403	134
Hawaii	2,758	354	Oklahoma	2,133	327
Idaho	737	459	Oregon[a]	2,957	843
Illinois	2,547	346	Pennsylvania	4,450	365
Indiana	834	193	Rhode Island	2,812	704
Iowa	1,211	191	South Carolina	721	203
Kansas	774	219	South Dakota	458	270
Kentucky	1,012	223	Tennessee	3,330	514
Louisiana	2,149	873	Texas[a]	5,484	1,389
Maine	658	351	Utah	663	367
Maryland	2,856	636	Vermont	485	157
Massachusetts[b]	5,400	223	Virginia	2,346	958
Michigan	1,752	682	Washington	929	155
Minnesota	3,139	113	West Virginia	2,105	370
Mississippi	2,819	435	Wisconsin	1,967	491
Missouri	1,879	165	Wyoming	213	121

Source: The Council of State Governments' survey of legislative agencies.

Note: Data from March 2007 and January 2006.

[a] Did not meet in 2006, so data for 2005 session reported.

[b] Bill introductions not available in 2006, so data for 2005 session reported.

to a legislator for introduction. While it is not mandatory that senators and representatives sponsor a citizen's bill, it is customary that they do so. However, they may indicate to colleagues that the bill is sponsored "by request"—a signal that they may not be ardent supporters.

Many bills, whether labeled or not, are introduced at someone's request—the governor, a department or agency of state government, or a constituent. But a bill has to be introduced by a legislator who is known as the sponsor or author of the proposal. In some chambers members are limited by rule as to how many bills they can introduce. Both chambers in California, Colorado, Indiana, Louisiana, Montana, Nevada, New Jersey, and North Dakota have limits, as do senates in Tennessee and Wyoming and houses in Arizona, Florida, and North Carolina.[3] Bill limitations keep the numbers lower than they otherwise would be, but they do not necessarily reduce the amount of work facing the legislature. There are diverse ways to get something enacted into law, including the introduction of amendments in place of bills. Take the case of California, where senators are limited to fifty bills and assembly members to forty bills each per session. This results in more omnibus committee bills, which include items that are not introduced separately and are negotiated by committee chairs.[4]

Legislatures start out with bills introduced by their members. Four out of five chambers have deadlines after which bills cannot be introduced, except by special procedures. They have a specified period of time to dispose of them, enacting some and rejecting or ignoring the majority. In almost half the chambers, the bills carry over from the first year of the biennium to the second year. In the rest, the bills die at the end of the first year of the biennium and have to be reintroduced at the beginning of the second year.[5]

Action on a bill, therefore, has to occur within a limited time frame—one or two annual sessions of the legislature. In the relatively full-time legislatures that meet for six months or longer, time appears to be less pressing. Even though these legislatures normally meet only three or four days a week, they may put in eighty to one hundred workdays a year. Nonetheless, during the final weeks of a session even full-time legislatures scurry to process bills that will expire unless passed by an adjournment date. Alabama, Arkansas, Florida, Georgia, Hawaii, Indiana, Kentucky, Louisiana, New Hampshire, New Mexico, South Dakota, Utah, Virginia, and West Virginia have fewer than sixty days a year for lawmaking. All these states have annual sessions except Arkansas, where the legislature meets biennially for no longer than sixty calendar days (unless the legislature by a two-thirds vote decides to extend its session).

How It Gets There

Every bill has one or multiple legislator sponsors, but just about every bill also is stimulated by a push from outside. The legislature is a place that deals with the problems facing the state; with requirements that have to be met; and with a variety of agendas from inside and outside of government, from constituents, and from ideas that legislators themselves are promoting.

Similar Problems

At any session, a number of items on the legislative agenda of one state are also on the agendas of other states. Legislation is becoming a national phenomenon. A bill introduced in New York may be quite similar to another introduced in Ohio or Arizona or any other state. In 2007, for instance, a number of problems were high on the agenda of many state legislatures. More than two hundred bills on data privacy had been introduced in thirty-nine states. Fifteen states were examining legislation to ban or limit trans fats in restaurants. Over 350 bills pertained to global climate change. Oklahoma and Arizona had enacted anti–illegal immigration measures, and another dozen states were considering passage of similar laws. A number of states—such as California, Florida, Illinois, Indiana, Massachusetts, and Texas—that were anticipating revenue shortfalls were considering selling or leasing their lotteries.[6] Since 2002 almost every state legislature increased taxes on tobacco in order to make up for revenue shortfalls. In 2008 a number of legislatures with budget problems turned to squeezing tobacco again.

Commonality of agendas derives from a variety of factors. In the first place, states have common problems. Furthermore, federal law and federal court decisions require state legislative response. Most important, national interest groups, especially those with state affiliates, push their proposals widely, not only in a few places. The exchange of information that is facilitated by national legislative organizations—the National Conference of State Legislatures (NCSL), Council of State Governments (CSG), State Legislative Leaders Foundation (SLLF), and American Legislative Exchange Council (ALEC)—and by the Internet also contributes to commonality among lawmaking agendas.

Year after year the issues of abortion and guns almost surely have a place on the agendas of many states. In the 2008 sessions of state legislatures, for example, the National Rifle Association (NRA) was tracking 208 pieces of gun-related legislation in thirty-eight states, some of which the organization supported and some of which it opposed.[7] Other issues with durable nationwide currency have included legalizing marijuana for medical purposes, outlawing racial profiling, making driving without a seat belt a primary rather than secondary traffic offense, granting paid family leave, and allowing convicted felons the right to vote after they have served their terms, among others.

Many problems are neither state-specific nor regional in impact. The cost of prescription drugs is a recent example. In 2001 Maine became the first state to regulate drug prices, forcing pharmaceutical companies to provide discounts to the uninsured. Since then legislatures in every state have had bills in play that involve pharmaceuticals. The exploration of what to do about costs and the availability of drugs continues practically everywhere. A relatively new issue concerns marketing practices pharmaceutical companies use to woo doctors. In 2008 over a dozen state legislatures considered bills that would force these companies to disclose the gifts—meals, travel, and other perks—they give to doctors each year.[8]

Laws enacted by Congress leave legislatures little choice—they have to engage. Federal highway safety regulations put pressure on legislatures to pass seat belt laws. Federal education law, laid down in the No Child Left Behind Act of 2002, causes upset in many legislatures, but they all comply to one extent or another. In 2005 the Real ID Act mandated states to adopt by 2008 uniform, tamper-proof driver's licenses and ID cards. A number of legislatures had serious objections to the mandate, mainly because of its costs. Legislatures in Maine, Montana, New Mexico, Vermont, Washington, and Wyoming considered legislation that would enable them to avoid compliance with the federal law, but by April 2008 all the states had complied.

Another example of a federal mandate requiring a legislative response nationwide is congressional action pressuring the states to lower the legal limit of the blood alcohol content level from 0.10 to 0.08 percent. If states do not agree by the specified date, they stand to lose 2 percent of their federal highway construction funds, with the penalty increasing in subsequent years. Within a few years of its enactment by Congress, half the states had complied and the issue is still being fought in the remaining states.

A scandal can reverberate far beyond the borders of one or several states. In 2007 New York's attorney general, Andrew Cuomo, charged that colleges and universities across the country had been receiving payments of one sort or another for recommending "preferred" lenders to students seeking loans. The so-called "college loan scandal" had immediate effects in the New York Legislature, but within a short time legislation was also pending in California, Indiana, Iowa, Pennsylvania, and Texas.[9]

The issues do not have to be blockbusters in order to make it on the agenda. Bills to require that cigarettes be self-extinguishing were debated in a number of places and were passed by legislatures in California, Illinois, Massachusetts, New Hampshire, and Vermont. Seventeen states that same year (2006) banned alcoholic vaporizers, which allow users to inhale alcohol and get intoxicated more quickly than by merely drinking it.

State Requirements

An extremely important part of a legislature's agenda is dictated by requirements generated within the state itself. The state constitution, for instance, requires that the legislature enact a budget either annually or biennially. The legislature must meet its responsibility of appropriating funds for the conduct of state government, including the operations of state agencies and the conduct of state programs, aid to localities, and capital expenditures. The budget, except in Vermont, is constitutionally required to be in balance, with expenditures offset by revenues. If a budget cannot be adopted before the fiscal year begins, or if a stopgap measure cannot be passed in lieu of the budget itself, parts of state government may be closed down.

Because of constitutional provisions, legislation cannot be avoided in other domains as well. For example, every ten years after the census is taken and announced, states have to enact a redistricting plan for Congress and for the state senate and house. Normally, the redistricting plan is the legislature's job, although in some states redistricting is delegated to commissions, with neither the legislature nor the governor having an official say. If the legislature or a commission fails to act or if its action is challenged, courts decide and often do the redistricting themselves or appoint a special master to do it for them.

Legislation Prompted by the Courts

The judiciary has the power to review the constitutionality of state law. It can declare legislatively enacted law unconstitutional. State and federal courts have had an enormous impact on legislatures in various policy domains, but nowhere as much as in the financing of public education. About forty states have been sued for failing to provide poor school districts enough money to meet what courts interpret to be constitutional standards. In the past quarter-century federal or state courts have ruled state formulas unconstitutional in about half the states. On each occasion, the legislature was compelled to respond with new law. In New Jersey, for example, the supreme court has been a major actor in education policy for over thirty years. The legislature has been forced to respond to a number of court rulings requiring more funding for schools in urban areas. Arkansas is another state with a history of legislative-judicial disagreement on school funding. A school district there sued the state in 1992, charging that it did not spend sufficient money on public education and that it was unfairly allocated. When the Arkansas Supreme Court ruled against the state in 2002 and 2005, the legislature had to react. By spending additional money it satisfied the court, which ruled in May 2007 that the schools were being adequately funded.

Judicial rulings of lesser magnitude also affect legislatures. The U.S. Supreme Court struck down Michigan and New York statutes banning the direct shipment of wine to consumers. This had the effect of changing the fortunes of in-state and out-of-state wine dealers, and so the legislature was called upon to deal with the court decisions.

The court's role vis-à-vis the legislature ranges broadly. It can require legislative action without actually overruling a statute. The Vermont Supreme Court, for instance, in December 1999 ruled in *Baker v. State of Vermont* that same-sex couples should receive the equivalent legal benefits of heterosexual married couples. The court left it up to the legislature to comply. The legislature reacted by passing a bill legalizing civil unions, which afforded gay and lesbian couples the legal rights associated with marriage (without legalizing same-sex marriage).

The judiciary may stimulate legislative action, rather than actually require it. After the U.S. Supreme Court in 2005 narrowly upheld the authority of New London, Connecticut, to condemn houses in a run-down neighborhood in order to develop private office space, condominiums, and a hotel, many legislators attempted to blunt the impact of the decision. Within weeks of the Court's decision, Alaska, Delaware, and Texas passed bills to limit the eminent-domain rights of local governments. Seldom has a Supreme Court decision had such an immediate legislative reaction, with Democratic and Republican legislators from California to Maine agreeing that something had to be done to protect their citizens' property rights.[10] The U.S. Supreme Court's ruling in April 2007 upholding a federal law barring so-called "partial-birth" abortion also affected state legislatures, in that it encouraged anti-abortion forces to push for more restrictions, such as waiting periods, strict licensing laws for doctors and clinics, mandatory ultrasound examinations, and mandatory counseling for women seeking abortions.[11]

The issues do not have to be of national relevance for the legislature to have to respond to legal action. For example, as a result of a lawsuit, the city of Boston and the U.S. Department of Justice reached an agreement that required that ballots be available in Chinese and Vietnamese. To alter language on a ballot in Massachusetts, the legislature had to enact a special law because the Chinese and Vietnamese populations did not meet the numerical threshold already established by statute.

It Has to Get Done

Some matters—of a very immediate nature—have to be handled expeditiously. In order to have the National Collegiate Athletic Association Women's Final Four—a national basketball competition—held in Boston, funding had to be provided in advance. Waiting for the Massachusetts state budget to be enacted would not do; the funding would arrive too late. If the legislature did not take quick action, the tournament would have to be cancelled and the state would suffer embarrassment.

If they are not renewed, some laws expire. Therefore, legislatures have to decide whether to extend them, and whether and how to revise them. In Massachusetts a law authorizing simulcasting at the state's four racetracks was expiring. If it were not renewed the racetracks would have to close down. That is because the ability to broadcast and accept bets on races throughout the nation is critical to the economic viability of these tracks. Closings would lead to the loss of employment and income for track workers.

It's Been around for a While

Many of the introductions in any legislative session have been around for years but have not been enacted into law. A new legislative session finds that hundreds of bills introduced in earlier sessions are introduced again. This time their sponsors and backers hope to pass them. In the 2006 session of the Massachusetts legislature hardy perennials included a proposal to decriminalize small amounts of marijuana, legalize clean needle sales in order to reduce the incidence of AIDS, and ban discrimination against women in insurance annuity policies. After a bill to permit the children of illegal immigrants to pay state tuition rates at state higher education institutions had failed, its proponents announced that they planned to file the bill in the next session. "We are not a community that's going away," one proponent said. The primary seat belt law was also defeated in the Massachusetts legislature that session. The response of the executive director of Mothers Against Drunk Driving (MADD) was straightforward: "As far as we're concerned, the bill will come back every session until it's passed." [12]

Most substantial or controversial legislation takes a while to get through. Repeated efforts are necessary before the requisite majorities can be assembled. Massachusetts legislators had spent six years trying to pass legislation requiring tobacco companies to sell only self-extinguishing cigarettes. It had passed in the senate but not in the house. Then in 2006 broad support was achieved in the house as well as the senate. It took a bill banning the sale of consumer products containing mercury six years to get enacted in the Bay State. A nurses' staffing ratio bill, first introduced in 1998, was on the agenda year after year but did not pass until 2006.

Some bills are nearly always around. Minimum wage legislation has a continuous presence. The law financing local education, known in Massachusetts as Chapter 70, is almost always under scrutiny in the legislature. The aid formula, which was part of the Massachusetts Education Reform Act of 1993, had not been changed substantially for six years, although minor adjustments were made annually. There were always bills to revise it in a more comprehensive way. In 2006 the legislature once again wrestled with the problem of coming up with a new formula to distribute the state's education aid to cities and towns. On this occasion, the legislature succeeded in enacting major change.

What the Governor Wants

In chapter 8 we refer to the governor as "chief legislator." Obviously, then, the most significant bills on the legislature's agenda will reflect the governor's priorities. Some governors have a virtual laundry list, but most concentrate on a small number of measures they want passed.

Take as an illustration Gov. Mitt Romney's 2005–2006 agenda for the Massachusetts legislature. In addition to his budget priorities, Romney was interested in accomplishing a number of statutory objectives. He wanted the state's automobile insurance system changed. Of somewhat lesser scope, he wanted anyone indicted for rape or sexual assault to be treated for HIV and other sexually transmitted diseases. Still another Romney bill would have forced noncustodial parents to pay for their children's health insurance. Another proposal would have prepared the state for an influenza pandemic, while still another would have allowed part of unexpended state funds to be spent on summer jobs for youths. Romney's signature bill, of course, was that pertaining to health care, which became the major focus of lawmaking in that session.

Not only governors but also the departments and agencies in the executive branch have items that they need enacted into law. A few are broad in scope, a few are controversial. The large majority is of an essentially "housekeeping" nature—measures that make changes in previously enacted statutes, accomplish fine-tuning, or are technical rather than substantive.

When he chaired the Environmental Affairs Committee in the Wisconsin Legislature, Mordecai Lee routinely sponsored bills the Department of

Natural Resources wanted. The department would bring him a draft and he would sponsor a bill. Often these bills were technical in nature, but sometimes they made "minor policy" changes. Lee agreed to sponsor a bill regulating lakeside boathouses. (Such legislation was not considered minor by the owners of lakeside homes who opposed such regulations.) His views coincided with those of the department and he gladly took it on, even though it was more controversial than most executive agency bills.[13] Less controversial "minor policy" was a bill initiated by the Department of Natural Resources in Maryland, which would have required children under the age of seven to wear life jackets while on board recreational boats. No controversy accompanied a Minnesota Department of Human Services bill that would permit a few nursing homes to share administrators.

There is no way to tell exactly how many, but large numbers of bills that legislatures process emanate from the executive branch. Relatively few of these come from the governor; many more come from the executive agencies, normally with the consent of the governor's office. According to C. J. Bowling and D. S. Wright, two experts on state administration, about half of all state legislation originates in the agencies.[14]

What Local Jurisdictions Need

Wisconsin's Lee writes about how agencies of municipal and county governments also originate bills and get legislators to sponsor them. In Wisconsin, as in some other states, local governments have no powers other than those assigned through law by the state. If a local agency wants to do anything, it requires authorization from the legislature. Each legislator would carry a number of bills requested by municipal and county agencies in the legislator's district:

> The veteran legislators would often encourage the first-term and junior members to be the lead sponsor of most of these bills. The mantra went like this: These bills are usually not very controversial, pushing them will show that you're being responsive to local needs, trying to get them passed will give you some experience in the legislative process and—most important of all—they have a good chance of passage.[15]

Most, but not all, bills of a local nature are limited in scope and arouse no opposition. Like Wisconsin, in Massachusetts the legislature is responsible for laws that affect cities and towns. Dozens of local bills are passed by the Massachusetts Senate or House on a session day. A few of these bills have general application, such as one that allows local jurisdictions to increase fines for violations of local snow- and ice-removal ordinances. The large majority, however, apply to specific jurisdictions, such as a bill related to city services in Somerville, a department of public works in Topsfield, borrowing money for road improvement in Brewster, enforcing delinquent sewer fees in Taunton, or regulating tax deferrals in Princeton. Other bills authorized Braintree to establish a city-council form of government and facilitate the repair of a public waterfront walkway in Chelsea. One would help first-time home buyers on Nantucket Island and another would rename Amesbury Bridge after a soldier killed in Afghanistan.

The Demands of Interest Groups

In addition to the large proportion of bill introductions attributed to executive departments and agencies, a significant number can be attributed to interest groups in the state. Indeed, roughly one out of five introductions is what is often called "special interest" legislation, intended to help an organized group that wants to advance or protect the interests of its members or its businesses.

Examples of interest group–inspired legislation range broadly. Maryland's independent service station owners got a bill introduced to restrict the predatory pricing of gasoline by large dealers. A bill in New York was designed to allow rental car companies to require customers to bear the cost of insurance for rental cars. Another bill furnished a new baseball stadium for the Minnesota Twins. All these bills could be (and were) justified in terms of public policy and the public interest. But they also promoted the narrower objectives of service station owners, rental car companies, and a major league baseball team. Meanwhile, Merck & Co., a large pharmaceutical company that had developed the Gardasil vaccine to combat human papillomavirus (HPV), was pressing for legislation in many states to add HPV to measles, hepatitis B, and polio as a disease against which school-age children should be inoculated.[16]

Like individuals, interest groups have the constitutional right to petition their government. That is what they are doing by proposing laws that will benefit them. These groups often have strong allies among legislators. Together with their legislator-allies, labor organizations, teacher associations, professional and occupational groups, senior citizens, environmental organizations, companies, police chiefs and sheriffs, sportsmen, MADD, and many others, they are promoting their causes.

As in any other legislature, the 2005–2006 session in Massachusetts featured numerous groups advocating legislative remedies for what was troubling them. During that period, the Massachusetts Medical Society was promoting medical malpractice reform, trying to get rid of "joint and several liability" and reduce the cap on "pain and suffering" payments. A proposal to create a Massachusetts Transit Fund in order to expand commuter rail service had as proponents a coalition of the state's construction industry and labor, along with environmentalists. Pharmacists backed a bill that would give them greater autonomy in managing patients' therapies and drug treatments. Libraries advocated a measure to match grants to public libraries with state money.

Of a different nature, but just as important, is the competition that takes place among interest groups striving to obtain funding for their programs in the state budget. They do not introduce bills as such, but rather use amendments to accomplish their purposes. Antidomestic violence advocates wanted a 69 percent increase over what the governor had proposed. The Phobic United Foundation sought additional money for the homebound. The Metropolitan Council for Educational Opportunity, which sends city students to suburban schools, wanted to close a $15 million gap in its budget. The Massachusetts Immigrant and Refugee Advocacy Coalition asked for more than the governor had included in his proposal. Afterschool programs required additional funds, as did teen pregnancy prevention programs. Groups advocating for the blind, homeless, deaf, and mentally ill also argued that they deserved additional state aid for their programs. These represented only a few of the hundreds of claims on the state budget by Massachusetts interest groups.

Many interest groups have nationwide agendas. The food industry is an example. When food and restaurant companies felt threatened by consumer lawsuits and large judgments against them, they appealed to legislatures.

What spurred them to action was the 2002 case brought by two teenagers who accused the McDonalds restaurant chain of making them fat and unhealthy. Led by the National Restaurant Association and its fifty state organizations, a coalition sponsored "commonsense consumption" laws, which would prevent lawsuits seeking personal injury damages related to obesity.[17]

Abortion is a long-standing issue that is always on legislatures' agendas, although final action is not always taken on all the bills introduced. From time to time a new national effort is made by one side or the other. For example, the U.S. Supreme Court ruling in April 2007 upholding the Partial-Birth Abortion Act precipitated abortion opponents to press state legislatures to pass more restrictive laws and chip away at the Court's decision in *Roe v. Wade* (1973). The Family Research Council underwrote the campaign, along with the National Right to Life Committee, and helped state legislators draft bills patterned after the federal law on "partial-birth" abortion. In response to the Court's decision, legislators in over thirty states sponsored "partial-birth" abortion prohibitions.[18]

Ideas from Constituents

Legislators in their representational role welcome constituents' ideas for legislation. Most of them will introduce bills on behalf of constituents; sometimes they champion them and sometimes they make no attempt whatsoever to get them enacted. It depends on the legislator's judgment as to the merits of the constituent's case. At the least, however, the case will make its way to the introductory stage.

Consider, for instance, how a New Jersey senator, Joseph Vitale, represents constituents in this regard. One bill he introduced was in response to the request of a constituent who had been assaulted. It would impose penalties on those who abet such crimes. Another asked that the law expand coverage of victims' compensation. A woman whose HMO was about to change her obstetrician in the middle of her pregnancy also prompted a bill. After one of Vitale's aides, on a visit to a veterans' home on behalf of the senator, was asked why residents had to pay the New Jersey sales tax, another bill was framed. This one exempted from the sales tax goods sold at concession stands in state-owned veterans' homes. Several of Vitale's bills passed.[19]

Every now and then a bill of broader scope comes as a result of a constituent's coming forward. A Baltimore developer read about a New York measure that encouraged developers to incorporate conservation features in new and rehabilitated buildings by offering them tax credits. The developer visited with Maryland delegate Sandy Rosenberg, who took on sponsorship of the bill. A request from Jewish residents of a condominium in his district to have a Sabbath elevator installed also got Rosenberg's support. Adjustment was not out of the question; a computer chip could make the elevator stop at every floor, so that observant Jews would not have to push a button for their floor (which would violate a religious prohibition of working on the Sabbath). Rosenberg's bill would have required a condo association or apartment owner to make "reasonable accommodation" for residents' religious practices.[20]

Rosenberg is not unlike his legislator colleagues around the country. They are on the lookout for opportunities to sponsor and promote legislation that will help people—especially people in their constituency. They welcome constituency groups and individuals who bring them problems and potential solutions. In Massachusetts, for example, Sen. Richard Moore received an e-mail from a constituent whose Labrador retriever had been brutally attacked and killed by persons who had no cause. Moore responded with a bill that increased penalties for cruelty to animals. Another legislator heard from a constituent who first learned of his child's cancer diagnosis months after it was made. By that time it was too late for a particular treatment. The legislative remedy was a bill to require that health care providers disclose patient test results covering life-threatening illnesses within ninety-six hours of their diagnosis.

An unusual but not unique instance of constituent-initiated legislation concerns noncustodial parents' access to students' records. When Henry Fassler, a dentist in Milford, Massachusetts, tried to help his seventeen-year-old daughter change her school schedule, school officials refused to release any information to him. They explained that he was not her custodial parent and state law barred anyone but a custodial parent from such access.

Fassler thereupon got in touch with his state senator and state representative, who undertook to change the law.

Multiple Sources

On many issues, and particularly on major policy matters, multiple sources give rise to legislative initiatives. The case of health care in Massachusetts illustrates the difficulty of tracing parentage on such a sweeping and persistent issue. As in most places, health care has been among the most pressing issues in the state for quite a while. People in Massachusetts have been critical of government because it had neither expanded health care services nor controlled health care costs.[21] Meanwhile, the health care industry, which includes insurance companies and health providers, had become the state's top employer, so its interests could not be ignored. No wonder that health care is high on the Massachusetts legislative agenda: about three hundred of the bills filed in 2005–2006 were related to health care.

For the sake of understanding, it would be convenient to pinpoint responsibility for the initiation of a major legislative achievement in 2006. But there is no single locus; rather, responsibility was shared broadly among the Romney administration, the legislature, and a coalition of advocacy groups.

Health care legislation did not spring up suddenly. Governors and legislatures had been struggling, trying to do whatever they could to narrow the gap between health needs and what was then being provided. In 1988 Massachusetts enacted a major law, but one that largely failed in implementation. Eight years later another health care effort was enacted, and it proved more successful.[22] Various groups had come together in a coalition to press for improvement. In 2002–2003 the Blue Cross Access Foundation began to develop a road map for universal coverage. At the end of 2004 Health Care for All, headed by John E. McDonough, a former legislator, announced a broad-based coalition in support of a health care package. It had taken about three years to build this coalition and get it on the radar screen. Once organized, however, it became a powerful force.

Furthermore, the state's top political leadership enlisted in the effort. As early as 2003 Gov. Mitt Romney had instructed Ron Preston, his secretary of the Department of Health and Human Services, to put together a plan that would ensure that everyone in the state had health care insurance. Preston responded with a white paper, which included among other things a tax on employers who did not cover workers. The governor embraced the idea, but shortly thereafter was warned off the employer mandate by political advisors. At about the same time that Romney was putting together his proposal, Senate President Robert Travaglini committed himself to the health care endeavor. Coming off an election in which he had helped turn back the governor's campaign to get more Republicans elected to the senate and house, Travaglini was feeling his oats. He publicly pledged in an address that access to health care would be at the top of his agenda. His speech received page one coverage in the *Boston Globe*, probably prompting Romney to act quickly. The governor responded with an op-ed piece that called for coverage of all the uninsured. He presented his plan to the legislature in 2005, only a few months after Travaglini had introduced his. Three months later the speaker of the house, Salvatore DiMasi, offered his own health care proposal. The top leaders were committed and engaged. Health care was very much on the legislature's agenda, having been put there by several of the state's leading political actors.

Legislators as Advocates

Ideas, requests, and demands for bills come into legislatures from all sides and all directions. But it is a mistake to think of legislators simply as waiting for the governor to announce his or her agenda, agencies to ask them to sign on as sponsors, interest groups to press their issues, and constituents to identify problems and offer remedies for their solution. Some legislators are inclined to wait. They are content to be reactive, picking and choosing among items that come their way. Other legislators are more proactive. They are on the lookout for problems that need solving and bills that need introducing. They want to look like they think lawmaking should look— introducing bills and getting them passed. Two observers of the process argue that "claiming credit for the introduction of legislation (without regard to its likelihood of passing) is a critical part of legislators' public relations and campaign strategies." [23]

Usually, legislators need to have some of their bills pass before they can feel or claim that they are effective. Lee explains this rationale:

> For legislators to feel that they are performing their role requires having an inventory of bills to push. Bragging rights at election time are rarely based on inaction or bills opposed. Rather, the political currency in reelection campaigns (or elections to higher office) focuses on the new laws that the legislator has passed.[24]

Not just liberals and Democrats but also conservatives and Republicans are in the business of making law. The result of all this is that in some legislatures—California's is an example—members get on average over 50 percent of their bills passed.

Legislators, however, do not only want to look good to their constituents; they want to do good by way of public policy. John Kingdon, in his study of decision making in Congress, recognizes that senators and representatives want to affect the shape of public policy, from the left or the right.[25] David R. Mayhew agrees. Life in Congress is more than merely carrying out the wishes of interests that exist outside, in his judgment.[26] Members of Congress, writes Frances E. Lee, "are also legislative entrepreneurs with their own ideas of the public interest . . . they have beliefs about what government should do and how it should do it." [27]

Experience

Legislator antennae search for problems that can be addressed by legislation. Such problems can surface as a result of the legislator's own experiences. In Colorado a lawmaker, moved by her daughter's ordeal as a victim of domestic violence, sponsored a bill to improve communication among law enforcement officials about restraining orders issued by judges against violent domestic partners. Another Colorado lawmaker sponsored a bill that would require the placement of special zebra-striped auto license plates on the cars of repeat drunk-driving offenders.[28] A New York assemblyman, after witnessing an accident caused by a driver talking on a cell phone, introduced a bill to ban the use of hand-held cellular phones while on the road.[29] A Florida senator had a bad experience at a restaurant in Tampa— no running water, no soap, and a jammed toilet in the men's room. "The next day at the office," the lawmaker told the Miami *Herald*, "I said. . . , 'We're doing a bill.' " The bill required that restaurants provide toilet paper and antibacterial soap in every restroom.[30] In Massachusetts one representative, the mother of an autistic child, pushed legislation that would ban the use of shock therapy on autistic and retarded students in state schools.[31]

One of my own representatives, New Jersey Assemblyman Reed Gusciora, was ticketed at the Princeton Junction train station when he parked in a permit-only space after he could find no available spaces in the daily parking lot. Gusciora explained his action, which took place after work hours, as follows:

> There were at least a dozen cars circling around looking for spaces. A woman in another car pulled up and asked what to do. Right across the way from the daily lot was a permit lot with about 100 or more empty spaces. We both parked there.

The assemblyman's reasoning was that NJ Transit (the commuter light-rail system) should not encourage its use if it could not provide enough parking. And people who are not daily commuters should be able to use excess spaces after normal work hours without being ticketed. Gusciora's bill would require NJ Transit to provide more parking spaces for those who travel only occasionally rather than daily.[32]

Events

Events often signal the existence of problems for which legislators derive legal remedies. Let us look at happenings in the state of Massachusetts during 2006. After a homeless man was attacked and set on fire in a Boston park, a bill was filed adding homelessness to a list of categories, such as race and religion, that are protected from "hate crimes." The death of a four-year-old and the alleged abuse of a twelve-year-old, both of whom were in the custody of the Department of Social Services, prompted an introduction that would change investigative procedures in child-abuse cases. After a teenager employed by a country club died in a golf-cart accident, a bill to make child labor laws more stringent was introduced. And "Patrick's Law" came as a reaction to the case of Patrick Holland, who was eight when his father murdered his mother. The bill permitted a child to sever ties with one parent who was convicted of murdering the other. Following the death of a young woman while exercising at a gym, a bill was introduced requiring defibrillators in health clubs. Indirectly at least, the sex abuse scandals involving Catholic priests led to legislation requiring more financial disclosure by religious organizations.

The legislature cannot resist addressing certain problems that surface either gradually or more suddenly. They either have effects touching many citizens of the state, or they have undeniable impacts in and on the state. Often they are put on the agenda by the media. One instance is when it was reported that the state of Massachusetts itself was employing illegal immigrants. This led to a bill that would impose sanctions on contractors to the state hiring illegal immigrants. During the 2006 session the cost of oil was rising. By the time the price of regular unleaded gasoline had reached three dollars a gallon, legislators were looking for ways to respond. Individual members drafted bills, such as one that would suspend the state's twenty-one-cent gas tax over the summer months. The Telecommunications, Utilities, and Energy Committee put the problem on its agenda. "Anything we can do to keep pricing down is what this issue is about," announced house chair Brian Dempsey. More sudden in its effects were five days of torrential rains and flooding in May, which imposed unanticipated costs on the Massachusetts budget (just at the time when the legislature was considering the budget) and brought to vivid attention the need for the state to put together a flood-relief measure and shore up a number of defective dams. It would have been unthinkable for the Massachusetts legislature—or any legislature, for that matter—not to attempt to remedy these situations by doing what it normally does: enact law.

Commitments

In the 2007 session the New Jersey Legislature passed a package designed to relieve the burden of property taxes on homeowners in the state. Property tax relief was by no means a new idea in the state. Successive governors and legislators had verbally committed themselves to reform. All sorts of proposals had been floated. Bills had been introduced at session after session, but not much had happened. Joseph Roberts, the new speaker of the assembly, came into office committed to property tax reform. "For me, the job is to tackle the big issues," he said. "The fun of the job is to do the heavy lifting." [33] Roberts became familiar with the problem during the years he served in local office. And since he started out in the legislature, complaints from constituents continued and increased. One statewide poll after another showed that property taxes were the most pressing concern for New Jerseyans. If the legislature was to have any credibility with the public and if Roberts was to maintain Democratic control of the assembly, something would have to be done. Roberts's commitment was not new, but his opportunity as speaker to advocate change was.

Many legislators have policy commitments when they arrive at the capitol. The commitments of others grow out of their work in the capitol. Either way, many legislators have policy concerns and policy domains in which they are especially active. For each major policy domain in any state, there are probably enough entrepreneurial legislators to keep the lawmaking pot boiling. The specific ideas included in bills that these members advocate may not be their very own, but they are ready to sign on to sponsor them and then champion them. More than likely, the ideas come from interest groups or academics, or derive from bills introduced elsewhere. If we look at the Massachusetts legislature during the 2006 session, we can see how lawmakers make commitments on a range of matters.

Sometimes they come up with narrow-gauge ideas on their own. A school curriculum on the subject of genocide can be attributed to Sen. Steven Tolman. He realized that such a curriculum could not be mandated by the legislature, so he introduced a bill that would allow the Department of Education to authorize its development. If legislators have backgrounds in particular areas they may well reflect their interests in legislation. Rep. Brian Dempsey had worked as a nursing home admissions director, so it is not surprising that he sponsored an amendment to the budget that would increase state financing for long-term care. Not coincidentally, the cochairs of a special legislative committee on foster care were foster-care children themselves, and the legislator sponsoring a bill to reduce the incidence of asthma by restricting cleaning materials used in schools, hospitals, and public housing was himself asthmatic.

While legislators are open to ideas of almost any stripe, they tend to devote much of their energy to ideas in specific policy domains. These demands are usually, but by no means always, associated with the standing committees on which they serve. At the congressional level, Kingdon writes of the tendency for committees to be populated by members who believe in the programs within their jurisdictions. Highway committees, he points out, have members who favor highway construction; health committees have members who wish to advance health care; and agriculture committees have members who want to help farming.[34] Although lawmakers and committees in the states are less specialized than those in Washington, D.C., a number of members have strong commitments in one policy area or another. This does not mean that legislators confine themselves to only one policy area; rather, they specialize in several, according to responses in the 2002 State Legislative Survey. Indeed, only 7.7 percent say they specialize in a single policy area; most spread themselves more thinly.

Committee chairs, however, tend to specialize on matters that fall within their jurisdictions, as the case of Massachusetts illustrates. The chairs of the joint Senate-House committees here are committed to and advocate for broad causes, such as economic development, education, cultural affairs, tourism, and mental health. These lawmakers work closely with the advocacy groups whose concerns parallel their own. Arm in arm, legislators and interest groups try to provide what they generally agree is in the public interest. The popular perception of legislators responding to pressure by interest groups is not without foundation. But it is only part of the story. Actually, on the majority of the big issues that legislators consider, it is more likely that the objectives of legislators and interest groups are in alignment. Legislators and lobbyists are simply on the same side pursuing the same objectives. Advocacy alliances are at the heart of the lawmaking process, even though specifics and details from time to time provoke disagreements even among allies.

Take medical malpractice reform, by no means a new issue in Massachusetts or most other states. Sen. Robert O'Leary thought that a workers' compensation model might be appropriate. To learn more about the issue, he met with a number of interest groups, all of which were stakeholders, as well as experts from the Harvard School of Public Health. He enlisted the support of one of his colleagues for a bill he had drafted, then took it to the stakeholders to enlist their support. It was a beginning, but it would take time to develop. His plan was to move his bill during the next legislative session. Putting together a coalition would require a lot of work. But O'Leary, like many of his colleagues, is a lawmaking entrepreneur.

The economic stimulus package in Massachusetts is a good example of joint advocacy—legislators and interest groups sharing common objectives and working together to get legislation enacted. The general aim was to grow the Massachusetts economy by creating more jobs. The initiative came mainly from the business community, but also with labor's strong support. A major push was provided by the University of Massachusetts, which stood to benefit from investment in research and workforce training. Within the legislature there were a number of champions, but the principal ones were the cochairs of the Joint Committee on Economic Development and Emerging Technologies, Rep. Daniel Bosley and Sen. Jack Hart, along with Sen. Steven Panagiotakos, who cochaired the Higher Education Committee.

In the field of public education, the two committee chairs advanced proposals that they thought would address problems and improve schools in the state. One of Rep. Patricia Haddad's aims was to improve the leadership skills of school principals, another was to strengthen the professional development of classroom teachers. One of Sen. Robert Antonioni's aims was to curb bullying in the schools. On this issue his consultations with the various stakeholders—including local board members, school administrators, teachers, and students—went on continuously. Rep. Eric Turkington, who chaired the Tourism, Arts, and Cultural Development Committee, turned into a leading advocate for the arts. His practice was to hold hearings at historical sites around the state. The more Turkington learned about the subject, the stronger his commitment became. As an advocate, his main job was to make an effective case to the House Ways and Means Committee for increased funding for the arts, including tourism and cultural development.

As chair of the Financial Services Committee, Rep. Ronald Martin was committed to making the auto insurance market more competitive. Senator Tolman was committed to helping personal care attendants and thereby serving the interests of seniors and disabled residents in nursing homes. Along with Rep. Ruth Balser, he also championed substance abuse programs. His advocacy did not require much by way of new law, but it did require additional funding, especially because of the cuts made in recent years. "You will save state money," Tolman and Balser argued, "if you invest in substance abuse programs."

The Massachusetts legislature's joint committee system, like committee systems elsewhere, provides great opportunity for specialized advocacy. The men and women who chair the twenty-six committees in Massachusetts tend to have backgrounds and/or interests in their jurisdictional areas. As Sen. Richard Moore put it: "Most bills I file because of my membership on the committee." A recent reorganization of the committee system by the two presiding officers divided up committees that previously had had broad jurisdictions, thus creating bodies with narrower jurisdictions. The former health committee, for example, was divided into three separate committees—one on health care financing, another on public health, and a third on mental health and substance abuse. As a result of the reorganization, interest groups now have better forums in which to present and pursue their cases, and members have a somewhat more concentrated focus for advocacy. In Massachusetts, at least, a number of these advocacy-type committees are fairly consensual.

The Massachusetts chairs, and some of their members, are "policy champions." They specialize, they craft, they promote, they shepherd within their jurisdictions. And they build support, although it may take a while. People like this are probably a vanishing—or even vanished—breed in term-limited states. That is the conclusion of recent studies of the effects of term limits.[35] Term limits means that lawmakers will be around for fewer years, and on a particular committee for less time than otherwise. Chairmanships are retained for only a few years—not enough time for a lawmaker to gain real control of a subject. Specialization and effective advocacy both suffer. The focus in term-limited legislatures tends to be more diffuse and even more short-term than otherwise.

Shepherding a Bill

No bill will get far in the legislative process unless the sponsor or author shepherds it along. Policy advocates or champions will do this as a matter of course, but lawmakers also deal with many measures of narrow scope and minor nature. On such bills there are no "champions" as such. Either way, however, a bill's passage through two houses does not happen automatically. It requires a push here and a shove there—and usually some orchestration of effort. It may even require hard work.

In virtually every legislative body legislators introduce bills at the request of others. They are asked by constituents and by lobbyists for interest groups to sponsor a bill. Although they may be agnostic on the subject, they agree to help out. After all, they can justify their sponsorship with the rationale that every idea deserves a hearing. But often they go no further, and under such circumstances their bill is likely to get bogged down once it is referred to committee. In many legislative bodies a committee chair will not bring the bill up for consideration unless the sponsor asks for such action. If lawmakers abandon their own progeny, a signal is sent that not enough interest exists for the committee to take valuable time to consider it.

"If they [sponsors] don't push them, that's pretty much the end of their consideration," said Representative Turkington in Massachusetts. In his legislature over five thousand bills are filed a year, largely because of the citizen's right of free petition. Massachusetts committees "hear" every bill, but if "no one shows up, nothing happens," according to Turkington. With no legislator to push them, most of the introductions do not go anywhere, They wind up being "sent to study" by the committee to which they have been referred. Ordinarily that is the death knell, the end of any consideration during the legislative session. Sponsorship is requisite but not sufficient for a bill to have a chance of becoming law. "You have to follow it all the way—answering questions, keeping it moving," is how Senator Panagiotakos puts it.

Even shepherding a bill may not be enough to get it very far. Many bills that are filed can be pronounced dead on arrival. Some have been filed session after session, and members regard them as losers from the outset. Some appear very impractical or extremely costly. Some are out of the mainstream, such as those to repeal the minimum wage, create a second state lottery, and require dogs to wear diapers. These are nonstarters. A lawmaker may file a bill to ban pharmaceutical advertising, which his colleagues view as unconstitutional. They realize that the sponsor just wants to rattle the pharmaceutical industry. Some bills are just off base. Each year a hundred or so measures are filed for the reclassification of individual state employees. The

Ways and Means Committee takes the position that the committee and the legislature should not be deciding such matters. In Massachusetts a large percentage of bills each session can be deemed nonstarters. "After a little while," says Senator Moore, "members know which ones they are." If by chance members do not know, the chairs of standing committees do.

The Degree of Controversy

During 2007 a wide range of legislation was taken up in legislatures around the country. In Florida the legislature had before it a bill to prohibit employees from bringing guns to the workplace. Iowa's legislature was debating whether to allow companies to apply for a statewide franchise to provide video services rather than negotiate agreements with individual jurisdictions. Oregon took up the issue of self-extinguishing cigarettes. Colorado was deciding whether to require a person convicted of animal abuse to submit a DNA sample to the state's criminal database and whether (in another bill) to allow licensed physical therapists to perform therapy on animals. Nevada had before it a measure that would keep people arrested for driving under the influence of alcohol in jail until their blood-alcohol level dropped to .04. Minnesota was deliberating over whether to pass legislation requiring the state to cut greenhouse gas emissions 80 percent by 2050. Indiana was debating the requirement that schools send home to parents information about a vaccine to avert cervical cancer in young girls, while South Carolina had to decide on a measure to require all girls entering the seventh grade to be vaccinated against HPV (human papillomavirus). Texas was considering legislation to permit law enforcement agencies to conduct surveillance via the Internet, cell phones, and multiple phone lines. Oklahoma debated legislation to ban the use of state funds to pay for abortions unless the mother's life was in danger. Washington was considering a requirement that motorists use a hands-free device when talking on a cell phone. And Wisconsin had to decide whether to allow grocery and liquor stores to give customers free six-ounce samples of beer.[36]

Legislative bill agendas are truly a mixed bag. They appear even more mixed if we sort further. Take Massachusetts during its 2006 session. The *Boston Globe* and other media channels reported on:

- Health care insurance
- Minimum wage increase
- New spending for education
- Embryonic stem cell research
- Antigang legislation
- Economic stimulus package
- Income tax rollback
- Family leave
- Sex offender legislation
- Death penalty
- Auto insurance reform

These were the major issues, but by no means the most representative ones, that the Massachusetts legislature confronted. An alternative selection (but not a random sample) of issues might include the following, all of which were in the form of bills on the agenda:

- Designation of Taj Mahal as the state's official blues artist
- Designation of Massachusetts History Day
- Limit on administrative costs of the Children's Catastrophic Relief Fund
- Reduction in time required for hospitals to keep patient records
- Establishment of first lieutenant position within state police
- Repeal of hunting prohibition on Sunday
- Program to serve victims of Shaken Baby Syndrome
- Commission to explore the regulation of medical spas
- Department of Public Works in Topsfield
- Safety education in course for new hunters
- Movement of registration of bottled water manufacturers from local boards to a state department
- Regulation of genetic counseling
- Authorization of liquid gas factory in Fall River
- Requirement that managers of two veterans' cemeteries be veterans themselves

This list of issues is no less relevant to the lawmaking job of the legislature than the earlier list of issues of broader scope and greater prominence.

How does one make a distinction among the bills that are shepherded through the lawmaking process in the state? The hundreds or thousands of bills that are introduced at every session of a legislature can be categorized in a variety of ways. Policy analysts tend to conceive of political systems as divided into separate policy areas, such as education, health, transportation, and so forth.[37] These policy domains differ from one another in content, personnel, and interests involved. Yet there is no evidence that the lawmaking processes in state legislatures differ by policy domain.

E. E. Schattschneider years ago pointed to what he regarded as most important—the scope of an issue, mainly how many people were affected and how many participated in its resolution.[38] Scope is important as far as lawmaking is concerned. Issues of broader scope are settled differently than those of narrower scope. Salience is another criterion for categorizing issues. Salient issues overlap with broad-scope issues, in that they include matters on which public awareness and concern are widespread. Yet, as Kingdon points out in his study of decision making in Congress, high salience may be more a product of interest group activity than of public attention.[39] Either way, salience is important. Visibility is still another means of sorting among bills in a legislature. It too overlaps scope and salience. As Carl E. Van Horn and his colleagues indicate in their book on policymaking, the mass media play a large part in telling people what issues are important and where they should direct attention.[40] The public's attention to issues tracks media coverage of those issues.

Visibility, along with salience and scope, are interrelated. All are important in distinguishing among the ways in which lawmaking proceeds measure by measure. Another obvious method by which to categorize various bills is according to the amount of controversy they engender. Controversy can be related to scope, salience, and visibility. Generally speaking, the broader the scope, the greater the saliency, and the higher the visibility, the more controversial the measure. But in legislative bodies there are many exceptions to any such rule. Narrow scope and invisible measures of little saliency may still arouse controversy. Controversy means conflict, and the degree of conflict is central to a bill's life chances in the legislative process. If any overriding objective of lawmaking exists, it is to build consensus and reduce conflict wherever possible—granting that often, as we shall see, it is not possible to do so. Many bills that are introduced in state senates and houses are noncontroversial at the outset; they do not arouse conflict. They make their way through the lawmaking process with little or no opposition.

It is not always obvious whether or not a measure will face opposition. Usually new regulations are opposed by one group or another, but not always. When the regulatory burden is minor, justification is clear, and potential opponents have been reassured, opposition may not arise. One Massachusetts bill would have required new hunters to take safety education courses, which was already law in the rest of the states. It had the support of those who would be affected, hunters and gun owners. However, sometimes bills that appear benign spark controversy. Genetic counselors, who provide information on the risks of passing on a genetic predisposition for certain diseases, were regulated in a number of states, but not Massachusetts. The counselors wanted to be licensed, in order to advance their status as a profession. A task force drafted a licensure bill. No one seemed to be on the other side as the bill made its way quickly through the legislature. Yet the governor vetoed the act because, in his view, a special regulatory system did not seem to be necessary when there were fewer than eighty genetic counselors in the entire state.

If a bill favors a "good cause," makes no extraordinary fiscal or regulatory demands, and does not advance one group's interests at the cost of another's, its chances of avoiding opposition are good. For example, a measure requiring several Massachusetts agencies to establish educational programs for new parents and develop programs to serve victims of Shaken Baby Syndrome aroused no opposition. Nor did a bill that set up a commission to explore the regulation of medical spas. Allowing local election officials to hire sixteen- and seventeen-year-old poll workers and workers from outside their municipalities provoked no controversy.

Many of the bills that are noncontroversial address local matters. But even local bills occasionally run into problems. Fall River, Massachusetts, wanted a bill authorizing a liquefied natural gas facility, legislation that the senate endorsed. But the house preferred to treat the issue in a comprehensive way rather than deal only with a single jurisdiction. A bill for a shopping and entertainment complex in Dedham met opposition from labor, which wanted guarantees that local union members would be hired for construction. From time to time the governor objects by casting a veto, such as a bill providing for investments in Brookline, one for a theater in North Adams, or ones related to housing programs in Concord and Mansfield.

When a bill raises questions or arouses opposition, the legislature—usually at the time the bill is still in committee—tries to work things out. If that is not possible the bill is likely to stall. For instance, state veterans organizations insisted on requiring the managers of two veterans' cemeteries to be veterans themselves. This was opposed by the governor's secretary of veterans affairs, which put the bill in a different category than otherwise. What may appear to be totally harmless can cause concern, even if only among a select group of people. There can easily be wrinkles in any piece of legislation. For instance, nothing could look as harmless as a bill requiring that hospitals and physicians notify parents whose child is being treated for drug overdose. Yet hospital officials indicated that while they supported the bill's intent, they had reservations that the notification requirement might discourage teenagers from seeking treatment. Similarly, a bill to give noncustodial parents access to students records appeared to be on a fast track. But since current law in Massachusetts had been designed to protect children and ex-spouses from domestic abuse, legislative sponsors had to reassure victims' advocacy groups (such as Jane Doe Inc.) that their work was not being undone.

Any bill costing the state dollars (much like any provision of the annual budget bill), however narrow in scope, cannot be considered minor as long as the dollars add up. There is just so much to go around, so requests for funds compete. State resources are limited, not to say scarce, so their allocation always has significance. Yet little controversy may accompany these bills because the spending is patently meritorious—substantively and/or politically. A measure that established a sick-leave bank for state employees or one that protected school employees from losing health insurance during the summer months was easy for lawmakers to support. Fuel assistance for low-income families by means of a tax credit was also easy in Massachusetts. Senate and house chairs worked together, the presiding officers backed the legislation, and the governor got on board. The leaders changed some provisions and the senate and house came up with slightly different versions, but within a few weeks differences were worked out, $20 million was committed, and the program became law. Just about everyone was supportive. It was not difficult, either, for legislators to rally around a provision one of their colleagues wanted in the budget. It would have allowed commuters to deduct up to $750 in transit expenses from their state income taxes, if they paid highway bridge and tunnel tolls electronically or if they purchased monthly passes for commuter rail, subway, or bus. With fare increases projected, the provision was easily agreed to—even though it would cost the state a chunk of money.

Bills that are not controversial and arouse no opposition sail through with just a slight push. Half the chambers in the states employ consent calendars to process such measures, and the rest expedite their journey by one means or another. By the time of third reading, or a vote for final passage on the floor, the overwhelming majority of bills pass by an overwhelming majority of votes, if not unanimously. Many of these bills are noncontroversial—that is, noncontroversial from start to finish. Some, however, have been challenged along the way—in committee, on the floor, or somewhere in between. Disagreements have been settled, compromises struck, and consensus built. By the time the bill gets to the floor, its proponents have given up enough to dispel opposition. In Minnesota, for example, during the 2001 session an omnibus energy bill passed in the senate by 59-0 after less than an hour's debate. The measure would appear to have been noncontroversial, but that was hardly the case. At the start of the session three different groups submitted energy legislation. The Minnesota Chamber of Commerce backed a bill that called for energy deregulation; the Department of Commerce proposed a bill that would have increased state planning; and a coalition of consumer, environmental, labor, and conservation groups pushed for increased conservation. The chair of the Senate Telecommunications, Energy, and Utilities Committee managed to take bits and pieces of each, forging a supporting coalition of disparate groups. A bill that was controversial at the outset of the process was consensual by its end.

Many bills do go through the legislative process uncontested and unscathed, with nothing needed to be worked out. The bill in the 2001 session of the Maryland General Assembly to make the calico the state cat is an example. It was sponsored by children in the Westernport Elementary School, who testified on its behalf before the house and senate committees in Annapolis. Since Maryland has a state dog, bird, insect, and even dinosaur, why shouldn't it have a state cat as well? No groups, lobbyists, or other cats emerged to challenge the calico, so it became the legal cat symbol for the state. Had there been a bloc for Persian, Angora, or alley cats, it would not have gone as smoothly; undoubtedly there would have been a catfight. In Ohio all did not go as well, apparently, when the smallmouth bass, the largemouth bass, and the walleye all vied to become the state fish.

If everyone agrees, there is no problem in enacting legislation. The problem, of course, is that on many matters, and even ones that appear inconsequential, there are at least two sides to the issue, and one of them is against its passage into law. Lawmaking by consent calendar is a completely different story from lawmaking by thrust and counterthrust. Both are part of the legislative process in the states.

Public Policy

Legislators believe their job is to make law, and that is what they spend most of their time doing when the legislature is in session. The 2002 State Legislative Survey asked the nation's legislators how many bills of which they were primary author became law. Almost 80 percent of senate members and almost 60 percent of house members claimed three or more enactments to their credit. That adds up to a lot of law.

Controversial or not, a lot of what goes in comes out as law, as public policy that is more or less consequential. Almost nineteen thousand bills became law in 2006 and more than twenty-four thousand became law in 2007. Table 9-1, on page 308, shows the number of bills enacted in each of the fifty states during the 2006 regular session. Even those states that pass relatively few bills put more than one hundred new laws on the books in a year. Minnesota, Nebraska, New Mexico, Ohio, Vermont, Washington, and Wyoming are in this category. At the opposite end are states that pass over one thousand laws—Arkansas and Texas—both of which only meet for one year of the biennium. Another dozen or so states, including four with biennial sessions, pass over five hundred bills in a year. California, Georgia, Michigan, and New York are among them. The rest, about three-fifths of the total, pass anywhere from under two hundred to over five hundred bills at a legislative session. In California and Colorado about two out of three of those introduced wind up as law. In New York and New Jersey only one out of twenty-five goes all the way.

Whatever the number and whatever the proportion, the question is, how do they negotiate the obstacle course that stands between the introduction of a bill and the enactment of a law?

Notes

1. Mordecai Lee, "Political-Administrative Relations in State Government: A Legislative Perspective," *International Journal of Public Administration* 29 (2006): 1035.
2. See B. Guy Peters, *American Public Policy*, 6th ed. (Washington, D.C.: CQ Press, 2004), 4–8.
3. American Society of Legislative Clerks and Secretaries, *Inside the Legislative Process* (Denver: National Conference of State Legislatures, October 2005), 3/1.
4. John Howard, "Part-time Legislature: Can It Be Done by Initiative?" *California Journal* (July 1, 2004).
5. American Society of Legislative Clerks and Secretaries, *Inside the Legislative Process*, 3/2, 3.
6. *State Net Capitol Journal*, August 6, October 29, and November 19, 2007.
7. *New York Times*, April 15, 2008.
8. A study reported in the *New England Journal of Medicine* found that 94 percent of doctors had a direct relationship with a drug company while 83 percent received food or gifts, and more than 25 percent were paid for consulting or getting their patients to agree to participate in new drug trials. *State Net Capitol Journal*, March 31, 2008.
9. *State Net Capitol Journal*, May 7, 2007.
10. *New York Times*, February 21, 2006.
11. *State Net Capitol Journal*, April 23, 2007.
12. Massachusetts State House News Service, January 2006; *Boston Globe*, May 24, 2006.
13. Lee, "Political-Administrative Relationships in State Government," 1033.

14. C. J. Bowling and D. S. Wright, "Change and Continuity in State Administration," *Public Administration Review* 59 (1998): 436.

15. Lee, "Political-Administrative Relationships in State Government," 1033.

16. *State Net Capitol Journal,* August 6, 2007.

17. *New York Times,* July 7, 2005.

18. *National Journal* (May 26, 2007): 28–32.

19. These instances are drawn from a May 3, 2002, paper by Dawn Thomas, who interned in Vitale's office as part of a Rutgers University program.

20. Diary of Del. Sandy Rosenberg, March 20, 2008.

21. Mass Insight Corporation, *State of the State: Quarterly Public Opinion Survey* (Boston: The Corporation, Winter 2006): 4.

22. John E. McDonough, *Experiencing Politics: A Legislator's Stories of Government and Health Care* (Berkeley: University of California Press, 2000), 199–284.

23. Jeremy M. Creelen and Laura M. Moulton, *The New York State Legislative Process: An Evaluation and Blueprint for Reform* (New York: Brennan Center for Justice, New York University School of Law, 2004), 38.

24. Lee, "Political-Administrative Relationships in State Government," 1035.

25. John Kingdon, *Congressmen's Voting Decisions* (New York: Harper and Row, 1973).

26. David R. Mayhew, "Actions in the Public Sphere," in *The Legislative Branch,* ed. Paul J. Quirk and Sarah A. Binder (New York: Oxford University Press, 2005), 70.

27. Frances E. Lee, "Interests, Constituencies, and Policy Making," in *The Legislative Branch,* ed. Paul J. Quirk and Sarah A. Binder (New York: Oxford University Press, 2005), 297–298.

28. John A. Straayer, "Colorado's Legislative Term Limits," Joint Project on Term Limits (unpublished paper, August 2004).

29. *New York Times,* June 22, 2001.

30. *State Net Capitol Journal,* April 23, 2007.

31. Massachusetts State House News Service, June 23, 2006.

32. *Star Ledger,* December 9, 2007.

33. Interview with Assemblyman Joseph Roberts, December 5, 2007.

34. Kingdon, *Congressmen's Voting Decisions,* 131–135.

35. See Karl T. Kurtz, Bruce Cain, and Richard G. Niemi, eds., *Institutional Change in American Politics: The Case of Term Limits* (Ann Arbor: University of Michigan Press, 1007), and Rick Farmer, Christopher Z. Mooney, Richard J. Powell, and John C. Green, eds., *Legislating Without*

Experience: Case Studies in State Legislative Term Limits (Lanham, Md.: Lexington Books, 1007).

36. These examples are reported in *State Net Capitol Journal,* April 23, 2007.

37. Andrew McFarland, *Neopluralism: The Evolution of Political Process Theory* (Lawrence: University Press of Kansas, 2004), 6.

38. E. E. Schattschneider, *The Semisovereign People* (New York: Holt, Rinehart and Winston, 1960), 2–13.

39. Kingdon, *Congressmen's Voting Decisions,* 42, 140.

40. Carl E. Van Horn, Donald C. Baumer, and William T. Gormley Jr., *Politics and Public Policy,* 3rd ed. (Washington, D.C.: CQ Press, 2001).

10

What Makes Lawmaking Tough

SINCE IT FIRST AIRED on ABC's *Schoolhouse Rock!* television series in 1975, Dave Frishberg's song "I'm Just a Bill" has been a civics education standard. Many of us can recall this ditty that charts a bill's progress in Congress, from constituent to congressperson to committee and on to the White House— that is, if everything works out:

> I'm just a bill.
> Yes, I'm only a bill.
> And I'm sitting here on Capitol Hill.

It is not easy to become a law, but this bill will. High school and college texts describe the same route, albeit in a more sophisticated way, when they lay out for students just "how a bill becomes a law." And in response to citizens' requests for information, legislative public information offices send out a very similar message about the legislative process. The cartoon figures and other graphics vary, but the route is the same: introduction, committee, and floor in each house.

The Stages by Which a Bill Becomes a Law

The formal process by which a bill moves from inception to enactment runs generally as follows.

Reference

The bill is sent to one or more standing committees in the body. Reference normally is automatic, depending on how the text of the bill matches up with committee jurisdictions.

342

Committee Decision

The initial screening of a measure is undertaken by a standing committee, and sometimes by a subcommittee as well. Practically every bill that is introduced receives consideration of one kind or another. A subcommittee refers its recommendations to the full committee. Similar bills can be on the agendas of committees in each chamber. Decisions in committee include: (a) whether and when a bill will be taken up; (b) to what extent a bill is rewritten or modified; and (c) whether a bill is reported out favorably—and how favorably—for consideration on the floor.

Leadership or Rules Committee Clearance

To get to the floor for consideration and a vote, a bill must be put on the daily calendar. Except in the minority of chambers where bills reported from committee automatically are put in line for floor consideration, legislative leaders or their designees exercise discretion. In houses scheduling authority normally resides with the speaker, who can facilitate, impede, or stymie a bill's progress. In senates a rules committee or its equivalent, which is usually a leadership body, has to act before a bill goes to the floor.

Passing on the Floor

A bill has to win majority votes in each house. It is taken up on two occasions. The first occasion, often called "second reading," customarily permits amendments to the bill. The second occasion, often called "third reading," may limit the amendatory process. In either case, a majority of those present and voting (as required in about three-fifths of the states) is necessary for the bill to pass. Amendments also are subject to majorities of those present and voting. A constitutional majority (a majority of all members elected to the chamber) is required in some places.

Conference Committees

Ordinarily a conference committee is the means by which the house and senate resolve differences on major matters of legislation. The budget is usually the most important and contentious bill to be dealt with by a conference committee. A conference committee may consist of three members from each house, or five from each house, or some other ratio depending on the state. Whatever the numbers, however, a majority of conferees from each chamber must agree on the conference committee report that is transmitted for adoption to the house and senate. Each chamber must ratify the conference report, if a law is to be enacted.

House and Senate Agreement

The bill that the governor receives must pass both legislative bodies in the same form. This means that if bills are not identical after enactment by each chamber, differing house and senate bills have to be reconciled through negotiation. This requires a vote in one or both bodies, with a majority recorded in favor. If a second house makes changes in a bill, it will seek concurrence from the first house. If a majority concurs, the bill goes to the governor. If not, the second house may recede from its amendments, or it can request a committee of conference whose recommendations have to be endorsed in each chamber.

Gubernatorial Consent

The governor must say yes, or at least not say no, to a measure that the legislature passes. If the governor vetoes a bill passed by both houses of the legislature, there is still a chance for a law to be enacted. But both houses have to override the veto. That requires an extraordinary majority—either three-fifths or two-thirds—voting to override in each chamber. In most states a bill becomes law unless a governor vetoes it, although in a number of states a bill dies unless it is signed.

The lawmaking process is pretty straightforward. What makes it difficult is that proponents have to build consensus and put together majorities all along the route. If measures are noncontroversial and no one really cares, consensus is practically automatic. Otherwise, building consensus and winning majority votes can be a very demanding process.

At the outset, proponents need the consent of the chair of the committee to which the bill is referred. This is to ensure that the bill is put on the committee's agenda. Then it requires a majority of votes in the committee, and perhaps subcommittee, in order to be reported out with a "do pass" recommendation of the committee.

If the bill makes its way forward, the consent of the house speaker or senate president (or their designees) is either requisite or helpful. Leadership opposition can usually kill a measure.

On the floor, majority votes are customarily necessary at both second and third readings. A constitutional majority (a majority of all members elected to the chamber) is required in about half the chambers, as is a simple majority of those voting in the others. When he served in the Illinois Senate, Barack Obama cast a number of "present" votes. They were the equivalent of "no's," since a constitutional majority—thirty of the fifty-nine members—was required to pass a measure on the floor. In New Jersey, even if only sixty of the eighty members of the assembly vote on a measure, forty-one affirmatives are needed. The same holds in Maryland, where seventy-one votes are required in the 141-member House of Delegates.

If a bill is passed in one house, its proponents have to build consensus and put together votes in the other house—perhaps in a standing committee and certainly in the chamber as a whole. Sometimes a bill is considered simultaneously in the two bodies; sometimes a bill gets passed in one chamber before being taken up in the other.

If they have gotten as far as this stage, proponents of a measure next have to worry about the product that emerges from conference. That means they have to be sure that a majority of conferees, in negotiating a senate-house agreement, will keep the major thrust of the legislation intact.

The conference committee report, then, has to be voted up or down in each chamber. It cannot be amended on the floor. If defeated, another conference is held and another version is reported for confirmation by the two chambers.

Last but by no means least, proponents have to ensure that the governor is on board with that final majority of one. If so, proponents have themselves a law. If not, proponents need to persuade legislative leaders to call for a vote override, if necessary, and persuade two-thirds or three-fifths of senate and house members to vote to override the governor.

Opponents of the measure can strike at any time. They do not have to defeat a measure at every step along the way, but only at one or two steps. Proponents have to put together multiple majorities; opponents have to deny them only one. Majorities have to be built, maintained, and rebuilt on different types of votes in different venues. The opposition has all the advantages of a well-armed insurgency in its effort to defeat or weaken a bill.

Sausage Making and Other Metaphors

Given the route a bill must take, the multiple affirmations it must gain, and the possibilities to derail it, it is little wonder that sausage making ranks as the leading metaphor for the lawmaking process.[1] Otto von Bismarck, chancellor of Germany in the late nineteenth century, is credited with the oft-quoted expression: "There are two things you don't want to see being made—sausage and legislation." Despite its one-hundred-year-long run and universal acceptance, for some time I harbored doubts about the comparison. I wondered whether the metaphor still applied (or if it ever did) and whether sausage and legislation were a lot different today than they were when Bismarck was in office. So several years ago, while observing legislatures for a book I was researching, I took advantage of an opportunity to visit a sausage factory, the Ohio Packing Company, in Columbus, Ohio.

The Sausage-Making Process

Established as a neighborhood butcher shop in 1907, Ohio Packing had two processing factories, one of which turned out forty-thousand pounds of sausage a day. This facility was medium-sized as sausage factories go.

Sausage making, I discovered, occurs in distinct stages, each of which takes place in a specified room or area of the plant. First comes the raw-materials cooler, where sausage ingredients are mixed according to computer formulation. A vat will hold two thousand pounds, one-quarter fat trimmings and three-quarters lean trimmings. At the second stage, the raw materials proceed to the sausage kitchen. A grinder processes up to forty thousand pounds per hour, a blender allows water and seasoning to be added, an emulsifier reshapes the contents with a new form, and natural hog casings are stuffed with ingredients.

The cooking process is the third stage. Huge processing ovens dry, smoke, cook, or steam the sausage. A gas fire, using hickory chips, provides natural smoking. The chilling or holding area is the fourth stage. Here, the sausage waits to be packaged in the fifth stage, which is accomplished by three large machines. With the assistance of ten to fifteen packagers, the machines wrap multiple sausages in plastic film. Sixth is storage in a large freezer with a capacity of about a million pounds. Finally, seventh is the shipping area where wrapped, packaged sausage waits to be loaded on trailer trucks.

The Sausage Link to Lawmaking

At first glance, sausage making and lawmaking appear to be a lot alike. Just as pork, beef, and chicken make their way stage by stage to the shipping docks, so a bill travels stage by stage from its introduction to its enactment. However, there is a major difference between the two processes. In sausage making what you see is what you get. In lawmaking, the "how a bill becomes a law" progression fails to capture the nitty-gritty of the legislative process. Let us compare the processes of sausage making and lawmaking in some of their significant dimensions and thereby see how different they really are.

Accessibility. It is not easy to get into a sausage factory, unless you work there or are a raw ingredient. Because of the possibility of liability and contamination, the public is barred. I needed a letter of introduction from the president of the Ohio Senate to gain entry. By contrast, the state house is very accessible. People can observe the legislature through C-Span coverage, which is aired in over half the states. Constituents can visit with their legislators at home or in the capitol. Members of the public, acting as individuals or more frequently as members of interest groups, can raise issues, seek action, and help shape what the legislature does. Contamination is welcome in the legislature; not so in sausage plants.

Coherence. The sixty people who make sausage in Ohio Packing work in different areas and engage in different operations. But they are all part of one team, molding a variety of products according to strict specifications. No one tries to introduce a substitute sausage or attach a bratwurst amendment to a frankfurter. No one wants to prevent sausage from seeing the light of day. By contrast, in the legislative process there is more than one team. At the least, there is a Republican team and a Democratic team, and a house team and a senate team. Then there are the regional, urban, suburban, rural, women, African American, and Hispanic teams in places. These teams, as well as others, do not agree on what the product should be. Indeed, they want to make conflicting products.

Regularity. Sausage making strives for uniformity. Constant testing takes place to ensure the proper measurement of ingredients—fat content, moisture, seasoning, and so forth. The process is closely regulated by the U.S. Department of Agriculture (USDA), whose applicable regulations currently run into thousands of pages and whose inspectors make daily visits to check on operations at the Ohio Packing Company. In addition, the process is monitored diligently in-house by quality-control personnel. Not so with lawmaking, where uniformity is virtually unheard of, measurement of content is illusory, and just about every bill—and certainly every important bill—gets individualized treatment. You can predict what will come out of the sausage factory; you cannot predict what will come out of the legislature.

Efficiency. If Ohio Packing is to survive and prosper, sausage making has to be done efficiently. Only a few weeks elapse from the time the raw materials are unloaded at the shipping dock to the time when the finished products are loaded onto trucks bound for distributors and retailers. The sausage spends most of the elapsed time on the shelf waiting for orders to come in. Not so with the lawmaking process. Noncontroversial bills can move quickly, but significant or controversial legislation may take years before enactment. Sometimes the legislature misses its budget deadlines: New York did so for about twenty consecutive years until recently, as did New Jersey in 2006 and Pennsylvania the following year.

Comprehensibility. The process of making sausage is complex, but in an hour-and-a-half tour of the plant, I could generally figure things out. However, even after many years of obsessively studying state legislatures, I cannot figure them out. The legislature is much too human, democratic, and messy to be as comprehensible as a sausage plant.

Product. There is no denying that sausage comes in many varieties. Ohio Packing produces 250 different items, although most are variations on a few themes: breakfast sausage, Italian sausage, bratwurst, frankfurter, bologna, and salami are the main items under the sausage umbrella. The brand names that Ohio Packing supplies also vary, although Harvest Brand is the company's own label. Whatever the brand, however, the labeling required by USDA provides customers with more information than they could possibly absorb: brand name; product name; ingredients by proportion, including seasoning; nutrition facts; inspection legend; net weight statement; signature line (that is, who manufactured the sausage); and a handling statement. The bill that is enacted into law may be as specific in its language and its definitions, but it is impossible to know what ingredients went into its production and what unanticipated consequences may accompany its implementation. There is little hint of just how it will taste.

The products as well as the processes of sausage making and lawmaking are almost entirely different. Bismarck has been at rest for more than a century. The metaphor he left us also should be laid to rest. If lawmaking did resemble sausage making in the late nineteenth century, it no longer does so today.

Other Metaphors

In his book on the California Legislature, William K. Muir Jr. runs through a long list of terms to which he had heard a legislature compared. The metaphors in alphabetical order are: arena, assembly, back alley, balance, bawdy house, branch of a tree, brokerage firm, bunch of horse traders, butcher shop, card game, cash register, circus, citadel, club, cockpit, collection agency, decision maker, engine, errand boy, factory, family, forum, group, house, inquisition, judge, jury, linchpin, locus of pressure, machine, magnet, marketplace, medium, mender of the social fabric, mirror, moral midwife, night club, organ of the body, pork barrel, pride of lions, rat race, referee, sausage maker, school, seminar, small town, stage, struggle, theater, and zoo.[2] Indeed, one of the metaphors Muir mentions provides a title for this book.

John A. Straayer contributes two additional metaphors.[3] The legislature can be seen as a casino full of tables and games. Stakes are high, cards are held tight, and self-interest prevails. There are winners and losers, but the outcome is never final, for there is always a new game around the corner. The legislature can also be viewed as an arena in which a number of basketball games are progressing, at the same time, on the same floor, and with participants playing on several teams at once. These players switch at will, opposing each other in some instances and acting as teammates in others.

It is interesting that there are so many different views of lawmaking. No metaphor seems to capture everything important—perhaps because the process is too multifaceted for an appropriate metaphor. It would appear that the lawmaking process in the states is *sui generis,* incomparable, not quite like anything else in one's experience.

Differences and Disagreements

If everyone agreed with everyone else, lawmaking would be a snap. It would proceed as smoothly as it does on noncontroversial items. Yet compared to other domains, legislative politics, according to Carl E. Van Horn and his associates, is "the most visible, open, chaotic, and human. . . . Legislatures embody a fundamental urge in the American experience—to have a place where the conflicts of public life are debated, deliberated, and decided in full view." [4] The starting point, then, is "the conflicts of public life." Probably the most important thing to keep in mind is that the lawmaking process is predicated largely on differences and disagreements as to what should and what should not be enacted into law, how much in state funds should be spent on what and when, and who should pay.

Lee Hamilton, a former member of the U.S. House, points out how extensive debate back and forth is written into the structure of the legislative system:

> At every level, from subcommittees through committees to the floor of each chamber and then to the conference committees that bring members

from each house of Congress together, there is the presumption of discussion, debate, disagreement, and argument.

The basis for differences in Congress is differences among people. Therefore it is hardly surprising that some issues are difficult to resolve. It may take "years of wrangling, arguing, and debate" to move forward.[5]

Exempted from a conflictual process are the narrow-scope, noncontroversial measures. Also exempted are those consequential measures where settlements have been negotiated in advance of their filing as bills. In Massachusetts, for instance, not much tweaking was needed on the "cork-and-carry" bill, which would permit people to bring bottles of wine home from a restaurant even after they had opened the bottle. If customers ordered sufficient food, resealed the bottle with a cork, and placed it in a see-through bag provided by the restaurant, the unfinished wine could be carried away. Consumers supported the bill because they felt it would benefit people who had not finished their wine. Restaurants supported the bill because they thought it would encourage people to purchase more wine, even though they might not plan to drink the whole bottle. Even Mothers Against Drunk Driving went along because the proposed measure could reduce the amount of alcohol consumed at one sitting. There was no problem for such a bill proceeding smoothly.

Disagreement as to the Merits

In many cases, however, agreements are hard to forge. This is because legislators, and others as well, disagree as to just what the problem is and/or how to deal with it. Much of the lawmaking process focuses on disagreement as to the substantive merits of a proposal or bill. One can distinguish between the "substantive" or "policy" merits of a proposal, on the one hand, and the "political" merits, on the other. The former, which far outweigh the latter in public discussion, relate to: What is the problem? What does the proposal do to deal with the problem? Who benefits? Who suffers? What are the costs, and who pays? What is being done elsewhere? How is the public interest affected? The latter relates to how the proposal is regarded by other lawmakers, the political parties, significant interest groups, the governor, and constituents in the legislator's district.[6]

Frederick Wiseman's documentary film *State Legislature,* which first aired nationally on PBS television stations in June 2007, shows the deliberation that goes on in committee, on the floor, and elsewhere in the capitol as people argue the merits back and forth. Wiseman filmed the Idaho Legislature's entire twelve-week session in 2004. Out of 160 hours of film, his edited product runs three hours and twenty-seven minutes, without any narration. What comes across most dramatically in the film is the diversity of issues—even in a small state like Idaho with a citizen legislature. There are more problems and issues in Idaho (not to mention California, Texas, or New York) than anyone could possibly imagine. And, except for a few items that Wiseman films, there are opposing points of view, issue by issue.

The differences among Idaho legislators usually reflect differences among organized groups and sometimes among the unorganized as well. For example, Idaho requires that one's primary residence be within a mile radius of a proposed site in order for individuals to have standing to testify before the unit of government making the siting decision. Some senators hearing the matter, on grounds of fairness, wanted to eliminate the residence restriction; others believed that letting anyone testify would be unfair to those most affected by the siting of a facility. Both arguments would appear to have had merit. And the committee divided 4-4 on the measure. In another instance, a bill to regulate smoking in public places separated those who thought the risk of secondhand smoke was too great from those who opposed further governmental regulation. In a floor debate some house members spoke in favor of requiring children to be enrolled in kindergarten by a specified age; other house members wanted to continue leaving it to parents to decide when their children started school. Wiseman's cameras nicely captured the deliberative aspects of lawmaking. Indeed, much of what transpires in any legislative body involves legislators (as well as individual citizens and lobbyists representing organized groups) arguing the merits of their case and others arguing the merits on the opposing side. Each side, of course, sees the merits and demerits very differently.

Monitoring of the 2006 session of the Massachusetts legislature reveals the same kind of disagreements that Wiseman filmed in Idaho. Even what would appear to be minor matters to most people are very important to others, no matter how few. A bill was introduced in the Massachusetts

House to permit special education students who failed the Massachusetts Comprehensive Assessment System examination required for graduation to attend their high school graduation ceremony. The director of the Federation for Children with Special Needs testified that he got complaints year after year from parents whose children were barred from attending graduation. The chair of the Education Committee, Sen. Robert Antonioni, was persuaded of the merits of the request "for those students that really demonstrate that they've tried." However, Thomas Payzant, the Boston superintendent of schools, had a different view of the matter. "We believe that if we lower the bar for these students," he said, "we're sending a message that we think they are capable of less." [7]

What we have here is a dispute over the merits of the issue in question. Two legitimate points of view are being expressed, and an argument is made for each. The overwhelming part of the discussion in the process of lawmaking—whether in committee or on the floor; whether in Massachusetts, Idaho, or elsewhere; whether among members themselves or by lobbyists to members—is over the merits of a proposed measure. Arguments—buttressed by evidence of one sort or another—are offered in support of a measure, and arguments—also buttressed by evidence—are offered in opposition to it.

Deliberation between proponents and opponents dominates the lawmaking process. The merits of the case cut both ways, and reflect the differences that people have on matters that are brought up in legislative bodies. Consider the opposing arguments made on the following measures before the 2006 Massachusetts legislature:

On a Bill to Authorize Slot Machines at Racetracks. Proponents pointed to saving five thousand jobs in the horse-racing industry and $500 million in revenues for the state. They cited a study by the University of Massachusetts that shows state residents spending $2.2 billion in 2005 at casinos in Connecticut and video lottery locations in Rhode Island. That money, proponents assert, would be spent in-state if tracks had the stronger pulling power that slots could provide. Opponents minimized the claims for job and revenue enhancement and argued that slots at tracks would not appeal to people who were drawn to Connecticut's casinos. Instead, slots would take money from local businesses, undermine the state lottery, create more compulsive gambling, and ultimately open up the state to large casinos and the gambling that goes with them.

On a Bill to Make Syringes Available. Supporters maintained that this bill would save lives by reducing the spread of HIV, AIDS, and hepatitis C stemming from intravenous drug use. Opponents maintained that it would condone illegal activity and promote the use of drugs.

On a Bill for Primary Enforcement of Seat Belts. Proponents claimed that a law allowing police to pull over drivers for not wearing seat belts would cut the number of deaths and serious injuries on the road, save taxpayers millions of dollars that Medicaid spends for the severely injured, and help the state regain federal highway funds that it lost because its seat-belt use was below 80 percent. Opponents claimed that such a law would restrict personal freedom, threaten civil liberties, and could lead to racial profiling.

On a Bill That Would Raise the Driving Age to Seventeen and a Half. Proponents maintained that increased maturity would result in fewer accidents, deaths, and injuries. Opponents pointed out that raising the driving age would keep some teenagers from getting to part-time jobs and after-school activities and would put an extra burden on family members who would have to drive them.

On a Bill Mandating a Higher Minimum Wage. Proponents based their case on fairness and maintained that past increases did not negatively impact business or the state economy. Opponents stressed the increased cost to consumers, the comparative advantages of retailing in neighboring states, and the negative consequences for teenagers looking for work.

On a Bill Requiring a Longer School Day. Proponents argued that children would be kept for a longer period in a safe learning environment; opponents pointed to the potential cost and impacts on school programs, teachers, and parents' ability to schedule.

On a Bill Regulating Mercury in Products. The health implications of mercury constituted the main case for regulation, but the case against it was that regulation might impede energy efficiency and lead to higher prices.

Institutional Bases of Conflict

Interest Group Conflict

Organized interest groups have different and conflicting views on issues. This is demonstrated by the disagreement between the Coalition to Protect Massachusetts Patients and the Massachusetts Nurses Association on one side and the Massachusetts Hospitals Association and Organization of Nurse Executives on the other. The former groups advocated the "Patient Safety Act," which would set a limit on the number of patients that could be assigned to nurses. They maintained that such a regulation would save thousands of lives each year, because currently nurses had too many patients to care for at one time. In opposition, the hospital association and nurse executives argued that the bill would take away the ability to assign the necessary number of patients to nurses depending on individual need.

As in the above case, often the interests of one group clash with those of another.[8] Some interest is likely to be adversely affected by just about anything of substance. A bill in Maryland to lower the cost of prescription drugs for senior citizens would hurt pharmacists. In Vermont gas station owners objected to a $7,000 increase in the fee for underground storage tanks.

In Massachusetts the clash between business and labor interests is ongoing. Most issues of common concern provoke at least a degree of conflict. Take the state minimum wage, which is typical. Labor wanted to raise it from $6.75 to $8.25 an hour. The Retailers Association of Massachusetts objected, arguing that it would force many employers to eliminate jobs and/or increase prices. What particularly upset the association was a provision that employers pay time-and-a-half for work on Sundays. Another typical issue separating business and labor is unemployment insurance. Massachusetts provides benefits for longer than other states, but Gov. Mitt Romney tried to reduce unemployment taxes on business in order to improve the state's economic climate for business. Although business and labor could agree on a few items, they could not get together on other major provisions of a bill that the legislature succeeded in passing, the governor vetoed, and the legislature overrode.

A family-leave bill, promoted by labor and other groups, also aroused opposition from business and taxpayer groups. The proposal would have required that employers grant employees paid leave to care for infants or elderly relations. Opponents, led by Associated Industries of Massachusetts, insisted that the cost would be much higher than estimated, and that payroll deductions could not support the costs. Moreover, the state mandate would displace paid family-leave programs that were already in effect and could also discourage companies from hiring additional employees. A proposed change in the child labor law, which had substantial support in the legislature, was opposed in its early form by the restaurant industry.

Business interests also come into conflict with consumer interests, as on a bill to narrow the scope of lawsuits brought under the state's consumer protection laws. In response to a series of court rulings, legislation was introduced to require that consumers demonstrate they suffered monetary loss in order to recover damages. Medical malpractice reform is an issue that pits doctors on one side against trial lawyers and patient advocates on the other. The Massachusetts Medical Society has tried for years to change the law by eliminating "joint and several liability" and reducing the cap on payments for "pain and suffering," but without success.

Interest groups are almost certain to oppose legislation that can do damage to their members or encroach on their turf. Interior designers wanted a law licensing them and giving them greater autonomy from architects. Architects were certified by the state and could bid contracts, with subcontracts going to designers. Architects objected, claiming that they and not designers shouldered responsibility for what got built. Physician assistants promoted a bill requiring insurance companies to reimburse care that they gave. They were opposed by the Massachusetts Association of Health Plans and the Massachusetts Medical Society.

The major package on health insurance, which was the main focus of the Massachusetts legislature during its 2006 session, nicely illustrates the different perspectives, interests, and objectives of various groups. There were the consumer and advocacy groups, banded together in the Health Care for All coalition. They wanted universal coverage. Then there was the health care industry, including hospitals, doctors, HMOs, pharmaceutical firms, and insurance companies. If there was to be a reshuffling, all of these service providers wanted to make sure that they gained rather than lost economically. Finally, there was the business community, which worried about being saddled with the costs of any expensive health care plan.

Partisan Conflict

Another important base of conflict is partisan in nature. State by state, Democrats and Republicans tend to represent different constituencies and different interest groups and tend to have different ideological bearings. The majority party, whether Democratic or Republican, tries to keep its members together on issues that are important to it. These normally include matters related to budgets and taxes, as well as several other policies. Depending on the state, these partisan issues may number one, two, or three dozen out of the hundreds or thousands of bills introduced.[9] But these partisan-related issues are among the most significant items each session. Whereas the majority party sets the agenda and has the upper hand, the minority tries to peel off majority party members from critical votes.

As mentioned in chapter 4, the approaching election permeates the legislative process in competitive states. Whether the majority succeeds in enacting its agenda or the minority succeeds in keeping the majority's accomplishments down will certainly be grist for the forthcoming election campaigns.

In a number of states partisanship plays less of a role than it does in places where either party has a chance of winning control of the senate and house. The more closely divided and competitive a legislative body, the greater the partisanship in lawmaking activity. In Massachusetts, for instance, while Republicans had been able to compete statewide and had elected governors for sixteen straight years before 2006, they had not been able to establish much of a foothold in the legislature. In 2004 Governor Romney tried to pick up seats for his party, and Republicans fielded 131 candidates in two hundred races. Yet the Democrats still gained seats.[10]

While the handful of senate and house Republicans generally support their governor's legislative initiatives, their votes are inconsequential as far as lawmaking in Massachusetts is concerned. Only on the rarest occasions will house Republicans band together, as when they proposed an amendment to ban tobacco products, which they knew would not pass. Otherwise, they conduct themselves in a nonpartisan manner. Senate and house Democratic leaders and rank-and-file members do not treat Republican colleagues as a partisan minority, as would be the case in a competitive legislature. But they do view the Republican governor in partisan terms.

Executive versus Legislative

In the Romney years, party was a consideration in the legislature. That is because of Romney's aggressive stance regarding the legislature, but also simply because Romney was governor. The Massachusetts legislature and the Massachusetts governor compete, more in institutional than in partisan terms. When the governor came out with an appealing proposal, legislative Democrats would respond with one of their own. The governor included a reduction in the income tax rate in his budget. The legislature responded with a reduction of its own, and the senate president sponsored a proposal that would more than double income tax deductions for child and dependent care expenses.

In Massachusetts, as in other states, some of the most significant disagreements between the executive and legislative branches are over the budget. The governor and legislature provided different amounts for school aid, higher education, and many other items. Generally, Romney opposed spending beyond anticipated revenues and balancing the budget by digging into the state's stabilization or "rainy day" fund. Spending, earmarking, and pay raises for judges, among other items, were in dispute. The House Ways and Means Committee recommended $72.2 million less for Chapter 70 education funds than the governor's proposal, while the budget passed by the house itself recommended more. Probably the principal differences between the governor and the legislature during 2005–2006 were over whether the income tax should be rolled back (Romney) or not (legislature), whether automobile insurance should be deregulated (Romney) or not (legislature), whether government spending should be lower (Romney) or higher (legislature), and whether the death penalty should be reinstated (Romney) or not (legislature).

The executive and legislative branches saw welfare reform differently, with (among other things) the former's plan requiring about 25,500 welfare recipients to work and the latter's requiring 16,000. The Romney administration opposed nurse staffing ratios, while the legislature favored them. Nor did the two branches see eye to eye on a massage therapists' licensure bill. They differed over legislation on direct wine shipments, as well as on whether Massachusetts should join an eight-state regional approach to greenhouse gas emissions.

The Republican governor and the Democratic legislature did reach agreement on health care, which was a remarkable achievement. Still, Romney vetoed several provisions of the health care package passed by the legislature: the new assessment on employers, the legislative plan to expand the Public Health Council, the requirement that the administration share information with the legislature regarding negotiations with the federal government on the health care waiver, and the provision of dental and eyeglass coverage. The house and senate had the last word, overriding Romney's vetoes by overwhelming margins.

Senate versus House

Disagreement between the parties is to be expected. So is institutional disagreement between the executive and legislative branches, although it may be tempered by the same party controlling the governor's office and the legislature. Similarly, if the senate and house are controlled by different parties, the chances of conflict are increased. But even when the senate and house are in the hands of the same party, conflict between the bodies occurs—and occurs much of the time. Conflict is endemic to the bicameral legislative system, just as it is endemic to the separation-of-powers system of the nation and states.[11]

First, the senate and the house are very different bodies, with dissimilar cultures and contrasting perspectives on their roles in the legislative process. In every matchup, houses exceed senates in size. As a result, house members have fewer committee assignments and can specialize to a greater degree than their senate colleagues. They share the feeling that they are the experts and do the most important work of the legislature. Because the senate is smaller, it is more loosely organized and more collegial. Ordinarily, partisanship is more muted in senates than in houses. Minority members tend to have more influence as individuals. Senates also are more stable in their memberships than are houses. This is because in most states senate terms are four years, while house terms are two. The fact that house members run every two years while senators run every four affects the way members deal with issues. Other things being equal, senators have greater opportunity to put politics aside, at least somewhat, and take into account other factors. In term-limited legislatures, wherever possible, a number of house members at the end of their tenure run for the senate, while fewer senators run for the house.

Second, not only are cultures and procedures in senates and houses dissimilar, but so are the standing committees that shape legislation. Often the jurisdictional committees correspond from one chamber to the other. To some extent, however, these committees are competing with one another. Each wants to be the major focus of influence within the policy domain under its jurisdiction. Members in each chamber see the same issues differently and are likely to disagree, at least to some extent, on how the issue should be addressed. Most important, different people—with different agendas and approaches—chair senate and house committees.

Third, the house and senate are rivals for influence generally. Each has institutional pride, at least regarding the other. Each wants to prevail. To add fuel to the fire, there is a lingering fear on both sides that the other body may team up with the governor to create a two-on-one situation in negotiating differences among the institutional participants.

Take Massachusetts, for instance. What explains the fact that the Democratic senate and Democratic house are so frequently at odds? In Massachusetts members of both bodies have two-year terms, so differences cannot be attributed to senate members being further away from popular control than house members. The fact that the districts of senators are four times as large, and are more heterogeneous and diverse, probably contributes to differences in views. Like only Maine and Connecticut, Massachusetts relies on joint committees, which ought to facilitate the development of senate-house concurrence relatively early in the process. But the fact is that the two chambers manage to shape different initiatives that have to be reconciled in conference; included in "sections"; or amended onto omnibus bills, such as the budget. This is because different members and different leaders in the two chambers see problems and solutions somewhat differently from one another. Furthermore, separate institutional cultures and arrangements and the rivalry between the two bodies all encourage dissimilar measures. Each side has a position and each jockeys to get the better of the other.

Sometimes in Massachusetts, as elsewhere, different versions do not get reconciled. In 2006 the Massachusetts Senate, for instance, by a 33-4 vote approved a measure to require more financial disclosure by religious organizations. The house voted the other way, by just as lopsided a vote, 147-3. Whereas the house voted to adopt a primary enforcement seat belt law, the senate voted against such a law. Another major division occurred on permitting slot machines to be installed at racetracks. By 26-9 the senate voted in favor, by 100-55 the house in opposition. A bill to change the auto insurance system gained support in the house, but not much in the senate; and the two bodies could not get together.

On any important piece of legislation the possibilities for disagreement between the senate and house are many. They may agree on twenty provisions of a bill but disagree on five or even one. If the differences are serious, and the stakes high, the bill may stall. The Massachusetts sale of surplus property illustrates the point. With the expiration of an earlier law, the state had not been able to sell surplus property. A large coalition was solidly behind the legislation, but the senate and house in conference committee had "very significant differences" (according to the chief senate conferee, Mark Montigny). The major one was that the house measure required legislative approval of all surplus sales, while the senate measure required approval of sales exceeding lots of twenty-five acres. That was enough to prevent a deal.

On many matters the two bodies start out with differences but do manage to resolve them through joint committee, conference committee, and leadership negotiations. On health care the basic house bill was introduced by Speaker Salvatore DiMasi, while the basic senate bill was introduced by President Robert Travaglini. The two differed in many respects and on dozens of specific issues. What received the most media attention was the disagreement on whether or not to assess a payroll tax on employers who did not provide health insurance to their employees. The house favored such a tax, citing fairness as a basis. The senate opposed it, pointing to the potential adverse effects on businesses and the economy in the state. The two competing principles of "employer responsibility" and "the well-being of the economy" had to be reconciled. Negotiations between the two chambers went on for months, with one chamber insisting on identifying spending targets and revenue projections and proceeding slowly, and the other wanting to move faster. When many issues had been settled, a final glitch in the negotiations involved a dispute over Medicaid rates for state hospitals, particularly those in the Boston and Cambridge districts of influential legislators.

Complexity and Detail

Disagreements are not confined to values, principles, and policy directions—to the broad matters where legislators may already be inclined to go one way or the other. Even though a majority of legislators may see eye to eye on the existence of a problem and even on a general way to address it, getting there is not as easy as it might seem. John E. McDonough is aware from his own experience in the legislature that "agreements in principle have a tendency to break down over details. . . ."[12]

Practically every piece of legislation has a number of detailed provisions. These are part of the initial drafts, which are subject to scrutiny and modification in committee. The specifications of the senate bill on the one hand and the house bill on the other frequently differ and have to be reconciled. On a major issue like health care the devil is in the details, as well as in the more general objectives and provisions.

In the Massachusetts health insurance package, for example, much of the negotiating among the governor, senate, and house was over provisions specifying just how a new program would work in practice. Participants might agree on what they wanted to achieve, but they held very different views on just what financial and organizational arrangements would be needed. The health care system as it existed and the legislation changing it were extremely complex. Although the employer tax stimulated the most notable conflict, participants disagreed over fifty or so other issues as well. Many of these disputes occurred because those closest to the issue had different judgments as to what would work best in practice and how every group's interests could be protected as fully as possible. No one could be sure in advance. When the media criticized the governor and legislative leaders for not settling on a comprehensive bill sooner, Senate President Travaglini replied:

> You need time to review and analyze. I mean, this is just part of the process. It has taken this much time, so a day here, a day there right now isn't a big deal to me.[13]

Former speaker Thomas Finneran defended the two legislative leaders. The length of time it was taking to reach agreement was not their fault, he said. It is the very subject matter of universal health care, he explained, that creates problems and is responsible for the impasse.[14]

Another example of complex and detailed legislation from Massachusetts is provided by an economic stimulus package, titled the Commonwealth Investment Plan. It contained many provisions, running to 276 pages when it was finally enacted in June 2006. Even though it was mainly put together by a joint committee, the senate, house, and governor differed over the level of expenditures and exactly how they should be made. It took a while for agreement to be reached on all of the provisions in a senate-house conference committee.

Legislators concern themselves with details—they have to. A bill requiring prospective employees within the Massachusetts Department of Mental Rehabilitation to undergo a national background check seemed simple enough in general. In the opinion of a critical legislator, however, it was vague and could create more bureaucracy and entail greater costs. Moreover, individuals would be unable to challenge these records. Details were also subject to question in an otherwise innocuous Massachusetts bill that permitted localities to require the licensing of animal control officers. When asked by a colleague for an explanation of his bill, the sponsor referred to it as a mere detail, a "technical clarification" that does not cost the state, cities, or towns any more, unless they pay for certification. In response, the interrogator made the point that somebody would have to pay for certification, as technical as it might be. He objected to the bill.

Probably no bill includes as much detail as the budget. The issues that arise over the budget are less over what programs and projects are worthwhile; nearly all of them are, at least to some extent and to someone. Issues that arise with regard to the budget are over just how the revenue pie gets sliced, how it might be increased, and from what source the money is going to come. Resources, however, are always limited. Thus, spending on some things precludes spending on others. In the interstices of the budget, legislators seldom choose between what is "good" and what is "bad." Rather, they choose among "goods," all of which are competing for dollars. Legislators have their own ideas regarding what programs merit additional monies and what projects ought to be written in.

The Massachusetts legislature, like every other legislature except Vermont's, is constitutionally required to balance the state budget. This means that expenditures cannot exceed revenues. If expenditures rise but revenues are not projected to keep pace, the legislature has to fill the gap by raising taxes or fees or finding more ingenious ways to achieve balance. Thus, any anticipated major costs are central to the legislature's budgeting. The health care plan in Massachusetts, for example, was projected to cost over one billion dollars in the initial three years of operation, but new state monies would constitute only a small proportion of the total. Nevertheless, until it was known just how much had to be set aside at the outset, no other commitments could be made by the legislature. Anything else requiring funding—including the budget itself—had to be put on hold. Other bills that required spending had to wait. "Everything that's been done up to this point has been held up," said Sen. Scott Brown. "Until you know what the dollars are that you have to work with, you really can't do much else." Among other items, the supplemental budget and the economic stimulus package had to be considered jointly with health care, since the three used a sizeable amount of the revenues that would be available.

Legislators have different preferences regarding what ought to get funded and at what levels. As mentioned earlier, they want to take care of their districts by bringing home projects and funding. They also want to advance the causes in which they believe, such as health, welfare, and education. Most of the Massachusetts legislature's work on the budget was done by the Senate Ways and Means Committee and the House Ways and Means Committee, operating separately but in close consultation with the leaders in each chamber. Each committee made hundreds of decisions in its formulation of a budget bill to recommend to its chamber.

In most states the committee recommendation is essentially the last word for decision making in the senate and in the house. Not in Massachusetts. Here, members proposed 949 amendments to the Ways and Means budget in the senate and 1,600 amendments to the Ways and Means budget in the house. On average, ten amendments were introduced by each representative and twenty-four by each senator. The amendments ranged from the parochial in nature, mainly earmarks for members' districts, to those that involved statewide public policy, including school and tax reduction, alternative fuels, and pay raises for judges. Hundreds of proposed amendments had to be screened and dozens consolidated into a relative few. It was up to legislative leaders, the chairs of the two Ways and Means committees, and committee staff in each house to decide which amendments to include and which to exclude from a consolidated measure. In the house, for example, a sixty-one-page amendment encompassed forty-nine individual amendments that were selected on behalf of the leadership.

The budget itself was complicated enough, but to add to its complexity the Massachusetts legislature addressed the funding formula, Chapter 70, for school aid. The House Ways and Means Committee recommended a budget that increased school aid, but less than the governor had done. Pressure by members on leadership to raise the funding level were widespread and intense, because the amount of school aid a district receives resonates throughout the state. The speaker was convinced of the need to up the Ways and Means proposal. It did not hurt the case for more money that the Senate Ways and Means Committee indicated that it was considering raising the ante by over $200 million and also changing the formula. Thereupon the house added $82 million to its committee's proposal, bringing forth a raise of $173 million. According to Sen. Richard Moore: "I don't think the House leadership was inclined to do as much, but Sen. Theresa Murray [the Ways and Means chair] gave the speaker a warning that said, 'Look, we are going to do this.'" In the competition to satisfy members and their districts, the house was forced to follow suit.

Several weeks later the senate brought forth its plan to spend $210.4 million more on Chapter 70 and to make significant changes in the formula, which took into account income, as well as property values, when calculating how much a locality could afford to pay for elementary and secondary education. It also adjusted the formula regarding how much a district needed to educate students. The new formula, like the old one, was extraordinarily complicated. Senator Murray acknowledged the complexity. "There is no one cookie-cutter approach that's going to give everybody what they need," she said.[15]

The house and the senate each had wrestled not only with the amount of funding for schools, but with the more challenging question of how (in both substantive and political terms) to distribute billions of dollars in aid equitably. Need, enrollments, growth, wealth, and other factors all had to be taken into account. A task such as this one is no small challenge for any legislature.

An Uphill Process

The budget, along with the funding formula for school aid, is a splendid example of complex legislation, replete with detailed provisions that individual members see somewhat differently. The budget is by no means the only piece of legislation that begins its legislative process with less than a majority of members in support.

Disagreement is simply a normal part of lawmaking in legislatures. In large part legislators' differences reflect the multiple values, interests, and priorities in state and district populations. In large part, too, conflict is built into the structure and processes of the legislature itself. Many bills are non-controversial and engender no conflict whatsoever. And on some bills, conflict is easily worked out. But on a number of measures differences arise. That is because in any legislature there are multiple sources of opposition to a proposal. Opposition is always possible—either because individual members have contrary agendas, committees within the same house come into dispute, the two parties take different positions, or the senate and house have contradictory views. All of these obstacles are part and parcel of everyday lawmaking.

Another major obstacle involves the limited resources available to pay for policy and programs, and the constitutional prohibition on the legislature's spending more on services to the public than it takes in by way of taxes and fees from the public. There can never be enough money to fund the many worthwhile programs and projects legislators and their constituents want. That is why the state budget, reflecting expenditures and revenues, is always among the most contentious issues the legislature handles. There are only obstacles to overcome here; yet somehow, and in some way, these obstacles are overcome—albeit never to everyone's satisfaction.

Notes

1. This section draws on Alan Rosenthal, "The Legislature as Sausage Factory," *State Legislatures* (September 2001): 12–15.
2. William K. Muir Jr., *Legislature: California's School for Politics* (Chicago: University of Chicago Press, 1982), 1.
3. John A. Straayer, *The Colorado General Assembly,* 2nd ed. (Boulder: University Press of Colorado, 2000), 7.
4. Carl E. Van Horn, Donald C. Baumer, and William T. Gormley Jr., *Politics and Public Policy,* 3rd ed. (Washington, D.C.: CQ Press, 2001), 121.
5. Lee Hamilton, "Debate Is Good for Our System," *Congress Newsletter* (November 9, 2007).
6. See also Paul Sabatier and David Whiteman, "Legislative Decision Making and Substantive Policy Information: Models of Information Flow," *Legislative Studies Quarterly* 10 (August 1985): 397.
7. *Boston Globe,* April 5, 2006.
8. This is by no means always the case, however. On Congress, see John W. Kingdon, *Congressmen's Voting Decisions* (New York: Harper and Row, 1973), 142.
9. Speaker Mike Busch estimates that out of 1,500 bills introduced in the Maryland House each year, only 20 to 30 split members along party lines. Tom Stuckey, "Masters of Consensus," *State Legislatures* (July/August 2007): 29.
10. In the election of 2006 for senate and house seats, the Republicans fielded only eighty candidates for two hundred positions.
11. This section draws on Alan Rosenthal, *Heavy Lifting: The Job of the American Legislature* (Washington, D.C.: CQ Press, 2004), 98–100.
12. John E. McDonough, *Experiencing Politics: A Legislator's Stories of Government and Health Care* (Berkeley: University of California Press, 2000), 103.
13. Massachusetts State House News Service, March 18, 2006.
14. Massachusetts State House News Service, February 2006.
15. *Boston Globe,* April 28, 2006.

11

How Majorities Get Made

IT TAKES NOT JUST ONE but a series of legislative majorities to enact a law. On noncontroversial items majorities come easily, but on more contentious matters work is required. Study, deliberation, and bargaining are all parts of the process of making majorities. But for a controversial measure to proceed very far, advocacy, sponsorship, and pressure are required. A bill has to have momentum at the outset, and that has to be sustained for the long haul.

Interest Group Lobbying

Lobbying activity by interest groups is important in maintaining pressure on the legislature, either to help a measure achieve a majority or to deny it a majority. Many issues, including ones of little general importance, stir the concerns of at least several groups in the legislative environment. While constituents qua constituents engage with very few issues, organized groups are in the business of providing representation to their specialized constituencies on as many issues as affect them. By way of illustration, let us look at interest groups in Massachusetts. Some of these groups have extremely narrow agendas and are active on only one or a few bills during a two-year legislature. In the 2005–2006 session, physicain assistants and genetic counselors focused on very discrete issues. Others had more imposing agendas. Senior citizens, organized in the Massachusetts Senior Citizen Council, had the following on their legislative agenda: advancing a constitutional amendment guaranteeing adequate and affordable health care, extending the "first refill" provision under Medicare Part D, full funding of Prescription Advantage, passing "nurse staffing" legislation, funding home care, restoring dental and eyeglass coverage under Mass Health, and giving support to the personal care and attendant industry. The Massachusetts Association of Realtors had on its legislative agenda: supporting legislation to control methamphetamines,[1] promoting uniform wetlands and septic system codes as well as expediting their permitting processes, and opposing a number of land-use bills and an affordable housing transfer tax on Martha's Vineyard and Nantucket Island.

A large and diverse lobbying industry has in the past thirty or forty years organized around the legislative process in every state. This industry includes direct lobbying, grassroots mobilization and campaigns, coalition building, public relations, advertising, and campaign fund-raising. Today there are more groups making their case and pressing claims than ever. It is hardly surprising, therefore, that the lobbying that takes place is continuous, multifaceted, and effective. Basic to the entire enterprise is the direct lobbying done by contract lobbyists or organizational leaders. The individuals regularly make the rounds of legislators' statehouse offices, and even visit members in their home districts. They make the case for their priorities and voice their opposition to proposals they believe harmful to their interests. Depending on the issue, direct lobbying can be rather heavy. Business interests, including individual industries and corporations, are probably most active here; they have the most directly at stake, state by state.

Also basic is the testimony on the merits of their case offered by interest group representatives at committee hearings. The lineup of witnesses for and against is important to legislators, as are the substantive arguments put forward by the various parties to an issue. Generally speaking, if a position is to be taken into account by the legislature, that position has to be presented at the hearing stage of the process. Lobbyists visit members' offices, attend political fund-raisers, and generally buttonhole members throughout the session. Each day they patiently wait in the rotunda outside the senate and house chambers to touch base with legislators who will be voting on the issue of concern to their groups and clients.

Direct lobbying and committee appearances are features of the "inside game" of lobbying. There is also an "outside game," which in the past twenty or thirty years has become almost a routine part of the process. Whenever possible, a group that can mobilize its members will do so, in one way or another. Legislators are impressed by grassroots, whereby rank-and-file citizens telephone, e-mail, write, or visit representatives on behalf of the position on a bill of the group with which they affiliate or that they support. Grassroots activity is a continuous element of the legislative session.

Interest groups bring members from around the state to the capital city with the purpose of winning over legislators to their cause. Many organizations sponsor a day in the capital during each legislative session. For example, on the National Association of Social Workers' Lobbying Day at the state house in Boston, members made the case for a number of bills, especially for budgetary items their organization favored. Legislators were listening. The chair of the House Ways and Means Committee announced: "As I go through the budget line by line, item by item, please know that your concerns have fallen on very receptive ears." He was an ally and would help. On another occasion, Residents' Day on Beacon Hill, young doctors and medical students lobbied for bills on booster seats, primary seat belt enforcement, school nutrition, physical education, and early childhood education.

Rallies on Beacon Hill occur more frequently as the session grinds on. It does not take many people to make an impression on legislators. With the bill authorizing slot machines at racetracks in Massachusetts about to be debated, only about forty opponents and four greyhound dogs demonstrated outside the state house. At the same time, only about twenty-five proponents were inside, chanting "Save our jobs!" outside the speaker's office. On another occasion, about twenty-five environmental activists rallied on the Boston Common in support of a bill that would put Massachusetts into a regional greenhouse gas initiative. Other rallies produced more people and more drama, as when two hundred individuals, many in wheelchairs or with walkers, demonstrated in the state house for a bill sought by the state's personal care attendants, or when three hundred motorcyclists circled the state house in support of a bill that would make wearing helmets optional. Some issues, such as those involving immigration or gay rights, rallied many people during the course of the 2005–2006 legislature, others relatively few.

In half the states, where the initiative allows the legislature to be bypassed and the electorate to decide, an additional weapon is available in the interest group arsenal. In Massachusetts, before an initiative can be put on the ballot it must be placed before the legislature (meeting as a Constitutional Convention) for a vote. It has to get only fifty votes out of a total of two hundred in successive sessions of the legislature. Nonetheless, its availability permits groups to exert additional pressure on the legislature, as was done on health care in 2005–2006. Right at the outset, advocates of expanded health insurance coverage decided to launch an initiative campaign. They gathered 112,000 petition signatures, more than enough to put the measure on the ballot. The initiative was far more liberal than any of the major bills being deliberated. The very existence of the initiative campaign impelled the business community to work with the plans introduced by the senate president and house speaker. The strategy of the advocates was also that of the speaker, who said: "I used the threat of the ballot measure to pressure the business community." [2] That helped overcome business's opposition to employers' fees, which could have been a huge stumbling block.

On significant issues or where key groups are stakeholders, appeals are made through the media. The purpose here is both to win over mass public opinion in the state and to suggest to legislators that mass public opinion has been won over. Newspaper and radio ads are generally the means of getting a message across. Tobacco Free Mass, a coalition of antismoking advocates, ran ads appealing for the restoration of funding for the Tobacco Control Program. The budget also generated a series of sixty-second cable ads in Boston and elsewhere and a thirty-second television ad in the Boston and Springfield markets and on cable statewide, sponsored by the Massachusetts Teachers Association, calling for the increased funding of public education. Health care also witnessed a media campaign during that session. Business groups ran ads independently that an employers' tax would hinder the state's economic growth, while health care advocacy groups ran ads urging support of the house plan for health insurance.

Interest groups can buy media, try to obtain free media, or do both. On any issue that gains some currency, a group will adopt a public relations strategy and try to get its side reported, or better still, editorially endorsed in the media. Group after group will issue a press release or hold a press conference. Depending on the spokesperson for a position and on the salience of the issue itself, a message can be communicated through the press.

What goes on in Massachusetts is likely to be going on in many other states as well. That is because many of the same issues are being advanced by the same groups. Many interest group campaigns are nationwide. Take the food industry's national lobbying effort in 2005 to make it impossible for it to be sued successfully for causing obesity-related health problems.[3] A few years earlier a lawsuit was filed blaming McDonald's for the obesity of two teenage customers. The campaign was led by the National Restaurant Association, based in Washington, D.C., and its fifty-state organization. State by state, food company and restaurant lobbyists led a coalition. They visited legislators, testified before committees, and increased their campaign contributions in their efforts to get legislatures to pass "commonsense consumption" laws. The food and restaurant industry was opposed by consumer advocates and trial lawyers.

A national campaign to kill legislation is illustrated by the pharmaceutical industry's lobbying against bills to reduce drug prices, to require disclosure of pharmaceutical operating expenses, and to restrict the commercial use of physician prescription data.[4] The industry was fighting hundreds of bills around the country, which it argued were unnecessary or misleading. It was led by the Pharmaceutical Research and Manufacturers of America (PhRMA), an interest group with ten regional offices around the country and contract lobbyists in practically every state. One New Hampshire legislator reported that her committee chair and vice chair told her that "they never experienced such intense lobbying pressure," and both had served for over a decade.

During a session of any state legislature, interest groups and lobbying activity are probably as visible as anything else. Discussion in committee and on the floor, and by lobbyists and interest group members with legislators, focuses on the merits of the issue. Each side puts forward its case on substantive grounds. But lobbyists and organized groups also convey an implicit message if their resources are at all credible—that of political pressure. It is popularly believed—a belief nourished by the media—that interest groups dominate the legislative scene and usually the most powerful among them prevail. That is much too simple a picture of how the process works and how legislators arrive at their decisions. There is no doubt, however, that group demands constitute a substantial part of the legislative agenda and are *an* important factor in the resolution of most issues that have to be decided.

How Legislators Decide

Let us illustrate the nature of legislative decision making with five hypothetical scenarios. Each relates to a different issue on which legislators have to take a position: (1) an increase in the sales tax; (2) abolishing the death penalty; (3) an increased cigarette tax; (4) allowing optometrists to use diagnostic drugs; and (5) a reduction in the voting age. Each specifies some of the *most important* factors that normally influence how legislators vote. The factors are: (1) the merits for and against passage of a bill; (2) the position of the interest groups that are involved; (3) a legislator's political party's position; (4) where one's constituents stand; and (5) the legislator's own convictions and record on the issue.

Given the specifications in each scenario, the question is, how would most legislators decide to vote and why? Although these scenarios are extremely simplified versions of a more complex reality, and although they exclude the effects of processes within the legislature itself (such as committee and collegial recommendations), they suggest how and why individual legislators make many of the decisions they do.

Scenario 1: Deciding How to Vote on an Increase in the Sales Tax by Two Cents

Merits of the Case. In favor of such an increase is the argument that it is necessary to fund a raise in state school aid to local districts, among other things, in order to keep property taxes from going up. Against such an increase is the argument that if local school boards did their job and kept educational expenditures down, property taxes would not rise.

Interest Groups. Most of the organized group activity is in support of the sales tax increase. Especially active are the statewide teachers association, the association of school boards, and groups representing local elected officials in the state.

Political Parties. The legislator's political party generally opposes raising either the income or sales tax but has not taken a position here.

Constituents. Constituents in the legislator's district support public education programs, but they are also opposed to tax increases at any level of government.

Conviction/Record. In the legislator's years in office, he or she has voted to raise taxes on alcohol and tobacco but has opposed raising either income or sales taxes.

How would *most* legislators vote, given the conditions stipulated in the scenario? This would be a relatively easy decision for most legislators. They would vote "nay."

The *merits of the case* for an increase are simply not strong enough, even for those who are advocates for public education in the state. Despite increased funding for education in the past, local property taxes have been rising. Many legislators would not be confident in the ability or will of local elected officials to hold expenditures down.

Most of the *organized group activity* supports the sales tax increase. The so-called "special interests" are mainly on one side. The teachers association is an especially important group because it has a relatively large membership statewide, and teachers live and work in the districts of every legislator in the state. Despite the strong organization, skilled lobbyists, and grassroots advocacy of its members, the teachers association is not likely to prevail if a legislator has to vote for higher taxes.

The dominant factor for the legislator here is *constituents* who object to having their taxes raised—at least income, sales, or local property taxes. There are very few issues about which people in a legislator's district are concerned, as indicated in chapter 3. The overwhelming number of issues that legislators handle does not register with constituents. So when an issue does make a mark, legislators pay careful attention and try their best to be responsive. Few constituency mandates exist that "direct" the legislator to act in one manner or another. But one that currently does, at least in most places, is "Don't raise my taxes." This mandate applies both to income and sales taxes but not necessarily to business or alcohol and tobacco taxes. Moreover, as shown in chapter 3, most legislators see eye to eye with their constituents on taxes.

In the scenario presented here, as in most actual instances, there is no real clash. The legislator's own *conviction and record* is opposed to raising both the income and sales tax. Moreover, the legislator's *political party*, in response to the electorate, stands in general opposition to tax increases.

Given these factors, it does not matter that most organized interests support the two-cent increase, while only a few oppose it. A "constituency mandate," especially one with which the legislator personally agrees, trumps everything else.

Scenario 2: Deciding How to Vote on a Measure to Abolish the Death Penalty (Which Currently Is Law in This Particular State)

Merits of the Case. The case against the death penalty is based largely on the belief that innocent people might be executed in error. In some cases, with new DNA evidence individuals convicted of capital crimes have later had their convictions reversed. The case for the death penalty is that, given the nature of crimes like premeditated murder, retribution is deserved and necessary.

Interest Groups. A number of groups are active here. Those opposing the death penalty are public defenders in the state and state affiliates of the National Coalition to Abolish the Death Penalty and Amnesty International. Those supporting the death penalty are state prosecutors and members of Justice for All.

Political Parties. Neither the Democratic nor Republican Party in the legislature has a position on the issue. Some Democrats support capital punishment, some oppose it; some Republicans support capital punishment, some oppose it.

Constituents. Most of the legislator's constituents—and certainly most of those who voted for the legislator—appear to favor the death penalty. But those who want it abolished have done more to organize themselves, contact the legislator, and express their views forcefully.

Conviction/Record. The individual legislator has been consistent in his or her belief that the death penalty is good public policy and in the past has voted in the legislature against its abolition.

How would *most* legislators vote on ending the death penalty, given the conditions stipulated in the scenario? Here too the decision is relatively easy. They would vote "nay."

If *constituency* and *conviction* did not exercise such strong influence, the argument against the death penalty might have had more impact on the legislator. But in arriving at his or her convictions, the legislator has already rejected the argument that mistakes that are made cannot be corrected if people are put to death. As to the *merits,* the legislator believes that the death penalty is deserved and necessary.

On an issue such as this one, the balance of advocates for and against does not matter that much for most members. They cannot be budged. Although *interest groups* may try, they make exceedingly few conversions. On an issue such as this one—a so-called "conscience issue"—the legislative *parties* are not likely to take a party position as such. They realize and accept that their members will be on both sides and will want to vote their conscience. What counts most heavily on this issue of capital punishment are the same factors that would count most heavily on abortion, gun control, and gay rights issues: what a legislator's constituency believes and the personal conviction of the legislator.

The scenario stipulates that most of the legislator's constituents appear to favor the death penalty, even though those who want to abolish it are better organized and more active. Of those constituents who are supporters of the legislator (that is, members of the legislator's party and of the legislator's voting base), most oppose abolishing the death penalty. Among their constituents, legislators look especially at their supporters (that is, members of their own party) to figure out where their constituency stands on an issue.

Scenario 3: Deciding How to Vote on an Increase in Cigarette Taxes

Merits of the Case. The main arguments for increasing the tax are as follows: First, the state is facing a tough budget and, without additional revenues, cuts will have to be made in a number of programs; and second, an increased price will discourage some people—especially teenagers—from smoking. The main arguments for opposing a tax increase are as follows: First, cigarettes are already heavily taxed, at $2.00 per pack; second, an additional tax is an unfair burden for those who choose to smoke; and third, higher cigarette prices will further encourage smuggling and the illegal sale of cheaper, untaxed cigarettes.

Interest Groups. The Tobacco Institute, supported by a number of tobacco companies, is opposing the tax. The institute contributed $500 to the legislator's last campaign. The state chapters of the American Heart Association and the American Lung Association, as well as several other health groups, have come out in favor of the tax. They do not make campaign contributions.

Political Parties. Members of the legislator's party have not taken a position on the issue.

Constituents. Only about one out of four of the legislator's constituents smokes. The smokers are not organized, but a number have written to the legislator's office objecting to the tax increase. Nonsmoking constituents have not taken any position; the issue is obviously less important for them than it is for smokers.

Conviction/Record. In the past the legislator has voted in favor of increased taxes on tobacco products and has voted to restrict cigarette smoking in the workplace. The legislator acknowledges that tobacco is harmful to one's health, but also feels that people should be allowed to smoke if they choose.

How would most legislators vote on an increase in cigarette taxes, given the scenario above? The decision is by no means as clear-cut as the legislator's decision to oppose an increase in the sales tax.

The *merits of the case* cut both ways, as they almost always do. There are good grounds to support legislation to bring about a higher cigarette tax: it will provide funds for state services and discourage some people from smoking. But there are also good grounds against raising a tax that is already high: it is unfair to some people and may result in illegal sales. Legislators could take either side on the basis of what they believe to be the merits.

The pressure, however, is coming mainly from the opposition to raising the tax on cigarettes—tobacco companies, represented by their organization, the Tobacco Institute, and a number of individual constituents who smoke. Neither smoking nor nonsmoking constituents are very organized on the issue. But a few national health organizations have taken positions in support of a measure that might discourage smoking.

At this point, neither *party* has taken a stand, for or against. However, if most of its members take one side or the other, members of the majority and minority parties will probably take a position when they meet together in caucus.

What appears decisive is the legislator's *convictions* and *record* on the issue. This particular legislator has an antitobacco record, even though he or she would not go as far as to try to outlaw cigarettes. The campaign contribution from the Tobacco Institute makes little difference when it runs counter to a legislator's beliefs, as it does in this case. Just as scissors cut paper, paper covers rock, and rock breaks scissors, so conscience outweighs contribution.

Most legislators would support this increase in the tax on tobacco, if the facts line up as they do in this scenario. If, however, half of the legislator's constituency—and a majority of the legislator's supporters—were strongly opposed to the tax, then the constituency would challenge the legislator's convictions. Under these circumstances, the decision could go either way.

Scenario 4: Deciding How to Vote on a Bill Allowing Optometrists to Use Diagnostic Drugs to Diagnose Eye Ailments

Merits of the Case. Optometrists argue that it would be cheaper for patients to use their services for routine examinations for eye ailments than to have to go to ophthalmologists. Ophthalmologists maintain that optometrists are not qualified to make such examinations, which entail the use of diagnostic drugs. Unlike themselves, optometrists have neither attended medical school nor been licensed as physicians. Therefore a procedure done by optometrists would not be as safe.

Interest Groups. Two interest groups are in direct competition here—the state association of optometrists on the one hand and the state association of ophthalmologists on the other. Members of both groups are actively lobbying the legislature on the issue. The optometrists have regularly made $500 contributions to the legislator's reelection campaigns.

Political Parties. The two political parties are not taking any position on the issue.

Constituents. Outside of the relatively few optometrists and ophthalmologists in the legislator's district, no one seems to care one way or another about the issue.

Conviction/Record. The legislator does not have strong feelings on the issue and has no voting record. He or she can see the merits on both sides of the issue.

How would most legislators vote—to allow optometrists to use diagnostic drugs or not—in view of what is described in the scenario? We have here an example of one of a large number of "special interest" issues that legislatures have to handle. On issues such as these, one or several groups are trying to gain an advantage through the enactment of law, while competitor groups do not want to be disadvantaged and oppose the enactment. In these cases the legislature is asked to decide between competing interests, either one of which is difficult to equate with the public interest or the constituency interest.

The issue in the scenario presented here reflects the classic battle, dubbed "Eye Wars," that is still being fought in states throughout the nation. It began when optometrists, who had been limited to giving eye examinations and prescribing glasses, tried to obtain authority to use diagnostic drugs for their examinations. They were opposed by ophthalmologists—eye doctors who had attended medical school and had the legal monopoly on such treatment. The groups involved in such issues are trying to pass or defeat legislation to promote or defend the interests of their members. Each group will argue the *merits of its case,* maintaining that what benefits them is also good public policy. The optometrists justify their position in terms of economy, arguing that they are lowering patients' costs. The ophthalmologists justify their position in terms of safety, arguing that they are more qualified than optometrists to conduct the procedure safely. Each side has a reasonable argument—economy, which would impact broadly, saving some money for consumers; or safety, which is more important but would put no more than a few people at greater risk.

An issue such as this is of very limited concern to the public. *Constituents* do not care, nor do the *political parties.* The overwhelming majority of legislators are not committed by conviction or record: they have many other items on their agendas. On this particular issue, and others that are similar, legislators can go either way. They have to decide, but no strong influence is pushing them one way or the other.

With everything else just about equal, the main difference between the two sides may be that one group has provided the legislator with campaign support, while the other has not. Although members of both groups at the state level are actively lobbying the legislature, the optometrists in this case have made $500 contributions to the legislator's reelection campaigns. They are among the legislator's supporters. That, if nothing else, distinguishes them.

In a case like this the legislator most likely pays more attention to the merits of his or her supporters' position. It is a reasonable and justifiable position. The legislator can feel comfortable deciding that little or no danger to the public health will be caused by authorizing the procedure for optometrists, and cost savings will accrue to patients. The merits of the case line up with the position of the legislator's supporters. Other things being equal, campaign support counts, but only if there is meritorious argument to accompany it, as there usually is.

Scenario 5: Deciding How to Vote on a Bill to Reduce the Age Requirement for Voting from Eighteen to Sixteen

Merits of the Case. The major reason advanced for the sixteen-year-old vote is that it would increase the likelihood that young people would "learn" to vote and get in the habit of voting. If their first eligible vote occurred when they were sophomores or juniors in high school, they could be taught more about voting in civics or government courses they took in the ninth or tenth grades. The opposition is based on the belief that sixteen-year-olds are neither mature nor responsible enough to be entrusted with this important right of citizens.

Interest Groups. The National Student Association supports the proposal, while no significant groups have declared opposition.

Political Parties. Neither party in the legislature has taken a position on this issue.

Constituents. Relatively few constituents have contacted the legislator on the issue. Most adults who have oppose the idea of sixteen-year-olds voting. But the overwhelming majority of people in the district are not at all concerned about the issue. On the other hand, several high school classes consisting of hundreds of students have sent petitions favoring the proposal.

Conviction/Record. The legislator has no record in this particular area, nor any strong feelings about the issue. The legislator would like more youngsters to be interested in and engaged in politics, but is not sure whether it is a good idea to allow them to vote at the age of sixteen.

How would most legislators vote on a measure to reduce the voting age from eighteen to sixteen, given the scenario just presented?

Legislators are inclined to ask, explicitly or implicitly, with regard to just about every contested issue: "How would its enactment affect my *constituency*?" and "How would my support of its enactment affect me with my constituency?" The answer in this case would appear to be not much, although a few constituents have informed the legislators of their opposition, and several school classes (of nonvoters) have petitioned the legislator in its favor. But how would the constituency respond if the measure permitting all sixteen-year-olds to vote were actually enacted? Maybe there would be no reaction, but maybe there would be.

Neither *interest groups* nor *political parties* play a role here. While a national association of students has taken a position, it is a remote force. So there is no real impact on the legislator from parties or interest groups as organizations.

Like so many other issues that legislatures handle, this one is not a central concern to the particular member. This legislator has no strong feelings and no record, one way or the other, on the voting-age requirement. The legislator is unconvinced by the *merits-of-the-case* argument that youngsters would be taught about voting in high school civics or government courses; there is no guarantee of that. On the other hand, reducing the voting age would be a major change in state policy, and neither the public support nor policy justification appear to be strong enough to justify such a change. It is probably better to leave things alone, to avoid trouble. Until the constellation of forces shifts, the likelihood is that *most* legislators would vote "nay." Even more likely, the bill would be buried in committee or somewhere en route and not come to the floor for a vote.

Reaching Individual Consensus

In the world of real—not hypothetical—legislators as described by a former member of the Massachusetts House, the sources of influence on a member's votes "are multiple, and change from official to official, issue to issue, and year to year." Included among these sources are "personal beliefs and interests, colleagues, party leaders, constituents, campaign contributors . . . , newspapers and magazines, TV shows, radio talk shows and other programs, friends, relatives, professional background and training, interests groups, lobbyists, books, religious leaders, and many, many more." [5]

On most major issues, members are disposed one way or another. Their ideological dispositions are not newly acquired.[6] Usually they have held views on the role of government, the efficacy of regulation, gay rights, affirmative action, and other subjects for most, if not all, of their political careers. They also are likely to be aligned with some interest groups but not others—for example, Democrats with labor and trial lawyers and Republicans with business. So on a number of the continuing issues in contest, it can be predicted right from the outset which way half or more of the members of a legislative body lean. Then, of course, there is the constituency that expresses a mandate on very few issues and rarely one that conflicts with the legislator's own orientations.

In his perceptive analysis of congresspersons' voting decisions, John W. Kingdon postulates that on controversial issues they take into account the "field of forces" that play upon them. These include constituency, interest groups, colleagues, and their own views on the issue. "Much of the time—even though there may be some conflict in the environment as a whole," Kingdon writes, "the congressman finds this more immediate field of forces that bears on his decision in agreement." [7] In addition, similar influence is exercised by a congressperson's preconsensus drive toward consistency. Past patterns of behavior help structure current decisions.[8] Current voting decisions, in short, tend to be consistent with prior ones.

Just which way legislators decide is less predictable on the many relatively minor bills that they consider, or on the specific provisions of the major bills that are the focus of attention in the process. On these matters, their decisions are in play. First and foremost, legislators want to avoid trouble whenever they can. What is most threatening is the potential for trouble from their constituency. They want to dodge issues and votes that will arouse objection from constituents.

Even in Massachusetts, where most districts are electorally safe for Democrats in a general election, the possibility of a primary always exists. Therefore, legislators do not want to deal with bills that can stir up people back home. These may be relatively small bills, but they could cause relatively big problems. Any legislator has enough problems without asking for more. So avoidance is a risk-minimizing strategy of many members.

A bill mandating health education in the Massachusetts school curriculum might seem noncontroversial. But sex education became a sticking point in its consideration. Parents, pro-life supporters, pro-choice advocates, health care providers, and educators all had something to say about the bill. Gov. Mitt Romney spoke out against any such requirement. The issue became so controversial that there appeared to be no way the committee hearing the bill could reach consensus. "Don't make us vote on this," members appealed to the chair. The chair responded to their request; the bill was put in a study, which meant that it was killed for the session. Legislators in Massachusetts would also rather steer clear of charter schools, even though a few dozen bills are introduced on the subject at each session. The problem is that the subject can impact every district, dividing parents into public school and charter school camps and, at the same time, upsetting the educational establishment. It is better to avoid the issue, unless one is an outspoken advocate. Needle bills and the decriminalization of marijuana are extremely controversial; many members would just as soon sweep them aside if they could.

Sometimes, of course, votes cannot be avoided, as was the case regarding the primary seat belt legislation. The Massachusetts House had deadlocked on the bill in both 2001 and 2003. Few constituents contacted their representatives in support, but more let their representatives know that they did not want the police given one more reason to pull them over. Three members who had voted yes on the bill in January 2005 changed their votes to no in May of the following year. One of them, Kathi-Ann Reinstein, had consistently voted against the bill until the January vote; she reversed herself when an associate died in a crash while not wearing a seat belt. After that Reinstein underwent another change of heart: "I've been getting calls from my constituents since January and up to today," she said. Her final position was: "I don't think it's right that you're just being pulled over for not having your seat belt on." [9]

When a bill promises to have direct effects on people back home, and when those who will potentially be affected express themselves, legislators sit up and take notice. On raising the driving age, Massachusetts legislators began to hear from constituents with teenage children. A higher driving age would create hardships for parents because no public transportation existed, and they could not be expected to drive their kids to after-school jobs and events. Rep. Bradford Hill indicated that he had received more than one hundred e-mails on the issue, only two of which supported the bill. Similarly avoided are bills regulating child labor. Constituents have personal stakes, personal experience, and conflicting positions. It is an issue that for legislators is very close to home and, therefore, combustible.

Even issues that are more remote from most constituencies can strike a responsive chord with people back home. When emotion combines with numbers, political merits trump other merits. That was certainly the case regarding a bill, supported by the Massachusetts Immigration and Refugee Advocacy Coalition, to allow undocumented immigrants to pay in-state college tuition if they filed for permanent residency in Massachusetts. In 2005 this bill quickly passed the senate by a 39-0 vote. The house brought the bill up early in 2006. The speaker supported the bill and a leadership poll showed over one hundred representatives backing it. Then media stories, e-mails, and telephone calls began to come in, and legislators began to defect. Another poll showed its supporters in the house had decreased to ninety, a comfortable majority but not enough to override a veto, which had been threatened by the governor. The speaker announced his support, called for a vote of conscience, and brought the bill up in the house. Two amendments intended to make the bill more palatable lost. The bill was defeated 95-57. Many of those who voted against it saw providing benefits to illegal immigrants to be a political liability in their district.

Emotions usually are directed by those outside the legislature, who have been impacted by an issue being decided within the body. But emotions can also come from within, and on issues that touch legislators directly. A bill to award a state pension, worth $44,000 a year, to former Massachusetts representative Michael Ruane, sparked the emotions of many of his colleagues. During his thirty years in the house, Ruane had neglected to join the retirement system. Now he was ill with lung and colon cancer and with no way to provide for himself or his wife. The bill would enable Ruane to select a retirement option and allow him to receive medical benefits. In considering the legislation, members had to choose between following their "hearts" or their "heads," in the words of Rep. Paul Donato. On the "head" side, to give Ruane a pension would be to provide special consideration for a former colleague but not for hundreds of other individuals who were looking for special consideration with regard to pension benefits. One legislator, whose views were overridden, described the bill as "unhealthy, inequitable and unfair to people who don't have political connections." On the "heart" side, members liked and respected Ruane, felt sorry for him, and believed that he was not aware that he could have joined the state retirement system. The bill, according to its supporters, was "just," "fair," and "reasonable."

Much of what goes on in a legislative body is beyond the substantive and beyond the political. It is personal. Members relate to one another as well as to lobbyists on a personal basis. How legislators decide on issues is informed by personal experience at some point in their lives. Maryland delegate Sandy Rosenberg notes in his diary just how the personal affects policymaking.[10] In a committee voting session in the Maryland House, a bill regarding joint custody of children was being discussed. "Both of my children have divorced," said one delegate, and "In one instance the court had to determine custody for my disabled grandson." She brought her personal experience to the issue. Another bill before the committee dealt with changing a child's last name if one of the child's parents had remarried. "My father died when I was eleven and my mother remarried," said one of the committee members. "As long as I remember my father, I want to bear his name." That legislator already had a position staked out.

Weighing the Merits

No measure gets very far without justification. Substantive merits are argued by proponents; substantive demerits are argued by opponents. Political merits and demerits are less likely to be featured in the debate, but they also are weighed. The merits advanced by either side can be persuasive. Indeed, people on opposite sides of an issue not only see different merits and demerits, they also interpret the facts of the case differently.

Some of the time the legislator endorses the merits as advanced by his or her political supporters and interest group allies. In such instances there is little need for persuasion; in other instances the legislator has to be persuaded. Either way, the legislator buys into the narrative that does not conflict with his or her ideology, constituency, or political allies.

Much of the time, however, deliberation pays off and the merits mainly carry the day. Despite the emphasis given to pressure by political groups, special interests, and campaign contributors in determining how lawmakers decide and what gets enacted into law, it is necessary to stress the importance of ideas and arguments. It is not simply all pressure. Edward L. Lascher Jr. emphasizes in his study of automobile insurance issues in several legislatures that decision makers not only react to pressure brought to bear on them but act on the basis of their own conception of the merits of policy choices.[11] Kingdon, while acknowledging the importance of concepts like power, influence, and pressure, insists that there is more to the policymaking process: "The contents of the ideas themselves, far from being mere smokescreens or rationalization, are integral parts of decision making. . . ."[12]

Legislators, like executive-branch officials, marshal evidence and argue in support of or in opposition to proposals. Such discussions are central to the legislative process, especially as part of the work that goes on in committees. Here, according to Frances E. Lee, "Members make their determination neither on the basis of constituency, interest groups, or ideology, but on 'the merits.' "[13] Or, as Francis L. Marini, the Massachusetts House minority leader, told legislators at an orientation for new members: "Most cases are ones in which conscience is not affected and no district will be hurt."[14] A member has to go by the merits, as he or she comes to see them.

Lascher's study of automobile insurance emphasizes the important role of ideas. He identifies "cues on the merits," relating to the content of policy alternatives, and develops two "causal stories" that provide alternative accounts of why a problem exists and what has to be done about it. Of impact, according to Lascher, is whether lawmakers embrace one story or the other. In Lascher's study, one story posits that insurance companies were mainly responsible for high and rising rates. The other story claims that the insurance industry was competitive and its profits not unreasonably high, but that rising claim costs forced providers to raise rates. Lawmakers who accepted the first story favored rate freezes or rollbacks and tighter regulation. Those who accepted the second story were more likely to accept a no-fault plan. Lascher recognized that ideology might have influenced which story was accepted by whom, yet there was no correspondence to the liberal or conservative orientations of lawmakers. Somehow, the alternative stories and the ideas, data, and arguments that comprised them penetrated ideological barriers.[15]

The merits of the case weigh heaviest on relatively minor matters (and on the specifics of relatively major matters). Often one feature of the meritorious case is that other states have the law, so why *don't we also pass it.* Twenty-nine states allow motorcycle riders to choose whether or not to wear helmets. Twenty-five states have a primary seat belt law. Thirty-six permit consumers to take unfinished wine home from restaurants. Eleven have decriminalized small amounts of marijuana without negative effects. How one state ranks among others—in terms of judicial or teacher salaries, for instance, or how much is spent per capita on the environment—also is used to persuade members to adopt a proposal or raise expenditures. Economic development benefits often form the basis of another strong argument as to the merits of a proposal.

Perhaps as frequent as any other justification is the resort to "fairness." This was the case regarding a bill before the Washington Legislature that would have made cutting in line to catch a ferry illegal. It was sponsored by Sen. Mary Margaret Haugen, whose district included Whidbey Island, a terminus of a ferry line from Seattle. For several years she had tried to respond to constituents who complained about commuters and tourists who bucked lines, blocked driveways, and generally did not follow the rules. Although there had been previous unsuccessful efforts in this direction, this one would succeed. According to the chair of the House Transportation Committee, while other issues simply amounted to "pet peeves," this one was about not being fair. "Everybody has a sense of fairness," she said.[16] That appeared to be persuasive enough.

How Legislatures Decide

How individual legislators decide on the one hand and how collective legislatures decide on the other are obviously related. Yet they are by no means the same thing. Decisions by standing committees, party caucuses, and legislative leaders, as well as intercameral and joint executive-legislative decisions, come about differently than individual decisions. These institutional decisions are reached through processes that require majorities and, finally, collective unanimity with the governor, the senate, and the house in accord on a measure.

Politics internal to the legislature matter enormously to the success of any controversial bill introduced. A few votes here or there may make the difference between a bill's enactment and its defeat. Internal politics is ubiquitous to the process. Members trade with one another. Debts are incurred or paid. A committee chair, while not a big supporter of a measure, votes for it anyway because of a commitment made to its sponsor. Conversely, legislators who do not like one another will not assist one another; some may occasionally try to do in a measure backed by a disliked colleague. Trading goes on intermittently. Favors are routine. Retaliation is always a possibility. At one time or another, a chair will hold a bill hostage in committee; in return for the chair's own bill advancing elsewhere in the process, the chair will agree to release the hostage. Or a chair may hold a bill at the request of leadership, whereupon it is up to the sponsor to try to pry it loose. In Massachusetts, for instance, Rep. John Quinn believed that Speaker Salvatore DiMasi was blocking a measure that would authorize a town in his district to pay the medical expenses of an official who had been injured while on duty. Quinn retaliated against his leader by objecting, on three successive occasions, to taking up bills that were not formally on the house calendar, thus blocking business DiMasi wanted to transact.

Studying, Deliberating, and Bargaining

However important internal politics are, study and deliberation are still the essence of the process. Study is a constant. On the health bill in Massachusetts, for example, the education of legislators was a significant part of what went on over the course of months. Legislative leaders and key legislators were briefed repeatedly by staff and by experts on one issue after another until they grasped the complexities of the package they were shaping. Teaching and learning were instrumental in enactment of the bill. On this issue, as well as so many others, deliberation is ongoing. Deliberation, according to Paul J. Quirk, refers to the processes of identifying alternatives, gathering and evaluating information, weighing considerations, and making judgments as to the merits. The primary vehicle is discussion in committee and on the floor, with some members discoursing and others listening.[17]

Deliberation on the substantive aspects of a proposal probably counts less on visible and salient matters that are affected by ideology, party, and constituency. It counts more on less visible and less salient matters and on details. A deliberative process requires that participants not only listen to the other side's arguments but that they also be open to persuasion (at least to some extent). Debate that takes place on the senate or house floor can have deliberative effects even though the debaters themselves have already decided. Debaters speak normally to one another; they also listen to one another; but their object is not to reach agreement among themselves, but rather to persuade the audience.[18] In a legislative body, however, debate is not only for show; it can actually sway undecided members, even though it will not win over staunch opponents.

Amy Gutmann and Dennis Thompson believe that deliberation can reduce disagreement and help people who disagree settle for mutually acceptable policies.[19] However, the more fundamental, the more deeply rooted, and the more reinforced the disagreement, the less likely that deliberation will affect many. But it may affect a few legislators who are not firmly connected to one position or another. That is why morally related disagreements—such as over abortion, gay rights, capital punishment, and gun control—cannot usually be settled by deliberation in a legislative body. Instead they either have to be avoided entirely or fought out.

In theory, deliberation relates to the weight of arguments, while bargaining relates to the balance of forces. The latter begins after the former has run its course. Michael Walzer offers the example of a jury as a rather pure form of deliberation. The idea is not for jurors in a criminal case to bargain with one another, so that one juror will vote guilty on one count in return for another juror's vote of not guilty on a different count. It is for jurors to weigh the evidence and come up with a verdict that is their best judgment as to guilt or innocence.[20] Often the merits of a bill are all that count. But often, too, proponents and opponents go well beyond deliberation in order to win.

In the legislative arena, it is impossible to distinguish between deliberation and bargaining. They occur simultaneously throughout the discussions, although the more public the forum the more likely deliberation predominates. Consider the operations of a standing committee. Hearings on a bill consist of testimony taken from legislator sponsors and public witnesses and questions posed by committee members. This stage of the process is mainly deliberative. When the committee marks up the bill and proceeds to a vote, deliberation may still predominate, but bargaining over provisions is also likely to occur. If the bill's sponsor or the committee chair is trying to build consensus on the committee, he or she may have to amend the bill in question or take action on an unrelated measure in order to win support. The smaller the forum, the more inclined members are to reach agreement by making one deal or another or splitting the difference.

Perhaps as good an example of study and deliberation as any is the New Jersey Legislature's handling of property tax relief in a special session in 2006. Legislative leaders and their staffs decided that the best way to address the problem was through a special session, in which four joint senate-assembly committees explored: (1) what are the causes of increasing property taxes; (2) what drives up costs; and (3) what can be done about it? Twelve of the forty members of the senate and twelve of the eighty members of the assembly served on four joint committees, each of which had six members, four Democrats and two Republicans. Meeting over the summer and into the fall, these committees held forty-one public meetings (each of which was broadcast on cable television and over the Internet), heard testimony from experts and practitioners, and received over 4,800 e-mails from New Jerseyans with ideas on how to reform property taxes. The result was four reports, with a total of eighty recommendations for legislative action. Two of the four reports had full bipartisan support.

For months members of these joint committees studied and deliberated, while other members of the senate and assembly were kept aware of the developments and asked for their reactions. It was mainly a deliberative period, but with soundings taken and negotiations going on simultaneously. Once the reports were issued, however, study and deliberation no longer received top billing. Negotiating and bargaining became the main business of the legislature, as affected interests responded to committee recommendations. The New Jersey Education Association, the League of Municipalities, the Professional Firefighters Association of New Jersey, and a dozen other groups thought one or another of the recommendations went too far. By the time the property tax package was introduced in the legislature, it had been scaled back in order to pacify the opposition it encountered from public employees, who were concerned about pensions and benefits, and local officials, who were worried about expenditure caps and consolidation.

Deliberation accounts for much of the conversation throughout the lawmaking process.[21] Yet it is seldom viewed as critical in changing the decisive votes or final outcome in close contests. Deals, bargains, payoffs, pressure, and less substance-based techniques are deemed to be the factors that finally put one side or the other over the top. That may indeed be true; but without all the votes influenced by substantive considerations, there would be no "decisive votes" to be won over by bargaining and other techniques. In his exploration of lawmaking in the U.S. Congress, Joseph M. Bessette asks how many votes are the result of judgments on the merits and how many are of bargaining. Even if bargaining is the capstone in putting together the bits and pieces and ultimate majorities, it may explain only a small part of all the votes cast. When reasoned appeals fall short in majority-building efforts, essentially nondeliberative techniques come into play, according to Bessette. Suppose, for instance, that the legislative body divided about evenly on the actual merits of a proposal, whereupon bargaining moved one member to create a majority. We could conclude that bargaining made a difference to the bill's enactment. But we could also determine that deliberation on the merits, which largely affected all but the deciding vote, made the biggest difference.[22]

The need to build consensus and fashion majorities injects explicit or implicit bargaining into the entire process. The substantive merits expand to include political merits, inside as well as outside the legislature. "A good deliberation," Bruce Cain and Gerald Wright write, "would include political as well as purely policy considerations. . . ."[23] Think of the budget bill as assembled by the Massachusetts General Court in 2006, probably the most complex measure of the legislative session. The "merits" of what goes into the budget and what gets left out are broadly construed. In the house 1,600 amendments were offered by legislators to the bill reported by the House Ways and Means Committee. In the senate 949 amendments were added. It was necessary for house and senate legislators to choose some amendments from among the many and consolidate them into one or a few to come up for a vote. The deliberation took place off the floor, with decisions being made as to what to include and what to exclude. Members for the most part wanted money for projects in their districts. These projects had both substantive and political merit, according to the legislators. Included in each consolidated amendment by the leadership were the amendments of enough members to ensure that the budget would pass in each chamber. The bargaining was done behind the scenes, while the deliberation that occurred when the bill came up on the floor was after the fact. The conversation was for the record, since the decisions had already been made. In the senate, for instance, although debate on the budget lasted during two days of floor sessions, according to Minority Leader Brian Lees: "There was certainly minimal debate. That can be perceived as a good thing or a bad thing. I don't know." [24] Everything had already been settled.

Developing Consensus

In his memoirs Willie Brown, the former speaker of the California Assembly, writes: "No matter how righteous your cause, you've got to do heavy political lifting to secure the consensus you need to get anything done. . . ." [25] Lawmaking is a consensus-building process. For legislative purposes, consensus is minimally a majority of those voting or of those eligible to vote. On most issues, however, consensus reaches well beyond a simple majority. By the time most bills, and most amendments, get to the floor of the senate and the house, substantial consensus has been built.

Many bills in the legislature fall by the wayside; a number of them are not actually intended by their sponsors to go very far, but are introduced to appease an interest group or constituents. The large proportion of such bills die in committee. The consensus-mode has worked, to kill rather than enact. Some bills get out of committee but languish on the calendar, while others pass one house but not the other or fail to be reconciled by negotiation or in conference. The differences between senate and house versions cannot be bridged. The legislature fails to reach agreement, which of course is a decision not to pass a measure. In such cases the necessary consensus for something simply could not be built.

On some issues the governor and legislature fail to reach agreement, a veto is cast, and there are not enough votes to override. The bill is defeated. Or two sides may duke it out on the floor with one side winning. Neither may be willing to compromise with the other. Even if compromises are made, they may not be enough to satisfy a majority. In most legislative bodies, bills will not be calendared for the floor unless proponents are confident that they have the votes to pass them. In some, however, anything can happen. The votes are not assured before a bill is brought up for second or third reading. Either side can win on the floor.

In his study of Congress Kingdon has analyzed consensus-building in the "policy stream" and the "political stream." In the policy stream, consensus is built largely by means of persuasion on the substantive merits. In the political stream, bargaining and the building of coalitions matter more, by means of concessions in return for support and clear benefits from participation.[26]

Consensus-building starts even before the lawmaking process *per se* begins. Interest groups backing legislation on one matter or another round up support from other organizations and try to reach agreement on a measure. If backers can engage groups that might take the other side and persuade them at the outset to buy in, the coalition of support will be a most formidable one. Legislators routinely insist that affected interest groups work things out among themselves before the legislature will take up a narrow-gauged, special-interest issue. If consensus can get built outside the legislature, it will likely get built within the legislature as well. Often agreements are worked out through negotiations even prior to committee consideration.

Once a bill has been referred to a standing committee, the sponsor or the chair ordinarily will try to get the concerned parties together to see if they can iron out any differences over the measure. In Massachusetts, for example, since the racetrack owners could not reach agreement on details of a simulcasting bill, the legislature postponed action until they could. Some issues get pushed aside, because the principal interest groups are not willing to compromise. A group may find no action preferable to the compromises its opponents offer. In that case the legislature just stands by. For years firefighters and electricians in Massachusetts tried to get together on whether low-voltage wiring should be regulated for fire and safety alarms and home entertainment. They were not successful. The legislature's response was simply, "If you can't figure it out, we can't." The bill continued to be filed, but the firefighters and electricians could not work out their differences.

Unless opposing interests can come to terms with one another on narrow-gauged issues, it is unlikely that the legislature will be able to do so. Typical of groups that cannot get together are architects on the one hand and interior designers on the other. In Massachusetts architects have state certification, interior designers do not. Architects have the authority to bid on contracts and also to commission interior designers to work on such contracts under their supervision. Interior designers want autonomy, licensure, and the right to enter into their own contracts. The architects object, arguing that they have ultimate responsibility for the building and therefore should have a strong say on the interior design. Members of the committee of reference split on the issue. The subcommittee chair sided with the designers, while the full committee chair believed that unless a compromise were reached the legislature would not pass a bill giving designers autonomy and, anyway, the governor would not sign one. The committee chair saw no risk to the public under the status quo and therefore no pressing reason why the bill should be taken to the floor. Although the committee chair tried to mediate the differences between the two sides, he was not able to do so. The bill did not move.[27]

Sponsors have to bring together concerned parties to work through disagreements that affect support for their bill. Most of the time disagreements are worked out during the stage of committee consideration. The effort starts well before members vote on whether to report a measure or not. In Maryland, for instance, "pre-meeting" committee meetings are common. The chair meets with a colleague or two to reach consensus before the public voting session. In the legislature, Del. Sandy Rosenberg observes, "you're taught not to take a vote if you don't know the outcome."[28] It is in the standing committees where consensus is not only built but also recorded for all to see. If a standing committee reports a bill out with an overwhelming endorsement of its members, chances are that such an endorsement will be repeated when the bill is brought up for a vote in the chamber. Consider, for example, the way standing committees operate in New York. About eight of ten votes in assembly committees on legislation that passed from 1997–2001 were unanimous. About nine of ten votes in senate committees on legislation that passed in 1998–2001 were also unanimous. Ordinarily a bill will not be placed on the committee's agenda until the chair and staff know that the votes are there to move the bill forward.[29]

By the time a bill reaches the floor, a consensus has usually been fashioned. In most states the votes for passage are there. In relatively few places and on relatively few issues will a bill's proponents be surprised by what happens on the floor; by then, the tough work has been done. New York exemplifies how the deliberative and negotiating processes take place before bills reach the floor of the senate or assembly. In 1997–2001 not one of the bills that reached the floor of the senate and assembly in New York was voted down.[30] Massachusetts contrasts sharply with New York. But even here, where amendments are adopted and bills beaten on the floor, by far the largest part of the senate and house agendas receives overwhelming support.

Compromise

At the core of the negotiating process by which consensus gets built is compromise that results from negotiations. Hardly anything goes on that does not involve some compromise—among a few legislators, among interest groups, across committees, between the senate and the house, or with the governor. The result is that the outcomes of the lawmaking process tend to flatten out, so that on a large proportion of measures no one wins everything, no one loses everything, and everybody can claim that at least some progress was made.

Legislators individually have to compromise their own ideas. What they believe in, what makes policy sense, and what serves their district may not be the same. And what they can get in a settlement may be entirely different. Most of the notable compromises, however, are not *within* members but *among* members. These compromises are negotiated in the initial formulation of a measure, at the committee stage, in caucus, during floor consideration, or with the other house. Look at some of the compromises made in the Massachusetts legislature during its 2006 session.

On legislation to address childhood obesity, action was postponed one month because the food and beverage industry objected. The bill was softened, with guidelines proposed regarding drinks acceptable for sale at different grade levels and maximum calorie amounts in school food. In return for a bill the industry could "live with," food and beverage interests went along. A bill to stiffen standards for teenage drinking would have raised the legal drinking age. Substantial opposition developed and this provision was dropped, while tough driver's education requirements and increased penalties were retained.

The Massachusetts Senate and House saw eye to eye on the need to raise the state minimum wage. But the bill passed by each body differed in the amount of the increase and whether future increases should be indexed to the cost of living. The house bill would have raised the minimum from $6.75 to $8.00 over three years, while the senate would have gone to $8.25 over two. The senate bill included indexing, the house version did not. According to the compromise, the senate prevailed on the two-year provision, while the house prevailed on not including an indexing provision. The chief sponsor in the senate had wanted to see the minimum wage tied to inflation, but had to settle for less. "Is it perfect? No," he said. But most important was increasing the wages of low-paid workers.[31]

Another clear-cut compromise was between the Massachusetts legislature on the one hand and the public higher-educational community on the other. The issue in contest was the tuition increases to which legislators, echoing their constituents, objected. In the give and take between legislators and representatives of higher education, it was agreed that the legislature would provide more financial assistance in return for caps on how much tuition could be increased by the institutions.[32]

On most issues that have substantial support to begin with, if objections arise negotiators are able to cut some deal. For example, the Massachusetts House and Senate pushed bills that would enable the Boston Convention and Exhibition Center (BCEC) to put on more shows, smaller ones as well as larger ones. The neighborhood community in which the BCEC was located objected; residents were concerned about the impact of increased traffic. An agreement was reached by which a new measure provided that each BCEC show pay a special tax that would go to a community mitigation fund in South Boston—ten cents per square foot of space used and one dollar per ticket sold.[33]

There are few better examples of the importance of compromise in the lawmaking process than the health insurance package in Massachusetts. Under the law, which required four months of negotiations to reach agreement, every resident of the state would be required to have health insurance. After the event, Governor Romney said simply: "We found a way to bridge the partisan divide, and to find a coincidence of interests among the various stakeholders in the health care community." He qualified his praise for the accomplishment by adding, ". . . it doesn't mean that everything in the bill is exactly how I'd like it." [34] Practically everyone applauded—the advocates united under Health Care for All, the health care providers, and the business community. They too were happy, but not entirely thrilled with every provision of the complex new law.

Yet it was no easy matter to get from the divergent proposals advanced by the governor, house speaker, and senate president at the outset to substantial agreement on a product at the end. "Substantial" agreement rather than "complete" agreement best describes the settlement, because Romney vetoed several provisions, recognizing at the time that the legislature was certain to override. At the end, too, the legislative leaders agreed that the final bill was a true compromise.[35] It was more than a "true compromise"; it was a virtual bundle of compromises. The most important and the most general compromises were those between liberals and conservatives, between Democrats and Republicans, between the house and the senate, and between the legislature and the governor. The measure brought together ideas from both the liberal and conservative camps into an unlikely mix of seemingly incompatible concepts. One side achieved universal coverage while the other maintained the role of the private sector in furnishing most of the coverage.

When asked if the bipartisan, executive-legislative accomplishment was conservative or liberal, Governor Romney answered: "It's liberal in the sense that we're getting our citizens health insurance. It's conservative in that we're not getting a government takeover.[36]

The right-wing Heritage Foundation helped craft the bill that the governor proposed. The left-wing New America Foundation was among a number of liberal groups that found that they could support the settlement.[37] "What's remarkable to me," said Romney in celebrating passage of the law, "is that such a disparate group of people could come together on a workable consensus." Sharing the platform with Massachusetts senator Ted Kennedy, Romney quipped that his son said that the two of them supporting the same piece of legislation would help slow global warming. That would be because hell had frozen over. Kennedy, who spoke immediately after the governor, quoted his own son: "When Kennedy and Romney support a piece of legislation, usually one of them hasn't read it." [38]

Among the many compromises that had to be made along the way was that regarding an employer's fee. Business had to be convinced that employers who did not offer health insurance should pay a fee. It was a tough sell, but business finally agreed. Speaker Salvatore DiMasi and Senate President Robert Travaglini both started out with a preference for a payroll tax to finance part of the package, but they settled on a $295 worker assessment on employers who did not offer health insurance on their own. The various groups that were affected by this measure had to give up something, but each got a piece of what it wanted. Business succeeded in eliminating the payroll tax, which was in the house bill, but it had to agree to a fee instead. Health care providers got to sell a subsidized insurance plan to new subscribers, but the costs had to be kept low without the policies being stripped down. Hospitals and physicians got increases in Medicaid rates for medical services, although insisting that it would still not be enough to cover their costs. Also, payments were tied to performance measures starting in fiscal year 2008. The hospitals in Boston and Cambridge did exceedingly well, thanks mainly to the support they received from the senate. People earning low incomes wound up with state subsidies for the private coverage they were required to purchase.[39]

The Massachusetts plan could be declared a victory for the legislative process. A significant measure was crafted and succeeded in winning overwhelming support. But, like any other complicated piece of legislation, there were no guarantees that the new health insurance system would work. Senate President Travaglini sounded a most appropriate note of caution:

This is just a blueprint. We must still implement the reforms, educate the public, and establish the guidelines and regulations that will make this legislation a reality.... And the legislature will have ... to evaluate the progress we're making and step in with the revisions whenever necessary.[40]

There was much to be done, not the least of which were the pay-for-performance specifications according to which hospitals and doctors had to show that they were meeting quality standards and controlling costs. And probably the most difficult task would be getting individuals without insurance to enroll. Health care in Massachusetts was truly a work in progress—beginning with a three-to-five-year implementation process that involved hundreds of moving parts.[41]

After a year's operation, the verdict was a mixed one. Critics pointed out that it had cost $153 million more than the $472 million the state had appropriated for fiscal year 2007–2008. Proponents pointed out, however, that the enrollment in Commonwealth Care, the new plan, had exceeded expectations, with 340,000 of an estimated 600,000 obtaining coverage. Meanwhile, legislators continued to introduce bills to improve on their health care accomplishments.[42]

Virtually everyone was satisfied with the outcome in Massachusetts. Normally, however, a number of participants in a settlement are at least somewhat unhappy with the result. Take the Vermont health care reform, which was passed at about the same time as the Massachusetts act. Republican governor Jim Douglas and the Democratic legislature had different ideas about a health care plan for the state. The governor favored a private system, while the legislature preferred a governmental one. After several attempts to get together on a package, the two finally compromised on some major items and a bill was signed into law. Not everyone was pleased, however. The liberal wing of the Democratic Party would have rejected the compromise and kept trying to achieve its goals, without having them diluted by the other side. The legislative leaders, who negotiated the settlement, came in for criticism by a number of members within their own caucuses.[43]

Massachusetts and Vermont exemplify the vital role that compromise plays in lawmaking. But sometimes the senate and house or the governor and legislature cannot resolve their differences. California illustrates the inability of Republican governor Arnold Schwarzenegger and a Democratic legislature to get together on a plan to extend health coverage to all uninsured people in the state. The governor, after being elected by an overwhelming margin in November 2006, pledged that California would lead the nation in covering all the uninsured. Schwarzenegger's proposal would have assessed doctors, hospitals, and employees who did not offer health benefits and would have mandated that individuals get coverage. Democratic leaders responded with a proposal that would have required employers to spend at least 7.5 percent of their payrolls on health care but would not make insurance for individuals mandatory. The two sides appeared to have stalemated. To break the impasse, the governor proposed leaving the financing of health care to a ballot initiative, for which he would campaign.[44] By early 2008 Governor Schwarzenegger and Speaker Fabian Nuñez managed to agree on a measure. The assembly went along, but the senate refused to follow suit. The compromises that had worked beautifully in Massachusetts, and less so in Vermont, had not yet succeeded in California.

Getting the Votes

Deliberation over substantive and political merits; building consensus in committee, caucus, and beyond; negotiations involving compromising and splitting the difference—these activities account for most of what happens in lawmaking in state legislatures. Part of the job of any bill sponsor is getting the votes. It begins with finding cosponsors for a bill. The crucial stage is at the time the bill is in committee. The sponsor has to get the bill reported favorably by the committee to which it has been referred. Getting the votes of the chair and members is tough work. And often the sponsor has to work a bill for votes, even as it is being debated on the floor. In Maryland Rosenberg was sponsoring a constitutional amendment regarding the election of judges on the Orphan's Court. He needed 85 (out of 141) votes, but fell one short. He asked that the vote be reconsidered the next day and his request was granted by the presiding officer. Rosenberg examined the roll call vote that had just taken place: four members who were present but did not vote, Democrats who voted no, and one Republican who voted for the bill in committee but against it on the floor. He approached several of these members. "No one asked me for my vote," said one. "If you need me tomorrow, I'll be with you," said another. No one asked Rosenberg to support their bill in return for their vote, but he did agree to put in a good word for their bills with his chair.[45] Sometimes additional effort has to be exerted in order to garner the last few votes, and occasionally such effort has to be made for more than just a few votes to put a bill over the top. The conventional wisdom is that almost every legislator's vote has a price. That is not the case; yet on some of the most significant issues in a legislative session a price may have to be paid. Ordinarily, the governor and the leadership of the majority party are the ones making payment and are the ones who decide if the price is right.

Ralph Wright differentiates among three types of members he knew as speaker of the house in Vermont. First, there were the issues people, who make up their own minds but could be counted on for forty or so votes of the seventy-six needed to pass a bill that the Democrats favored. Second, there were those Republicans who would vote against what the liberal speaker wanted. Their numbers almost equaled those of Wright's liberals. Third, there were those that Wright labels "the what's-in-it-for-me group." These were the people who recognized the importance of compromise in the legislative process. For them compromise meant, "You get something, and I get something." They might have wanted an appointment to a committee for themselves or an appointment to a board or commission for a constituent. These members used what leverage they had. Wright describes the process of getting their votes, once he learned that they did not think they could support one of the measures the leadership was pushing:

> Then it was just a matter of finding out what they wanted. Sometimes it was simply an audience with the Speaker to air a gripe or reestablish themselves as players; other times it might be a commitment for some help in getting their pet bill out of a committee or on the calendar.[46]

It does not usually take much for leaders to persuade the last few members to go along. But at the very least it takes asking for a colleague's vote. Just the attention paid to a member may be sufficient to win that member over. However, it is not only flattering to be asked for one's vote by the leader, it may also be intimidating. What will happen if the member refuses? What sanctions might be exercised in the short run, or in the longer run? Legislators cannot be certain, but they realize that at some point, sooner or later, they will want a favor from their leader.

John E. McDonough recounts his experience in the Massachusetts House. On a bill to give a tax break to Raytheon, a large defense contractor in the state, McDonough pushed the red "no" button on his desk. Almost immediately the majority whip informed him that Speaker Charlie Flaherty wanted a "yes" on the bill, even though he already had enough votes for passage. McDonough looked up to the speaker's rostrum where Flaherty stood staring at him. McDonough switched his vote. He explained that he had mixed feelings on the subject and could have gone either way. His constituents were not concerned, so he had a free hand there. But what he did know was that during the session, "I would be bringing to the floor my own controversial legislation on health care access expansion, and I fervently hoped that when my turn came, the Speaker would deliver the votes of the recalcitrant members as he was now delivering me." McDonough asked himself whether his switch was an example of "opportunistic self-interest" or simply a "trade-off necessary to achieve a higher good?" Either answer contained some degree of truth.[47]

Probably "pork" constitutes the most substantial benefit leaders can provide members whose votes they need. Indeed, without the ability to distribute district benefits to members, leaders would have a more difficult time passing the budget than they already do. For the most part, what legislators can do for their districts depends on majority party leadership, and the governor as well. Leaders are not entirely free agents here. Funding for local projects normally is distributed roughly on the basis of loyalty to the majority party, safety of a minority party member's district, service on a committee where allotments are made, overall fairness, and a majority party member's need for electoral help.

The amount of money dedicated to "earmarks" (as they are referred to in the U.S. Congress), "pork" (as referred to in general), "turkeys" (in Florida), "member items" (in New York), or "Christmas tree items" (in New Jersey) is a tiny part of the state budget. In some states, such as New York, the total amount is determined in advance. Here each year the legislature sets aside $200 million: $85 million for the senate, $85 million for the assembly, and the rest for the governor. The majority leader in the senate and the speaker in the assembly have the power to divvy up their allotments as they see fit. In other states, such as New Jersey, decisions as to the total bill for pork are made from budget to budget. Still, leaders have some discretion in how much is distributed to each member.

From time to time—and on budget bills more than anywhere else—leaders offer district benefits in return for the member's vote. The bartering arrangement is clear. More often, however, if the leader asks persuasively, a member will go along (unless conscience and/or constituency pull strongly in the other direction); that way there is no question of receiving benefits for the district then and also in the future. Moreover, a number of legislative leaders adhere to the principle that if a member votes against the budget, he or she is not entitled to any provision within the budget. No vote for the majority party, no pork for the district.

Reaching Agreement

Trying to forge agreements on major issues is probably the most difficult work in which legislators engage.[48] As tough as anything else are the negotiations toward the close of the legislative sessions, mainly on the budget but on other items as well. Former senator Ember Reichgott Junge describes budget negotiations at the end of the Minnesota Legislature's 2000 session. The leadership had closed the "big picture deal," and it was up to general conference committees to work out the details:

> Throughout the weekend, conferees walked around bleary eyed, with no sleep. Many stayed up between 24 and 48 hours straight; some even got to 62 hours. No wonder tempers flared, tears flowed, legislators walked out, and even-tempered legislators showed frustration. . . . Virtually nothing goes on in public. Conferees meet privately in offices where they can't be found. Conference committee meeting rooms look the way a transatlantic plane looks after the end of a long flight: food everywhere, papers strewn about, chairs tipped, legislators and audience with big bags under their eyes. People doze in their chairs, spread out over two or three chairs if they can. Time doesn't exist. It's like Las Vegas, where there are no clocks on the wall. There are clocks, but they don't mean anything. Conferees announce they'll reconvene at 8 p.m. and maybe they'll get there at 10:45 p.m. They announce another offer for maybe five minutes. No response from the other side. Recess until 2 a.m. That's how it goes.[49]

Negotiating is an iterative, and frustrating, business. Deals are proffered, rejected, recast, and accepted; and then they fall apart. On Wednesday prospects for a settlement look bright, on Thursday they are dim, and on Friday participants are still at it. Sometimes negotiations fail, but on big-ticket items they tend to succeed. Negotiated compromises are probably the best lawmakers can do. The Washington Legislature received the ultimate in praise from one of the state's daily newspapers. After the session concluded, the *Olympian* editorialized: "The 2002 legislative session wasn't pretty, but lawmakers did tackle tough issues—resolving most." [50] Not pretty, but probably the best that could be done *under the circumstances*—the circumstances of representative democracy.

Notes

1. Methamphetamine laboratory operators tend to dump toxic waste down drains or in yards, which affects the values of properties and neighborhoods.
2. *New York Times,* April 6, 2006.
3. This account is based on an article that appeared in the *New York Times,* July 7, 2005.
4. This account is based on an article that appeared in the *Star-Ledger,* August 26, 2007.
5. John E. McDonough, *Experiencing Politics: A Legislator's Stories of Government and Health Care* (Berkeley: University of California Press, 2000), 126–127.
6. See Frances E. Lee, "Interests, Constituencies, and Policy Making," in *The Legislative Branch,* ed. Paul J. Quirk and Sarah A. Binder (New York: Oxford University Press, 2005), 299.
7. John W. Kingdon, *Congressmen's Voting Decisions* (New York: Harper and Row, 1973), 330–332.
8. Ibid., 254.
9. *Boston Globe,* May 24, 2006.
10. Diary of Maryland delegate Sandy Rosenberg, March 25, 2005.
11. Edward L. Lascher Jr., *The Politics of Automobile Insurance Reform* (Washington, D.C.: Georgetown University Press, 1999).
12. Kingdon, *Congressmen's Voting Decisions,* 125.

13. Lee, "Interests, Constituencies, and Policy Making," 298.

14. Remarks at orientation session for Massachusetts legislature at the University of Massachusetts, Amherst, December 13, 2000.

15. Lascher, *The Politics of Automobile Insurance Reform,* 20–21, 41–44, 121.

16. *New York Times,* April 11, 2007.

17. Paul J. Quirk, "Deliberation and Decision Making," in *The Legislative Branch,* ed. Paul J. Quirk and Sarah A. Binder (New York: Oxford University Press, 2005), 316–317.

18. Michael Walzer, "Deliberation, and What Else?" in *Deliberative Politics,* ed. Stephen Macedo (New York: Oxford University Press, 1999), 61.

19. Amy Gutmann and Dennis Thompson, *Why Deliberative Democracy?* (Princeton: Princeton University Press, 1999).

20. Walzer, "Deliberation, and What Else?", 62.

21. This paragraph draws on Alan Rosenthal, *Heavy Lifting: The Job of the American Legislature* (Washington, D.C.: CQ Press, 2004), 121.

22. Joseph M. Bessette, *The Mild Voice of Reason* (Chicago: University of Chicago Press, 1994), 71, 99.

23. Bruce Cain and Gerald Wright, "Committees," in *Institutional Change in American Politics: The Case of Term Limits,* ed. Karl T. Kurtz, Bruce Cain, and Richard G. Niemi (Ann Arbor: University of Michigan Press, 2007), 75.

24. Massachusetts State House News Service, May 26, 2006.

25. Willie Brown, *Basic Brown* (New York: Simon and Schuster, 2008), 24.

26. Kingdon, *Congressmen's Voting Decisions,* 159–160.

27. Interview with Rep. Vincent Pedone, March 8, 2006.

28. Diary of Maryland delegate Sandy Rosenberg, February 28, 2008.

29. Jeremy Creelen and Laura M. Moulton, *The New York State Legislative Process: An Evaluation and Blueprint for Reform* (New York: Brennan Center for Justice, New York University School of Law, 2004), 6.

30. *New York Times,* July 22, 2004.

31. Sen. Marc Pacheco, quoted in the *Boston Globe,* July 7, 2006.

32. Massachusetts State House News Service, February 2006.

33. Massachusetts State House News Service, July 27, 2006.

34. Massachusetts State House News Service, April 3, 2006.

35. *Boston Globe,* April 4, 2006.

36. *New York Times,* April 6, 2006.

37. Massachusetts State House News Service, April 12, 2006.

38. Massachusetts State House News Service, April 12, 2006.

39. *Globe,* April 5, 2006.

40. Massachusetts State House News Service, April 12, 2006.

41. Interview with John E. McDonough, April 17, 2006.

42. *New York Times,* April 5 and 17, 2008.

43. Remarks of Rep. Gay Symington, Eastern Leadership Academy, Council of State Governments, Philadelphia, September 9, 2007.

44. *New York Times,* September 9, 2007.

45. Diary of Maryland delegate Sandy Rosenberg, March 7, 2008.

46. Ralph Wright, *Inside the Statehouse* (Washington, D.C.: CQ Press, 2005), 98–104.

47. McDonough, *Experiencing Politics,* 119–120.

48. This section draws on Rosenthal, *Heavy Lifting,* 161–163.

49. Ember Reichgott Junge, unpublished manuscript, 2000.

50. *Olympian,* March 17, 2002.

12

How Well Do Legislatures Work?

AT THE BEGINNING of this book we looked at what the public thought about state legislatures and why the public thought what it did. The conclusion, which comes as no surprise, is that Americans are not at all satisfied with their legislative bodies—not with the U.S. Congress and not with state legislatures. The question is, how well are state legislatures working?

What standards ought we to use in an assessment of a legislature's performance? I suggest that three types are available. The first is what people think, as indicated by public opinion polls. Polls are not the answer, however. Too few people have any idea of what a legislature is doing for the public to make an informed judgment. While public opinion polls should not be ignored, they are by no means adequate indicators as to how well legislatures are working.

Another standard is the laws or policies that the legislature produces. Here, people have some idea, but there is little agreement on how such a standard would be operationalized for purposes of measurement. What would good law or good policy be? More enactments rather than less, or vice versa? A larger proportion of introductions enacted, or smaller? If quality rather than quantity ought to count, then what is "good" and what is "poor" in terms of the quality of law or policy? Democrats would have one idea of "good," Republicans another; and even members of the same party would not agree on just what "good" is and what "poor" is. Environmentalists would interpret "good" from their perspective, developers from theirs, and business groups and consumers from quite another. Each and every legislator has his or her own ideas as to what a good bill is and what it is not. So does the governor.

Legislative performance, in my judgment, ought to be judged on the basis of process rather than product. This is because the legislature is not only a means to an end, that end being public policy. *The legislature is also an end itself, in that it provides the key mechanism in our representative democracy for deciding what public policy should be.* The workings of the legislature as an institution and the processes it employs are what distinguish better from poorer legislative performance.

Although a focus on process steers us in the right direction, it does not make assessment any easier. In the book they edited on Congress, Paul J. Quirk and Sarah A. Binder acknowledge that questions about congressional performance are difficult to answer. But for them the important questions also relate to process:

> Does Congress respond and give reasonably proportionate weight to public opinion, interest-group pressure, and other sources of policy demands? . . . Does it deliberate intelligently, taking account of relevant knowledge? Does it face up to the real effects of policy choices. . . ? Does it avoid gridlock?[1]

Establishing "proportionate" weights for public opinion, interest group pressures, or other sources of policy demands would be a daunting task, to say the least.

The standard that I have used for the assessment of legislative performance is similar in some degree to those offered by Quirk and Binder. How, and how well, does the legislature do its job? In *Heavy Lifting* I maintain that there are three principal aspects to the legislature's job: representing constituents and constituencies, lawmaking, and balancing the power of the executive.[2] These three aspects are not separate and distinct but overlap substantially. How legislators express the views of constituents relates to how legislatures deal with a number of issues in the lawmaking process. How the legislature and governor deal with one another also is reflected in lawmaking.

I would add two other aspects to the legislature's job. The first is legislative oversight, which involves the legislature's ongoing review and evaluation of how effectively enacted policies are being implemented and how effectively they are working. The second is legislative maintenance, which involves attention to the well-being and strength of the legislative institution.

An Assessment of Performance

The views that members have of their own legislature's performance contrast dramatically with those of the public. It is not surprising that "insiders" and "outsiders" do not see eye to eye on institutional performance. They seldom do.

Consider, for instance, the views of baseball fans and baseball players toward Barry Bonds. In a *USA Today*/Gallup Poll (May 18–20, 2007), people were asked (before Bonds broke the record), if he were to hit his 756th home run to pass Hank Aaron, "Who do you consider to be the greatest home run hitter in baseball history?" Only one-third responded that they would consider Bonds the greatest, while approximately another third chose Aaron, and still another third selected Babe Ruth. The 750 active players of major league baseball were asked the same question, and 72 percent of the 493 who replied picked Bonds as the best home run hitter in history. Asked to explain the disparity, Derek Jeter of the New York Yankees answered: "If you have enough people writing bad things about you, people start believing it." Bonds certainly was not the favorite player of the nation's sportswriters.

In the survey I conducted of legislators in five states (Maryland, Minnesota, Ohio, Vermont, and Washington) in 2001–2002, I asked "insiders" about their legislature's performance in "representing constituents," "lawmaking," and "balancing executive power." Percentages giving positive ratings of "excellent" or "good" varied among the states, but overall 88 percent of the legislators rated "representing constituents" positively, 69 percent rated "lawmaking" positively, and 41 percent rated "balancing executive power" positively.[3] My own observations and assessments, which appear throughout the book, are not far out of line with what legislators themselves think.

Representing

Legislatures do an excellent job representing constituents and constituencies. They serve the needs of their constituents and the interests of their districts. They provide access and help to individuals and get whatever benefits they can for the district. Although performance varies from state to state and member to member, it tends to be in the high range. This kind of representation is something that legislators want to do and feel that they are expected to do and have to do. As far as expressing the views of the constituency, the picture is murkier. This is mainly because on the overwhelming number of issues that legislatures consider, constituents are essentially unaffected, completely unaware, and totally unconcerned. It would be unreasonable to expect otherwise. On the few issues about which constituents care, normally the views of the constituency majority and the representative coincide. In the few cases where conflict exists, the legislator may still vote according to the preferences of the constituency (or may try to get out of voting altogether). The system is one in which elected representatives decide without constituency input in many instances, listen to their constituencies—and primarily to political supporters within their constituencies—when there is something to which to listen, and only in the rarest cases have to worry about conscience and constituency clashing.

Even though the representational system may appear to work satisfactorily to most people, some maintain that not everyone in the state or district is represented equally.[4] Shouldn't more women, minorities, blue-collar workers, and younger people be holding seats in the legislature? The problem is that more have not run and more have not been elected. Greater representation for underrepresented groups might make a difference as far as public policy is concerned.

There is evidence that the increase of women in legislatures since the 1970s has resulted in the incorporation of so-called "women's issues" onto legislative agendas. This would have been less likely without women spearheading such issues in the legislature. Although both men and women supported these measures in similar proportions when they came to a vote, it was essentially women who brought them to a vote.[5] African American and Hispanic legislators also make a difference, even if their numbers are not substantial. They too raise issues that otherwise might not be seriously considered.

If gender, race, and ethnicity matter even somewhat, why not construct a system that more accurately represents such characteristics? Such a system of "descriptive representation" would mirror the population. If 54 percent of a state's population were women, then women would constitute 54 percent of the state senate and house. But what social characteristics besides gender would be entitled to proportional representation? Race? Ethnicity? Income? Social class? Age? An argument can be made for each category. Imagine implementing a system of descriptive representation for even a single category, let alone for a number of categories! The mechanics of achieving such representation, by means of an electoral (rather than a sampling or lottery) process, would be overwhelming.

The current system is also criticized for underrepresenting partisan minorities. Who represents Republicans who live in heavily Democratic districts or Democrats who live in heavily Republican districts? Without some system of proportionality in legislative elections, the winner will take all. And the winner will more likely reflect the views on a number of issues of voters of his or her own party rather than those of the opposition party. Multimember districts may leaven the effects of winner-take-all, but not necessarily or significantly so. The system that used to exist in Illinois provided that the 177 members of the house were each elected from a three-member district. Under a cumulative voting arrangement, at least one Democrat and one Republican had to be elected from each district. But in 1980 the Illinois Constitution was revised to reduce the size of the house, provide for single-member districts, and eliminate cumulative voting.[6]

Some assert that if districts were more competitive voters would feel better represented. At any time, some voters—in fact, even more voters than in noncompetitive districts—would feel unrepresented because the candidate elected would be from the other party. Thomas L. Brunell makes a strong argument that voters prefer winning elections to participating in competitive elections. Therefore, the more competitive the district, the more losers and the fewer winners there are among the electorate. In a noncompetitive district, there are many more winners than losers. In a competitive district, however, losers might feel that they had a chance to elect one of their own the next time. [7] That might assuage their sense of disappointment, but it would not necessarily mean that their views had greater weight. Unless, that is, the competitiveness of the district forced their representative, no matter what his or her party affiliation, to take a position in the middle, straddling both sides. To do so, however, would be to ignore one's partisan base and give rise to the possibility of a primary challenge if one stepped too far out of line. Moreover, there is reason to believe that legislators from safe districts would vote with their constituency more often than do those from competitive districts. This is because the safer the district the easier it is to define what the dominant constituency view on an issue is.[8]

This is not the place to explore the benefits and disadvantages of competitive districts or the standards and procedures for legislative redistricting. Suffice it to say that even under a winner-take-all system the views of a district's partisan minorities do not really go unrepresented. As far as the service aspects of representation are concerned, everyone gets represented. Few legislators distinguish among constituents' partisan identifications in responding to requests for help of most kinds. Nor does a legislator make partisan distinctions when fighting for local-aid formulas that give more money to the district or for projects that benefit localities or groups in the district. And as far as the issue aspects of representation are concerned, the views of partisan minorities do get represented—not necessarily by the legislator from the district where they reside, but by legislators of their party who represent districts elsewhere. A Democratic legislator represents the views of many Democrats, no matter where they live in the state; a Republican legislator represents the views of many Republicans, no matter where they live in the state. Political parties (and interest groups), in addition to a district's elected legislators, are significant channels of representation for people's views.

Similarly, African American and Hispanic legislators often speak for many African Americans and Hispanics, whether they live in their districts or not. And many women legislators take on the advancement of women generally as one of their jobs. Younger legislators have their own generation's perspective and perhaps to some extent advocate for those few issues that may be peculiar to a younger generation. In any case, the views constituents have do get represented, not always directly but one way or another. Whether they get enacted into law depends on much more than the representational part of the legislature's job, however.

In sum, representation by the legislature works remarkably well (which is not to say there is no room for improvement). Members give constituents access, connection, recognition, and service. They provide their districts with whatever benefits they can wrestle from the state. On salient issues, they attend to constituency views—particularly the views of the electoral majority, their supporters. Those constituents who participate in the political party or in organized interest groups have greater influence than those who do not. But, as far as lawmaking is concerned, the district is only one of a number of factors that affect how issues are resolved. And on the large majority of issues a legislator's district is not much of a factor at all.

Lawmaking

Fundamental to the system of representative democracy is the diversity of the nation and the state—with the differing values, interests, and priorities held by citizens, interest groups, political parties, and lawmakers. The concerns of all of the above come to bear in the lawmaking process.[9] And often when they do, they impact in opposite directions and with contradictory effects. When Speaker Joseph Roberts brought up a major property tax reform package in the New Jersey General Assembly on January 29, 2007, he acknowledged that the legislature found itself right smack in the middle of contradiction. Roberts addressed his fellow New Jersey legislators:

> On the one hand, our residents support merging governments by a 2-1 margin—but when it's proposed in their own zip code, some start to see it in a different light. On the one hand, a majority of residents believe public employee benefits should be brought in line more with the private sector. . . . On the other hand, according to last week's Quinnipiac poll, half oppose requiring public employees to pay higher health premiums or accept reduced retirement benefits. A majority of our residents want a new school aid formula—but a majority also is happy with how our schools are currently funded. In some ways, the public's message to the Legislature is to "go shake up the status quo, but at the same time please stay the course."

What should citizens expect from the lawmaking process as performed in bodies that handle differences and conflict? First, the issues in contest must be studied. Information and knowledge ought to make a difference, and they generally do. They are especially important for the detailed provisions of law, and possibly somewhat less so for the general thrust. It is up to the legislature to have some mastery of the substance of policy it is considering. Second, deliberation ought to be an important part of the process. This entails proponents and opponents arguing the merits of their case, including justification at the macro level and the micro level as well. Depending on the issue, deliberation may lead to some legislators making up their minds and others, perhaps, changing their minds on both the larger and smaller aspects of an issue. Not every legislator has to be engaged for deliberation to work, but at least some must be listening to the arguments back and forth and some must be open to persuasion on one point or another.

As we have seen, study and deliberation play a large part in lawmaking. Not all bills receive the same amount of attention, however. Uncontested bills are reviewed and given some consideration, but not serious study or deliberation. There simply is not enough time available to study and deliberate over each matter. Where opposition exists, even on bills of very limited scope, information and arguments make a difference. And on the broader-scope issues, study and deliberation are ongoing matters, taking place from one session to the next and often during interim periods as well.

It is at the committee level where study and deliberation particularly hold sway, weighing heavily in both the formal and informal proceedings. The hearings and staff memos inform members, and discussion and markup sessions allow for back-and-forth. In two-party, competitive bodies, committees are where minority party members have their greatest say in shaping legislation and affecting final outcomes. Minority party members who do their homework, engage in discussion, and have no partisan axes to grind are given a real chance by the majority party to contribute to the committee's work. Particularly if they do not insist on credit (such as bill authorship), their ideas are considered and they have the opportunity to exercise influence. Study and deliberation peak at the committee stage, but they continue beyond it, at leadership meetings, party caucuses, and on the floor on many issues.

Negotiating is a constant feature of lawmaking. It includes strategizing, bargaining, dealing, compromising, and settling—all of which fuse together in a kaleidoscopic process that goes on until a bill is sidetracked, defeated, or signed into law. Anything and everything would seem to go into rounding up the votes and reaching intercameral agreement necessary for enactment. The final word is the vote, endorsed by a majority of members or rather, successive votes, endorsed by majorities. "Democratic government," writes Richard A. Posner, "allows people to disagree—that is, to acknowledge that there is no better method of resolving disputes than by counting noses." [10]

What, then, constitutes better legislative performance at lawmaking? Each legislature engages in lawmaking in a somewhat different fashion depending upon the situation, circumstances, and personalities. The process is not the same from house to senate, day to day, or issue to issue. It is said that there are many ways to skin a cat; it can also be said that there are many ways to make a law. As Maryland delegate Nancy Kopp observed: "We get there . . . eventually." "Eventually" may require years, modification, arm-twisting, or practically anything. Just about every bill takes a somewhat different course. In all of this, negotiation is unlikely to be neglected. If proponents want to get a law enacted, they must concern themselves with obtaining the votes. Sometimes majorities are distributed solely according to how members interpret the merits. More often majorities require political work.

What sort of political work, however, is acceptable and what is not? Suppose the majority party puts together all the votes and does not have to negotiate with the minority? Is that acceptable, or should the minority always be brought on board? Suppose the minority refuses to participate? Suppose the two parties have different positions on a highly divisive issue? Is compromise called for or is stalemate an appropriate outcome?

Take a dispute over the state budget. Should each party give ground? At what point? When the Minnesota budget was in dispute in the 2001 session, the Republican speaker of the house, Steve Sviggum, had one view of how to settle:

> If one side or the other—the Democrats, the Republicans, the House, the Senate, or the governor—had totally receded from or caved in on their philosophy, we would have finished this session not only on time, but in March. We need more cooperation.[11]

Sviggum's own house majority leader had another response to the question of why the legislature did not get its work done earlier. "The answer," said Tim Pawlenty, "is we couldn't have gotten our goals if we would have finished this session in late May. We could not have gotten the tax package as big and bold as it is now."[12]

Participants disagree as to when or whether deals should be struck. When does compromise constitute a selling out of one's principles? It is impossible for an observer, such as myself, to judge. It would seem that one would have to allow considerable leeway for the political aspects of the lawmaking process to run their course. But just how far should partisanship be taken? We shall return to this question later.

It is easier to judge the study and deliberation that go into lawmaking. Although we could disagree on just how much study and deliberation should go into each issue, we would agree that too little would not be desirable. The principal means of study and deliberation are the standing committees of the legislature. Here is where measures are reviewed, shaped, and agreed on. Committees are the workhorses of the legislature and are key to most of the decisions that the legislature makes. Insofar as committees are weak, negligent, or bypassed in the lawmaking process, study and deliberation are likely to be shortchanged as well.

The lawmaking job of legislatures is easy to second-guess; everyone does it. But the process is so variable, depending on contingencies of all kinds. As long as there is disagreement among members, interest groups to deal with, another house to worry about, or a governor who wants a say, the process can go any which way. Proponents will zig while opponents will zag. Lawmaking is truly a collective endeavor, but it is one in which people are pulling in different directions.

Balancing

The job of balancing the power of the executive overlaps that of lawmaking.[13] Indeed, it is mainly in lawmaking that legislatures exercise their balancing function. As far as legislators themselves are concerned, as the Five-State Survey shows, among the three top jobs this is the one that is done least well. Balancing requires that the legislature share with the governor participation in setting the priorities and policies for the state.

As discussed in chapter 8, the governor has the upper hand here. The governor's ability to focus and communicate, which stems largely from the oneness of the office, cannot be matched by the legislature. Furthermore, if the two houses of the legislature are controlled by the same party as that of the governor, the latter's advantage is even greater. In a few places legislatures appear to hold the predominant position, largely because of the budgetary powers they exercise. In most places, however, legislatures have to assert themselves if they want to balance their governor. This happens usually when the governor is of the opposite party, but occasionally with a governor of the same party. However, the trend over past decades appears to have been toward stronger governors and weaker legislatures. Perhaps more than any other factor, term limits have shifted the balance further toward the executive in the fourteen states where they have already gone into effect. Formerly strong legislatures in Arkansas, California, Colorado, Florida, Maine, and Ohio have been weakened by the turnover of legislators and legislative leaders.[14]

Allowing for structural differences between the branches, the balance of power depends to some extent on arrangements that have been customary and to some extent on personalities and politics. Power shifts, but not quickly and not usually in the legislature's direction. Coequality requires the legislature to have almost the same unity or oneness as the governor; and with two houses and two parties this is difficult to achieve. What is necessary for the legislature to do its balancing job is a recognition that it ought to do it, a will to try to do it, the ability to actually accomplish it, and the persistence to see it through. That is a tall order for a legislature that has so many other things members want to get done.

Oversight

One of the legislature's jobs is overseeing the executive—reviewing and assessing how enacted policies are being implemented and how effectively they are working. It is not a task that appeals to many legislators, who prefer making law to figuring out whether past law they have made is working. Legislators are not accustomed to looking backward; they look ahead, albeit not much further than the end of the session or the next election.

In the 1970s and 1980s a number of legislatures undertook to develop structures for conducting oversight on a systematic basis. Some legislatures assigned the task to audit agencies, and particularly to performance auditing units. Minnesota's and Wisconsin's audit operations, for example, produced many useful audits and evaluations of state programs and state agencies. A few legislatures assigned the task to special commissions and their staffs. Most notable here is the Joint Audit and Review Commission (JLARC) of the Virginia legislature, which over the thirty years of its existence has probably been the most effective such operation in the states.

Despite the studies undertaken and the reports produced by audit and evaluation staffs, oversight still has involved relatively few legislators and has had relatively little impact on the legislative process or on how legislators go about their jobs. That is not to say that results have been lacking. Programs have been modified, funding has been redirected, and administrative and management practices have been altered. Yet systematic oversight is still not something to which legislators or legislatures give much attention. More commonly, the kind of oversight that gets done by legislatures is haphazard. It surfaces when constituents or interest groups complain that policies and programs are not working as they should. If an agency is administering a law too firmly or too laxly, if interest groups or legislators are unhappy with a program—that is when questions get asked.[15] Oversight also occurs during the course of budget hearings, when legislators inquire into an agency's operations and are not completely satisfied with the answers they get. Oversight does take place, but for the most part it is subsumed in the conventional processes of lawmaking and budgeting. It is not, by far, the legislature's strongest suit. And given the nature of the enterprise and the fact that it offers few incentives for the participation of members, it is not likely to become stronger in the near future.

Legislative Maintenance

Anyone elected, or even appointed, to high public office has a responsibility to the office he or she holds. Governors can be expected to work to preserve the health of their constitutional office, safeguarding its powers from encroachment by the legislature or other political institutions. Judges sitting on the highest state court concern themselves with the independence of the judiciary and its peculiar role as interpreter of the state's constitution and law. Those elected to serve in legislative office have a comparable responsibility to the legislature.

The genius of representative democracy in America lies mainly in its legislative bodies. Legislators themselves have to work at maintaining the well-being of these bodies as political institutions. Yet institutionally inclined legislators are in short supply today. Indeed, they have always been in short supply. Legislators have so many other, immediate, concrete matters to consider—their constituencies, their agendas, and their careers, among other things. Furthermore, in many states legislators are not in the capitol long enough to develop much of an institutional sense. Their sessions may be biennial rather than annual, or they may be relatively short. Or legislators may simply choose to spend the largest part of their energies on their districts and the bulk of their time back home.

Those who serve in legislatures with term limits have shorter time horizons. They know they will be leaving the senate or the house in six, eight, or twelve years. They have no option, unlike legislators in non-term-limited states, to spend twelve or more years in the senate or house, if they can get reelected. Term-limited members are passing through their legislatures on their way to other public office or back to private life. It makes little sense to make a commitment to an institution in which their membership will be relatively brief.

Time is always in short supply—more so in term-limited legislatures, but in the rest as well. And it takes time for institutional commitment on the parts of members to be seeded and grow. It probably takes having leadership responsibility as well. Rank-and-file legislators, whose focus is on their districts and personal agendas, usually have more of an individual perspective. Legislative leaders and committee chairs, whose focus is on building consensus and putting together the votes, can be expected to have more of a team perspective. It is the latter group, consisting of experienced members with leadership responsibility, who are more inclined to be appreciative of the legislature as an institution. They are the ones who recognize the need to maintain it and keep it as strong as possible. But even among legislative leaders, these institutionalists constitute a select breed.

Legislative Reform

Over years of observation and study, I have found that legislatures work well—by no means perfectly, but well. As indicated in this book, they do a noteworthy job representing constituents and constituencies and a less than noteworthy job balancing the power of the executive. They get their lawmaking done but are roundly criticized for just how they do it and for the results of what they do. Of course, there is always room for improvement. State by state, one can conceive of each legislature working better. Improvements can always be made and legislatures have the responsibility to make them.

Recommendations for legislative improvement, or "reform" as it is called, abound. Citizen groups and legislators themselves have proposed reforms for everything ranging from financial disclosure requirements for legislators to limits on bill introductions to the number and size of legislative bodies. Whether or not many of the proposed reforms actually have addressed institutional problems or focused on institutional ailments is another matter entirely. Before discussing the ailments that beset state legislatures today, let us look at some of the most prominent legislative reforms advanced in the past fifty years or so.

Increasing Legislative Capacity

Following the reapportionment revolution of the 1960s, a period of legislative reform lasted into the 1980s. Most of the reforms offered and adopted in states across the nation related to providing legislatures with the wherewithal to do the job.[16] Procedural and structural improvements were part of the mix. But emphasis was on legislative time, information, staff, and facilities. This reform movement was extremely successful for a number of reasons. Legislative leaders and legislative rank and file all agreed on the need. Citizen groups mobilized as part of the reform coalition, and implementation was relatively easy to accomplish. These reforms touched on most legislatures in the country, resulting in expanding professional staffing, making more information available, adding time during and between sessions, and creating new and restored facilities.

Improving Legislative Ethics

Through the entire period legislative ethics reforms have come in fits and starts. Proposals that would enhance the ethics of legislators are constantly promoted by reformist groups, but their adoption comes about largely in two related ways. First, they have been enacted after the indictment and conviction of legislators, often stemming from federally launched sting operations. Second, they have been enacted when nothing illegal has transpired but after a media campaign portrays legislator behavior and practice as scandalous.[17]

Adopted ethics reform has included more and more stringent financial disclosure requirements, waiting periods before former legislators can lobby, limitations on outside legislator employment, and bans or limits on the gifts legislators can accept from lobbyists or their employers. Some ethics laws probably did very little to raise the integrity of legislators or legislatures, but some did have a positive effect. It would appear that bans and/or restrictions on gifts have helped transform capital cultures in many places like Sacramento, Tallahassee, and Austin so that legislators and lobbyists no longer can cozy up to one another as in earlier days, when lobbyists were picking up the tab.[18]

The downside of these reforms is that, with less socializing taking place, legislators find it harder to communicate not only with interest groups but also with constituency groups. Nor do they develop the relationships with one another that they did in earlier years. It is more difficult for them to build trust. At a recent gathering in Sacramento, for instance, three former legislators bemoaned the cultural change that had taken place. Pete Wilson, who also served as governor, said that "These guys, like teetotalers, need to lighten up a bit." John Burton, a former senate pro tem, regretted the loss of the lobbyist-sponsored lunches that enabled lawmakers to get to know one another better. And Willie Brown, a former assembly speaker, lamented the loss of back-room wheeling and dealing.[19] None of them thought that the legislature worked as well as it did in the old days.

Greater Efficiency

One of the objectives that reformers prize highly is efficiency. In one of its reports the Brennan Center at New York University describes what an efficient legislature would look like:

> An efficient legislature produces legislation for the governor's signature without unnecessary delays, unduly high ratios of bills introduced to bills passed, or unnecessary barriers to final passage of a single bill by both chambers. The financial costs of the legislative process are no greater than necessary to accomplish the goals outlined already; staff and other legislative resources are directed where they are most effectively used. A well-functioning legislative process may not be cheap, but it need not be inefficient in its use of resources.[20]

This may be a worthy goal for a sausage factory, but not for a legislature.

Few people nowadays would maintain that legislatures are efficient organizations; they are anything but. The U.S. Congress was not designed by the framers of the Constitution to be efficient. Nor were state legislatures designed that way. But the longing for more efficient legislatures endures. In a number of states, legislative bodies appeared to reformers to be too large to be efficient. Therefore, the size of the Connecticut House was reduced—twice as a matter of fact—from 294 to 177 seats and then to 151. In Ohio and Vermont the houses were downsized by 38 and 96 seats, respectively. In Massachusetts the house was cut from 240 to 160. Several states made smaller reductions; more recently Rhode Island slimmed down to 75, from 100. Whatever gains were achieved in efficiency, a price had to be paid. With fewer legislators, the size of legislative districts grew. Moreover, the talent pool within the chambers diminished; smaller numbers of members meant fewer people were available for specialized committees and for party and committee leadership positions.

Getting rid of one house would be the ultimate in consolidation for the sake of greater efficiency. But while unicameralism has been proposed and considered in a number of states, it has not caught on. At the time of the Constitutional Convention, three of the thirteen colonial legislatures were unicameral. But by the time of the Civil War not a single state had a unicameral legislature. Then in 1934, Nebraska by popular initiative traded in its bicameral legislature for a unicameral one. Nebraska has been inviting other states to follow suit, but to date none have. All but Nebraska have resisted the arguments that one chamber is more efficient, lowers costs, and ends the bickering and deadlock that occur with two chambers.

Other reforms also have had as their objective the enhancement of legislative efficiency. The late 1960s and the 1970s brought many changes in standing committee systems in the name of efficiency. In about three-quarters of the states the number of committees and committee assignments for members were reduced. Each committee was given greater jurisdictional responsibility and each member had a better chance to focus his or her attention.

More Democracy

Legislatures are probably the United States' most democratic political institutions. Yet, according to critics, they are not democratic enough. Essentially two sets of proposals are aimed at further democratization of state legislatures. The first would give rank-and-file members more power and legislative leaders less. The second would give citizens more power and legislatures less.

The power of leaders relative to members has been on the decline since the 1960s. Prior to the legislative modernization movement, leaders had a monopoly on critical information and staff. As a result of modernization, however, staff and information were made available to everyone. If knowledge is power, its distribution became wider and flatter. Legislative leaders still control resources that members need, but their ability to discipline or deny members is limited. Even their allocation of campaign funds is challenged, by colleagues inside and critics outside. Not many authoritarian presiding officers are around anymore, and fewer and fewer states have leaders who have held the reins for over ten years, let alone twenty.

Voters have always had the power to choose who would represent them and lobby whomever they pleased to have their grievances redressed. Legislators do not often decide independently of their constituents, organized interests, and the public generally. On some questions, particularly those amending the state constitution or issuing bonds, the electorate is required by law or invited by the legislature to decide on its own.

Twenty-four states go further by providing processes—the initiative and referendum—whereby the electorate can vote on particular issues without a role (or only a limited role) being played by the legislature.[21] In fifteen states the initiative can be used to enact statutory law or amend the constitution. In six others it can be used only to enact statutes and in three others only to amend the constitution. The initiative is a mechanism that provides for maximum citizen participation in governmental decision making. Between 1898 and 1918 nineteen states adopted the initiative; the other five adopted it since 1959, with Mississippi being the last. A number of states have seriously considered the initiative more recently, but none have decided in its favor.

The initiative process allows citizens to draft laws or constitutional amendments, place them on the ballot, and have their fate decided by voters in an election. If a proposal goes directly to the ballot, as it does in most states, it is a direct initiative and the legislature has nothing to do with it. Maine, Massachusetts, Mississippi, Nevada, and Ohio, however, all have an indirect initiative process (and Utah and Washington have both direct and indirect initiative processes), whereby the legislature gets a crack at the proposal before it is put on the ballot for popular referendum. The states have varying requirements for proposals to qualify as initiatives, primarily in terms of the number of signatures that have to be collected and secondarily in the vote needed for adoption. The states also vary in how much the initiative process is used, with California, Oregon, North Dakota, Washington, Colorado, Arizona, and Montana being the principal users. In 2006, for instance, seventy-nine citizen initiatives were on the ballot (the third-highest number in one hundred years, with ninety-three in 1996 ranking highest). Lately, initiatives on subjects such as gay rights, tobacco, abortion, fiscal limits, insurance, and English as a state's official language have been fought out at the polls.

Proponents of the initiative, who advocate its adoption throughout the country, argue the following points.[22] First, the initiative is necessary when the legislature refuses to act. Indeed, simply as a threat, it can goad the legislature into action. Second, it expresses the popular will directly, without the distorting effects of the representational process. Third, it reduces citizens' alienation by enabling people to express themselves on issues. Fourth, it maximizes the potential of citizens as they personally engage in the democratic process. Fifth, it results in more informed citizens. Sixth, it reduces the abuse and corruption that are endemic to legislatures. And seventh, it lessens the power of interest groups that have an advantage in the legislature.

Despite such arguments, the initiative process has less than a stellar record. Many of the initiatives that are passed are declared unconstitutional by the courts. Signature drives have sometimes been misleading or deceptive. The drafting of the language in initiatives has often caused confusion. There is also the problem of voters comprehending just what a stated proposition entails. Furthermore, many initiative campaigns appeal to passions and prejudices, not reason.[23]

Even more fundamental, opponents of the initiative process argue, the initiative suffers by comparison with the legislative process itself. First, the electorate has available much less information on which to base a decision than do legislators. Second, voters are not able to consider how an initiative proposal affects other policies and programs, or how it might affect state revenues and appropriations.[24] Legislators, however, usually take into account how an initiative fits in with past policies and how it affects present ones, especially spending and revenues. Third, while the legislative process is a deliberative one, with members engaging in arguments as to the merits of a measure, the initiative is a one-way process, in which backers attempt to persuade voters in any way they can. Fourth, with the initiative, there is no compromise between proponents and opponents: one side wins, the other side loses. In the legislative process normally the two sides make adjustments in order to reach a settlement: neither side wins everything, neither side loses everything. Thus, both sides have at least some stake in what is enacted. And fifth, citizens are not accountable for how they vote and how the initiative works out in practice. Legislators, by contrast, are accountable for the votes they cast in the lawmaking process. If they back a measure that their constituents do not like, when they run for reelection they risk losing votes and perhaps their seats.

More direct democracy does not appear to be a promising solution for problems confronting legislatures. Indeed, the rise of direct democracy and the decline of representative democracy, as I have suggested elsewhere, is more of a problem than a solution.[25]

Term Limits

The initiative is primarily responsible for term limits, which are currently in effect in fifteen states. Term limits were the product of the initiative or threat of the initiative in twenty of the twenty-one states that at one point or another adopted this reform. Proponents had different justifications for limiting the terms of legislators, but they all seemed to touch in some way on the need for responsiveness and/or responsibility.[26] One argument by proponents was that legislators whose terms were limited would be less inclined to cave in to lobbyists and more likely to represent their constituents' interests. Another argument was that new legislative blood was necessary for new ideas and more responsible lawmaking. Whatever the argument made by organizations spearheading the movement, voters in practically every state where referendums were held supported term limits as a way of sending a message to political people and political institutions in whom they had lost confidence.[27]

The effects of term limits have been the subject of research by political scientists, including a dozen associated with the Joint Project on Term Limits spearheaded by the National Conference of State Legislatures (NCSL), the Council of State Governments (CSG), and the State Legislative Leaders Foundation (SLLF).[28] The results of this research show that the effects of term limits are somewhat mixed from state to state.[29] Term limits surely accomplished one objective of proponents: reducing legislator tenure and experience and cycling in more new members.

But term limits did not alter the composition of legislatures. The people who run and get elected are no different than their predecessors; most of them would like to spend careers in public service. Nor do they differ in their political backgrounds or demographics to any significant extent. Yet term limits had behavioral effects, ones that were not intended by proponents. New members in term-limited legislatures now approach their work with a special sense of urgency. The future is now, not years ahead. The idea of apprenticeship does not mean much in legislatures generally, and even less in term-limited bodies. Specialization in one policy domain or another does not appeal to members who are on their way out as soon as they arrive.

The most profound effects appear to be on organizational aspects of the legislature. Since few members have the advantage of experience or expertise, legislatures have been leveled out. Members are more equal than they might otherwise have been. Where legislators can run for the other body when their terms expire, house members tend to run for the senate more than vice versa. Thus, experience and expertise in senates outweigh those in houses, giving one chamber a personnel advantage over the other. The top leaders in term-limited legislatures also suffer a disadvantage. They have little time to train for their jobs or to learn while in their jobs. With power more dispersed, not only top leaders but committee chairs have less ability to steer the process. And, to some extent, the decision making normally done by standing committees has moved to the majority party caucus. At the same time, legislators are less likely to defer to committee recommendations.

Research findings on the influence of legislative staff and lobbyists as a result of term limits are inconclusive and/or inconsistent. It may be that the influence of nonpartisan staff has remained about the same or even been diminished as a consequence of term limits. However, the influence of partisan staff may have increased. The more rapid turnover of legislators requires lobbyists to devote greater efforts to establishing relationships and educating members. Close legislator-lobbyist relationships are much less likely. The job of lobbyists is tougher, but the influence of lobbyists tends to vary. For example, it seems to have increased in California and Colorado but not in Arizona, Arkansas, or Maine.

The most significant institutional impact of term limits has been on the balance of power between the executive and legislative branches of state government. The evidence is clear and consistent: as a result of term limits, the legislature has been losing ground to the governor and executive branch. This is nicely demonstrated in the budgeting process, where Thad Kousser finds that legislatures do worse in bargaining over budget items, controlling budget lines, and shaping policies. "Every state with term limits," he writes, "shows a substantial decline over the past decade in how much legislatures are able to alter the governor's requests." [30]

Term limits is a reform that has gone awry. Voters wanted to punish their legislature, and they did. They probably did not want to punish their own legislators so much as punish all the rest. They succeeded, but they had to throw their own babies out with the bath water. Proponents failed to accomplish most of their objectives,[31] but they did succeed in weakening the legislature as an institution while strengthening the executive in the process. This is not what they intended.

Remedying the Ailments That Exist

If nothing else, the experience of term limits suggests that reformers ought to think carefully about the likely, and the not-so-likely, consequences of institutional change. It is possible, of course, to make things better, but it is also possible to make them worse. So when it comes to engaging in "legislative reform" or "just tinkering," it would be wise to follow one of the tenets that bind physicians: "First do no harm." If nothing else, some of the legislative reforms noted above suggest that before reformers prescribe a remedy, they should be sure that it is designed to treat an ailment that in fact exists. Too often proposed reforms have little to do with actual problems.

The first question, therefore, is what are the major problems legislatures confront today? Not every legislature faces the same problems, but many have ailments in common. We ought to diagnose what they are before we can prescribe remedies to alleviate them.

The Effects of Partisanship

Legislators, among others, are distressed by the increase in partisanship and the consequent decline of civility in state legislatures since the 1990s. Both the U.S. Congress and state legislatures are accused of being too polarized, too rigid, and too partisan. Fifty years ago, the opposite seemed to be the case: informed opinion complained about too little partisanship. The two political parties were seen as not much different than Tweedledum and Tweedledee. The American Political Science Association (APSA) issued a report recommending change that would lead to a clearer ideological differentiation between the Democrats and Republicans. What the political scientists called for was indicated by the title of the APSA report, *Toward a More Responsible Two-Party System.*

A more responsible two-party system exists nationally and in most states today. The parties represent different bases with different views. As two political scientists write, "The tremendous personal, partisan, and ideological differences that polarize Democratic and Republican politicians are paralleled among the voters that make up the rival parties." The liberal wing of the Democratic Party is a substantial majority among voters who claim to be Democrats. The conservative wing of the Republican Party is a substantial majority among those who call themselves Republicans.[32] It is not just the party politicians who are polarized, it is the party people as well. Party agendas differ, so voters have a choice. The parties are competitive nationally and for statewide office as well in more than half of the legislative bodies across the country. So heightened partisanship is to be expected.

What has exacerbated the partisan condition is the increased role that legislative parties now play in elections. Earlier, campaigns for the legislature were run by candidates themselves, with an auxiliary role played by state, county, and local parties. Now, campaigns for targeted seats in the competitive districts are run by legislative parties and legislative party leaders. In the large states with professional legislatures the campaign never ends; indeed, it becomes fused with the governing process that is the business of the legislature. Both legislative parties position themselves for the approaching election; the majority party buttresses its incumbents who are threatened, while it tries to undermine the targeted members of the opposition party. Partisan combat now is a form of trench warfare, hand to hand. Is it any wonder then that legislatures are more contentious and relationships across party lines less civil than before?

In that they organize the political struggle and offer voters a real choice, parties and partisanship are a good thing. Incivility, however, is not. There is experimental evidence that uncivil discourse has negative effects on political trust and on support for political institutions.[33] But what can be done about incivility without negating the positive aspects of partisanship? There is also much to be said for the role of legislative parties in elections, even though the governing process is thereby affected. How can partisanship be kept within bounds, and be functional rather than dysfunctional? In Louisiana, for example, there has been an implicit agreement that legislative leaders and legislators themselves refrain from targeting incumbents of the other party. Will such an agreement be maintained? Will it help?

The Issue of Legislative Integrity

Although I believe that the overwhelming majority of lawmakers in the legislatures in the fifty states are people of integrity, whose motives are primarily to serve the public and whose ethical behavior is commendable, most citizens believe the opposite. Not much empirical evidence exists to bolster one belief or the other.

Legislatures are responsible for their members, but they do not select them. They have little, if any, control over who gets nominated and elected district by district. They have to accept whomever the voters send. Despite the legislature's inability to determine its composition, it still is accountable for the integrity of its members. Even if only a few of the nation's 7,382 legislators are ever convicted, indicted, or even accused, the effects are amplified by the media. As a consequence, the negative views of the public are reinforced. The maintenance of legislative integrity is a problem, as is the communication to the public of the positive state of legislative ethics.

The enactment of legislative ethics laws, which has been demanded by the media and also by the public, is the main way in which legislatures have responded. The results have been mixed. Clean election laws, gift bans, and other reforms have helped somewhat. But as long as state legislatures have "citizen" rather than "professional" status, members will have outside employment and the possibility of conflicting interests or the appearance of conflicts. And as long as legislators raise and spend money on campaigns, they will be subject to charges that they have sold the votes that they cast, the help that they give, and the access that they provide. What can the remedy possibly be here? More regulation? More law?

The Erosion of Study and Deliberation

Standing committees traditionally have been the workhorses of legislative bodies. It is in committee where much of the substantive study and deliberation take place. Standing committee systems in a number of legislatures were strengthened, thanks to the legislative modernization movement of the 1960s and 1970s. Work by standing committee during interim periods, between legislative sessions, increased. Still there were legislatures, like those in Illinois, New York, New Jersey, and Delaware, where committees were less central and their participation in study and deliberation left a lot to be desired.

With increasing partisanship and the expansion of partisan staffing in many senates and houses, partisan considerations have grown in importance while substantive considerations have declined. Standing committees have ceded some of their authority to majority party caucuses and top legislative leaders. Term limits have exacerbated such a trend, depriving committees of their experience and expertise and diminishing their standing in the chamber. Study and deliberation in term-limited states has declined, in part because of the weakening of their committee systems.

In more than a few states, there is a need for more conscientious study and deliberation. If it is not done in standing committees, where can it be done?

Diminished Responsibility

Legislatures have become more open, more democratic, more accountable, and more responsive. As legislators, members have multiple responsibilities—to their colleagues, their parties, their constituencies, their states, and their own agendas and political careers. Nevertheless, nowadays one can question just how responsible legislatures are as political institutions.

Just look at the financial hole that many states are in today, because legislatures were so responsive to demands and so reluctant to impose burdens. A number of states face serious structural deficits in their budgets, partly because of the heavy debt they have to pay. At the end of 2007, for instance, Gov. Arnold Schwarzenegger announced that California's budget deficit had grown to between $10 billion and $14 billion. Few doubted that the system needed fixing, but neither the governor nor the legislature seemed to have the will or ability to do the job.

New Jersey is another state in a budgetary hole. For instance, it is one of seven states where pension costs have increased as a result of early retirement packages. Sen. Shirley Turner, who in 2002 was a prime sponsor of an early retirement bill, admitted her mistake five years later. "We want to please people, we want to make them happy," she said. "But it has to be paid for. That's how we've mortgaged the future." [34] New Jersey's former governor, Brendan Byrne, pointed out the bind in which elected public officials find themselves. Nobody wants to allocate money to reduce the deficit. Spending programs—for education, transportation, and others—take precedence over retiring debt.[35] Gov. Jon Corzine's budget message in February 2008 recognized the enormous fiscal problems the state faced, and it proposed strong medicine as a remedy. Just how much of that medicine could be swallowed is the question.

Illustrative of the fiscal difficulties facing the states is the condition of their pension funds. According to the Pew Center on the States, almost half the states have been underfunding their retirement plans—by a total of $731 billion—for public workers. New York and California are about $50 billion behind. The further behind a state falls, the more money it has to come up with each year to catch up. The center's report cautions: "Large underfunded long-term liabilities put future budgets—and taxpayers—at risk." [36]

Responding to the needs of organized interest groups and even those of an inchoate public makes sense in a democratic political system, but it may ignore future costs of current action: Is it responsible for legislatures to provide benefits in the present, if it means shifting tax burdens to future generations? Yet democratic accountability and competitive elections encourage legislators to provide expanded public services with no additional taxes. This is responsiveness at the expense of responsibility.[37] As political scientist Morris Fiorina explains, specifically with regard to Congress: "Ironically, if our legislators were less vulnerable and less responsive, they might be more willing to make tough but nationally beneficial decisions. . . ." [38]

The disposition of elected politicians is to please. Not only do they want to please their electorates, they also want to please their colleagues. Pleasing the electorate entails giving people what they want, here and now and not later. It means not saying no to demands that have popular support and appeal. In state after state, one house will pass a popular bill figuring that the other house will kill it. Legislators can be on record as in favor of a bill and still be confident that it will not be enacted into law. Or both chambers will enact legislation about which most members have serious doubts (but against which they feel they cannot afford to vote), expecting that the governor will veto it. Although such behavior is disingenuous, it may not prove harmful as long as each chamber and branch behaves as expected. But what is expected does not always happen, and sometimes a measure that most lawmakers really oppose gets passed.

While such behavior may be tolerated, there are more serious examples of irresponsibility at the committee level. In most legislative bodies standing committees are expected to screen bills, separating the wheat from the chaff. Bills with little or no support are killed in committee or reported out with a recommendation that they do not pass. Increasingly, however, committees in a number of legislative bodies are refusing to kill bills, abdicating responsibility and passing decisions on to the caucus or entire chamber. Given the norm of reciprocity, which still exists in legislatures, members prefer not to vote against colleagues' bills lest their colleagues vote against their own bills. They would rather pass the buck than take the heat.

It is no simple matter to achieve a balance between responsiveness on the one hand and responsibility on the other. Nor should we expect legislators to ignore the norm of reciprocity and willy-nilly reject their colleagues' pet bills. Allowances have to be made for the give and take of politics. Nonetheless, legislatures ought to pay attention to a standard of responsibility.

The Erosive Effects of Public Cynicism

Our portrayal of public attitudes toward representative democracy and legislatures is a discouraging one—cynicism, cynicism, and more of the same. Legislatures cannot buy a break. Take the case of the New Jersey Legislature, which courageously took on the issue of property taxes in 2006–2007. The legislature went through an exemplary process of study and deliberation but could not put together the votes to beat public-employee unions on pensions and benefits. Still, the legislature enacted a program providing property tax rebates, capping local expenditure increases, and instituting several longer-range reforms. The media's interpretation of what happened was that the New Jersey Legislature caved in to the special interests and the inference was that what was achieved was not worth the effort. After the property tax legislation was signed into law, the Monmouth University/Gannett Poll reported that "caps and credits," in the view of the public, amounted to a whole lot of nothing. Of those polled, only 37 percent were satisfied and 49 percent were dissatisfied with what the legislature had done.[39] This was the public response after one of the New Jersey Legislature's finest hours.

Do the high level of cynicism and the low level of public support really matter? Not to the extent that the political system is in peril, writes John R. Hibbing (regarding the U.S. Congress), but there are negative consequences:

> Indications are that when Congress is unpopular, qualified individuals are dissuaded from running for reelection or from seeking election in the first place; members' willingness and ability to tackle unpopular but necessary issues are lessened; the appeal of simplistic institutional reformers . . . is enhanced; and citizens' tendency to comply with the action of the institutions is diminished.[40]

In short, the orientations of the public toward legislatures create a context in which legislatures work. If public orientations are negative, legislatures will not work as well as otherwise.[41]

There is no doubt whatsoever that legislators are keenly aware of the public climate in which they function. Indeed, many are demoralized by it, as public opinion consultant and strategist Frank Luntz found at NCSL's 2001 meeting, where he conducted an interactive session attended by about one thousand state legislators from around the country. He did an instant electronic poll of a sample of 250 of them, asking among other things what they liked *least* about being a legislator. He offered the following items from which they could choose: constant fund-raising, constant campaigns, lack of financial compensation, media scrutiny, partisanship, personal family sacrifice, lobbyists, and public cynicism. While all the items mentioned were considered burdensome, the sample of legislators ranked public cynicism most burdensome.

Legislators still like what they do, but a few drop out as a result of the distrust they encounter. For instance, during Walter Baker's tenure in the Kentucky General Assembly, some of his colleagues were convicted of corrupt practices in connection with an FBI sting known as Boptrot. The media vehemently assailed the entire legislature and called into question the integrity of every member, even though only a small number were guilty. Baker, an outstanding legislator and the fourth generation of his family to serve in the general assembly, announced his retirement soon afterwards. Baker's son could have chosen to run, but in view of the climate he was not willing to continue the family tradition of legislative service. Baker did not try to persuade his son to do otherwise.[42]

More numerous than those who drop out because of public distrust are those who never even get into politics because of the nasty climate. Years ago, anyone who ran for the state legislature had to be willing to sacrifice income, outside career, and family to undergo the strains of legislative life. Nowadays, legislators also risk their reputations. Whoever they are and however they behave, their lives are prime targets for the political opposition, the media, and law enforcement. Unless the fire is really burning in their bellies, they are likely to pursue career paths that are not so heavily mined. It is not possible to estimate just how many people are discouraged from running for the legislature because of today's atmosphere. However, Beth Rosenson has given it a try. Most ethics laws that have been enacted since the Watergate scandal are based on the distrust of people in public office.[43] Rosenson has analyzed legislative ethics laws, state by state, to determine whether the stringency of regulation is associated with candidacy for legislative office. She has found that the stringency of ethics laws deters some people from running. Financial disclosure laws reduced the number of candidates who ran for open seats in state legislative primaries as well as the number of business owners serving. Ethics laws limiting the practice of lawyer-legislators contributed to the decline of lawyers who were members of the legislature. "What is problematic," she writes, "is that ethics laws may be deterring highly qualified individuals from these occupations from serving." [44]

Not only are the politically disposed dissuaded from running, but the less politically disposed are further discouraged from participating. Rank-and-file citizens already have a wealth of reasons for not participating. Why should they even consider doing their civic duty, if public service does no good because the people and the system are untrustworthy and, indeed, corrupt?

Public cynicism has also had a direct negative impact through the imposition of term limits. We have already discussed how term limits have weakened state legislatures. Such institutional weakening has not only occurred in the term-limited legislatures, however, but in a number of others as well. Most legislatures are weaker political institutions today than they were in the 1970s and 1980s. One consequence is that the process of consensus-building is adversely affected, and reaching agreement becomes even more difficult than it normally is. It is much more difficult to satisfy people now than it used to be.

The result of all this is an erosion—albeit slow—of representative democracy, while two alternative means of governing are gradually gaining sway. One is *executive dominance,* whereby governors work their will and legislators act more or less as rubber stamps. The other is *direct democracy,* whereby the study, deliberation, and negotiation of representative assemblies are supplanted by public initiatives or referenda that vote major issues up or down after hard-fought issue campaigns.

Lack of Institutional Commitment

Last among the major ailments afflicting state legislatures is the lack of commitment by members to the legislature as an institution. In discussing one of the legislature's major functions—that of maintaining itself—we touched on why (especially but by no means only in term-limited states) legislators are not inclined to pay much attention to their institution. If they do not devote themselves to their institution's well-being, who can they expect to do the job for them? The public? The media? The profession of political science? Legislators might get help along the way, but the responsibility is primarily theirs—and it is not being adequately shouldered. One of the most important and most difficult challenges facing state legislatures is mobilizing members in support of their own institutions.

What Can Be Done to Improve Legislatures

Legislatures are a work in progress, so tinkering with one thing or another has to go on continuously—a change in the committee structure, a new staffing pattern, a revised code of ethics, tighter scheduling—all may matter in one place or the next. There are no quick fixes and certainly no permanent ones. I would suggest, however, that certain fundamental efforts have to be undertaken. The key would be what might be termed a "New Legislative Institutionalism." From the late 1960s through the early 1980s, we witnessed a strong wave of legislative institutionalism. Many members of the generation of legislators elected as a consequence of the reapportionment revolution were committed to improving the legislature as an institution. Legislative leaders were in the forefront of the modernization movement and were responsible for a capacity-building enterprise that legislatures had not previously witnessed. Although legislators went about their regular work, they also found time to pay attention to the institutional needs of their legislature.

Legislators are already committed to their constituents, their parties, their interest group allies, their policy causes, and other items on their agenda. Now they have to make an additional commitment—to the institutions in which they serve. How can such an institutional commitment be developed? It may evolve over time on the job itself. It may grow with increasing responsibility. But legislatures can no longer leave the development of institutional commitment to chance. They have to jump-start it, and continue to nurture it. This will require "indoctrination"—or, more tactfully, in-service education and training—much more than is currently offered.

For years legislatures have conducted training programs, mainly for new members.[45] The seriousness with which states approach training and the resources they commit to it range widely, but on the whole the training of new members ranks rather low among leadership priorities. Term limits brought a heightened sense of urgency to the states that were impacted, but even in these states training has varied from place to place and time to time. In only a few states—Georgia, North Carolina, and Alabama are principal examples—has legislator-training been delivered with gusto. Georgia probably surpasses any other state in the education and training of its members, which is done by the Carl Vinson Institute at the University of Georgia. It takes place biennially; lasts for several days; is held on the university campus in Athens; and is attended by all legislators, including legislative leaders. This highly successful endeavor has been supplemented by additional training for legislators who are being groomed for leadership positions. The case of Georgia demonstrates that education and training are not only possible, but can become a regular part of legislative service.

Giving legislators an institutional sense and institutional commitment requires even more than Georgia presently offers. Programs have to be especially designed to promote institutional appreciation and commitment. This will not be easy to accomplish, but it is possible if legislators learn more about the history, traditions, and functioning of the legislature and about its key role in American democracy. Such learning has to go on periodically and involve veterans as well as junior members. It has to take place in retreat settings, where legislators have informal time together—juniors with seniors, representatives with senators, and Democrats with Republicans. The purpose of such learning is to alert members to problems their legislatures face, problems such as those identified earlier: term limits, ethics, partisanship, the job of standing committees, and the tension between responsiveness and responsibility. Learning is no substitute for experience, but it can guide and channel experience and, most important, be integrated with experience.

How can commitment to the senate, house, or legislature be encouraged when division and conflict are at the core of the process? It will not be easy;

it will take leadership, imaginative planning, and superb teaching. Such education and training, moreover, should not depend on contributions from the private sector, but ought to be provided for in the legislative budget. The conduct of training could be contracted out—to a university within the state or to one of the national membership organizations of state legislatures. In each legislature a training officer would help plan, coordinate, and manage the endeavor. The support and involvement of legislative leaders would be requisite.

It might appear to be something of a conflict of interest—or, at the very least, a conflict of perceptions—for an educator like myself to recommend more education as the remedy for ailments that affect state legislatures. Nevertheless, the only way for legislators to develop more of an institutional sense would be by getting together and discussing matters related to legislative organization, procedures, and functioning. Dealing with term limits, the operations of standing committees, complying with ethics laws, and the matter of appearance—all of these subjects would be on the agenda. Such programs, moreover, would enable members to meet with one another informally, thus breaking down barriers and developing or reinforcing relationships.

In-service education on a continuing basis, which is done in a number of professions, is part of the answer to some of the ailments currently afflicting legislatures. Another part of the answer relates to the legislature's responsibility to help educate citizens on the legislature and representative democracy. The objective of such education would be to dispel some of the cynicism that exists and replace it with an appreciation of the legislature and legislative process. NCSL has taken a lead in civic education; legislatures in Massachusetts, Minnesota, Wyoming, Washington, and New Jersey, among other states, have undertaken programs aimed at the schools. Civic education is a long-haul, retail enterprise. Positive results will not be easy to achieve. Nevertheless, the state legislature has an obligation to inform people about its role. Otherwise, people have to rely on the media and on what they might have learned in school, neither of which is sufficient for appreciation or understanding. If legislators engage in serious and substantive outreach programs, aimed at adults as well as youngsters, they themselves will develop a stronger commitment to the institutions in which they serve.

With considerable effort, and over time, an alternative perspective will become available to citizens in the states.

In the meantime, the state legislature is doing its job, and doing it well—albeit not as well as we would like. The legislative engine chugs along, continuing to push the train up the hill. "I think I can, I think I can, I think I can," it puffs. And it can. We citizens ought to be cheering it on.

Notes

1. Paul J. Quirk and Sarah A. Binder, "Congress and American Democracy: Assessing Institutional Performance," in *The Legislative Branch*, ed. Paul J. Quirk and Sarah A. Binder (New York: Oxford University Press, 2005), 525–550.
2. Alan Rosenthal, *Heavy Lifting: The Job of the American Legislature* (Washington, D.C.: CQ Press, 2004), 8–11, 232–243.
3. Ibid., 233–234.
4. This section draws on ibid., 235–237.
5. See Susan Thomas, *How Women Legislate* (New York: Oxford University Press, 1994); Cindy Simon Rosenthal, *When Women Lead* (New York: Oxford University Press, 1998); and Susan Carroll, ed., *The Impact of Women in Public Office* (Bloomington: Indiana University Press, 2001).
6. Christopher Z. Mooney and Tim Storey, "The Illinois General Assembly, 1992–2003," Joint Project on Term Limits (unpublished paper, August 16, 2004).
7. Thomas L. Brunell, *Redistricting and Representation* (New York: Routledge, 2008), 29–49.
8. John W. Kingdon, *Congressmen's Voting Decisions* (New York: Harper and Row, 1973), 61. See also Brunell, *Redistricting and Representation*, 75–89.
9. This section draws on Rosenthal, *Heavy Lifting*, 237–241.
10. Richard A. Posner, *Law, Pragmatism, and Democracy* (Cambridge: Harvard University Press, 2001).
11. *Legal Ledger*, May 24, 2001.
12. *St. Paul Pioneer Press*, June 30, 2001.
13. This section draws on Rosenthal, *Heavy Lifting*, 241–243.
14. Richard J. Powell, "Executive-Legislative Relations," in *Institutional Change in American Politics: The Case of Term Limits*, ed. Karl T. Kurtz,

Bruce Cain, and Richard G. Niemi (Ann Arbor: University of Michigan Press, 2007), 148–164. The field research for the term limits study, which was completed in 2005, indicated that in Ohio the legislature had maintained its position vis-à-vis Gov. Bob Taft. This balance was attributable more to the peculiar weakness of Taft as a governor than to the institutional strength of the Ohio General Assembly. With Taft's successor, Ted Strickland, the balance has shifted more to the executive than to the term-limited legislature.

15. Mordecai Lee, "Political Administrative Relations in State Government: A Legislative Perspective," *International Journal of Public Administration* 29 (2006): 1024–1025.

16. See, for example, Citizens Conference on State Legislatures, *The Sometime Governments* (New York: Bantam, 1971).

17. See Beth A. Rosenson, *The Shadowlands of Conduct: Ethics and State Politics* (Washington, D.C.: Georgetown University Press, 2005).

18. See Alan Rosenthal, "The Effect of Legislative Ethics Law: An Institutional Perspective," in *Public Ethics and Governance: Standards and Practices in Comparative Perspective,* ed. Denis Saint-Martin and Fred Thompson (Oxford: Elsevier, 2006), 155–177.

19. *State Net Capitol Journal,* December 10, 2007.

20. Jeremy M. Creelen and Laura M. Moulton, *The New York State Legislative Process: An Evaluation and Blueprint for Reform* (New York: Brennan Center for Justice, New York University School of Law, 2004), 3.

21. See Alan Rosenthal, *The Decline of Representative Democracy* (Washington, D.C.: CQ Press, 1998), 32–35.

22. Thomas E. Cronin, *Direct Democracy: The Politics of Initiative, Referendum, and Recall* (Cambridge: Harvard University Press, 1989), 207–219.

23. Elizabeth Gerber, *The Populist Paradox* (Princeton: Princeton University Press, 1999), 100; and Todd Donovan and Shaun Bowler, "Responsive or Responsible Government," in *Citizens as Legislators: Direct Democracy in the United States,* ed. Shaun Bowler, Todd Donovan, and Caroline J. Tolbert (Columbus: Ohio State University Press, 1998), 249–273.

24. Donovan and Bowler, "Responsive or Responsible Government," 257–258.

25. Rosenthal, *The Decline of Representative Democracy,* 325–346.

26. Jennie Drage Bowser and Gary Moncrief, "Term Limits in State Legislatures," in *Institutional Change in American Politics: The Case of Term Lim-*

its, ed. Karl T. Kurtz, Bruce Cain, and Richard G. Niemi (Ann Arbor: University of Michigan Press, 2007), 16–17.

27. It should be noted that term limits were defeated on the ballot in Mississippi and North Dakota twice and in Idaho once. In Idaho this reform had been adopted as statute by popular initiative and then repealed by the legislature. It was put on the ballot again, but this time failed to pass. In a few states efforts have been made to modify term limits, but the voters have rejected such modifications. California voters rejected one modification several years ago. Most recently, in 2008, they rejected Proposition 93, which would have reduced the total time lawmakers could serve in the California Legislature from a total of fourteen to twelve years, but permitted them to serve those twelve years entirely in one chamber or divided between the two.

28. The results are published in Kurtz et al., *Institutional Change in American Politics;* and in *Legislating Without Experience: Case Studies in State Legislative Term Limits,* ed. Rick Farmer, Christopher Z. Mooney, Richard J. Powell, and John C. Green (Lanham, Md.: Lexington Books, 2007).

29. This section draws on Alan Rosenthal, "Living with Term Limits," in *Legislating Without Experience: Case Studies in State Legislative Term Limits,* ed. Rick Farmer, Christopher Z. Mooney, Richard J. Powell, and John C. Green (Lanham, Md.: Lexington Books, 2007), 207–223.

30. Thad Kousser, *Term Limits and the Dismantling of State Legislative Professionalism* (New York: Cambridge University Press, 2005), 25, 76, 339.

31. Bruce Cain, Karl T. Kurtz, and Richard G. Niemi, "Conclusion and Implications," in *Institutional Change in American Politics: The Case of Term Limits,* ed. Karl T. Kurtz, Bruce Cain, and Richard G. Niemi (Ann Arbor: University of Michigan Press, 2007), 186–189.

32. Earl Black and Merle Black, *Divided America* (New York: Simon and Schuster, 2007), 3.

33. Diana C. Mutz and Byron Reeves, "The New Videomalaise: Effects of Televised Incivility on Political Trust," *American Political Science Review* 99 (February 2005): 1–15.

34. *New York Times,* June 15, 2007.

35. "Summing up Corzine's Year," *Star-Ledger,* December 30, 2007.

36. *New York Times,* December 19, 2007; *State Net Capitol Journal,* December 24, 2007.

37. See Gary C. Jacobson, "Modern Campaigns and Representation," in *The Legislative Branch*, ed. Paul J. Quirk and Sarah A. Binder (New York: Oxford University Press, 2005), 115.

38. Morris P. Fiorina, *Divided Government* (New York: Macmillan, 1992), 55.

39. Monmouth University/Gannett Poll, February 18, 2007.

40. John R. Hibbing, "Images of Congress," in *The Legislative Branch*, ed. Paul J. Quirk and Sarah A. Binder (New York: Oxford University Press, 2005), 462.

41. Hibbing, "Images of Congress," 462.

42. See also Alan Rosenthal, Burdett A. Loomis, John R. Hibbing, and Karl T. Kurtz, *Republic on Trial: The Case for Representative Democracy* (Washington, D.C.: CQ Press, 2003), 5–6.

43. See Rosenson, *The Shadowlands of Conduct*.

44. B. A. Rosenson, "The Costs and Benefits of Ethics Laws," in *Public Ethics and Governance: Standards and Practices in Comparative Perspective*, ed. Denis Saint-Martin and Fred Thompson (Oxford: Elsevier, 2006), 143–144.

45. This section draws on Alan Rosenthal, "Education and Training of Legislators," in *Institutional Change in American Politics: The Case of Term Limits*, ed. Karl T. Kurtz, Bruce Cain, and Richard G. Niemi (Ann Arbor: University of Michigan Press, 2007), 165–184.

Selected Bibliography

American Society of Legislative Clerks and Secretaries. *Inside the Legislative Process.* Denver: National Conference of State Legislatures, October 2005.

Barber, James D. *The Lawmakers.* New Haven: Yale University Press, 1965.

Baumgartner, Frank R., and Beth L. Leech. "Interest Niches and Policy Bandwagons: Patterns of Interest Group Involvement in National Politics." *The Journal of Politics* 63 (November 2001): 1191–1213.

Beyle, Thad. "The Governors." In *Politics in the American States*, 8th ed., edited by Virginia Gray and Russell L. Hanson. Washington, D.C.: CQ Press, 2004.

———. "Governors: Elections, Campaign Costs, and Powers." In Council of State Governments, *Book of the States*, vol. 37. Lexington, Ky.: The Council, 2005.

Bishop, Bill. *The Big Sort: Why Clustering of Like-Minded America Is Tearing Us Apart.* New York: Houghton Mifflin, 2008.

Blanco, William T. *Trust: Representatives and Constituents.* Ann Arbor: University of Michigan Press, 1994.

Bowler, Shaun, Todd Donovan, and Caroline J. Tolbert, eds. *Citizens as Legislators: Direct Democracy in the United States.* Columbus: Ohio State University Press, 1998.

Bowser, Jennifer Drage, Keon S. Chi, and Thomas H. Little. *A Practical Guide to Term Limits: Final Report of the Joint Project on Term Limits.* Denver: National Conference of State Legislatures, July 2006.

Boyarsky, Bill. *Big Daddy: Jesse Unruh and the Art of Power Politics.* Berkeley: University of California Press, 2008.

Brown, Willie. *Basic Brown: My Life and Our Times.* New York: Simon and Schuster, 2008.

Brunell, Thomas L. *Redistricting and Representation.* New York: Routledge, 2008.

Bulger, William M. *While the Music Lasts: My Life in Politics.* Boston: Houghton Mifflin, 1996.

Cappella, Joseph N., and Kathleen Hall Jamieson. *Spiral of Cynicism: The Press and the Public Good.* New York: Oxford University Press, 1997.

Carey, John M., Richard G. Niemi, Lynda W. Powell, and Gary F. Moncrief. "The Effects of Term Limits on State Legislatures: A New Survey of the 50 States." *Legislative Studies Quarterly* 31 (February 2006): 105–134.

Chi, Keon S. *State Legislator Compensation: A Trend Analysis.* Lexington, Ky.: Council of State Governments, 2006.

Cigler, Allan J., and Burdett A. Loomis, eds. *Interest Group Politics,* 6th ed. Washington, D.C.: CQ Press, 2002.

Clucas, Richard A. "Improving the Harvest of State Legislative Research." *State Politics and Policy Quarterly* 3 (Winter 2003): 387–419.

_____. "Legislative Professionalism and Power of State House Leaders." *State Politics and Policy Quarterly* 7 (Spring 2007): 1–19.

Cooper, Joseph, ed. *Congress and the Decline of Public Trust.* Boulder: Westview Press, 1999.

Creelan, Jeremy M., and Laura M. Moulton. *The New York State Legislative Process: An Evaluation and Blueprint for Reform.* New York: Brennan Center for Justice, New York University School of Law, 2004.

Ehrenhalt, Alan. *The United States of Ambition: Politicians, Power, and the Pursuit of Office.* New York: Times Books, 1991.

Farmer, Rich, Christopher Z. Mooney, Richard J. Powell, and John C. Green. *Legislating Without Experience: Case Studies in State Legislative Term Limits.* Lanham, Md.: Lexington Books, 2007.

Fenno, Richard F., Jr. *Home Style: House Members in Their Districts.* Boston: Little, Brown, 1978.

Fiorina, Morris P. *Divided Government.* New York: Macmillan, 1992.

Francis, Wayne L. "Leadership, Party Caucuses, and Committees in U.S. State Legislatures." *Legislative Studies Quarterly* 10 (May 1985): 243–257.

Gerber, Elizabeth. *The Popular Paradox.* Princeton: Princeton University Press, 1999.

Goldstein, Kenneth M. *Interest Groups, Lobbying, and Participation in America.* New York: Cambridge University Press, 1999.

Gray, Virginia, and David Lowery. "Interest Representation in the States." In *American State and Local Politics: Directions for the 21st Century,* edited by Ronald E. Weber and Paul Brace. New York: Chatham House, 1999.

_____. *The Population Ecology of Interest Representation.* Ann Arbor: University of Michigan Press, 1996.

Hall, Richard D., and Frank W. Wayman. "Buying Time: Moneyed Interests and the Mobilization of Bias in Congressional Committees." *American Political Science Review* 84 (September 1990): 797–820.

Hall, Thad E. "Changes in Legislative Support for the Governor's Program over Time." *Legislative Studies Quarterly* 27 (February 2002): 107–122.

Hibbing, John R. "Images of Congress." In *The Legislative Branch*, edited by Paul J. Quirk and Sarah A. Binder. New York: Oxford University Press, 2005.

Hyatt, Richard. *Mr. Speaker: The Biography of Tom Murphy*. Macon, Ga.: Mercer University Press, 1999.

Jewell, Malcolm E., and Marcia l. Whicker. *Legislative Leadership in the American States*. Ann Arbor: University of Michigan Press, 1994.

Keyserling, Harriet. *Against the Tide*. Columbia: University of South Carolina Press, 1998.

Kingdon, John W. *Agendas, Alternatives, and Public Policies*, 2nd ed. New York: Longman, 2003.

Kousser, Thad. *Term Limits and the Dismantling of State Legislative Professionalism*. Cambridge: Cambridge University Press, 2005.

Kurtz, Karl T., Bruce Cain, and Richard G. Niemi. *Institutional Change in American Politics: The Case of Term Limits*. Ann Arbor: University of Michigan Press, 2007.

Kurtz, Karl T., Gary Moncrief, Richard G. Niemi, and Lynda W. Powell. "Full-Time, Part-Time, and Real Time: Explaining State Legislators' Perceptions of Time on the Job." *State Politics and Policy Quarterly* 6 (Fall 2006): 322–338.

Lascher, Edward L., Jr. "Assessing Legislative Deliberation: A Preface to Empirical Analysis." *Legislative Studies Quarterly* 21 (November 1996): 501–519.

_____. *The Politics of Automobile Insurance Reform*. Washington, D.C.: Georgetown University Press, 1999.

Lee, Mordecai. "Political-Administrative Relations in State Government: A Legislative Perspective." *International Journal of Public Administration* 29 (2006): 1021–1047.

Loftus, Tom. *The Art of Legislative Politics*. Washington, D.C.: CQ Press, 1994.

McDonald, Michael P. "A Comparative Analysis of Redistricting Institutions in the United States, 2001–02." *State Politics and Policy Quarterly* 4 (Winter 2004): 371–395.

McDonough, John E. *Experiencing Politics: A Legislator's Stories of Government and Health Care*. Berkeley: University of California Press, 2000.

Macedo, Stephen. *Deliberative Politics*. New York: Oxford University Press, 1999.

Mathews, Joe. *The People's Machine: Arnold Schwarzenegger and the Rise of Blockbuster Democracy*. New York: Public Affairs, 2006.

McFarland, Andrew. *Neopluralism: The Evolution of Political Process Theory*. Lawrence: University Press of Kansas, 2004.

Moncrief, Gary F., Richard G. Niemi, and Lynda W. Powell. "Time, Term Limits, and Turnover: Trends in Membership Stability in U.S. State Legislatures." *Legislative Studies Quarterly* 29 (August 2004): 357–381.

Moncrief, Gary F., Peverill Squire, and Malcolm E. Jewell. *Who Runs for the Legislature?* Upper Saddle River, N.J.: Prentice Hall, 2001.

Muir, William K., Jr. *Legislature: California's School for Politics.* Chicago: University of Chicago Press, 1982.

Patterson, Thomas E. *Out of Order.* New York: Vintage Books, 1994.

Pensoneau, Taylor. *Powerhouse: Arrington from Illinois.* Baltimore: American Literary Press, 2006.

Pitkin, Hannah F. *The Concept of Representation.* Berkeley: University of California Press, 1967.

Posner, Richard A. *Law, Pragmatism, and Democracy.* Cambridge: Harvard University Press, 2003.

Preston, Noel, and Charles Sampford, eds. *Ethics and Political Practice: Perspectives on Legislative Ethics.* London: Routledge, 1998.

Quirk, Paul J., and Sarah A. Binder, eds. *The Legislative Branch.* New York: Oxford University Press, 2005.

Reeher, Grant. *First Person Political.* New York: New York University Press, 2006.

Richardson, James. *Willie Brown.* Berkeley: University of California Press, 1996.

Rogers, James R. "The Impact of Bicameralism on Legislative Production." *Legislative Studies Quarterly* 28 (November 2003): 509–528.

Rosenson, Beth A. "The Costs and Benefits of Ethics Laws." In *Public Ethics and Governance: Standards and Practices in Comparative Perspective*, edited by Denis Saint-Martin and Fred Thompson. Oxford, UK: Elsevier, 2006.

_____. *The Shadowlands of Conduct: Ethics and State Politics.* Washington, D.C.: Georgetown University Press, 2005.

Rosenthal, Alan. "Appearance as an Ethical Standard: Its Consequences for U.S. State Legislators." In *Ethics and Political Practice: Perspectives on Legislative Ethics*, edited by Noel Preston and Charles Sampford. London: Routledge, 1998.

_____. *The Decline of Representative Democracy.* Washington, D.C.: CQ Press, 1998.

_____. *Heavy Lifting: The Job of the American Legislature.* Washington, D.C.: CQ Press, 2004.

Saint-Martin, Denis, and Fred Thompson, eds. *Public Ethics and Governance: Standards and Practices in Comparative Perspective.* Oxford, UK: Elsevier, 2006.

Schattschneider, E. E. *The Semi-Sovereign People.* New York: Holt, Rinehart and Winston, 1960.

Schlesinger, Joseph A. *Ambition and Politics: Political Careers in the United States.* Chicago: University of Chicago Press, 1966.

Smallwood, Frank. *Free and Independent.* Brattleboro, Vt.: Stephen Greene, 1978.

Smith, Michael A. *Bringing Representation Home: State Legislators among Their Constituencies.* Columbia: University of Missouri Press, 2003.

Squire, Peverill. "Measuring State Legislative Professionalism." *State Politics and Policy Quarterly* 7 (Summer 2007): 211–227.

Squire, Peverill, and Keith E. Hamm. *101 Chambers: Congress, State Legislatures, and the Future of Legislative Studies.* Columbus: Ohio State University Press, 2005.

Straayer, John A. *The Colorado General Assembly,* 2nd ed. Boulder: University Press of Colorado, 2000.

Thompson, Dennis F. "Paradoxes of Government Ethics." *Public Administration Review* 52 (May–June 1992): 254–259.

Van Assendelft, Laura A. *Governors, Agenda Setting, and Divided Government.* Lanham, Md.: University Press of America, 1997.

Van Horn, Carl E., ed. *The State of the States,* 4th ed. Washington, D.C.: CQ Press, 2006.

Weber, Ronald E. "State Legislative Redistricting in 2003–2004." In Council of State Governments, *Book of the States,* vol. 37 (Lexington, Ky.: The Council, 2005): 116–124.

Weber, Ronald E., and Paul Brace. *American State and Local Politics: Directions for the 21st Century,* New York: Chatham House, 1999.

Whitney, Gleaves. *John Engler: The Man, the Leader, and the Legacy.* Chelsea, Mich.: Sleeping Bear Press, 2002.

Wright, Gerald C., and Brian F. Schaffner. "The Influence of Party: Evidence from the State Legislatures." *American Political Science Reader* 96 (June 2002): 367–379.

Wright, Ralph. *Inside the Statehouse.* Washington, D.C.: CQ Press, 2005.

Index

Figures, tables, and notes are indicated by f, t, and n following page numbers.

budget deficit in, 431
committees in, 205, 208
constituency service in, 83
Democrats in, 281, 282
districts in, 74, 76, 77, 111
ethics issues in, 210, 211, 224n38
family life adjustments of legislators in, 56
full-times legislators in, 47
fund-raising in, 230
health care issues in, 399–400
Hispanic legislators in, 35
interest groups in, 148, 151
legislative compensation in, 54
legislative reform in, 184
legislative staffing in, 187, 188
opinion of legislature in, 18
professional legislature in, 190
public relations campaigns in, 164
redistricting in, 136–137
term limits in, 258, 299, 441n27
unicameralism in, 196, 279
U.S. House seats in, 130
California Teachers Association (CTA), 165
Campaign funding and contributions. *See also*
    Money and financial matters
caucuses and, 122–123, 124–125
corporations and businesses, 166, 168
grassroots organizations and, 163
incumbents and, 112–113
interest groups and, 148–149, 156, 176,
    181n60, 215, 369, 377, 380
lawmaking process and, 166–170
leadership responsibilities and, 229–231
media views of, 24
parties as governing bodies, 122–126
Campaign managers, legislators as, 229–232, 256
Campbell, Carroll, 273, 278
Cancimilla, Joe, 297
Capacity building, 189–190, 250, 288, 420, 436
Capital punishment issue, 97, 100, 373, 375–376,
    389
Cappella, Joseph N., 25
Carl Vinson Institute (University of Georgia), 437
Carnegie Corporation, 2
Caucuses
campaign funding and, 122–123, 124–125
committees and, 204, 205, 209, 257, 414
consensus-building in, 242–243
governors and, 279, 298
ideology and, 228
leadership roles and, 227, 228, 260
legislative responsibility and, 432
as legislative structure, 202
liberal, 228, 257
negotiations and, 243, 244
punishment of legislators and, 255
vote getting and, 245, 246

CCSL (Citizens Conference on State
    Legislatures), 185
Celebrity status, 45
Cemeteries and crematoriums, 143
Census figures, 129–130, 312. *See also* Demo-
    graphics; Populations
Center on Congress (Indiana University), 14
Checks and balances, 265, 275
Chi, Kean S., 68n14
Chief legislators, governors as, 275–288, 316
Christmas tree items. *See* Pork (political
    spending)
Cigarettes. *See* Tobacco issues
Cigler, Allan J.
on importance of information, 158
on interest groups, 140, 142, 170–171, 179n2
on politics, 122, 156
Citizen groups. *See* Interest groups
Citizen initiatives. *See* Ballot initiatives
Citizen legislators, 49, 76, 190–191, 352, 430
Citizens Conference on State Legislatures
    (CCSL), 185
Civic education. *See* Education issues; Training
    programs
Civility, 64, 110, 129, 428, 429
Civil rights issues, 32, 99, 168
Clarenbach, David, 36
Clucas, Richard A., 251
Coalitions
health care issues and, 329
interest groups and, 168, 175, 369, 372
leadership roles and, 227, 260
lobbyists and, 159
reform of, 420
Codey, Richard, 103, 284
Coherence in legislative process, 348
Coleman, Bonnie Watson, 37
Collier's Magazine on Samish, 151
Colorado
bills in, 339
budgets in, 270
committees in, 208
constituency service in, 84
districts in, 77
Hispanic legislators in, 35
length of legislative sessions in, 48
term limits in, 194
Committees
agencies and, 208, 343, 345
appointments to, 232–234
bills and, 202, 205–208, 331, 343, 345
budgets and, 343–344
caucuses and, 204, 205, 209, 257, 414
conference, 343–344, 345, 403
ethics issues and, 216–217
house vs. senate and, 361
leadership and, 228, 257

medical malpractice and, 328–329
Romney and, 244, 322–323, 359, 397
Mathews, Joe, 165, 279, 295
Mayhew, David R., 324
McCally, Sarah, 174–175
McCarthy, Leo, 58, 122
McCarty, J. D., 249
McDonough, John E.
on campaign funding, 112
on conscience-constituency clash, 97, 99,
100–101, 103–104
constituency and, 77–78, 83, 89, 91–92
on corruption, 213
on disagreement in lawmaking process, 362
on fund-raising, 169
health care issues and, 322
job departure of, 64
on legislative power, 253
memoirs of, 6
on party leadership, 257
as policy entrepreneur, 61
political heritage of, 36–37
public support of, 18
on vote getting, 245, 247, 402
McGreevey, James, 284–285
McInnes, Gordon, 59
McWherter, Ned, 266, 286, 293
Media. *See also* Public relations
agenda setting of, 326
blogs, 9
Boptrot, 434
campaign funding and, 24
constituent education and, 80
ethics issues and, 209–210, 213, 215, 216,
220–221, 420
executive-legislative balance and, 300
governors and, 277–278
health care issues, 164, 371
interest groups and, 163–164, 178, 371
legislative integrity and, 429–430
legislatures, 22–25, 363
political views and, 9
private lives of legislators and, 57
protecting institution of legislature and, 248
public attention and, 334
Medicaid and Medicare, 144, 145, 354, 362,
368, 398. *See also* Health care and
pharmaceuticals
Merchants and merchandise. *See* Retail industry
Merits, consideration of
bargaining and, 391
bills and, 351–354
in committees, 205
deliberation and, 413
interest groups and, 146–147, 152, 158, 172,
173, 369
legislative decision-making and, 373–382
majorities and, 386–388

Metaphors for legislature, 346–350
Methamphetamines, 369, 404n1
Miami Herald on restaurant hygiene law, 325
Michigan
base salaries in, 52
full-time legislators in, 47
fund-raising in, 124
legislative staffing in, 188
professional legislatures in, 190
Miller, Mike, 242
Miller, Zell, 197, 266
Minimum wage legislation, 271, 282, 316, 354,
355, 396
Minnesota
constituents in, 81–82, 84, 92
controversy in legislative issues in, 337
ethics issues in, 211, 218
family life adjustments of legislators in, 56
hours per week on job in, 49
interest groups in, 156
legislative staffing in, 188
legislature size in, 74
length of residency of legislators in, 44
local project spending in, 87
prior experience of legislators in, 45
recruiting of candidates in, 231
redistricting in, 132
state aid in, 85, 86
trustee vs. delegate role of legislators in, 94
veto power in, 275
Minority parties. *See also* Majority parties;
Political parties
committees and, 233, 414
complaints about legislative process, 22
control of legislature and, 21, 127, 128
Democrats in, 22
division of labor in legislatures and, 200
leadership in, 225–226, 232
local funding and, 402
partisan conflict and, 357
Mississippi
base salaries in, 52
budget in, 270
length of legislative sessions in, 48
Modernization, legislative, 184–185, 190, 249,
288, 423, 436
Moe, Roger, 88, 241, 242
Moncrief, Gary, 193
Money and financial matters, 24, 166–170. *See
also* Campaign funding and contributions
Monmouth University/Gannett Poll on New
Jersey legislature, 433
Montana
base salaries in, 52
biennial legislative sessions in, 47
citizen legislators in, 49
Mooney, Christopher Z., 69n14
Moore, Richard, 321, 330, 332, 365

divided parties in, 116
family life adjustments of legislators in, 56
legislative compensation in, 54
legislative staffing in, 187, 188
member items in, 86–87
opinion of legislature in, 16, 18
outside work of legislators in, 54
pork-barrel spending in, 88
power distribution in, 251
prior experience of legislators in, 45
professional legislatures in, 190
recruitment by local and state party
    leaders, 38
veto power in, 273–275
New York State Bankers Association v. Wetzler
    (1993), 269
New York Times
on ethics, 214
investigative reporting by, 24
on lobbyists, 150
on New York Legislature, 299
on party differences, 119
on pork-barrel spending, 88
on Spitzer, 287
Niemi, Richard G., 69*n*14, 72
Nixon, Richard, 210
NJRMA (New Jersey Retail Merchants Associa-
    tion), 171–172
No Child Left Behind Act of 2002, 311
Nonpartisanship. *See* Partisanship
North Carolina
constituency service in, 84
veto power in, 302*n*17
North Dakota
base salaries in, 52
biennial legislative sessions in, 47
citizen legislators in, 49
legislative staffing in, 187
opinion of legislature in, 16
personal and congratulatory resolutions in,
    106*n*12
professional legislatures in, 190
senate and house overlap in, 74
Nownes, Anthony J., 168
NRA (National Rifle Association), 311
Nuñez, Fabian, 297, 400

Obama, Barack, 345
Obesity legislation. *See* Food industry
Occupational adjustments, 54–56
Ohio
base salaries in, 52
committees in, 209
constituents in, 78–79, 81, 83–84, 92–93, 96
controversy over legislative issues in, 338
executive-legislative power in, 289
full-time legislators in, 47
fund-raising in, 230

hours per week on job in, 49
legislative reform in, 185
length of residency of legislators in, 44
opinion of legislature in, 18
prior experience of legislators in, 45
recruiting of candidates in, 231
redistricting in, 136–137
size of districts in, 74
state aid in, 85
term limits in, 440*n*14
trustee vs. delegate role of legislators in, 94
Ohio Packing Company, 346–347, 348, 349
Oklahoma, term limits in, 191–192
O'Leary, Robert, 328
Olympian on Washington (state) legislature, 404
O'Malley, Martin, 293
Ombudsmen, 59–60
Omnibus legislation, 198, 307, 309, 361
Optometrists and ophthalmologists, 144, 373,
    378–380. *See also* Health care and pharma-
    ceuticals
Oregon
biennial legislative sessions in, 47
committees in, 207
Organizations
interest groups as, 120–121, 152
legislators as managers of, 234–235
structure of legislatures, 183, 195–209
Oversight, legislative, 204, 306, 408, 417–418

PACs. *See* Political action committees
Panagiotakos, Steven, 329, 331
Partial Birth Abortion Ban Act of 2003, 320
Parties. *See* Democrats and Democratic Party;
    Political parties; Republicans and Republi-
    can Party
Partisanship
committees and, 204, 209, 430
efficacy of legislatures and, 428–429
gubernatorial elections and, 137*n*9
houses and senates, 360
increase in, 119
institutional rivalries and, 281
legislative campaigns and, 110
political parties and, 114, 117, 120, 128–129,
    226, 357–358, 367*n*10
public differences and, 13
redistricting and, 133–134, 135–136
staffing and, 126–127, 187–189, 188*f*, 232
underrepresentation of minorities, 411–412
unicameralism and, 196
The Party's Over (Broder), 11
Pataki, George, 88, 269, 273, 274, 286, 294–295
Paterson, David, 215–216
Patrick, Deval, 275, 292
Patterson, Thomas E., 23, 25
Pawlenty, Tim, 275, 415
Payzant, Thomas, 353

Pennsylvania
  base salaries in, 52, 53
  budget in, 300
  districts in, 76
  full-time legislators in, 47
  legislative pay raises in, 105
  legislative staffing in, 188
  opinion of legislature in, 18
  professional legislatures in, 190
Pensions. *See* Retirement and pension issues
Pensoneau, Taylor, 6, 68*n*2
Perdue, Sonny, 282
Performance and performance ratings, 16, 17*t*,
    18, 194–195, 407–419
Personal lives of legislators, 4, 30–71
  adapting to legislative life, 46–62
  ambition and, 37–39
  balance and, 66–67
  doing good and doing well, 41–42
  family life adjustments and, 56–57
  financial adjustments and, 50–54, 53*t*, 65
  job departures, 62–66
  motivation to run for office, 31–42
  occupational adjustment and, 54–56
  opportunities and resources, 42–46
  other adjustments, 57–62
  power and, 31–34
  public service and, 40–41
  sociology and, 34–37
  time requirements, 47–50, 48*t*, 51*t*–52*t*
Personnel directors, legislators as, 232–234
Pew Center on the States, 431
Pew Research Center for the People and the Press,
    119
Pharmaceutical Research and Manufacturing
    Association (PhRMA), 144, 372
Pharmaceuticals. *See* Health care and
    pharmaceuticals
Pitkin, Hanna F., 91, 93, 96
Pogemiller, Lawrence, 86, 257
Policy. *See also* Lawmaking
  commitments of legislators, 327–328
  domains in, 334, 360
  governors and, 270–272
  interest groups and, 152–153
  lawmaking and, 338–339
  legislators as entrepreneurs, 61
  parties promoting, 116, 118–120
  policy champions, 330
  reform, 40
  representative democracy and, 408
  underrepresented groups and, 410
Politeness. *See* Civility
Political action committees (PACs)
  campaign contributions and, 169
  fund-raising and, 123, 124, 156
  interest groups and, 166, 167–168
  in Maine, 231

Political experience, 19, 27
Political families. *See* Political heritage
Political heritage, 18–19, 36–37
Political parties. *See also* Democrats and Democ-
    ratic Party; Elections; Majority parties;
    Minority parties; Republicans and Republi-
    can Party
  change in, 43, 68*n*31
  elections and, 114–116, 115*t*
  as governing bodies, 116, 121–129
  governors and, 281–284
  gubernatorial leadership of, 281–284
  as identity groups, 116–118, 118*t*
  ideologies and, 117, 118
  interest groups and, 149, 176, 182*n*61
  legislative decision-making and, 373–382
  liberals and conservatives in, 117, 118, 324, 428
  as organizations, 116, 120–121, 122
  as policy promoters, 116, 118–120
  redistricting and, 133–136
  representative democracy and, 11–12
Politicos, 60, 94
Populations, 130, 132, 134–135, 139*n*31. *See also*
    Census figures; Demographics
Pork (political spending), 86–87, 88, 107*n*17,
    402–403. *See also* Earmarks
Posner, Richard A., 102, 414
Powell, Lynda W., 72
Powell, Richard J., 69*n*14
Power
  Brown (Willie) and, 32, 248, 258
  efficacy of legislatures and, 416–417
  of governors, 276–281, 288–301
  of interest groups, 170–178
  leadership and, 248–260, 252*t*–253*t*
  lobbyists and, 174
  of local government in Wisconsin, 317–318
  of political parties, 12
  running for office and, 31–34
  term limits and, 426, 427
Powerhouse: Arrington from Illinois (Pensoneau),
    68*n*2
Presidents (senate)
  bill passage and, 345
  in *factotum* role, 237
  majority party and, 22, 121–122
  protecting institution of legislature, 248
  speaker role of, 277
  vote getting and, 245
Press. *See* Media
Preston, Ron, 322–323
Professionalism, 183–195, 195*t*. *See also* Ethics
Public interest, 13, 152, 170, 318. *See also* Interest
    groups
Public opinion, 26–27, 278
Public relations, 163–164, 277–278, 371. *See also*
    Media
Public service, 40–41

Pulitzer Prizes, 24
Punishment of legislators, 254–255, 256, 423, 427

Quinn, John, 388
Quirk, Paul J., 389, 408

Rankings. *See* Performance and performance
    ratings
Readings of bills. *See* Bills
Reagan, Ronald, 45
Real-estate industry, 143, 145, 149, 369, 404*n*1
Real ID Act of 2005, 311
Recruitment of candidates, 38–39, 116, 126, 155,
    231
Redistricting, 111, 129–137, 287–288, 291,
    312–313. *See also* Districts
Red states. *See* Republicans and Republican Party
Reeher, Grant
    on incumbent safety, 112
    on job departures, 63
    on job satisfaction, 66
    on legislative workload, 57–58
    on media, 25
    on occupational adjustments, 54, 55
    on political candidacy, 36
    on prior political experience, 45
    on public service, 40
    on recruitment of candidates, 38
Reelections, 41–42, 66, 102, 103–105, 229
Reference (bill process), 342–346
Referendums, 14, 191, 268, 423–424, 425–426
Referrals, 236, 255
Reform, legislative, 184–185, 419–428
Reinstein, Kathi-Ann, 384
Religion of candidates, 34–35
Rell, Jodi, 20, 297
Rendell, Ed, 282, 300
Representational role of legislatures, 73, 306, 320,
    409–413, 419
Representative democracy. *See also* Democracy
    cynicism and, 8, 433
    diversity and, 413
    education of constituents in, 80
    efficiency of system in, 6, 404
    erosion of, 435
    legislative maintenance and, 418
    NCSL and, 7
    practices of, 8–14, 10*f*
    public policy and, 408
Republicans and Republican Party. *See also* Con-
    servatives; Political parties
    American voting patterns and, 11
    constituencies and, 117, 118*t*
    elections and, 114, 115–116
    interest groups and, 382
    liberals and, 401
    lobbying of, 160
    minority parties and, 22

numbers of, 116
partisanship and, 357–358, 367*n*10, 412, 428
polarization of, 119
representation by, 140
in South, 114, 127
Republic on Trial (Rosenthal), 7
Reputations
    committees and, 206
    credibility and, 44–45
    cynicism and, 434
    financial status of legislators and, 50
    lobbyists and, 174
Residency requirements, 44
Responsibilities of legislatures, 431–433
Retail industry, 171–173, 355
Retirement and pension issues, 385, 431
Reynolds v. Sims (1964), 130
Rhode Island
    family life adjustments of legislators in, 57
    legislative reform in, 185
Richardson, Bill, 297
Richardson, James, 6, 30, 67*n*1, 242
Riffe, Vern, 230, 231, 255
Riley, Richard, 292
Risser, Fred, 36, 62–63, 66
Rivers, Cheryl, 85
Roberti, David, 230
Roberts, Joseph, 284, 300, 326–327, 413
Roe v. Wade (1973), 320
Role models, legislators as, 238–240
Roll-call voting, 170
Romney, Mitt
    on consensus, 398
    education issues and, 164, 383
    executive-legislative balance and, 358–359
    health care issues and, 244, 316, 322–323,
        359, 397
    legislature and, 292
    partisan conflict and, 357
    power sharing and, 270–271
    statutory objectives of, 316
    tax issues and, 355
    veto power and, 273, 275
Rosenberg, Sandy, 61, 245, 321, 385, 394, 400–401
Rosenson, Beth A., 210, 434–435
Rosenthal, Alan, 70*n*34
Ruane, Michael, 385
Rubio, Marco, 255

Salaries, 52, 185, 189, 196, 217. *See also* Income;
    Legislative compensation
Salience of issues, 334, 371, 389, 412
Salter, Joe, 291
Samish, Artie, 150–151
Sanchez, Raymond, 258
San Diego Tribune, investigative reporting by, 24
Sarbanes, Paul, 65–66
Sausage making metaphor, 346–350, 421

Sviggum, Steve, 125, 231, 260, 415
Swing voters, 128

Taffett, Gary, 285
Taft, Bob, 284, 289, 440n14
Takeda (pharmaceutical company), 144
Taxes
    constituency views on, 97, 98, 100, 103
    ethics issues and, 219
    interest groups and, 142, 177
    legislative responsibility and, 432
    payroll fees, 398
    public spending and, 366
    Romney and, 355
    sales tax, 373–375
    on tobacco/cigarettes, 310, 373, 376–378
Taylor, Cas, 85–86, 87, 104, 258
Teachers. *See* Education issues
Tennessee, constituency service in, 84
Term limits
    advocacy and, 330
    balance of power and, 417
    ballot initiatives and, 280
    Brown (Willie) and, 63, 258
    Bulger and, 238
    committees and, 208–209, 430
    cynicism and, 435
    demographics and, 35
    efficacy of legislatures and, 425–427
    executive-legislative balance and, 289
    fund-raising and, 230
    governors and, 291
    houses and senates, 360
    job departures and, 63
    leadership and, 227–228, 258–260
    legislative maintenance and, 419
    legislative terrain and, 183, 191–192, 192t
    lobbyists and, 155, 174
    political ambition and, 39
    Risser on, 62
    study of, 6, 68n14–69n14
    training programs and, 437, 438
    turnover and, 193–194, 194f, 427
Term Limits Survey (2002), 178
Terrain. *See* Legislative terrain
Texas
    base salaries in, 52
    biennial legislative sessions in, 47
    budgets in, 270
    constituency service in, 83
    districts in, 76
    executive-legislative balance in, 291–292, 304n63
    family life adjustments of legislators in, 56
    interest groups in, 148
Theiss-Morse, Elizabeth, 9
Thomas, Clive S., 175
Thomas, Dawn, 340n19

Thompson, Dennis, 220, 389
Tobacco issues, 310, 373, 376–378, 424
Tolman, Steven, 327, 329–330
Torpey, Michael, 285
Toward a More Responsible Two-Party System (American Political Science Association), 428
Townsend, Jim, 84
Traffic controllers, legislators as, 235–236
Training programs, 210–211, 214, 219, 239, 437–438. *See also* Education issues
Transportation industry, 152
Travaglini, Robert
    action on floor and, 207
    biotechnology industry and, 148
    family-leave legislation and, 206
    health care issues and, 244, 323, 361, 363, 398–399
    legislative power and, 253–254
    payroll taxes and, 398
Travis, David, 36
Treen, David, 292–293
Trial lawyers, 149, 155, 356, 372, 382
Trust. *See* Credibility
Trustees vs. delegates, 93–97
Tucker, Don, 64
Turkington, Eric, 169, 329, 331
Turner, Shirley, 431
Turnover
    fund-raising and, 230
    leadership change and, 258
    professional vs. citizen legislatures, 191
    term limits and, 193–194, 194f, 427

Unconstitutionality. *See* Courts
Unicameralism
    in California, 196, 279
    legislative efficiency and, 422
    in Nebraska, 73–74, 121, 137n6, 185, 196, 422
Uniformity in legislative process, 348
Unruh, Jesse
    Brown (Willie) and, 58
    campaigning and, 122
    fund-raising and, 230
    Hertzberg and, 2
    legislative power and, 33, 251, 253
    legislative reform and, 184
    on winning elections, 109
Urban areas, 76–77
U.S. Congress, 196, 311–312, 324, 422, 428, 433.
    See also U.S. House of Representatives
U.S. Department of Agriculture (USDA), 348, 349
U.S. House of Representatives, 130, 229. *See also* Houses (state); U.S. Congress
U.S. Senate, 196
USA Today/Gallup Poll on Bond's hitting record, 409